Vedanta

Seven Steps to Samadhi

OSHO

Vedanta

Seven Steps to Samadhi
Talks on the Akshi Upanishad

)) **DIAMOND BOOKS**

Published by Diamond Pocket Books Pvt. Ltd.
X-30, Okhla Industrial Area, Phase-2, New Delhi-20
Tel : 011-40712100 Fax :011-41611866
E-mail : sales@dpb.in website : www.diamondbook.in

The material in this book is a transcript of a series of original OSHO Talks,
Vedanta: Seven Steps to Samadhi, given to a live audience. All of Osho's talks
have been published in full as books, and are also available as original audio
recordings. Audio recordings and the complete text archive can be found via the
online OSHO Library at www.osho.com/library

Printed in India by G.S. Enterprises

ISBN 978-93-5083-631-6

Contents

Preface

Meditation surely leads to no-mind, just as every river moves toward the ocean without any maps, without any guides. Every river, without exception, finally reaches to the ocean. Every meditation, without exception, finally reaches to the state of no-mind.

But naturally, when the Ganges is in the Himalayas wandering in the mountains and in the valleys, it has no idea what the ocean is, it cannot conceive of the existence of the ocean. But it is moving toward the ocean because water has the intrinsic capacity of always finding the lowest place, and the oceans are the lowest place. So rivers are born on the peaks of the Himalayas and start moving immediately toward lower spaces, and finally they are bound to find the ocean.

Just the reverse is the process of meditation. It moves upwards to higher peaks, and the ultimate peak is no-mind. No-mind is a simple word, but it exactly means enlightenment, liberation, freedom from all bondage, the experience of deathlessness and immortality.

Those are big words and I don't want you to be frightened, so I use a simple word, *no-mind*. You know the mind, you can conceive of a state when this mind will be non-functioning.

Once this mind is non-functioning, you become part of the mind of the cosmos, the universal mind. When you are part of the universal mind your individual mind functions as a beautiful servant. It has recognized the master, and it brings news from the universal mind to those who are still chained by the individual mind.

In fact when I am speaking to you, it is the universe using me. My words are not my words; they belong to the universal truth. That is their power, that is their charisma, that is their magic.

1   Towards the Truth

The Akshya Upanishad.

Aum, may my speech be rooted in my mind,

and my mind rooted in my speech.

O self-illumined Brahman, be manifest unto me.

Speech and min

d form the basis of my knowledge,

so please do not undo my pursuit of knowledge.

Day and night I spend in this pursuit.

I shall speak the law; I shall speak the truth.

May Brahman protect me;

may he protect the speaker, protect the speaker.

Aum, shanti, shanti, shanti.

The ultimate truth is not far away, it is not distant. It is near you, close, closer than you are to yourself, but still you go on missing it, and you have been missing it for millions of lives. This continuous missing has become a habit. Unless this habit is broken, the closest remains the most distant; unless this habit is transcended, God, truth, or whatsoever we may call it, remains just a myth, a theory, a doctrine, a belief, but not an experience.

And unless the divine is your experience, the belief is futile. It is not going to help you; on the contrary it may hinder you, because just by believing in it you deceive yourself that somehow you have known it. The belief becomes the deception. It doesn't become an opening, it closes you. It makes you knowledgeable without knowing it; it gives you a feeling of knowledge without any intimate experience of it.

Remember, untruth is not such a great hindrance as the belief in the truth. If you believe you stop seeking; if you believe you have already taken it for granted. It cannot be so. You will have to pass through a mutation; really you will have to die and be born again. Unless the seed that you are dies, the new life cannot sprout out of it. Belief becomes a barrier; it gives you a false assurance that you have known—but that is all you have got. Belief is just borrowed. A Buddha says something, a Jesus says something, or a Mohammed, and then we go on following it, believing in it. This can create such a situation within you that the distant will appear close and the closest will continue to appear distant—it creates an illusory mind.

I have heard one Sufi story. Once it happened that a fish in the ocean heard somebody talking about the ocean, and the fish heard for the first time that there exists something like the ocean. She started to search, she started to ask and in-quire, but nobody knew where the ocean was. She asked many fish, great and small, known and unknown, famous and not so famous, but nobody was capable of answering where the ocean is. They all said they have heard about it; they all said, "Sometime in the past our ancestors knew it – it is written in the scriptures." And the ocean was all around! They were in the ocean; they were talking, living in the ocean.

Sometimes it happens that the closest, the nearest, is so obvious that you can forget it. The nearest is so near that you cannot look at it, because even to look at something a certain distance is needed, space is needed. And there is no space between you and the divine; there is no space between the fish and the ocean – no gap. The fish is part of the ocean, just like a wave; or the ocean is just the infinite spread of the being of the fish. They are not two; they exist together, their being is joined together. Their bodies may appear different but their inner spirit is one, it is unitary.

The same is the situation with us. We go on asking about God – whether God exists or not – and we argue much for and against. Some believe, some disbelieve; some say it is just a myth and some say it is the only truth, but they all depend on scriptures, nobody has an immediate experience. When I say immediate experience I mean experience that has grown into you, or into which you have grown...intimate, so intimate that you cannot feel where you end and that experience begins.

God cannot be an object of any search; he remains the very subjectivity. You are not going to find him somewhere because he is everywhere, and if you start looking for him somewhere you will not find him anywhere. All that is, is divine. God just means the whole existence, the totality, the ocean that surrounds you, the ocean of life.

The first thing to remember before we enter into this intimate search and inquiry, into this intimate experience that people have always called God, or Buddha has called nirvana, or Jesus has called the kingdom of God – names differ, but the experience indicated is the same – the first thing to remember is: it is not far away, it is where you are. Right now you are sitting in him, breathing in him, breathing him, through him.

This has to be continuously remembered, constantly remembered; don't forget it for a single moment, because the moment you forget it the whole search becomes wrong. Then you start looking somewhere. Maintain it; remember it continuously at least for these eight or nine days – that it is exactly where you are. The very center of your being is its center also.

If this is remembered the whole search will become qualitatively different. Then you are not in search of something outside, but something inner. Then you are not in search of something which is going to happen in the future, it can happen right now; it is already happening. And then the whole thing becomes very relaxed. If the truth is somewhere in the future then you are bound to be tense, then you are bound to be worried, a deep anxiety is bound to be there. Who knows whether it will happen in the future or not? The future is uncertain; you may miss it – you have been missing so long. But if the divine is here and now, the very existence, the very breath, the very you, then there is no uncertainty, then there is no worry, no anxiety.

Even if you go on missing, you cannot miss him. You may have missed him for so many many lives, but really you have never missed him because he has always been hidden there, waiting for you to turn within. You have been looking outside, you have been focused on the objective world, and that which you are seeking is hidden within, it is your subjectivity.

God is not an object; God doesn't exist as an object. Whatsoever theologians say, they are absolutely wrong – God doesn't exist as an object. You cannot worship, because he is hidden in the worshipper. You cannot pray, because he is hidden there from where the prayer arises. You cannot seek him without, because he is your within-ness.

The first thing to remember is this, because if it is remembered then the whole effort becomes qualitatively different. Then you are not going somewhere, then there is no hurry, then there is no impatience. Rather, on the contrary, the more patience that happens to you, the easier becomes the search; the more you are not seeking him, the closer he is to you. When you are not seeking at all, when you are just being, not going anywhere, after anything, you have reached, the thing has happened.

This search is going to be qualitatively different. This search is, in a way, a no-search; this seeking is, in a way, a no-seeking. The more you seek, the more you will miss. If he was far away then it would have been alright. He is here, he is now. This very moment God is happening to you, because you cannot be without him. He is the ocean, you are the fish.

So don't be in a hurry and don't be impatient. There is no goal; the very effort is the goal. We will not be meditating to gain something, to achieve something; the very meditation is the goal. Meditation is not a means, it is the end. So don't force yourself; rather, relax. Don't run after something, some ultimate, some God, some x, y, z; rather stand still. The moment you are in a total standstill you have reached. Then there is no more. And this can be done any moment. If you understand, this can happen this very moment. God is life, God is existence, God is the case.

But there are problems; theologians have created them. The first problem they have created, and because of which this remembering becomes impossible – to remember that you are already divine becomes impossible – is a very deep condemnatory attitude. You go on condemning yourself: you are the sinner. They have created guilt in you. So how can a sinner be, right this very moment, the divine? He will have to get rid of the sin; he will have to suffer for his sins, and time will be needed. He will have to pass through purifications, and only when he has become holy, a saint, will he have a glimpse of the divine.

Particularly in the West, Christianity has given everybody a deep guilt complex. Everybody is guilty – not only about your own sins that you have committed, but also about the sin that Adam committed in the very beginning. You are guilty for it. You carry a burden, a long burden of guilt, so how can you think, imagine, conceive, that right this very moment God is happening to you? The Devil can happen, can be imagined, but not God. You can think of yourself as the Devil but never as the divine.

This creation of a guilt complex was needed not for you, but for religions. Their business can continue only if they create guilt in you. The whole business of religion depends on the guilt feelings that they can create in the masses. Churches, temples, religions exist on your guilt. God has not created them, your guilt has created them. When you feel guilty you need a priest to confess to; when you feel guilty you need someone to lead you, to purify you. When you feel guilty you have lost your center – now somebody can lead you.

You can become a follower only when you have lost your center. If you are right in your center, no question of following arises. You can become part of a crowd only when you are not yourself. So you belong to Christianity, or Hinduism, or Mohammedanism – these "belongings" are simply guilt feelings. You cannot be alone. You are so guilty you cannot rely on yourself, you cannot depend on yourself, you cannot be independent. Somebody, some great organization, some cult, creed, is needed, so under its blanket you can hide, and you can forget your guilt. And then you need some savior, you need someone who can suffer for your sins. This is just absurd.

Christians say Jesus suffered for the sin of the whole humanity. The whole logic is absurd. Adam committed the sin, you are guilty for it! Then Jesus suffers for you, and your guilt is forgiven, your sin is forgiven. So the whole deal is between Adam and Jesus – you are just puppets. Sometimes Adam leads you so you move into sin, sometimes Jesus leads you so you move into the kingdom of God, but you yourself are nothing. But to exploit, religions had to create the guilt feeling. Because of that guilt feeling that you are not accepted as you are, you cannot conceive of yourself as already in the divine, being divine.

With me this guilt feeling has to be dropped. You are not a sinner and you are not guilty. Whatsoever you are the existence accepts you. Whatsoever you are playing, whatsoever game, it is so because the divine wills it so. As you are, you are accepted.

This is the second thing to remember: don't condemn yourself, otherwise nothing can be done. Don't reject yourself, don't be an enemy to yourself. Be loving, be friendly, and accept whatsoever you are. I am not saying that there is nothing wrong in you. I am not saying that you don't need any transformation. You need it, there are many wrongs, but those wrongs are not sins; they are illnesses, diseases.

Someone has a fever: he is not a sinner, he needs our compassion, our help to come out of it. If we just condemn then he will also condemn his fever and then the whole thing goes wrong, because once you condemn your fever you start suppressing it. Then the man cannot say to others, "I am feeling fever, I am feverish," because the moment he says it everybody will think he is a sinner. So he goes on saying, "I am healthy. Who says that I have a fever? If the thermometer shows it the thermometer must be wrong. I am okay." He cannot accept his fever and then nothing can be done. He goes on hiding and suppressing. That is what you have been doing.

There are many wrongs, but remember, those wrongs are just illnesses, not sins; errors, mistakes, but not sins. You are not guilty. You may be ignorant; you may not be knowing as much as is needed to live a pure and innocent life, but that means you are ignorant, innocent – not guilty. Try to understand the distinction very well, because on it depends much.

In this camp, to me you are divine. You may be erroneous, the god within you may be ill, the god within you may be ignorant, the god within you may be committing many mistakes – but the god is not committing any sin. What is the difference? When you commit a mistake you don't condemn yourself, you try to understand why you committed it. The mistake is condemned but not you. When you call it a sin, *you* are condemned – *you* are wrong, not an act.

Your acts may be wrong, but you are not. You are totally accepted as you are. Your being is the highest flower that has happened to this earth. You are the salt of this earth. Howsoever erroneous, you are the very glory of existence.

Remember this: I accept you and I want you to accept yourself.

Not that there is going to be no transformation, but that only through this acceptance transformation becomes possible. Once you accept your being there is no suppression, once you accept your being the whole being comes into consciousness. There is no need to hide and to push some parts, fragments, into the darkness, into the unconscious.

The unconscious is a by-product of Christianity. There is nothing like the unconscious. If you accept yourself, your whole mind will be conscious. If you deny, reject, condemn, then the condemned parts will move into darkness. Not that they will not act now, they will act more, but their action will be now hidden, perverted, disguised. It will not be apparent, it will take a hidden course. You cannot face it directly but it goes on working. The unconscious is created by guilt.

Once you accept that there is no unconscious, the barrier has gone, the boundary disappeared, and the conscious and unconscious become one – as they are really, as they should be. And when your conscious and unconscious are one you can meditate, never before it. Once your inner divisions disappear, once you become one inside, a deep silence descends upon you, a great blissful moment is reached – just by the disappearance of the boundaries, divisions, fragments.

When you become one you become healthy; when you become one you feel a silent well-being. Moment to moment you feel grateful to existence, a gratitude happens to you, and this gratitude I call prayer. It is not a prayer to some god. This gratitude is an inner attitude towards existence which has given you life, love, light; towards this existence which has blessed you in millions and millions of ways, and which goes on showering upon you more and more blessings – but a unity is needed within.

So this is the second point to remember: don't feel guilty, don't feel yourself a sinner, don't feel that you are wrong. If you were wrong you would not have been. You are there because God wants to preserve you. You are there because God loves you. You are there, that's why the whole existence supports you. You are there because you are worth the trouble. Accept yourself, have a loving attitude towards yourself.

Jesus says somewhere: Love your enemies as yourself. But no one loves himself, so how can you love your enemies as yourself? You simply hate yourself. If you love yourself, to me you have become religious. And a person who loves himself, only he can love others; a person who hates himself deep down cannot love anybody.

If you cannot love yourself how can you love anybody? If you cannot accept yourself how can you accept anybody? So your so-called saints who go on condemning themselves, they go on condemning the whole world – they are condemning everybody. The moment they condemn themselves they condemn the whole world. You are the nearest; if existence in you is condemned, then how can you accept existence that is far away from you, existing in others? No guilt, no condemnation. Wrongs are there, but those wrongs are not in your being but in your doing; in your acts, not in you. And your acts are wrong because you are not aware – not that you are a sinner. Those wrongs exist because you are not alert. The god is asleep in you, fast asleep; sometimes you can even hear the snoring – fast asleep.

My effort in this camp is going to be to make that god a little alert, to disturb the inner sleep, to help him awake. It is not condemnatory. And once you start being alert, you have started being different. Perfectly aware, you have reached; perfectly aware, you are in nirvana, in the kingdom of God.

The third thing to remember: in this camp we will be doing many things, many techniques, many methods, but hidden behind every technique and method is the basic thing and that is, search for awareness, search for more consciousness. So whatsoever you are doing here, remain alert, remain conscious, remain a witness. Doing meditation remain conscious, remain a witness. Doing meditation, dancing, doing *kirtan* and singing, remain alert, don't become unconscious.

Whatsoever is happening, a center within you goes on looking at it, a center remains a watcher. Your body may be going mad, your body may be jumping, shrieking, screaming, your mind may have become a whirlpool – but a watcher remains. Go on constantly remembering that you are watching, because that watcher is the thing. That watcher has to be brought more and more into force. So while your body is doing many things, your mind is doing many things, one thing deeply hidden within you goes on looking at it all. Don't lose contact with that.

I am going to create a situation in these days in which your body will become very active, your mind will go through many catharses, much activity will be there, but simultaneously, side by side, remain alert, passively looking at all that is happening as if you are not only the actor but the audience also. Doing, watching – this watching must be continued moment to moment, not only while you are meditating. You are walking, you are eating, taking a bath, talking with someone, going to sleep – go on watching everything that is happening.

For these eight days devote all your energies to moving towards being a witness. Eating, let the body eat – you watch also. Walking, let the legs move – you watch also. Hearing me, listening to me, let the ears listen, let the mind absorb – you watch also. You remain a witness. Continuously hammering for the witness will help your god to be awake, and once your god is awake you yourself are a Jesus, a Buddha, a Krishna – then you don't lack anything. Right now also you don't lack anything, except that the god in Krishna or Christ is awake and in you fast asleep.

There is nothing wrong in sleep also, but in sleep many errors are committed. You move in sleep, then you commit many mistakes. If you love committing mistakes then there is no problem, but remember that when you commit mistakes you suffer also. That suffering doesn't come from Adam's sin – it comes from you. If you commit a mistake you suffer, pain results. All suffering is a by-product of ignorance. So if you enjoy your suffering then it is okay, then don't make any effort for any change. Sleep is good and you enjoy your suffering. But if you don't enjoy your suffering then something has to be done. Prayers won't help, only conscious effort will help you.

A few instructions and then I will move to the sutra.

When you go to sleep tonight and every night following, before going to sleep put off the light, sit on your bed, close your eyes and exhale deeply through the mouth with the sound O – Ooooo. Go on exhaling with the sound O, as deeply as possible. Your stomach goes in, the air moves out, and you go on creating the sound O. Remember, I am not saying aum, I am saying simply O. It will become aum automatically. You need not make it, then it is false. You simply create the sound O. When it becomes more harmonious and you are enjoying it, suddenly you will become aware it has become aum. But don't force it to become aum, then it is false. When it becomes spontaneously aum then it is something vibrating from within. And this sound aum is the deepest sound, the most harmonious, the most basic.

When it happens and you enjoy and you flow in its music, your whole body and your brain relax. With the sound aum you will go on relaxing and your sleep will have a different quality, altogether different. And your sleep has to be changed, only then can you become more alert and aware. So we will start by changing the sleep.

In the night put the light off, sit on the bed, exhale deeply through the mouth with the sound O. When you have exhaled completely and you feel that now no more exhalation is possible, the whole breath has gone out, stop for a single moment. Don't inhale, don't exhale – just stop. In that stop you are the divine. In that stop you are not doing anything, not even breathing. In that stop you are in the ocean.

Just remain in the stop for a single moment and be a witness – just look at what is happening. Be aware where you are: witness the whole situation that is there in that single stopped moment. Time is no more there, because time moves with breaths; breathing is the process of time. Because you breathe you feel the time moving.

When you don't breathe you are just like a dead man. Time has stopped, there is no process anywhere, everything has stopped...as if the whole existence has stopped with you. In that stopping you can become aware of the deepest source of your being and energy. So for a single moment stop. Then inhale through the nose, but don't make any effort to inhale.

Remember, make all the effort to exhale, but don't make any effort to inhale; just let the body inhale. You simply relax your hold and let the body take the inhalation. You don't do anything. That too is beautiful and works wonders. You have exhaled, stopped for a moment, then you allow the body to inhale. You don't make any effort to inhale, you simply watch the body taking the inhalation. And when you watch the body taking the inhalation you will feel a deep silence surrounding you, because then you know your effort is not needed for life. Life breathes itself. It moves by itself of its own cause. It is a river, you unnecessarily go on pushing it. You will see that the body is taking the inhalation. Your effort is not needed, your ego is not needed – *you* are not needed. You simply become a watcher, you simply see the body taking the inhalation. Deep silence will be felt. When the body has taken a full inhalation, stop for a single moment again. Again watch.

These two moments are totally different. When you have exhaled completely and stopped, that stopping is just like death. When you have inhaled totally and then stopped, that stopping is the climax of life. Remember, inhalation is equivalent to life, exhalation equivalent to death. That's why the first thing a child does when born is to inhale, and the last thing the same child will do when old, dying, will be to exhale. On this earth, the first thing you did while entering life was inhalation, and the last thing you will do will be exhalation. No one can die inhaling. When you die you have to exhale, you die with exhalation. And no one can be born with exhalation, you have to start by inhalation.

Those who know, and those who have watched their inner life process deeply, they say – and you will come to feel it yourself – that with every inhalation you are born again and with every exhalation you die. So death is not something in the end, and birth is not something in the beginning; every moment there is birth and death, every moment you die and are born again. And if you die beautifully you are born again more beautifully, if you die totally you are born totally.

So exhale as totally as possible; that will give you a death moment. That's beautiful, because a death moment is the most silent, the most peaceful – that is nirvana. Then let the body inhale to the full, and then stop. That moment is a life moment: the climax of energy, power, bioenergy at its peak. Feel it, and feel both. That's why I say stop twice: when you have exhaled, then; and when you have inhaled, then – so you can feel both life and death, so you can watch both life and death.

Once you know this is life, this is death, you have transcended both. The witness is neither death nor life. The witness is never born and never dies; only the body, the mechanism. You become the third. These two moments are very significant. This very night you have to do this meditation, for twenty minutes you go on doing this and then fall down and go to sleep.

In the morning when you feel the sleep has left you, don't open your eyes immediately. The mind has the tendency to open the eyes immediately. You miss a great opportunity...because when sleep leaves you and life energies are wakening inside, you can watch them, and that watching will be very helpful for going into deeper meditation.

The mind is fresh, the body is fresh after the whole night's rest; everything is fresh, unburdened. There is no dust, no tiredness – you can look deeply, penetratingly. Your eyes are fresher; everything is vital. Don't miss that moment. When you feel sleep has left, don't open the eyes immediately. Remain with closed eyes and feel the energy which is changing now from sleep to waking. And that's what I am going to teach you: how to change all your energies from sleep to waking. So just watch.

You may be lethargic in that moment, you would like to turn over and go to sleep again, so do one thing: for three minutes with closed eyes stretch your body like a cat. But with closed eyes; don't open the eyes and don't look at the body from without. Look at the body from within. Stretch, move, and let the body energy flow, and feel it.

When it is fresh it is good to feel it; the feeling will remain with you the whole day.

Do this for two or three minutes –if you enjoy it, five minutes. And then for two or three minutes laugh loudly like a madman, but with closed eyes, don't open the eyes. With closed eyes laugh loudly. The energies are there, flowing; the body is awake and alert and vital. The sleep has gone. You are filled, flooded with new energy.

The first thing to be done is laughter, because that sets the trend for the whole day. If you do it, you will feel within two or three days that your mood remains the whole day the mood of laughing, enjoying. Don't be afraid of what others will say, because they may be just waiting for you – so laugh and help them to laugh.

Remember, the first thing in the day sets the trend, and the last thing in the night also sets the trend. So begin your sleep with a deep relaxation so the whole night becomes samadhi, the whole night becomes a deep meditation – relaxed. Six, seven, eight hours – it is a long time. If you live for sixty years, twenty years you will be in your bed. Twenty years is a long time, and if you can change the quality of sleep you need not go to a forest to meditate; twenty years – enough! No need to go anywhere, no need to do anything. If you can change your sleep there is no need to go like Mahavira in the forest for twelve years, or like Buddha for six years. Twenty years is a long time, and you are not doing anything in that sleep so meditation is easy, because meditation is more like nondoing than like doing. It is a deep relaxation.

Relax when you go to sleep and laugh when you come out of sleep. That laughter should be the first prayer. Remember that if you can laugh, sooner or later you will come to believe in God. A person who laughs cannot remain an atheist for long, and a person who is sad, whatsoever he may say, cannot be really a believer in God, because sadness shows that he rejects, sadness shows that he is against, sadness shows that he denies, condemns. Laughter shows a deep acceptance, laughter shows a celebration, laughter shows that life is good.

First thing in the morning stretch your body like a cat so you can feel energy, move like a cat, and then laugh, and only then get out of the bed. Then the whole day is going to be different. Then we will be doing three meditations in the day.

In the morning a meditation of four steps, the last really not a step but a jump. The first step: ten minutes of fast chaotic breathing. This breathing is used just like a hammer to hammer your energies, particularly energies which are hidden in the sex center. And you exist right now as a sex center, because your whole energy moves into that center. Your contact with the world is through that center, you are related to the world through that center. And unless energy erupts upwards, flows upwards to other centers which are there, nonfunctioning, you cannot change, you cannot be transformed.

The higher the energy moves, through higher centers you are related to the world. When from the highest center you relate to the world, you have become divine and the whole world is divine; from the lowest center, sex, you are an animal and the whole world is also animal. Darwins and Huxleys and others who have worked hard to prove that man has evolved out of animals are right, their research is right, but they have not studied a buddha; they have studied the ordinary human being. The ordinary human being is related with the animal kingdom. He remains an animal, just a little more sophisticated. Mark Twain writes somewhere that the cauliflower is a cabbage with a college education. That's the only difference between animal and man – a little more sophisticated animal with a college education, with a culture. But he remains an animal, and because he is educated he becomes more dangerous.

The higher your energy moves, the more new realms of existence will be revealed to you. And if the Upanishads, if Vedantins, Buddha and Jesus and people like them have declared that everyone is divine, they could say so only because they were related to the universe from their highest center. Your energy has to be moved from the sex center to the *sahasrar,* that which is hidden in your head.

This chaotic breathing, the first step, is just to be used as a hammer. It works, it is not a theory; you can do it and you can know it, and you *will* know it.

The second step for ten minutes will be of catharsis. You have to bring out, act out, whatsoever you have been suppressing up to now. Whatsoever you have suppressed has to be thrown out, because only then can you become flowerlike, weightless, and only then can you fly, only then can you rise upwards. All the burden has to be dropped down.

I have heard one story about Hotei, a Zen master. One day he was passing through a village. On his shoulders he always carried a very big bag full of many toys, chocolates and sweets for children. Somebody asked him, "Hotei, we have heard that you are just playing a role, acting. We have heard that you are a Zen master, so why do you go on wasting your time just giving toys to children? And if you are really a Zen master then show us what Zen is." Zen means the real spirit of religion.

Hotei dropped his bag, immediately he dropped his bag. They couldn't follow, so they said, "What do you mean?"

He said, "This is all. If you drop the burden, this is all."

They asked, "Okay, then what is the next step?"

So he put his bag again on his shoulders and started walking. "This is the next step. But now I am not carrying. I know now that the burden is not me. Now the whole burden has become just toys for children and they will enjoy it."

The second step is to drop the bag that you are carrying, and carry it again only when *you* are not carrying it. Then you can carry the whole world; then there is no problem – you are not identified with it. The second step is to drop the bag. So be Hotei, and drop whatsoever you have been carrying so long. And it is just ugly, whatsoever you are carrying. Sadness, ugliness, hatred, suffering, anger, jealousy – things like this you are carrying. And if you have become a big wound it is no surprise, it is what you are carrying. So in the second step you have to throw down whatsoever there is in it.

You will look mad, because madness is there. You have been suppressing it up to now. Your sanity is false, it is just on the surface, not even skin-deep. You can be made insane immediately. Someone hits you and the sanity is gone, someone insults you and the sanity is gone. It is not even skin-deep, it is just there boiling. You are carrying yourself somehow. You are a miracle. How do you go on with so many madnesses within? How do you manage it? In the second step don't manage, just throw it out. Become mad, go mad.

Remember, when you become mad consciously you remain a witness. Mad-ness is beautiful if you are conscious – you enjoy it. The more you throw it out the less burdened you are, and you feel that your energy is purified. You feel that now you can fly in the sky. Now there are no boundaries to you, you have be-come weightless. Now the whole gravitation of the earth cannot pull you down to the earth, you have become greater. You can transcend this pull now; this pull works because you carry so much burden. The second step is to go mad consciously. Those who are intelligent will go mad consciously, those who are stupid will go on holding. So don't be stupid; be a man of understanding and try it.

The third step is a Sufi mantra, *hoo*; not w-h-o, just h-o-o – hoo without meaning. This is just a sound with no meaning at all; it has a significance but no meaning. It is just a technique. This sound hoo goes deepest in you, hits your deepest center, releases energy. Your whole body becomes aflame with a new energy that you have not known because you have never hit it.

You are so afraid of yourself that you never hit your sources of energy, because you don't know what you will do if much energy comes to you, and you are also afraid you may do something wrong if energy comes to you. So people remain consciously weak. If you are afraid of sex you will be afraid of energy, because if energy comes it will start moving in the sex center. Then what to do? So these so-called saints go on starving their bodies just to remain weak; their whole saintliness is nothing but a sort of weakness, a sort of impotence. And an impotent person can never be holy – because you don't have energy to be holy. If you don't have energy to be unholy, how can you have energy to be holy? The same energy moves from unholiness to holiness.

The third is just a technique, a sound which hits your hidden sources of energy which you are scared to hit. Your whole body will become aflame with new life, new energy, new heat, new electricity, and when your whole body has become vital, every cell of it, only then the jump can be taken, never before it.

Religion is not for weak people. Of course, if you go looking in temples, mosques and churches you will find weak persons there, kneeling down, praying – just weak. They are there because they are weak and they are in search of some help: somebody to protect them, somebody to give them security, safety.

But I say to you, religion is not for the weak, it is only for the strong, because it is such a jump. It is a total jump from the known to the unknown. The weak cannot take it. They can travel step by step, but they can never take a jump.

And remember, if you travel step by step, gradually, you are never transformed; you are at the most modified. You remain the same. A little refined, modified, a little change here and there, but you remain the same. A little better looking, but all ugliness hidden inside, just colored. Only those who are strong enough, who are erupting with energy, exploding with energy, can take the jump.

And this is the greatest jump and the greatest challenge – from the known into the unknown. Whatsoever you are you know, and where I am trying to indicate is the unknown. In all these days the abyss will be just near you. Any moment you can jump, but you will have to create energy.

This third step is to create energy, to make a volcano – and then I will leave it to you. When I see that now you are boiling, exploding, I will say, "Stop." And when I say stop, don't go on doing things. Whatsoever you were doing, stop immediately, go dead, because if you go on doing you will lose energy and the jump will not be possible. When I say stop, stop exactly at that moment. When you hear me say stop after the third step, you stop as you are. Even if the posture is uncomfortable don't change it, don't make it comfortable, because here we are not in search of comfort. And don't deceive, because you are not deceiving anybody except yourself.

When I say stop, it is meaningful that I am saying it at that particular moment. It is when I feel that now you have worked up, you have created the energy; now the right peak has been reached. When I say stop, stop immediately. Become a statue, a stone, a rock – no movement. Don't allow the energy to be expressed in any way, so the energy becomes integrated within and it comes with such a force that you can take the jump. The jump will happen by itself; you just create the energy. When I say stop, you stop.

The fourth step is a jump. You remain silent, just like a rock. In that moment of silence and stoppage, energy will be there – so much you cannot hold it; it will have to explode. And it will move from the sex center upwards. As it moves upwards you will feel a transformation, a change. You are not the same; moment to moment something else is coming into being. When this energy touches the head center, the last center, sahasrar...Hindus have said it is as if a lotus of one thousand petals has opened suddenly. You are filled with benediction, bliss, beatitude. This for the morning.

In the afternoon, from four to five, we will be doing kirtan – singing and dancing. Twenty minutes dancing, singing; twenty minutes silence, waiting; then twenty minutes expressing your joy, your happiness – celebration. For the first twenty minutes you have to do it so much, so deeply, so totally, that your whole bodymind is exhausted. It has to be exhausted. So don't save yourself, don't try not to get tired. That is the whole point: you have to be tired, so tired that the body and the mind, the old pattern, simply drops through tiredness, exhausted. So get exhausted. Go mad fast!

For twenty minutes you have to exhaust all your energies so the pattern cannot hold, and then you drop into relaxation. For those twenty minutes, if you are really exhausted you will feel some unknown source has become open to you, as if some unknown ocean is dropping into you. You will be filled with new life, and then celebration becomes possible. Then celebrate it, then dance and go mad, but remain constantly alert and watch whatsoever is happening.

In the morning, evening and night we will be doing group meditations; these are group meditations. One meditation is for you to do individually. From four to five we will do kirtan – singing and dancing. From three to four you move alone. Don't go with anybody, just move alone. Go under a tree, near a rock, or anywhere. If you cannot find any place then just sit outside your room, but be under the sky, don't do it in the room. This is to be done individually, and everyone has to do it; don't try to escape it.

Move to a tree, sit, look at the sky. Don't look at anything in particular, just look vacantly with empty eyes so that the whole sky can be in contact. When you look at something you are narrowed. Then you are focused, then your eyes can take in only one thing; they are exclusive. Just look vacantly so the whole sky becomes available to your eyes. Looking at the sky, for twenty minutes start talking gibberish, just nonsense. Because the sky cannot understand your language, don't use your language, it is useless – the sky cannot understand it. Gibberish….

You may not be aware from where this word gibberish comes. It comes from a Sufi saint whose name was Jabbar, and he used to talk nonsense. He would talk in such a way that nobody would be able to understand what he was saying. So because it started with Jabbar, people started calling it gibberish. The English word gibberish comes from the Sufi mystic Jabbar.

So become Jabbar: talk gibberish, nonsense, sounds, gestures, to the sky, not to anybody else. You are talking to the sky. There is a Christian sect who call this type of meditation glossolalia – talking in tongues. And as far as I know, in the whole of Christianity only that sect knows something. Whatsoever comes in the mind, say it: sometimes just sounds, sometimes animal sounds, sometimes screaming, howling, yelling, whatsoever. And don't try to create any sense, because that will be nonsense – creating sense with the sky. You are not talking to any human being; you are talking to the vast sky which cannot understand any language and which can understand anything.

Language will not be helpful. Why? – because if you go on with the pattern of language you never transcend your mind. When you talk with the sky without meaningful communication the mind simply drops; it has no use, it cannot continue. The mind will try to say to you, "What nonsense are you doing? Are you mad?" Don't listen to it. Just tell it, "You wait, and let me do whatsoever I am doing." Enjoy it.

For twenty minutes go completely Jabbar-like, gibberish, and then for twenty minutes silently relax. Go on looking at the sky if you feel like it, or if you don't feel like it, close your eyes and look to the inner sky. After these twenty minutes of nonsense you will feel so silent, so skylike, such a vast space within you, that you cannot imagine what can happen out of it.

But go alone, because if someone is there your mind will start playing tricks. If someone is there you would like to create some sense of whatsoever you are doing, because everybody is such an exhibitionist. Or you may create some nonsense just to impress others that you are creating nonsense. That is not the point. You have to be authentic about it. It is not for somebody else, it is for the sky.

And you cannot deceive the sky. The sky has known millions and millions and millions like you. You also for millions and millions of lives the sky has known. We all come out of it and we all go back into it. Be in contact with space. If you can be in contact with space a space is created within you, and when these two spaces meet there is ecstasy. This is to be done individually, then kirtan in the group.

In the night we will have a third meditation, a group meditation. You have to stare at me – it is a *tratak*. I will be standing here; you have to stare at me without blinking. The eyes will get tired, tears will start rolling down – let them. Go on staring at me so that I can meet you, you can meet me. Just by talking meeting cannot take place. I talk only to persuade you into something else which cannot be given through talk. So talk is just a seduction for something else, for something else which cannot be communicated through words.

That's why this meditation is the last in the night. The whole day I prepare you. I prepare you to go more and more mad, so by the time night comes you are already insane and you can do something which the mind would not have allowed you to do – stare at me with nonblinking eyes. Why nonblinking eyes? When you blink, mind changes. You may not be aware that your blinking depends on the mind. When you are really interested in something blinking stops. That's why your eyes get tired in a film.

Watching a film, the film is not destructive to the eyes, but your eyes stop blinking. You are so interested you forget blinking. You go on staring, that's why your eyes get tired. And staring at a film is dangerous because you are staring at something which belongs to the lowest of the centers. So if you go to see a movie, if at all you go, continuously blink. Be less concerned with seeing and more concerned with blinking, so you are not hypnotized and the film cannot provoke your lowest center. All films are hitting at the sex center, that's their appeal.

In this third method in the night, you have to stare at me. I want to hit at your sahasrar, the peak, the last, the highest center. Unblinking will be needed as it is needed for the lowest center. Unblinking you look at me: the mind stops. Then a flow starts; then you and I are not two, a bridge is there. I can move in you, you can move in me – a deep communion is possible.

You will be standing while doing this, and you have to go on jumping with your hands raised so that you forget the feeling of the body and you become energy – jumping, moving, dynamic. As you are, your body has become static. With static energy communication is not possible; only with a moving energy, a jumping energy, is contact possible. When energy is static it becomes like ice – dead, frozen. When energy is moving the ice melts, it becomes a river, flowing. And if you go on moving, a moment comes when your energy is not even like water; it becomes like vapor – invisible, rising upwards.

Remember, ice is static, cannot move; water is moving, dynamic, but can only move downwards; vapor is invisible, moving, but can only move upwards. These are the three states of your energy also. Every energy can have three states: the solid, the liquid, the vaporous.

You have to go on jumping with raised hands so you become a movement. Everybody will be jumping, and soon static energies will mingle with each other, they will become a dance. And you will be constantly, simultaneously, using the mantra hoo, so you are hitting your energy deep. Your energy starts moving upwards; your body has become flexible, liquid, vaporous, jumping, a dance; and constantly your eyes are static towards me, staring towards me, fixed to-wards me, and I can work on your highest center.

The whole situation is created: your energy moving, hoo constantly hitting at the source – the lowest source of energy – forcing it to move upwards, you jumping, your eyes staring, mind in a stop, and me constantly working on your sahasrar.

I will be moving my hands just to give you hints. When I move my hands like this you have to go completely mad and become dynamic; just a dance, the dancer is lost. And sometimes, as I move my hands upwards, you have to bring more and more energy to movement. You don't know how much energy you have got; you are holding it. Don't be a miser, allow it. Let it flow, let your totality come into it.

Then there will be some moments when I will put my palms downwards. When I put my palms downwards that shows that now you are in such a vaporous state that a contact can be made. Now I can come to you, now I can touch your sahasrar. So when I put my palms downwards you have to bring all energy, whatsoever there is, to become the dance, the jump, the hoo. Bring your total energy in that moment, because in that moment a contact is possible, a *shaktipat* is possible.

And you will feel...if you really move with me you will feel the lotus in the head flowering. You will feel the silence that comes through it, the bliss that comes through it. You will feel the perfume that happens within through its flowering. Once this flower starts flowering you can never be the same again. Now you are on the path, now nothing can stop you. Now you can move alone, no master is needed.

A master is needed only up to that point when your budlike sahasrar opens. Once the master has helped you to open it, once the petals have started opening, you can be alone. Now no one is needed, now you have gone beyond all possibilities of falling. You can rise and only rise now, there is no possibility of any fall. You have come to the point which is called by Buddha the point of no return. Only up to that point is a master needed.

These will be the meditations that we will follow. I thought it would be good if I told you about everything so there would be no need again to talk about them.

Now the first sutra. It is an invocation.

Aum, may my speech be rooted in my mind, and my mind rooted in my speech. O self-illumined Brahman, be manifest unto me. Speech and mind form the basis of my knowledge, so please do not undo my pursuit of knowledge. Day and night I spend in this pursuit. I shall speak the law; I shall speak the truth. May Brahman protect me; may he protect the speaker, protect the speaker. Aum, shanti, shanti, shanti.

We are not alone, and no one is an island. Existence is one. So when you are seeking you need the help of the whole. Just the attitude of asking for the help becomes the help; just the attitude to invoke, to call the whole, the center of the whole existence to help you, becomes the help. There is no one to give you help, there is no person.

Whenever the Upanishads invoke, they are not invoking any personal god – there is none. Then to whom is their invocation addressed? It is not addressed to anyone; really it is not addressed at all. Then why call it an invocation? Then why start with it? There is something totally different.

Upanishadic *rishis* feel and know that every ego exists in conflict, struggle. You exist as your ego because you go on fighting. The more you fight, the more you are; the more you are in conflict and struggle, the more the ego is strengthened. This effort to know the ultimate cannot be ego-based. It can only be an egoless effort.

This invocation is just for the seeker, for the rishi himself. It is an effort to drop the struggle, the conflict, the violent resistance which we are having every moment with existence. This invocation is just to say, "I will not swim in the river; now I will flow, float. I will not fight with the river of existence, I will just allow the river to take me wherever it leads." This is a surrender, and this surrender is very very significant.

Unless you surrender there is no possibility – because you are the disease. The very concept that "I am" is the problem. Every 'I' is false, because I cannot exist without existence. If I cannot exist without existence, what is the meaning of calling myself 'I'?

The Upanishads say, "If God is there, only he can call himself 'I', nobody else." But he has never called himself, he has not asserted anything. There is no one to whom to assert. There is no thou, so how can he say 'I'? He *is* only. This invocation is just to say, "I am not struggling against you, I'm ready to flow with you. I will become the river."

Aum. That's why no name – Allah, Ram, Yahweh – no name has been used, just aum. The Upanishads say that aum is the very structure of this existence. When you are totally silent and the mind has dissolved and the thoughts disappeared, when the ego has ceased, then you hear the sound of aum – it is a soundless sound. No one is creating it, it is there. It is the very existential sound; it is how existence happens to be – just a humming sound of existence. Existence is there, alive – that aliveness creates a sound; or, to that aliveness a sound happens. That sound is not created by anybody; it is uncreated, *anahat*.

If you have heard about Zen masters...they go on telling their disciples to go and meditate, meditate on the sound of one hand clapping. We can create a sound by clapping *two* hands. Zen masters say to their disciples, "Go and find out that sound which comes out of only one hand: the clapping of one hand, not with anything else."

We know this is absurd. A sound can come only with conflict, with two things clashing. Two hands can create sound, not one hand. Zen masters also know that, but still they have been giving this meditation for centuries. From Buddha up to now, Zen masters go on giving it. They know, their disciples know, that this is absurd. Then what is the significance? One has to watch, meditate, and move towards a sound which is already there, which is not created. That is the meaning of the sound of one hand.

I have heard a story. A small boy, just ten or twelve years of age, lived in a Zen monastery. Every day he would see many seekers coming to the master to ask for help, methods, techniques, guidance. He also became attracted, so one day he also came in the morning in the same way a seeker comes to a Zen master. With deep reverence he bowed down seven times. The master started laughing: "What has happened to this boy?"

And then he sat in the way seekers should sit before a Zen master. Then he waited, as seekers should wait, for the master to ask, "Why have you come?"

The master asked, "Toyo" – Toyo was the name of the boy – "why have you come?"

So Toyo bowed down and said, "Master, I have come in search of truth. What shall I do? How should I practice?"

The master knew that this boy was simply imitating, because everybody he heard came and asked the same questions, so just jokingly the master said, "Toyo, you go and meditate. Two hands clapping can create a sound. What is the sound of one hand clapping?"

Toyo bowed down seven times again, went back to his room, started meditating. He heard a geisha girl singing, so he said, "Right, this is the thing." He came immediately, bowed down.

The master was laughing. He said, "Did you meditate, Toyo?"

He said, "Yes sir, and I have found it: it is like a geisha girl singing."

The master said, "No, this is wrong. Go again, meditate."

So he went again, meditated for three days. Then he heard the sound of water dripping, so he said, "Right now, this is the thing – I have got it." He came again, the master asked...he said, "The sound of the water dripping."

The master said, "Toyo, that too is not it. You go and meditate."

So he meditated for three months. Then he heard locusts in the trees, so he said, "Yes, I have got it." He came again.

The master said, "No, this too is not right."

And so on and on. One year passed. Then for one year continuously he was not seen. The master became anxious: "What happened to the boy? He has not come." So he went to find him. He was sitting under a tree, silent, his body vibrating to some unknown sound; his body dancing, a very gentle dance, as if just moving with the breeze.

The master didn't like to disturb the boy, so he sat there waiting. Hours and hours passed. When the sun was setting and it was evening, the master said, "Toyo?"

The boy opened his eyes and he said, "This is it."

The master said, "Yes, you have got it!"

This aum is that sound. When all sounds disappear from the mind, then you hear a sound. The Upanishads have made that sound the symbol of the whole, because whenever the whole happens to the part, it happens in that music of aum, in that harmony of aum.

Aum, may my speech be rooted in my mind, and my mind rooted in my speech.

The master is saying, "O ultimate, the whole, the total, aum, help me so that my speech is rooted in my mind." A master should not speak of anything that is not deeply rooted in his mind, in his experience; that which he has not known he should not speak of. He should only speak of that which he has known, for which he can stand the witness, for which he can say, "I *May my speech be roote*am the witness" – only that.

May my speech be rooted in my mind – in my experience. Mind is your experience, the way you have experienced the world, the existence. The master says: *May my speech be rooted in my mind, and my mind rooted in my speech.* And whatsoever I say, I should not only say it, I must flow through it. Not only should my words relate, through my words I must move; my consciousness must use words as vehicles.

Ordinarily we use words without moving with them, even such beautiful words as love. We go on saying to people, "I love you," not meaning it at all. You may not even be aware of what you are saying. If you were aware, you would be very guarded. How can you say such a sacred word, love, so easily? You go on saying, "I love my car, I love my dog, I love my wife." You can love anything – even chocolate, ice cream. Your love is not rooted anywhere, you are not moving in it. How can a man love ice cream? And if you can love ice cream, then whenever you say, "I love," it is not reliable. Then don't say "I love" to any person, because no person would like to become like ice cream or chocolate.

But we go on using words not to express something, but on the contrary, to hide something. Just watch: when you say to someone, "I love you," you may be just hiding hate. It was so bubbling you were afraid the other may come to know it; immediately you have to hide it. You say, "I love you." This must be some type of screen, some form of hiding, suppression.

The master says:

Aum, may my speech be rooted in my mind, and my mind rooted in my speech.

Whatsoever I say, I must move in it, otherwise I should not say it. And whatsoever is said must be my experience, I should not say it on anybody else's authority. The Vedas say, The Bible says, the Koran says – they may be saying, but that's useless unless I know. They cannot be authorities; only my own experience can be the authority. If I know, they can be witnesses to my knowledge. Then I can say, "The Koran also says this." But the Koran is not right because it is the Koran; it is right because it is my experience, and the Koran supports it. I remain, my own experience remains, the center.

O self-illumined Brahman, be manifest unto me.

Very paradoxical….

O self-illumined Brahman, be manifest unto me.

Brahman is self-illumined, he doesn't need any other source of illumination. We are here; if the light is put off we cannot see each other. We are not self-illumined, the light is needed. If light is not there we are in darkness. But Brahman, the total, is self-illumined – no other light is needed.

The rishi says:

O self-illumined Brahman, be manifest unto me.

And then he says, "You are self-illumined; no light is needed to know you. You are self-evident; no proof is needed to prove you. Still, I am ignorant, my eyes are closed, I am finite. Because of my finiteness, because of my eyes, I cannot see you who are self-illumined. Be manifest unto me." This must be the attitude – a humble, receptive attitude.

Speech and mind form the basis of my knowledge, so please do not undo my pursuit of knowledge. Day and night I spend in this pursuit.

The rishi says, "Mind, thinking, are my means and methods, so don't undo my pursuit of knowledge. I don't have anything else; I have only the mind." And the rishi knows that the mind cannot be the right source of knowing the Brahman, but that is the only source you have. You can know the ultimate only when the mind is no more. But right now you have just the mind and nothing else.

So the rishi says, "Help me. I have nothing else, only this mind. And I know well that this mind cannot lead to you, but that's all I have got. So help me, and don't undo my efforts. Just because through mind you cannot be known, don't undo my efforts. My mind will lead me to a point where it itself becomes the no-mind. But wait and don't undo my efforts."

It is just like a child who says, "I have got legs to walk, but they are weak, unaccustomed – I have never walked before. I have only got these small, weak, unadjusted, yet-to-be-adjusted legs, and I have to walk with them. Don't undo my efforts. A moment will come when this weakness will disappear, so be patient with me."

That's what the rishi is saying to the universe: "Be patient with me. I may commit many errors, mistakes. I may move on a wrong path, but be patient with me."

I shall speak the law; I shall speak the truth. May Brahman protect me; may he protect the speaker. Aum, shanti, shanti, shanti.

Before the rishi starts his discourse, the Upanishad we will be discussing in these days, he says, "I shall only speak the law. I will not speak any creed, any theory. I will not talk about any doctrine. I will talk only about the law, that which is."

There are temptations to create theories, there are temptations to create systems. And it always happens that whenever a man finds a fragment of truth, immediately around that fragment he creates a system. The whole system is speculation.

This Upanishadic seer says, "I shall only speak the law, whatsoever it is, and I will not add anything to it. I shall only speak the truth. Whatsoever the consequence, whatsoever the result, wheresoever it leads, I will only speak the truth. But I am weak, so protect me, O Brahman."

May he protect the speaker...may he protect the speaker

Twice he repeats – the fear is there. Whenever one starts speaking, the fear is there that mind may tempt, mind may add something, distort the truth or create something which is untrue, or substitute something which is not there.

When one English poet, Coleridge, died, he left thousands of poems incomplete. Just before he died somebody asked him, "Why have you not completed them?" A few poems were missing only one line, so they said, "Why don't you complete them? – they will become masterpieces. Just because of one line…. Why can't you add one line to them?"

Coleridge is reported to have said, "I cannot do that. I have taken a vow that I will not add anything. These lines have descended to me, I have not done anything. In a moment of ecstasy they have been revealed to me; I have noted them down. I am simply a vehicle, not the creator; a medium, an adjunct – so I have noted down. The last line has not come yet and I am waiting, I cannot do anything. If it comes it comes, if it doesn't come, nothing can be done. I am helpless."

This is the attitude of the right seeker – he will not add anything, because a fragment of truth will become a lie if you add something to complete it. And the whole truth is not known, and cannot be known. Only fragments are known. The whole cannot be known. The whole is so vast; only glimpses are known. So the mind is tempted to create a system; the system becomes false. Hegel, Kant, Plato, Aristotle – they all had a few fragments of truth, but they destroyed them because they created vast edifices around them. And the fragrance is lost, you cannot find where it is.

These Upanishadic seers are different, their attitude absolutely different. They have not systematized whatsoever they have asserted. The Upanishads are unsystematized fragments, just fragments – no system, no logic, no reason. Whatsoever is revealed, they have noted it down. So the master says:

I shall speak only the law; I shall speak only the truth. May Brahman protect me…the speaker…may Brahman protect the speaker.

Aum, shanti, shanti, shanti.

2   Attaining Real Eyes

The sage Sankriti once visited Adityalok, the abode of the sun god,

and bowing to him he worshipped him with what is known as

chakshusmati vidya.

Aum, salutation to the sun god who illumines the organ of vision!

Salutation to the sun who is a great warrior!

Salutation to the sun who represents the three conditionings:

tamas, rajas and sattva (dark, red and white)!

O Lord, from untruth lead me to truth, from darkness lead me to light,

and from death lead me to the eternal. Salutation to the sun,

the son of Aditi, who is the light in our eyes.

And we dedicate all that we have to the sun who rules the universe.

Much pleased with being worshipped with chakshusmati vidya,

the sun god said:

A Brahmin who recites this vidya – knowledge – every day will not suffer from eye diseases, nor will anyone in his family ever be struck blind.

The power of this vidya is obtained if it is taught to eight Brahmins,

and knowing it one achieves greatness.

Man is blind. He cannot see that which is. We have eyes, but we can see through them only that which is illusory. Only the appearance is seen, not the real — the real is missed. That's why those who have known have called man blind.

Jesus goes on saying to his disciples, "If you have eyes, look; if you have ears, then listen." Of course, his disciples were not blind, nor were they deaf. They were as with eyes as we are, they had all the senses we have got. Then he must be referring to some other eyes, to some other senses.

These eyes which can look only outwards, which can only look into the without, are blind unless they also become capable of seeing within. If you cannot see yourself you are blind, and one who cannot see himself, what else can he see? And whatsoever he sees, whatsoever his knowledge, it remains based on a deep blindness. Unless you become self-seeing, unless you turn within, unless you can have a look at the reality that you are, whatsoever you encounter in the world is going to be just the appearance. The same will be the proportion: the more you penetrate within the more you can penetrate without, because reality is one.

If you are not acquainted with yourself, all your acquaintance, all your knowledge is just false. Without self-knowledge there is no possibility of any knowledge. You can go on knowing and knowing; you can go on collecting more and more information, but that information will remain information — dead, borrowed. It will never become a knowing eye.

How to attain those eyes which can penetrate the illusory and can encounter the real? This is going to be the base of this whole Upanishad. In the old days it was called *chakshusmati vidya*, the wisdom through which eyes are attained. But the first thing to be constantly remembered is that as we are, we are blind; as we are, we are dead; as we are, we are illusory, the stuff dreams are made of.

Why cannot our eyes see the real? They are so much filled with dreams, so much filled with thoughts, that whatsoever you see, you are not seeing that which is; you project your ideas, your thoughts, your dreams upon it. The whole world becomes just a projection screen, and you go on projecting things. Whatsoever you see outside, you have put it there. You live in a man-created world, and everyone lives in his own world. That world consists of his own projections.

Unless your eyes are completely vacant, unless there is no content within your eyes, no thoughts, no clouds; unless you become mirrorlike, pure, innocent, contentless, you cannot encounter the real. The real can be seen only through naked, empty eyes; it cannot be seen through filled eyes.

This is all the art or the science of meditation consists of: how to make your eyes mirrorlike, nonprojecting – just looking at that which is, not creating it, not imagining it, not adding anything to it...just encountering it as it is. You never see things as they are, you always see through your mind; you color them.

A girl looks beautiful to you or a man looks beautiful. The same man or the same woman was not beautiful a day before, and the same man or the same woman may not be beautiful again. So what happened? How does a person suddenly become beautiful? And your whole logic is illogical. You say, "I love this person because this person is beautiful." The contrary is the case: this person becomes beautiful because you love. The beauty is not the cause but a side-effect.

When you are in love with someone the person becomes beautiful. To others that same person may not be beautiful, and to others the same person may even be ugly. To you also the same person was not beautiful before, and later on the same person can become ugly – to you also. But at this moment, in this mood of love, you project something on the person. You project your dreams, the person becomes just a screen. The whole beauty is put there by you. It is you who create the beautiful face, the beautiful face is your interpretation. It is not the real, because the reality is neither ugly nor beautiful.

If man disappears from this earth what will happen? Will the hills be beautiful, the flowers beautiful, the thorns ugly? – what will happen? With the disappearance of man, beauty and ugliness will disappear. The earth will be there as it is. The sun will rise and the moon will be there in the night, and the sky will be filled every day with stars. Flowers will flower, trees will bloom, the hills will be as they are. Everything will be as it is, but there will be no beauty and no ugliness.

With the disappearance of man all his interpretations disappear. The reality is neither beautiful nor ugly – it is there. You interpret it according to yourself. That's why a certain thing can be beautiful in China and may not be beautiful in India. A certain type of face is beautiful in Africa, it may not be beautiful in England.

When for the first time Christian missionaries came to Africa, they were in a great difficulty. The Bible was to be translated, and God is always depicted as white and the Devil as black. So it was a problem – how to tell the black people that the Devil is black and God is white? They could conceive of God as black and the Devil as white. And that was natural, they had always depicted their God as black; their Devil had always been white. You may not be aware of what the Christian missionaries had to do. In African translations of The Bible, God is depicted as black and the Devil as white; otherwise there could be no communication, no possibility of any meeting.

We conceive of things through our mind; that mind goes on interpreting. But we can understand about beauty and ugliness – what about other interpretations? If man disappears there will be no good and evil in the world, nothing will be moral and nothing will be immoral. All our morality, all our judgment is through conceptions.

A lion jumping on an animal and eating it, tearing it – is he bad or good? Is he evil? If we interpret then it looks very evil, violent. But the lion is not doing anything, he is simply eating. He is not aware of anything – of what is good and what is bad. And he is not doing anything bad; he is taking his lunch, as you take your lunch. If man disappears, then there is nothing good and nothing bad.

And the same happens to the sage. When a man becomes enlightened the man has disappeared from him with all the interpretations, judgments. He has become pure, as if he is no more. The mind has been dropped. He is conscious, fully conscious, but with no contents to project. He looks at the world as it is, without any interpretation. And for the first time he comes to know reality.

Man cannot know the real because man goes on projecting his ideology; and all ideologies are home-made, the existence doesn't support them, you create them. That's why it is said again and again, all over the world – Eckhart says it in the West, Boehme says it in the West, Rinzai says it in Japan, Lin Chi says it in China, Buddha says it in India – all over the world, wherever a mirrorlike mind has appeared, it has said that nothing is bad and nothing is good. There is no evil and no God – existence is one. And if you can accept this existence without any interpretation, for the first time you are creating a way which can lead to the truth.

You cannot carry your mind to the truth. If you carry your mind, whatsoever you come to know will not be the truth. You may encounter the truth but you will not know it, because the moment you see something you have interpreted. You pass through a garden and you see roseflowers. You have not seen them and immediately the mind says, "Beautiful." The flowers have disappeared, your concept has come in. You have projected, you have judged. Jesus says, "Judge ye not." Don't judge.

I have heard about one Mohammedan Sufi mystic. He used to sell small things in the village, and the people of that village became aware that he had no judgment. So they would take the things and give him false coins. He would accept them, because he would never say, "This is wrong and this is right." Sometimes they would take things from him and they would say, "We have paid," and he would not say, "You have not paid." He would say, "Okay." He would thank them.

Then from other villages also people started coming. This man was very good; you could take anything from his shop, you need not pay, or you could pay in false coins, and he accepted everything!

Then death came near to this old man. These were his last words: he looked at the sky and said, "Allah, God, I have been accepting all kinds of coins, false ones also. I am also a false coin – don't judge me. I have not judged your people, please don't judge me." And it is said that how can God judge such a person?

Jesus says, "Judge ye not, so ye may not be judged."

If judgment disappears, you have become innocent. If you don't divide things into good and bad, ugly and beautiful, acceptable and nonacceptable; if you don't divide things, if you look at reality without any division, your eyes will come into existence for the first time. This is chakshusmati vidya, the signs of gaining eyes.

If you divide you will remain blind, if you judge you will remain blind, if you say this is bad and this is good, you will persist in your blindness...because existence knows nothing. There is nothing good and nothing bad – existence accepts everything. And when you also accept everything you have become existence-like. You have become one with it.

So remember, morality is not religion. Rather, on the contrary, morality is one of the hindrances in gaining religion, just like immorality. Morality, immorality – both are hindrances. When you transcend both you have transcended the mind, the dual, the dualistic attitude. Then the sage and the sinner have become one. Then you remain in your self, you don't move to judge. And when you don't judge, your mind cannot project: the mind projects through judgment.

You may have heard this story, so famous, but Christianity goes on missing the meaning of it. In a village a crowd came to Jesus, and they had brought a woman who had sinned in the eyes of the crowd. So they said to Jesus, "This woman is a sinner, and she has confessed. So what should we do now? It is written in the old scriptures that she should be killed by throwing stones at her, she should be stoned to death. What do you say? What should we do?"

They were trying to put Jesus in a dilemma, because if he said not to kill her...as it was expected he should say, because he was saying, "Love. And if someone strikes you on one cheek, give him the other cheek; if someone forces you to carry his burden for one mile, go two miles with him; if someone snatches your coat, give him your shirt also." This man could not say, "Kill, murder, stone this woman to death." And if he said, "No, don't kill her," then they could say, "You are against the scriptures, so you cannot be a prophet. You don't belong to us. You are a destroyer."

But Jesus escaped their dilemma – because the dilemma exists only for the obsessed mind. When there is no mind dilemma disappears, because dilemma consists of division. You divide things in two, in opposites, and then there is the question, What to choose, how to choose? Then the problem arises. But if there is no mind, there is no question of choice – a choicelessness has happened.

So Jesus said, "It is right, it is written in the scriptures to stone this woman to death. It is okay. Bring the stones and kill this woman – but only that man is allowed to stone this woman who has himself not committed sin in his actions, or in his mind."

Then those who were leading the crowd started dispersing, because there was none who had not committed adultery in act or in mind. And there is no difference whether you commit it in action or you commit it in the mind, it is the same for the consciousness. There is no difference. Whether you think of killing a person or you actually kill, there is no difference, because you have killed inwardly when you have thought. If, just in your mind, you want to rape a woman, you have raped. Your whole being has done it. Whether it has become actual in the world of events or not, that is irrelevant, that is secondary. As far as you are concerned the sin has been committed.

Nobody could throw a stone at that woman. The crowd disappeared, only the woman was left. So the woman said to Jesus, "But I have committed…I have done a wrong. I am immoral. So whether the crowd is going to stone me to death or not, you can punish me. I confess."

Jesus said, "Who am I to judge? It is between you and your God, you and the ultimate, you and the all – who am I to judge? It is something between you and existence. Where do I come in?"

This is the mind of the sage, the no-mind of the sage. He cannot divide, so he cannot judge; he cannot say this is good and this is bad. Only this type of consciousness can attain eyes – eyes that can see penetrate into the real.

Now we will enter the sutra.

The sage Sankriti once visited Adityalok, the abode of the sun god, and bowing to him he worshipped him with what is known as chakshusmati vidya. Aum, salutation to the sun god, who illumines the organ of vision! Salutation to the sun who is the great warrior! Salutation to the sun who represents the three conditionings: tamas, rajas and sattva!

A person is called a sage who has become choiceless; a sage means one who cannot judge. A sage in India is not the same as he is in the West. In the West they have been doing many absurd things. One of them, the peak of foolishness, has been this: the pope gives sainthood to people. It is like a certificate or a degree. The pope has to declare that a certain person has become a sage. The council of bishops has to agree, confirm it. So it's just like a university giving a doctorate – LL.D or D.Litt. or something.

So sometimes this has happened, as it happened with Joan of Arc. She was killed, murdered, burned; and she was burned because of the pope, because of the church. They thought she was against Christianity. Then later on the judgment was changed, later on other popes found that the pope who condemned her was wrong. So later on when she was dead, posthumously she was awarded sainthood, she was made a saint. She became Saint Joan of Arc.

But what to do with the man who had condemned her? What to do with the bishop who was solely responsible for her burning and murder, who had proposed to the pope that she should be condemned? He was dead, so what was to be done with him? So his bones were taken out of the grave, out of the town, and they were beaten, insulted, thrown to the dogs. Now Joan became a saint by the decree of the pope.

In the East this looks like the peak of foolishness, the climax of foolishness. Nobody can make a man a sage – nobody, no judge. This is not something like a degree to be given by somebody else; it is an inner achievement, an inner realization. It doesn't depend on anybody else. A sage is a person who has become enlightened. Now he has no choices. For him nothing is bad and nothing is good. He has become natural. He is, just like a tree or like a hill, like a river or like the ocean. He has no mind to say anything, to interpret. He doesn't divide.

It is said of one Zen master, one Zen sage…. He lived in a small hut three or four miles outside a village. One night he found that a thief had entered his hut. He was very much disturbed, because there was nothing in the house, and this thief had traveled for three or four miles in the night and he would have to go back empty handed. The sage started weeping and crying. The thief also became concerned. He said, "What has happened? Why are you crying so much? Are you disturbed that I may take something from your hut?"

The sage said, "No, that is not the thing, I am disturbed because there is nothing here. At least you could have been a little more gentlemanly, you could have informed me before; I would have arranged something for you to steal. There is nothing – what will you think of me? And this is such an honor, that you traveled three or four miles in this night, this cold night, to come to my hut. No one has given such an honor to me before. I am just a beggar and you have made me a king, just by the idea that something can be stolen from me. And there is nothing, so I am crying. So what should I do now? You can take my blanket."

He had only one blanket, otherwise he was naked, just under his blanket he was naked. And the night was very cold. He said to the thief, "Please have some compassion on me and don't say no, because I have nothing else to give to you. Take this blanket, and whenever you again think of visiting, just send a hint. I am poor, but still I will arrange something."

The thief could not understand what was happening, but he saw the man crying and weeping so he took compassion on him; he couldn't say no. He took the blanket and disappeared. And that night this Zen monk wrote a small haiku, in which he said…he was sitting still at his window, the night was cool, cold, the full moon was in the sky, and he says in his haiku:

God
if I could give this moon
to that thief….

This is the mind of a sage, or, the no-mind. With this same sage, again a thief happened to come to his hut. He was writing a letter, so he looked at the thief and said, "For what have you come? What do you want?"

And this sage was so innocent that even the thief couldn't tell a lie. So he said, "Looking at you, so mirrorlike, so innocent like a child, I cannot tell a lie. Should I tell the truth?"

The sage said, "Yes."

He said, "I have come to steal something."

The sage said, "There in that corner I have got a few rupees. You can take them" – and then he started to write his letter again.

The thief took the money, was trying to go out, and then the sage said, "Stop! When somebody gives you something you should thank him. The money may not be of much help, but thanking a person will go a long way and will be of help to you. So thank me!" The thief thanked him and disappeared into the dark.

Later on the thief was caught, and it was discovered that he had been to this sage's hut also, so the sage was called to the court. The sage said, "Yes, I know this man very well – but he has never stolen anything from me. I gave him some rupees and he thanked me for them. It is finished, it was nothing wrong. The whole thing is finished, the account is closed. I gave him some money and he thanked me for it. He is not a thief."

This mind, or no-mind, of a sage is the base.

The sage Sankriti once visited Adityalok.

This is a parable. *Adityalok* means the abode of the sun or the abode of light, enlightenment. The sun is just a symbol. The sun is not only a life-giving source, it is a light-giving source also. So the sun is symbolic. Sankriti, a sage, visited the abode of the sun.

It means that only sages can visit the abode of light. We remain in darkness, we remain in dark nights – not because there is night all around, but because our eyes are closed. Filled with so many projections, we cannot see the light all around. The light is there, the abode is everywhere. You need not go to visit the sun – the sun reaches everywhere. To every nook and corner of the earth the sun reaches, but only one who has become a sage can enter into its abode.

The sage Sankriti once visited Adityalok, the abode of the sun god, and bowing to him he worshipped him with what is known as chakshusmati vidya.

He bowed down to the sun and worshipped him, and this worship was done by the science of attaining real eyes. This is beautiful, because this is the only way you can worship light. The only way to worship light is to attain eyes; the worship is finished. If you can look at the light without any projection, this is the worship. If you project, you have changed the light into darkness. You are behaving like a blind man.

No other worship is needed. There is no need to go and kneel down on the earth and say a prayer to the sun. That is useless. The only worship is to attain those eyes which can see light. So the sage, Sankriti, worshipped the sun, bowing down to him with what is known as chakshusmati vidya. If you attain those eyes which can see the real you have become a worshipper, and only that worship can be accepted by existence, no other.

Your prayers are nothing but demands, your prayers are nothing but childish, foolish demands. They are of no use. You cannot persuade existence to move according to you. But go to the churches, to the temples – what are people doing there? They think they are worshipping, praying, meditating. They are not doing anything like that. They are just persuading the divine power to follow them, to do whatsoever they desire, to be according to them. They are giving advice. They know more than the divine; they know more what is to be done than the divine knows, so they have come just to give some advice.

They are trying to persuade, but there is no way to persuade the whole, be-cause the whole always knows more than the part. And the whole cannot follow the part, the part has to follow the whole. The whole cannot follow you. And it is good that it doesn't follow you, otherwise you would create a chaos – you don't know what you are asking.

You may have heard this story. Once it happened that a man was worshipping Shiva. He worshipped and worshipped, prayed and prayed for years. Then Shiva appeared and he said, "You can ask for three blessings, three gifts; three boons can be given to you."

The man had been worshipping for so long that he really had forgotten why he had started. His mind was so constantly changing. The worship had become an obsession. He had forgotten for what, so he said, "Let me think."

Then he asked for one gift. The gift was given. Then he became aware that this wouldn't do; he had asked for something wrong. He was angry with his wife, so he had said, "Kill her!" Immediately she was dead. And this can happen to any husband or any wife. They are fighting, filled with hate. But hate is also not total, there is love also. Mind is divided: you love the person and you hate the same person. It is always fifty-fifty. He asked that the wife should be killed, and the wife was dead; immediately she fell down. The moment she was dead he became aware that he loved her very much, so he said, "Please, revive her again." So the second gift was wasted. Two gifts wasted: first she was killed, second she was revived – only one was left. Then he said, "Now, give me time enough to think; otherwise I will again make a mistake, and then there is no fourth."

Shiva waited and waited. Years passed and he would come again and again and he would ask, "Now you ask for the third."

The man was so puzzled he couldn't sleep. He became almost insane just thinking about the one wish, because only one was left. He went visiting all the persons he knew who were wise, and they suggested many things, but nothing seemed worthwhile. Then he asked Shiva himself. "You tell me. I am going mad!"

And what Shiva told him is to be remembered. He said, "There can be only one wish, one desire which is worthwhile. Ask for desirelessness, otherwise nothing is worthwhile. Whatsoever you ask, the next moment you will want something else, even just the opposite of the first."

The mind is divided; our prayers are through that divided mind. A sage is a person who has become undivided. He cannot pray; his prayer is not through words, his prayer is through his being. The way he is, is his worship. So when this sage, Sankriti, looked at the sun, the god, the god of light, the very look, the way he looked, was his worship. The way he was, was his prayer. Those pure eyes, with no dreams, no clouds, no tears, no demands, not asking anything;

just simple, innocent, childlike, just looking at the god – that was the worship.

O Lord, from untruth lead me to truth.

And when the sun god was happy and was ready to bless him, this was his wish.

O Lord, from untruth lead me to truth; from darkness lead me to light; and from death lead me to the eternal.

This is what every seeker is asking: From untruth lead me to truth, from darkness lead me to light, and from death to deathlessness. This is all that everyone is seeking.

The sun god is holy; he is without parallel. The sun god holds all manifestations, and is adorned with a garland of constellations. He is all fire, luminous like gold, effulgent and hot. With a thousand rays and presenting himself in a hundred ways, this sun makes itself manifest to all creatures. Salutation to the sun, the son of Aditi, who is the light in our eyes. We dedicate all that we have to the sun who rules the universe.

Much pleased with being worshipped with chakshusmati vidya the sun god said: A Brahmin who recites this vidya – knowledge – every day, will not suffer from eye diseases, nor will anyone in his family ever be struck blind. The power of this vidya is obtained if it is taught to eight Brahmins, and knowing it one achieves greatness.

Many inner meanings have to be understood. That which is to be said is said through a parable. Don't be much concerned with the parable, don't be much concerned with the words that have been used. Rather be concerned with the significance, the inner meaning.

*Much pleased with being worshipped with…*the science of real eyes….

Existence is pleased with you when you are real. When you are unreal existence is not pleased with you. Not that there is someone who is pleased and unpleased. The way existence behaves is like any natural law, for example gravitation. If you walk in a balanced way gravitation is pleased with you, the gravitation will not be destructive to you. But if you lose balance you will fall down on the earth. You may become crippled for your whole life, you may break your bones. Gravitation is unpleased with you, not pleased with you. But there is nobody deciding – this is a natural law. If you follow the law you will be happy, if you don't follow the law you will be unhappy.

This is what in the East has been called the law of karma, the law of action. If your action follows the ultimate law, you will be attaining more and more bliss. If you go against it, immediately you will fall into suffering. There is no one like a grand manager deciding everybody's actions, who is doing wrong and who is doing good, and who is to be sent to the heaven and who is to be thrown into hell – there is no one. With every movement you create your heaven and your hell. If you follow the ultimate law, you are creating heaven for yourself moment to moment. If you go astray, if you go against the law, *you* are creating hell, not the law.

This is just a way of saying that the god was pleased. Why was he pleased? He was pleased because this man, Sankriti, this sage, Sankriti, had the real eyes to look with. He had become pure, innocent. His eyes were vacant of all theories, doctrines, scriptures. He was not projecting anything from his eyes. He was simply absorbing. His eyes were used to look, not to interpret.

Much pleased with being worshipped with chakshusmati vidya, the sun god said: A Brahmin who recites this vidya every day, will not suffer from eye diseases.

We are all suffering from eye diseases. This is just symbolic. Not that we use specs – those eyes are not what is meant. Even a blind man suffers from eye diseases and he has no eyes. These eyes, these visible eyes are not what is meant.

The world that we create around us is created through our eye diseases. We go on looking wrongly, we go on dividing. The universe is one, but our eyes go on dividing. That division is the disease. The existence is just as it is. We go on condemning or appreciating, that is the eye disease. We go on judging. Facts are just facts, there is no way to judge.

One Zen monk, Bokuju, was passing through a street in a village. Somebody came and struck him with a stick. He fell down, and with him, the stick also. He got up and picked up the stick. The man who had hit him was running away. Bokuju ran after him, calling, "Wait, take your stick with you!" He followed after him and gave him the stick. A crowd had gathered to see what was happening, and somebody asked Bokuju, "That man struck you hard, and you have not said anything!"

Bokuju is reported to have said, "A fact is a fact. He has hit, that's all. It happened that he was the hitter and I was the hit. It is just as if I am passing under a tree, or sitting under a tree, and a branch falls down. What will I do? What can I do?"

But the crowd said, "But a branch is a branch, this is a man. We cannot say anything to the branch, we cannot punish it. We cannot say to the tree that it is bad, because a tree is a tree, it has no mind."

Bokuju said, "This man to me is also just a branch. And if I cannot say anything to the tree, why should I bother to say anything to this man? It happened. I am not going to interpret what has happened. And it has already happened. Why get worried about it? It is finished, over."

This is the mind of a sage – not choosing, not asking, not saying this should be and this should not be. Whatsoever happens, he accepts it in its totality. This acceptance gives him freedom, this acceptance gives him the capacity to see. These are eye diseases: shoulds, should nots, divisions, judgments, condemnations, appreciations.

A Brahmin who recites this vidya every day….

Recites means lives. Through his whole being the recitation continues, through his whole being he is just a looker, not a judger. His eyes are just working like a mirror, whatsoever comes before them is mirrored. The moment it passes the mirror is again vacant. It does not cling; it does not think about the past, it does not look into the future.

The mirror remains in the present – whatsoever passes is mirrored. When it has gone the mirror is vacant again, nothing is left. You cannot destroy its mirrorlike innocence. This is the recitation. The whole day, moment to moment, one who lives this vidya, this knowledge, this seeing, will never suffer from eye diseases.

…Nor will anyone in his family ever be struck blind.

By family, the natural family is not meant. When a master is there his disciples are his family, not his sons and daughters. That has been called *kul*, the family. In the East, particularly in India, the house of the master, his ashram, was called *gurukul* – the family of the master. His disciples were really his descendants.

And if a master lives constantly seeing mirrorlike, his disciples will never be blind; blindness will never strike his family – those who belong to him in spirit, not in body. Ordinarily those who belong to you in body, they are your family, but for a master his family is those who belong to him in spirit. Those who belong to him in knowing, in discipline, in yoga, in *sadhana*, they are his family. And if a master lives constantly mirrorlike, the disciples are bound to be transformed just by his presence – even if they don't do anything, even if they just sit by the side of the master.

The word *upanishad* is very meaningful. It means sitting by the side of the master. The word upanishad means just sitting in the presence of the master, not doing anything. It is not a question of doing, it is a question of being – absorbing the master. That's what is meant in Christianity when Christ said, "Eat me. I will become your food."

When you are near a master who is living this innermost science of being mirrorlike – mind has ceased, a simple consciousness, a flame – you can eat him, he can become your blood and bones. Nothing is to be done, you have simply to remain receptive in his presence – intimate, close, receptive, not fighting it, just open. He will flow, he will become a flow within you. He will come to you, he will fill you to the very deepest center. Just living with the master, not doing anything, just being in his presence, you are eating him. And he wants to be eaten, he wants to become the food.

But the food is very subtle. It is so subtle that if you are a little disturbed, judging, arguing, fighting in the mind, resisting, you will miss it. It is such a subtle music. You should be as if you are absent when you are in the presence of the master; as if you are not – just a passage so he can travel. He is not going to do it by his will – there is no will. If you are open he simply travels...that's how it happens. If you are open he simply flows in you.

...Nor will anyone in his family ever be struck blind. The power of this vidya is obtained if it is taught to eight Brahmins, and knowing it one achieves greatness.

This is also to be understood. This is the secret of why a Buddha goes on trying for almost forty years, traveling from one village to another village seeking disciples; why Jesus is ready even to go to the cross; why Mahavira suffers so much – just to make contacts, to commune whatsoever he has attained.

A responsibility falls on you when you are enlightened, and that responsibility is not a duty enforced from without; it is something that is coming from within. When you become enlightened you have to share it. So it has never been otherwise; a person who has become enlightened, he has to share it. It is not a question of his decision to share or not. He has to share it, the very phenomenon is such that he has to give it to others. He has to find persons who can receive, who can eat him, for whom he can become food.

Buddha came to a village one evening. The whole village gathered, but he was waiting, as if for someone. Then somebody asked, "Why are you waiting? Everybody has come, now start your sermon."

Buddha said, "The one for whom I have come is still absent. I will have to wait. You can hear me but you cannot listen. The person for whom I have come...."

They were very much disturbed, because all the respectable persons were present. All the rich were present; all the good, saintly, religious were present. For whom was he waiting? And then a girl came – a very ordinary, poor girl. She was coming back from her field. The moment she came, he started. So they asked, "You were waiting for this girl? We were not even aware that she lives in this village."

Buddha is reported to have said, "In this village only she is receptive. For her I have traveled. She does not know much, she is not a scholar, she is not rich in any way. She is not respectable, she belongs to the untouchables, is poor, unknown, but she is receptive, and she has called me. Her receptivity is such that I became aware in the neighboring village that someone was calling me to flow. I have come to this village because of her."

A disciple is one who is ready to receive, who can become like a womb, who is passive, open, vulnerable. And a master is one who is flowing, overflowing, dispersing his last body into the existence. And the best way is to become food for those who are seekers. This is Jesus' sacrament. That is why the last thing he did on this earth was to call his disciples for the Last Supper. That is a symbol: before he leaves they should eat him totally.

The power of this vidya is obtained if it is taught to eight Brahmins....

But to find eight brahmins is very difficult. Eight brahmins means eight seekers – seekers of Brahman. It is very difficult; you have to go all around the world, then you can find eight. And even then it is not certain. Jesus had only twelve disciples.

Very few are there who are ready to receive; very few are there who are really in search; very few are there whose effort is authentic. Curious are many, but their curiosity is childlike, childish. They are curious about new things, but not authentically interested, not ready to do something, not ready to be transformed.

So the sun god says that the power of this vidya grows greater if you can share it with at least eight persons. A Buddha becomes more a Buddha, a Jesus becomes more a Christ the more he shares. This is the nature of bliss – the more you share it the more it grows. If you can share it with the whole existence it becomes the ultimate. But our minds are very miserly, we cannot share.

I have heard, once it happened: one man's wife died in a Buddhist land, somewhere in China. The man called a Buddhist monk to pray for his wife who was dead now and had gone on a new journey – just to pray to protect her. The monk prayed, meditated, and then he said, "Everything will be good. Don't you worry."

The man asked, "But I heard you saying something like 'for all the beings of the earth.' You never mentioned my wife in particular. You were asking blessings, you were asking bliss for all the beings of the earth, but you were not mentioning my wife in particular. Mention her name in particular!"

The monk said, "It is difficult, because Buddha has said that whenever you ask for something, ask for all. It has to be shared with all. I cannot ask only for your wife. And if I ask only for your wife she will not get it. If I ask for all, only then is there a possibility." Then the man said, "Okay, but at least make one exception – just my neighbor. Exclude him! – and ask for everyone else. But at least make one exception. Exclude him, because I cannot bear this idea that he is also getting blessings of the divine."

This miserliness, this mind of jealousy, hatred, cannot understand how to share. You never share anything. You may give something to somebody, but there is always a hidden bargain. Remember the difference. You can give many gifts to your husband, to your wife, to your friends, but they are deep bargains – you are expecting something to be returned. That is not sharing.

Sharing means you are never expecting anything in return, you are simply giving. You are not even expecting thankfulness.

It happened with Dozo, one Zen monk. A rich man came to Dozo with ten thousand gold coins. That is very much, a big amount. He was going to make that a gift for the temple where Dozo was the priest. Dozo accepted as if it was nothing. The man became disturbed. He said, "Do you know these are ten thousand gold coins?"

Dozo said, "You have said it so many times, I have heard it so many times. You have said it already too many times – do you think I am deaf?"

The man was just asking for thanks, only thanks, nothing more. Then he said, "Ten thousand golden coins is a big amount, even to me. I am a very rich man, but that amount is very big."

Dozo said, "What do you want? What are you really asking? Are you asking for some gratitude? Are you asking that I should be thankful to you?"

The man said, "At least that much can be expected."

So Dozo said, "Take your gold coins back. Or, if you want to give them to this temple, you will have to be thankful to me that I accepted."

On the temple it is written even still...it is written that the giver should be thankful; only then is it a sharing. Somebody accepted your gift. This is such a great thing, because he could have rejected. Somebody accepted you through your gift. He could have rejected, there was no necessity to accept it. The giver should be thankful. Then it becomes a sharing, otherwise it is always a bargain. You are expecting something – something more valuable than you have given.

When someone becomes enlightened he can share, and he will do whatsoever he can just to share it.

3   With Your Total Heart

One friend has said that he is a devotee of Sai Baba, and therefore he is reluctant to call anyone else Bhagwan, but he wants my help, guidance. He says:

Osho,

I feel I have surrendered to Sai Baba, but still I feel the necessity of working with another teacher or guru. Is this possible?

The first thing is to remember that the master really does not work. He is there, his presence works, but the presence can work only if you have trust. If you don't have trust, nothing can be done.

So really, if you feel you have surrendered to Sai Baba, what is the need to come to me? If the surrender has really happened, then asking for another master is futile. I doubt your surrender, your trust, because when trust has happened nothing more is needed. And if something more is needed, trust has not happened; you are still in search. If you cannot trust me, it is impossible to work. Not that I have any conditions, my door is open unconditionally, but it will remain closed to you because you can see it as open only when you have trust.

It is good if you feel an intimate closeness with Sai Baba, or anyone else. It is good. But then don't wander here and there, then don't go to anybody else, because this is impossible. Your trust remains with Sai Baba, then no one else can do anything; it is impossible. But you are not certain. You may be believing that surrender has happened. It has not happened, because then to ask for help from somebody else is just absurd. And if you ask for help, surrender will be needed. The reason is:

I cannot do anything positively.

I am available.

If you trust me then the contact is made.

It is just like this: light is there, but if you are sitting with closed eyes, the light cannot do anything in order for your eyes to open. Not that the light has any conditions for you. It is available, it is already there, it is already giving itself to you, but your eyes are closed. And if you say, "In this room I cannot open my eyes, because I have surrendered my eyes to some other room, to some other light," then here you will have to remain in darkness. Not that light is not available, but you are not receptive.

If you have come here, that shows that you may believe you trust in Sai Baba but you don't trust. You think you have surrendered, but your thinking is wrong, illusory. If you have surrendered then move to Sai Baba, open yourself to him so that he can work; then don't go seeking here and there. I am ready to help, but for that you will have to be receptive. I cannot be aggressive to you, nobody can be. The very work is impossible with such aggression. If you trust me, something becomes possible. Then without any aggression the work starts. If you don't trust, then I can only be violent to you, forcibly I have to open your eyes. That cannot be done. You cannot be forced into nirvana, you can only flow into it.

If you don't trust my river, how can you flow with me? Then deep down you will be struggling; then you will be wasting your time, my time, and it is useless. So be clear about it. It may not only be the case with one man, it may be with many of you. Your heart belongs somewhere else? – then go there. Be wherever your heart is. If your heart is with me, only then is something possible; otherwise don't waste your time and energy. This has to be understood clearly.

Your trust means that you are open. Your trust means that now you are ready to go into the unknown, into the uncharted. How can you move with me if you don't trust me? And what you call me is insignificant to me, but not to you. Whether you call me Bhagwan or not, it is the same to me, but not the same to you, because your feeling will decide many things. If you cannot call anybody Bhagwan other than Sai Baba, then go to him, because then he is your temple, and only in his presence will you be transformed. And nothing is wrong in it.

But you have come here. That shows that the touch has not happened; you have not moved in deep, close intimacy. The relationship has not happened, the love has not happened. You can go on deceiving yourself. That will not be of much help. So be clear, analyze your own mind. If your heart is here, then there are possibilities. If your heart is not here, then go wherever your heart leads you.

I know you will have to come back, because you have been with Sai Baba, as you have said in this letter, and nothing has happened there. You are here, and I know that now you will move to some other teacher, and there you will say you have been with me and nothing has happened. And you are not here with me! Just physically being here doesn't mean anything.

I know this must have been the case with Sai Baba also. You may have been there physically, as you are here, but it is not a question of physical presence, it is a question of inner opening. Then you may be on another planet and I can work. You are not needed to be here; space doesn't mean anything, nor does time mean anything. You may be on another planet, you may be in another time, but if you are receptive you are here close to me. You may be just here, existing this very moment, but if your heart is not here then there is no possibility of any bridge.

There are many who go on wandering from one master to another. The total result may be simply confusion, because each master works in his own way, he has his own methods, and you go on accumulating information. That information is bound to be contradictory. Then you will get confused, you may even go insane. It is better to stick to one master and give your heart totally to him. If then nothing happens, move. But be finished with that master, don't be in an incomplete relationship. Be finished. Either you are transformed, or you come to know that this master is not for you. Then the relationship has broken, there is no incompletion. Then you can move to another master with your total heart.

Now you are here and you are thinking of Sai Baba. This division will become a hindrance. First go back to Sai Baba, be finished with him. Either you are transformed, then there is no need to find anyone; or Sai Baba is not your master, it is proved. Then come to me.

And the same applies to my own disciples. If you are here with me, be finished with me. Be totally with me, so that either the mutation happens and then there is no need to find anyone or to go anywhere, or you come to realize, "This man is not for me." Then you can leave me totally, then you can move, then somewhere else.... But being here with me halfheartedly and then moving to someone else halfheartedly will not do. Rather, it may be dangerous. You may become so split, so divided, with so many voices in you, that you may become a crowd. This has already happened to many. They know too much and they have drunk from so many sources that now they cannot decide where they stand, who they are. And they go on adding more confusion.

Patience is needed. If you are totally devoted to one master the thing is bound to happen. And I would say that even if the master is not true, the thing can happen if you are totally devoted. Even if the master is false the happening is possible if you are totally devoted – because the happening doesn't happen through the master, it happens through total devotion. So even a dead master, or a master who has never been, just the name, will do. The real alchemy, the science of mutation, is within you. The master is at the most just a catalytic agent, nothing more.

Go back to your own master and be with him. And don't try to judge him; you have got no way to judge anybody. All that you can do is give your total heart to him. And what have you got to lose? So why be so afraid? You have got nothing to lose, so why be so untrusting? Give yourself totally. Just this giving totally becomes the base of your transformation. Many times it has happened that a disciple was transformed through a master who was not a master at all. And many times the contrary has also happened: the master was true but the disciple was not transformed. The ultimate thing depends on you, not on me. You are the deciding factor.

So wherever you go, make it a law: go with your total heart. Otherwise you will move with empty hands everywhere. And the more you move, the more you go to this master and that, the more there will be confusion, suffering, and finally you may decide that there exists no one who can transform you. Or, you may come to conclude that there is nothing like transformation, this is all hocus-pocus. And the reason will only be this – that you were never anywhere with your total heart.

The next question:

Osho,

Does reason or intellect have any place at all in sadhana?

Only this much: that reason has to show you that reason is useless, reason has to commit suicide – only this much. One of the greatest Tibetan mystics, Marpa, is reported to have said…. Somebody asked him, "Can't scriptures help?" He said, "They can. They can help you to go beyond scriptures. That is their only use. Read the scriptures, study them; they will help you to understand that scriptures are useless, and the truth cannot be attained through them."

Reason can help you only in this way. Reason out, analyze, argue, and through this whole effort you will come to understand that reason cannot lead you to truth. But this is one of the greatest possibilities. Once you realize this you can drop reason, and when reason is dropped, for the first time you start functioning from a totally different center of your being, and that is the heart. And the heart can trust. Reason can never trust, reason by nature is untrusting. Remember, reason can analyze, but can never synthesize. Reason can cut and divide, but can never create a unity or harmony. Reason is just like scissors, scissors can cut and divide.

It happened once that somebody presented Bayazid, one Sufi saint, with a pair of golden scissors. They were valuable, there were some diamonds on those golden scissors, and the man who was presenting them was very happy that it was a rare, unique gift. But Bayazid said, "Take them back, because my whole being is not to cut, not to analyze, not to divide. Rather, you bring a needle and some thread for me, because synthesis is my goal. I want to join things together, not to cut them apart. Golden or not golden," Bayazid said, "a needle will do. The scissors may be very valuable but they are not for me."

Reason is scissorlike: it cuts, divides, analyzes. That's why science cannot do without reason. It doubts, that's its basic function. It is good – for a particular purpose it is good. As far as matter is concerned, as far as the world of the outside is concerned, reason is the method. Science cannot do without reason, because science is analysis, dissection. That's why science finally reached the atom, the ultimate division. And now they have divided even the atom, and they have reached electrons. They will go on dividing.

Science reaches to the atomic, and religion reaches to the divine. Religion goes on joining things together, and the ultimate unity is God. The totality has been taken in. Religion cannot work with reasoning, just as science cannot work with trust. If you are a scientist you have to doubt, doubt is the very base. But in religion, if you doubt you are lost. In religion you have to trust.

These dimensions are diametrically opposite. Science moves in religion moves into the within. They move diametrically opposite, their dimensions are opposite, so obviously religion must be opposite to the scientific approach. Science means reason, doubt; religion means trust, faith. So only one thing can be done by your reason and that is to realize that reason will not be of much help in the world of sadhana, in the world of inner discipline. Then drop it and allow another center of your being, the heart, to function.

When the heart starts functioning you will have a different world around you – because you create your world. If you are doubting you create a world which is filled with doubt, depression, sadness, darkness. If you work through the heart you create a different world

– of radiancy, of love, of prayer, of joy – but that is totally different. And you cannot change from one world to another, you will have to change from one center to another. And these centers are within you, the center which doubts and the center which trusts.

When you fall in love, what is the use of reason? How can you use your reason while falling in love? That's why reason says it is a fall: "falling in love." Who created this phraseology, "falling in love"? Why not "rising in love?" Reason has condemned love, reason says it is a fall. And in a way it is, because from the head you fall to the heart. You start functioning from a different center. But how can you use your reason in love? Is there any way to use it? If you use it, you will destroy the whole phenomenon. The first thing reason will say is, "Doubt!" The first thing reason will say is, "Is there anything in existence which you can call love? Is there anything like love? Dissect it." And if you dissect, love disappears.

Love is a unity and a very delicate harmony; it cannot be dissected. It is just like a small child jumping, dancing, enjoying. He is alive. You cut the child, dissect him; you put him on a table, a surgeon's table, and dissect him to find out where life is, what it was that was alive – you will not find it. Not that it was not there; the way you are trying to find it means you will miss, the very method prohibits. The moment you dissect the child he is dead, the life has disappeared, and by dissecting you will come to death, not to life.

Science ultimately leads to death – Hiroshima and Nagasaki are not accidental. And if man still follows science for one more century…even one century is too optimistic; these coming twenty-five years…. If man continuously follows science it may prove a global suicide, because dissection cannot lead to life; the ultimate result is bound to be death. And science cannot believe in life, because you cannot find it anywhere, in any laboratory. You dissect, and life disappears. You dissect your beloved, and love disappears. You go to a surgeon and let him dissect your heart, or take x-rays of your heart to find out whether love is there or not. He may find a cancer there, but he cannot find love. Death can be detected, love cannot be detected. There is no way to have an x-ray of love. Death can be detected; if it is there, if cancer is there, it can be detected, science can find it out.

Go to a library and look at medical encyclopedias to find a definition of health. You will not find it. You will find every disease defined, but you cannot find any definition of health. Science cannot define health, because health can-not be detected. If you go to a doctor he can tell you that you are ill, but he cannot give you a certificate that you are healthy. He can give you a certificate that you are not ill – that's another matter, negative; he cannot give you a certificate that you are healthy. And there is no definition of what health is.

Science goes on fighting with a method, the very method creates the world of science. Religion doesn't work with that method. Religion works through a different type of methodology – the heart is the center. And if you can become headless, only then is religion something meaningful for you. If you are too much in the head, religion is not for you. If you are too much in the head, then prayer is very distant, even love is impossible. You can exploit people, you can kill them, but you cannot love them through reason. Or, reason can create such deceptions.

I was just looking at a Peanuts joke-book. Charlie Brown says there, "I love mankind; it is people that I can't stand." "I love mankind; it is people that I can't stand." The head can love mankind, because there is no one like mankind. You will not find mankind anywhere. Wherever you go you will find people, and the head cannot stand people.

It is easy to love a country, to love humanity, to love the nation, to love Christianity, to love Islam, to love Hinduism. It is very difficult to love a real person, very difficult, because for the real person the heart will be needed. And these concepts, abstract concepts – humanity, Hinduism, Islam, Christianity, or even God – the head can work with, there is no problem, because only thinking is implied, no lived experience is needed. You are not asked to get involved in anything where your heart will be required: just concepts, just logic, mathematics. The head can do that. Science is head work: religion is heart work. You can use your reason only to destroy reason, to help reason to commit suicide.

My whole effort is to persuade you to become headless.

Live without the head, then you will have a life which is totally different from this life you are leading. The life that you are leading is exactly how hell is defined in old scriptures. And if you go into hell, you may not be able to recognize that it is hell; you will think it is only an extension of the old world. You will find everything that you have got already, hell now cannot give you anything new. Man has himself created everything here on this earth.

Help your reason to commit suicide.

Fall within to the heart.

Let love, prayer, meditation, become the center of your world.

But in the beginning help will be needed, because in the beginning you cannot do anything else – you are there, existing in the head. That's why I go on talking so much. These talks are useless, they are not needed, but you exist in the head, so somehow you have to drop out. I am not giving you theories, I am not giving you some stuff to think about. I am simply helping your reason to come to a point where it itself realizes that just living in reason is missing life in its totality.

In the beginning it is needed. The first step has to be taken out of the head, so the head has to be approached. The moment you have taken that first step, then there is no need. But the first step is most difficult. You are so much obsessed with reason that whatsoever is said, your reason starts working around it. Whatsoever you read here becomes food for your reason.

Religious discourses are really poisons, they are poisonous food. Buddha talks, Krishna talks, Lao Tzu goes on preaching to the disciples. What are they doing? They are doing only one thing: they are giving you poison which looks like food to reason. Reason immediately absorbs it, but it is poison, and reason will have to die. And once reason is dead, for the first time you will be alert, conscious, awakened, and you will see the whole world in a new light.

The world remains the same but you are different, you have changed. Now you can look through different eyes. Then this world is not evil; then there is no suffering in the world. Then the whole world is just the dance of Shiva, just a divine celebration. And the whole life is a play. That's why Hindus have called it *leela:* leela means play, a play of divine energy.

Hindus have said that it is not a creation, it is a play. It is not a serious thing, it is simple play – a play of too much energy. But right now you cannot think in that way, that door is closed. Put reason aside, start functioning in a loving way. Bring more heart into your behavior, into your actions, into your movements. Then whatsoever Krishna and Jesus and Lao Tzu have said, that will become a truth to you, it will be revealed. You just need fresh eyes which can see it, hence so much emphasis on trust.

The third question:

Osho,

If the divine is right here and now, then what prevents us from seeing him? Why do we cling to our dream life, even though it has become a misery for us?

No, it has not become a misery for you yet, otherwise you could not cling to it. No one can cling to misery. You still have hopes, you have not yet become totally hopeless. Even in your misery you are hoping. You are thinking that today is misery but tomorrow the doors of paradise will open, and this misery is just a means to reach that paradise tomorrow. Unless the tomorrow dies completely, unless the tomorrow drops completely, unless you become totally hopeless, no hope...only then will you see what misery is there where you are living. And once you become aware of the misery that you are living, you will drop it – there will be no need for me to tell you.

Somebody came to Buddha and asked him, "You go on saying that life is suffering, *dukkha;* you go on saying that the house is on fire, and I realize that this is so, but how should we come out of that house which is on fire?"

Buddha said, "You are not seeing that the house is on fire. If the house is on fire you will not come to ask me, you will simply jump out of that house." You won't go to find a master to learn techniques, you won't consult The Bible and Koran to find out how to get out of the house which is on fire. When the house is on fire, you will leave your Koran and Bible inside, and you will jump out. And even if a Buddha is sitting there, you will remember only when you are out of the house that Buddha has been left inside, the master has been left inside. When you realize the house is on fire, you simply jump out of it; there is no method.

All methods are postponements. You are in search of a method so that you can postpone, because a method will need time, so you can say to yourself, "How can I jump right now? It will take three years, six years, lives, to practice. It is such a difficult thing, so I will first practice how to jump, and then I will jump. But unless I practice, I cannot jump."

And you have been doing this practice, this rehearsal, for many lives. You are not here for the first time to ask me – you have asked many times. The same questions you have been asking in every life, but you never do anything, be-cause Buddha may be saying that the house is on fire, but you look...it is a palace, nothing is on fire. Just out of consideration for Buddha you don't deny him. Otherwise you know he is crazy; the house is not on fire. Or he may be talking in symbols, he may be meaning something else. Or he is such a great man that you cannot understand what he is saying, so just out of respect you don't deny him, you say yes. Your yes doesn't mean any more than your no. Your yes, your no are meaningless.

I have heard that Mulla Nasruddin was in love with a woman, but very worried, depressed, always sad, so one friend asked, "What is the matter?"

He said, "Everything is finished, and I am contemplating suicide."

The friend said, "But you have been contemplating so long. Tell me what the matter is – maybe I can help you."

Nasruddin said, "I asked the woman to get married to me."

The friend said, "Yes, no need to say anything more, I have understood. She must have said no. But you are a fool. Don't believe it when a woman says no; she always means yes."

Nasruddin said, "I know that wisdom, and if she had said no, then there would have been no problem. But when I proposed she said, 'Rats.' So now what to understand? She said, 'Rats'; she never said no. Had she said no, then yes could be understood."

Everybody's mind is just like that woman. When you say no, the yes is hidden behind it. If somebody has slightly penetrating eyes, he can see your yes hidden behind the no. When you say yes it is just skin-deep, the no is hidden behind. And your yes can be turned into no without any effort. Your no can be turned into yes without much effort. Your yes and no are only different in degrees, not in quality. They can be changed, they continuously go on changing.

Even a small child knows this. The father says, "No, you are not going to the movie today." But even a small child knows that yes is hidden behind it. He starts a tantrum, he starts crying, and within minutes the father says, "Go, go! Go away from here." The child knows the yes is hidden behind the no. It can be brought out immediately, a little effort is needed. And no child believes in your yes or no because you can change so easily; no child trusts you. But this is how the human mind is.

So the first thing: you are not in misery. Buddha has said so, I may be saying so, but you know that you are not in misery. You go on feeling, hoping, that tomorrow something is going to happen. And tomorrow is the drug; through the tomorrow you intoxicate yourself, and then the day which is present, today, you can suffer it. It is not much, only a question of a few hours and then the tomorrow will be there; it is coming nearer and nearer. Because of the misery on this earth, we conceive of heaven as somewhere in the other life; that heaven is our tomorrow extended. Just to carry on anyhow this misery that is around us, we look somewhere ahead. We never look right now, here.

You are not in misery. I may be saying so; you go on believing that happiness is just near, you are just on the verge of it. The goal is so near, so why leave? Just continue a little more, be patient. If you realize that you are in misery, then there is no need to ask how to drop it. Then masters will be needed to teach you how to cling to it, and even then you will not listen to them.

Once you know that your life is misery, even a buddha cannot persuade you to cling to it. But the penetration is not there. It is not your realization. This knowing is not your knowledge, this wisdom has not been achieved through your own efforts. It is borrowed, it is cheap. You have heard that life is misery, but you have not realized it. And you say, "Why do we go on clinging to this dream life?" It is not a dream life to you; it is real. When you see a dream the dream is real. Somebody who has awakened from sleep may go on saying that whatsoever you are seeing is just a dream, but the person who is dreaming, he is dreaming a reality, not a dream. In a dream, howsoever absurd, you cannot feel it as a dream. You believe in it, because once you feel it is a dream the dream disappears. The dream cannot remain there, your cooperation is withdrawn. You can cooperate only with reality, not with dreams; and if you cooperate dreams become reality – it is through your cooperation.

In the night, deep in sleep, you dream that you have become a king. You may be a beggar, or vice versa: you may be a king and you dream that you have become a beggar. But in that dream you are so identified you cannot think that it could be a dream. If you can think that it could be a dream, the dream will stop immediately. It will be broken, you will come out of it.

Try this. Try this with ordinary dreams. While going to sleep at night, every day just go on thinking only one thought: "When I dream, I must remember that this is a dream." It will take many months for this thought to drop down into the unconscious, but it will reach there. After three weeks to three months it will reach if you persist, if you don't forget. Every night while falling into sleep, you go on thinking that when a dream starts you will immediately recognize that it is a dream. After three weeks to three months this will happen; suddenly one day you will start dreaming and you will have the realization, "This is a dream." Immediately the dream will disappear and your eyes will be open.

If you realize in dream that it is a dream the dream is broken, the dream cannot exist. It exists through your cooperation, your identification is needed. If you are committed to it, if you get involved in it, only then can it continue. And the same happens with the greater dream which is life. When you realize this is a dream, immediately you have become a buddha, you are enlightened. But this enlightenment cannot happen to you by others' knowing, others' wisdom.

Buddha may go on calling to you that this is a dream you are living, but you will only feel that this man is a disturbance, a constant nuisance, he is disturbing your life. That's why we kill such persons. Socrates – we poisoned him because he was a great disturber. Jesus – we crucified him because he was a nuisance. Everybody is dreaming such beautiful dreams, and these persons unnecessarily, and without being invited, go on disturbing people and saying to them, "Wake up! You are dreaming. This is a dream." And the man may have been dreaming such a beautiful thing that he could throw away all life for that dream.

Now psychologists say that for the ordinary mind, for the normal mind, dreaming is a must. If you cannot dream, if you are not allowed to dream, you will go mad. Previously it was thought that sleep is a necessity, now the new research says a totally different thing. The new research says that sleep is not a must; it is not sleep which gives you rest, it is dreaming which gives you rest. And if you are allowed to dream you will remain happy, if you are not allowed to dream you will go insane.

The whole night there is a rhythm: sleep period, then dream period, then sleep period, then dream period, of almost the same duration. If you sleep for eight hours, at least for four hours you are dreaming: forty minutes dreaming, then forty minutes sleep, then forty minutes dream, then forty minutes sleep – just like day and night, a rhythm.

They have tried many experiments, because now it can be known from the outside whether you are dreaming or not. Not many devices are needed. When a person is sleeping you can simply go on looking at his eyes. When he dreams the eyes move fast. He is looking at the dream, so the eyes move fast. When he is fast asleep the eyes stop and become dead. So just sitting by a person who is asleep, you can note down when he is dreaming and when he is asleep.

They have tried to disturb persons while they are asleep, in their sleep periods of forty minutes. When they are dreaming they don't disturb them; when they start sleeping they disturb them. Many nights you can disturb a person while he is asleep but allow the dream period, and he will be happy and okay, no problem; he will not feel tired in the morning. But do otherwise: when he is asleep let him sleep; when he starts dreaming wake him. If continuously the whole night, for only three nights, you don't allow a person to dream, then he will go insane. Why? It is so much needed. Your ordinary mind feeds on dreams, and if a person is not allowed for three days to dream he will start dreaming while awake. It is such a great need. He will be awake, sitting in his chair, and dreaming. He will have to fulfill the quota, in the day he will have to dream.

And if you insist for many weeks, if for at least three weeks a person is not allowed to dream, he will become hallucinatory. He will be awake and talking to a man who is not present. He will become just like madmen. Now psychologists say that these madmen whom we have pushed into madhouses may be simply persons who have been starved as far as dream food is concerned. They need more dreams to be readjusted to normal life. What is the problem? Why are dreams needed so much? Why can't you live without dreams? Because your life is so miserable that only through dreams can you exist. If you come to know life as it is, in its nudity, without any dreams, you will commit suicide.

Albert Camus has written that the only philosophical problem is whether to commit suicide or not, and that is the big problem. If you come to realize that the whole life is just nonsense…. What are you doing? What is happening? Nothing is happening, and you continue in suffering. If you are reasonable, you will start thinking of committing suicide.

Dreams help you to not commit suicide. They help you to create worlds of your own in which you can be happy, in which you can enjoy, in which you can become emperors, in which you can become conquerors, in which you can fly and reach the planets, in which you can do anything. You are free only in your dreams. The whole life is a slavery, only in your dreams can you destroy the whole world and create a new one.

You can have a beautiful woman in your dreams, a beautiful man. Life is not so beautiful. And howsoever beautiful a woman, you come closer and the flowers disappear and only thorns are left. Howsoever beautiful a man, a person, if you are far away the beauty is there, but the closer you come, the more the beauty starts evaporating. Sartre says, "Hell is other people – the other is the hell." The closer you come to the other, the more a hell is created. Only in your dreams can you be in paradise.

So don't say that you know that your life is suffering and dreamlike – it is real to you. To you I say it is real; to a buddha it is unreal. But you are not a buddha yet, so remain with your reality, and remain with your real mind. Don't move with borrowed things, because once you move on borrowed things you will never come to the reality again.

"If the divine is right here and now, then what prevents us from seeing him? Why do we cling to our dream life even though it has become a misery for us?" Think again. Contemplate on it. If it is a misery for you – for you I insist again and again, not for me – if it is a misery for you, don't do anything. Remain with the fact that your life has become a misery to you, because if you start doing something about it you may again create hope in the tomorrow. Just remain with the fact. If it is hell, remain in hell, don't do anything. Just remain alert that this is hell. And if you can be patient and alert and wait, just through waiting the hell will disappear, it will fall down. It needs your cooperation. It is just like dreams.

That's why Shankara and Buddha say your life is a dream life – because it can be just dropped like dreams. If you become alert a dream disappears; if you become alert of your misery, the misery disappears. You cling to it because you think it is not misery, or some happiness is hidden somewhere in it. It may be misery outwardly, but a deep treasure is hidden behind it, so you have to cling to it for that treasure. Your life is misery – but not for you. Realize its misery, it falls down. The very truth transforms you. And the moment misery falls the divine is revealed. To a miserable mind the divine cannot be revealed. To a celebrating mind the divine is revealed.

Remember, only to a celebrating mind, to a mind which is happy, blissful, enjoying moment to moment, ecstatic, is the divine revealed. To a miserable mind the divine cannot be revealed, because a miserable mind is closed. The divine is here and now, but you are not here and now. If you are also here and now then the divine will be revealed to you. The whole of my effort is to bring you here and now. This very moment, if you can be here, then nothing is hidden.

The last question:

Osho,

The rishi of the Upanishad fears he may speak some untruth, and so he prays, "May my speech be rooted in my mind." Does that mean that when he comes down to earth to speak, he comes out of his enlightened consciousness to do so, back into the ordinary mind again? If he is permanently in divine consciousness, how can nontruth come in?

There is no way of coming back to the ordinary state of the mind. Once you are enlightened there is no way to become blind again, no way to fall into the darkness – because this light is not something accidental. When you become enlightened you have become the light, so wherever you go, even in darkness, it will be light there. It is not something external, the light is not something accidental. Enlightenment means you have become the light, so now there is no way to fall into the darkness again. Wherever you go, even if there was darkness before, just by your reaching there the darkness will disappear. So there is no way of falling back.

Then why is this rishi afraid? Why does he fear? He fears for a deep reason. The fear is not that he can utter untruth, the fear is that the moment the truth is expressed in language it becomes distorted. He is not going to utter any untruth, but the medium of language is such that whatsoever you express through it, it changes, its nature changes. It is just like this: a river is flowing and you push a straight stick down into the water. The moment it penetrates the water it is no longer straight, the medium of the water and the refraction of light rays change it – the straight stick is no longer straight. Pull it out again, it is straight; push it down again, it is no longer straight. The stick remains straight, but because of the medium of water it appears as though it is not straight.

The truth is realized in a silent mind where there is no language, no words, no verbal existence…total silence, soundlessness. In that silence the truth is realized, and then it has to be expressed through language. That which has been known beyond language, that which transcends language, has to be forced again into language to communicate. And with you there is no other way to communicate it. You cannot understand silence.

I can remain here silent; you cannot understand it. If you can understand silence then there is no need to express, but then you will not be here, then there will be no need to come here also. If you can understand my silence you can understand the silence of the sky, because the language is the same. You can understand the silence of the rocks, you can understand the silence of the night. You can understand the silence with which the cosmos all over is filled. There is no need to come to me because silence is everywhere – if you understand it.

You don't understand it. That's why you don't go to a rock, you don't go to a tree, you have come to me...because the tree cannot express it in language, the rock cannot express it in language. The rock also exists in the divine as much as I, but the rock cannot express it through language. You need language. The fear is because of you, the fear is because of the very medium of language. Truth said becomes untrue.

Lao Tzu has said, "The Tao that can be said is no more Tao. The truth that can be said is no more true." Why? – because language, the very mechanism of language, depends on duality. For example, if you ask me whether God is light or darkness, if I say light, it is wrong, because he is also darkness. If I say darkness, it is wrong, because he is also light. If I say he is light, then the question arises, "Then darkness exists. Where does it exist? Then there must be something other than God where darkness exists." If I say God is life...then death? Who is death? If I say God is death, then who is life? And if I say God is both life and death, then it becomes a paradox. If I say God is both light and darkness, then you will say, "You are not saying much, it is a paradox. How can one be both?"

These are the four ways: either I can say God is light or darkness, or I can say God is both, or I can say God is not both, but the problem remains. And these are the only ways to express. That's why Mahavira has developed *saptabhangi* – sevenfold logic. You ask one question and Mahavira will answer seven answers. And if you can stay with him to listen to his seven answers, you will be more confused than when you came to him.

If you ask about God, he will say God is; immediately he will say God is not; immediately he will say God is both, is and is not; immediately he will say God is both not, is and is not – and he goes on. Sevenfold will be his answer, because he says, "I cannot be untrue. This is the whole truth." But you remain the same as you were and even more confused. You need a clear answer, you want that he either says God is, or God is not.

That's why Buddha remained silent. You asked about God, he would remain silent. He said that he would not answer eleven questions, and those eleven questions are the base of the whole of philosophy; all metaphysics consists of those eleven questions. He would not answer because he said, "Whatsoever I say will be wrong, or I will have to say it in such a way that nothing will become clear – as Mahavira is doing."

This rishi is going to try to communicate exactly, meaningfully, not creating paradoxes; linguistically understandable statements he will try in this Upanishad. That's why he is afraid – because the nature of language distorts.

Secondly, the moment something is said and you have heard it, you will destroy it. Firstly it will be destroyed by the medium of language; secondly, it has entered your mind, and your mind is a madhouse. Once it enters your mind, what meaning will come out of it no one can say. How you will interpret it, how you will follow it, what you will do according to your interpretation, no one knows.

Buddha has said somewhere that it is dangerous to talk to ignorant people, because whatsoever you say they think they have understood, and then they are the masters. You are no more in possession of your truth; they also possess it, and they will interpret it. That's why so many philosophies exist.

Buddha died. At least twenty-four systems immediately were there, twenty-four leaders saying, "This is the meaning of Buddha" – and they all were contradicting each other. Twenty-four schools, and each school against the other twenty-three: "Those twenty-three others are absolutely wrong!" This happens even when a master is alive, nothing can be said about what happens when a master is dead.

I remember, once it happened: Freud was old, and just before he died, two or three years before…. And Freud was not a religious man at all, not a man of trust and faith, but a man of doubt, logic and reason. But still he was working in a very dangerous field – the mind – so he had become a master in his own right. He had disciples, a great following, a big movement, so thinking that he was going to die soon as he was ill and old, all his great disciples gathered, just to meet him for the last time.

Twenty people were there, Freud was sitting with them and they were discussing. They were discussing, and they forgot that Freud was still alive. They were discussing what Freud meant about certain principles and each one had his own interpretation. They discussed, argued, and there was chaos, and there was no possibility of their coming to one conclusion – and Freud was sitting there! He suddenly stood and said, "My friends, you have completely forgotten – I am still alive! You can ask me what my meaning is."

But if I had been there I would have said to Freud, "Even that will not help, because they can ask what your meaning is, but again they will interpret the meaning. Then again there will be twenty interpretations. 'What is the meaning of your meaning?'"

You cannot escape disciples. That is the fear.

4   The Supreme Knowledge

The sage Sankriti then said to the sun god:

O Lord, please teach me the supreme knowledge.

The sun god said:

I shall now explain to you this most rare knowledge, upon the attainment of which you will become free while yet dwelling in this body. See in all beings the Brahman, who is one, unborn, still, imperishable, infinite, immutable and conscious; so seeing live in peace and bliss. Do not see anything except the self and the supreme. This state is known as yoga.

Rooted thus in yoga, carry out your deeds.

The mind of one who is thus rooted in yoga gradually withdraws from all desires, and the seeker feels blissful while engaging himself each day in meritorious acts. He has no interest whatsoever in the contrary efforts of the ignorant.

He never betrays the secrets of one to another,

and he occupies himself solely with lofty deeds.

He performs only such gentle acts as do not disturb others. He fears sin and does not crave any self-indulgence. He utters loving and affectionate words. He lives in the company of saints and studies the scriptures. With complete unity of mind, speech and action he follows them. Seeking to cross the ocean that is the world, he cultivates the above-mentioned ideas. And he is called a beginner, one performing his preliminaries. This is called the first stage.

The sage Sankriti then said to the sun god: O Lord, please teach me the supreme knowledge.

The Upanishads know only the supreme knowledge. What is this supreme knowledge? And why is it called supreme? The Upanishads call that knowledge supreme which is not gathered from without, which is not gathered at all. You cannot be educated in it, it cannot be taught; it happens within, it flowers in you.

The first distinction to be made is that there is knowledge which can be taught. The Upanishads call that knowledge lower knowledge. Precisely, they call it *avidya* – ignorance with information – because that which can be taught to you remains in the mind, it never reaches exactly to you. You remain untouched, your center remains untouched, your being is not in any way changed, transformed. Only the mind collects it, only the brain cells collect it, so it is the same as when we feed a computer – in the same way your mind is fed.

From the very childhood you have been taught many things. They have not reached you, and they will never reach you. The mind gathers them, the mind becomes filled with them. And the mind is so complex that in a single mind all the libraries of the world can be fed; a single head can contain all the knowledge that exists in this world – but the Upanishads say you will not become knowing through that. It is mechanical, consciousness is not needed for it. If even a computer can do it, then it is not worth it.

What the computer cannot do is supreme knowledge. The computer cannot become self-knowing, there is no possibility for the computer to become self-conscious. That which has not been fed into the computer cannot happen to it, and if the same is the case with man then there is no soul, then you are also a natural biocomputer. If everything that comes out of you has been fed into you, if exactly the same amount comes out that has been fed in, if nothing new happens within, then you have no soul; then you are a very complex mechanism, that's all.

So the whole religion depends on the phenomenon of supreme knowledge. Is it possible that something can happen within, absolutely new, which has never been taught to you, which has not been cultivated in you? If something so original happens to you, only that can prove that you have a soul; otherwise you are simply a brain, a complex mechanism but still a mechanism, and then there is no possibility of any transformation.

The Upanishads call that knowledge supreme which happens within. That's why religion cannot be taught. You can teach science, you can teach many other things, but you cannot teach religion. And if you teach religion, religion becomes false. That's what missionaries of all the religions have done to this earth. They have been teaching religion on just the same lines as science is taught, so they fill your mind with certain knowledge and you start repeating that knowledge. You may even start living that knowledge, but you will remain a computer, a robot.

The Upanishads say there is a possibility and there is a way to attain the supreme knowledge. So what will the master do if it cannot be taught? That's why I say a master is not a teacher. The master is not going to teach you; he is going to create a situation around you, only the situation. He will create devices around you, he will create only the soil – the seed you have already got within you.

The situation can be provided and the seed will start sprouting, the dead seed will become alive. The seed will die, but a plant will come in its place. And this seed, this seedling, this growing plant, will become a tree. But this is something which happens within you. You can be helped, but you cannot be taught.

A master can create a situation around you – just a situation, remember. And whatsoever he teaches is not knowledge, he teaches only how to create the situation. He teaches you methods; he cannot give you the conclusion – he can only help indirectly. That's why it is such a delicate phenomenon. And only one who has got it within him, one who has passed through all the stages, one who has become a big tree, flowering – only he can create the situation around you. So a person who has not become enlightened himself cannot help you; on the contrary, he may hinder you.

If it was just a teaching, then even scriptures would be helpful: The Bible would do, the Koran, the Vedas, the Upanishads would do. But you can read The Bible, you can memorize it, you can become an expert, you can become a scholar – but you will not become a religious man. Just by memorizing The Bible, Christ is not going to happen to you. The Christ can happen to you only when the situation is created around you, and your own inner seed grows. Religion is not a teaching, it is a growth. And what is supreme knowledge? – when you grow, when you know, when for the first time you have your own eyes to see into reality.

So the first thing: supreme knowledge is that knowledge which happens to you but cannot be taught. The second thing: all knowledge is about something other than you – supreme knowledge is absolutely about you. Or, it may even be wrong to say that it is about you. It is not about, because whatsoever it is about is about something other than you. It will be better to say that it is you, not about you...because many things can be taught about you. It can be asked, "Who are you?" Someone can say, "You are Brahman, you are the divine, you are the absolute, the soul, *atman*." But this is about you; this is not supreme knowledge – somebody else is teaching it to you.

When you become knowledge, when you become the knowing center, when your very consciousness becomes the door, then supreme knowledge has happened to you. Mathematics is about something, physics is about something else, chemistry about something else, psychology is about the mind – supreme knowledge is you. No university, no school is of any help. Directly, nothing can be done about it, only an indirect help is possible.

The sage Sankriti then said to the sun god: O Lord, please teach me the supreme knowledge.

He is asking an absurd question: *Please teach me the supreme knowledge*. It can-not be taught – but that's how a disciple has to reach the master. The disciple cannot know that there is something which cannot be taught; every disciple has to come to the master and ask to be taught. It is absurd for the master, because he knows it cannot be taught, but every seeker thinks that everything can be taught – even the supreme knowledge can be taught.

It happened in Upanishadic days that one young boy, Svetaketu, was sent by his father to a gurukul, to a family of an enlightened master, to learn. He learned everything that could be learned, he memorized all the Vedas and all the science available in those days. He became proficient in them, he became a great scholar; his fame started spreading all over the country. Then there was nothing else to be taught, so the master said, "You have known all that can be taught. Now you can go back."

Thinking that everything had happened and there was nothing else – because whatsoever the master knew, he also knew, and the master had taught him everything – Svetaketu went back. Of course with great pride and ego, he came back to his father.

When he was entering the village his father, Uddalak, looked out of the window at his son coming back from the university. He saw the way he was walking – very proudly, the way he was holding his head – in a very egoistic way, the way he was looking all around – very self-conscious that he knew. The father became sad and depressed, because this is not the way of one who really knows, this is not the way of one who has come to know the supreme knowledge.

The son entered the house. He was thinking that his father would be very happy – he had become one of the suprememost scholars of the country; he was known everywhere, respected everywhere – but he saw that the father was sad, so he asked, "Why are you sad?"

The father said, "Only one question I have to ask you. Have you learned *that* by learning which there is no need to learn anything any more? Have you known *that* by knowing which all suffering ceases? Have you been taught that which cannot be taught?"

The boy also became sad. He said, "No. Whatsoever I know has been taught to me, and I can teach it to anybody who is ready to learn."

The father said, "Then you go back and ask your master that you be taught that which cannot be taught."

The boy said, "But that is absurd. If it cannot be taught, how can the master teach me?"

The father said, "That is the art of the master: he can teach you that which cannot be taught. You go back."

He went back. Bowing down to his master's feet, he said, "My father has sent me for an absolutely absurd thing. Now I don't know where I am and what I am asking you. My father has told me to come back and return only when I have learned that which cannot be learned, when I have been taught that which cannot be taught. What is it? What is this? You never told me about it."

The master said, "Unless one inquires, it cannot be told; you never inquired about it. But now you are starting a totally different journey. And remember, it cannot be taught, so it is very delicate; only indirectly will I help you. Do one thing: take all the animals of my gurukul – there were at least four hundred cows, bulls and other animals – and go to the deepest forest possible where nobody ever comes and moves. Live with these animals in silence. Don't talk, because these animals cannot understand any language. So remain silent, and when just by reproduction these four hundred animals have become one thousand, then come back."

It was going to be a long time – until four hundred animals had become one thousand. And he was to go without saying anything, without arguing, without asking, "What are you telling me to do? Where will it lead?" He was to just live with animals and trees and rocks; not talking, and forgetting the human world completely. Because your mind is a human creation, if you live with human beings the mind is continuously fed. They say something, you say something – the mind goes on learning, it goes on revolving.

"So go," the master said, "to the hills, to the forest. Live alone. Don't talk. And there is no use in thinking, because these animals won't understand even your thinking. Drop all your scholarship here."

Svetaketu followed. He went to the forest and lived with the animals for many years. For a few days thoughts remained there in the mind – the same thoughts repeating themselves again and again. Then it became boring. If new thoughts are not felt, then you will become aware that the mind is just repetitive, just a mechanical repetition; it goes on in a rut. And there was no way to get new knowledge. With new knowledge the mind is always happy, because there is something again to grind, something again to work out; the mechanism goes on moving.

Svetaketu became aware. There were four hundred animals, birds, other wild animals, trees, rocks, rivers and streams, but no man and no possibility of any human communication. There was no use in being very egoistic, because these animals didn't know what type of great scholar this Svetaketu was. They didn't consider him at all; they didn't look at him with respect, so by and by the pride disappeared, because it was futile and it even looked foolish to walk in a prideful way with the animals. Even Svetaketu started feeling, "If I remain egoistic these animals will laugh at me – so what am I doing?" Sitting under the trees, sleeping near the streams, by and by his mind became silent.

The story is beautiful. The years passed and his mind became so silent that Svetaketu completely forgot when he had to return. He became so silent that even this idea was not there. The past dropped completely, and with the dropping of the past the future drops, because the future is nothing but a projection of the past – just the past reaching into the future. So he forgot what the master had said, he forgot when he had to return. There was no when and where, he was just here and now. He lived in the moment just like the animals, he became a cow.

The story says that when the animals became one thousand, they started feeling uncomfortable. They were waiting for Svetaketu to take them back to the ashram and he had forgotten, so one day the cows decided to speak to Svetaketu and they said, "Now it is time enough, and we remember that the master had said that you must come back when the animals became one thousand, and you have completely forgotten. Now is the time and we must go back. We have be-come one thousand."

So Svetaketu went back with the animals. The master looked from the door of his hut at Svetaketu coming with one thousand animals, and he said to his other disciples, "Look, one thousand and one animals are coming." Svetaketu had become such a silent being – no ego, no self-consciousness, just moving with the animals as one of them.

The master came to receive him; the master was dancing, ecstatic. He embraced Svetaketu and he said, "Now there is nothing to say to you – you have already known. Why have you come? There is no need to come now, there is nothing to be taught. You have already known."

Svetaketu said, "Just to pay my respects, just to touch your feet, just to be grateful. It has happened, and you have taught me that which cannot be taught."

This is what a master is to do: create a situation in which the thing happens. So only indirect effort can be made, indirect help, indirect guidance. And wherever direct guidance is given, wherever your mind is taught, it is not religion. It may be theology but not religion; it may be philosophy but not religion.

The supreme knowledge is that which cannot be taught. But the sage Sankriti asked: *Teach me the supreme knowledge.*

The sun god said:

I shall now explain to you this most rare knowledge, upon the attainment of which you will become free while yet dwelling in this body. See in all beings the Brahman, who is one, unborn, still, imperishable, infinite, immutable and conscious; so seeing live in peace and bliss. Do not see anything except the self and the supreme. This state is known as yoga. Rooted thus in yoga, carry out your deeds.

The first thing he said was: *See in all beings the Brahman.* This too is to create a situation, remember. This is not a teaching, this is giving a device. What do you see? You see trees, you see rocks, you see men, you see dogs, you see cows – you see many things, but not one. You go on counting waves but you don't see the hidden ocean.

The sun god said to Sankriti that the first thing is to see the one. Apparently there are many, but behind the many the one is hidden. So whenever you see the many, remember this is the surface, not the soul. Penetrate deep; forget the surface and try to know the center, the depth. The depth is one.

Go to the sea, there are millions of waves. You never see the sea, you always see the waves, because they are on the surface. But every wave is nothing but a waving of the sea, the sea is waving through all the waves. Remember the ocean and forget the waves – because waves don't really exist, only the ocean exists.

The ocean can exist without the waves but the waves cannot exist without the ocean. If there is no ocean there can be no waves – or can there be? Then what will wave in them? They cannot be, but the ocean can be. There is no need for the waves, the ocean can be silent. If there is no wind blowing the ocean will be there, silent.

The ocean can exist without the waves, but the waves cannot exist without the ocean. So waves are just the surface, and waves are accidental – through the action of the winds they have come into existence. They have come into existence from without, some accident has created them. If the wind is not blowing the ocean will be silent and non-waving. So waves are accidents created from without, on the surface; the ocean is something totally different.

And the same is the case with all beings. The tree is also a wave, and the man is also a wave, and the rock is also a wave. And behind the rock and the tree and the man the same ocean is hidden. That ocean is called by the Upanishads the Brahman. The Brahman, the ultimate soul, the absolute soul, is just the ocean. So look at a man but don't cling to the surface, immediately move to the depth and see the Brahman hidden there.

You can do this. Just try it in this camp. Whenever you have time, sit with your friend, your beloved, your wife, your husband, or anybody – a stranger will do – just sit and look into each other's eyes without thinking, and try to penetrate the eyes without thinking. Just look deeper and deeper into each other's eyes. Soon you will become aware that the waves have been crossed and an ocean has opened unto you.

Look into each other's eyes deeply, because eyes are just the doors. And if you don't think, if you just stare into the eyes, soon the waves will disappear and the ocean will be revealed. Do it first with a human being, because you are closer to that type of wave.

Then move to animals – a little more distant; then move to trees – still more distant waves; then move to the rocks.

If you can look deep down into the eyes, you will feel that the man has disappeared, the person has disappeared. Some oceanic phenomenon is hidden behind and this person was just a waving of a depth, a wave of something unknown, hidden. Try this; it will be something worth knowing. That's what the sun god said to Sankriti: *See in all beings the Brahman, who is one...* not many.

So wherever you feel any distinction, know that you are on the surface. All distinctions are on the surface; "many" belongs to the surface. In English we have a word, "universe," that is almost parallel to Brahman. "Uni" means one, but whatsoever you see around you is not "universe." You may call it a universe, but it is not, it is a multiverse. Many you see, not one; names you see, not the nameless; waves you see, but not the ocean.

This is to create a situation. Look deep and don't be deceived by the surface, and soon you will become aware of an ocean all around. Then you will see that you are also just a wave, your ego is just a wave – behind that ego, the nameless, the one, is hidden.

See in all beings the Brahman, who is one, unborn...

...Because only waves are born, the ocean remains the same. The many are born, the one remains the same. You are born and you will have to die; hence the fear of death, so much fear of death, but the Brahman in you is unborn and undying. Everyone is afraid of death. Why this fear? And nothing can be done about it; only one thing is certain in life, and that is death.

It is said of one Zen master, Tojo, that he remained silent his whole life, he would not speak. When he was a child it was thought that he was incapable of speaking, but he was so intelligent that sooner or later people realized that he was just keeping silence, he was not dumb. His eyes were so radiant, intelligent, wise; his behavior, his actions, were so intelligent that people became aware that he was simply keeping a deep silence – maybe continuing some vow to remain silent that he may have taken in his past life. And he remained silent for eighty years.

The first and last statement he made was on the day he was going to die. The morning he was going to die, just as the sun was rising, he collected his followers – many had started following him. He was not speaking, but he was living something, and that living something became so significant to those who could understand that there were many who followed him; many were his disciples. They would just sit around Tojo, they would just be in contact with his silence, and many were transformed.

He collected all his followers and said, "This evening when the sun sets, I will die. This is my first and last statement."

So somebody said, "But if you can speak, why did you remain silent your whole life?"

He said, "Everything else is uncertain, only death is certain. And I want only to speak about something which is certain."

Once born, death is certain; everything else is uncertain. Why is death so certain? Nothing can be done about it. Science may help to prolong life, but death cannot be destroyed, because it is implied in the very phenomenon of birth; it has happened already. Death is one pole of the same phenomenon of which birth is the beginning, the other pole.

It is just like a magnet: on a magnet you have two poles – the positive and the negative. You can cut off the negative pole, you can cut the magnet in half, but immediately the negative pole will appear on the place where you have cut. Now there are two magnets, and each magnet will have two poles. Before there was one magnet and it had two poles, negative and positive. Now you have cut it into two pieces. The one which has the positive pole will immediately create the negative, and the one which has the negative pole will immediately create the positive. You can go on cutting the magnet, but howsoever many fragments you cut, each fragment will have two poles – because a magnet cannot exist with one pole, it is impossible.

Life has two poles: birth is the positive pole, death is the negative. You cannot destroy, you can at the most prolong. You can at the most make a bigger magnet, but the other pole will be there. You can cut it and make a small magnet, but the other pole will be there. This polarity is absolute. So whatsoever science thinks or imagines, it can never happen. Death cannot be destroyed; through science, remember, it is impossible to destroy death.

Once born you have to die. But right now, behind this ego, the unborn is flowing. If you can look and see and feel the unborn, the fear of death disappears – and there is no other way to destroy the fear.

Death is there and you are going to die, you cannot be immortal as an ego. But if you look deep, and if you can find the depth of your ego where ego is no more, if you can see the ocean beyond the wave, you are already immortal. But that one which is hidden behind was never born and it will never die. Unless you come to know something which is not born, you cannot become deathless.

See in all beings the Brahman, who is one, unborn, still, imperishable, infinite, immutable and conscious; so seeing live in peace and bliss.

Once you can see that, bliss is just the by-product, peace simply happens. And it cannot happen before. Death is there – how can you be at peace? Death is there – how can you be at home? Death is there – how can you rest? Death will create tensions, anguish, worries. Death is there constantly hammering on your head – how can you be silent? And how can you love this existence? And how can you feel grateful to the divine? Impossible! Death is there. You can forget it for moments, but it is hidden; it is always there behind the mind. And whatsoever you do, knowingly or unknowingly, the phenomenon of death influences you. It is always there just like a shadow, it darkens your life.

People come to me and they say, "We are sad, depressed, and we don't know what the cause is. There is no visible cause for our being sad and depressed. We have everything that life can give, still we are sad and depressed."

They will remain sad and depressed. They may not know what the cause is; the cause is there – the death always around you, around the corner, waiting for you. And wherever you are moving, you are moving to the death; whatsoever you do, every act, leads you to the death.

I have heard one Sufi tale. Once it happened that one king had a dream. In the night when he was fast asleep he dreamed he saw a shadow, a very dark, dangerous looking, ferocious shadow, standing just behind him. He asked, "Who are you?"

The shadow said, "I am your death, and before the sun sets tomorrow, I am coming to meet you. I have come just to inform you."

The king wanted to ask, "Is there any way to escape from you?" but he became so afraid that he was awakened. He couldn't ask, and the dream disappeared. So in the middle of the night he gathered all his wise men and he said, "There is no time, so you decide immediately what this dream means. What does this symbol mean? Interpret it."

All the Freuds and Jungs and Adlers of his day were called immediately to interpret the dream. They came with their big scriptures, books and charts, and the king became afraid. He said, "Don't waste time! You have to decide immediately!"

They said, "It is a very intricate thing, very complex, and it has never happened before so there is no precedent. We cannot decide immediately, it has to be analyzed and it will take time."

But the king prayed to them, "Do it as soon as possible, because I have to decide and do something. The sun is just going to rise, and once the sun has risen it has already set – then there is no time. The sun will move and set, and within twelve hours everything will be finished!"

They started discussing, and there was much discussion – as it always happens with persons whose minds are filled with knowledge. Everyone was of a different opinion and the king was still more confused.

The king had one old servant. The old servant came near to him and whispered in the king's ear, "Don't wait. I know these people. Even if you have one hundred years to live, they will not come to any conclusion – they have never come to a conclusion. For centuries they have been discussing; conclusion is not their goal at all, discussion is their interest. These are philosophers. For thousands of years they have been discussing and have reached no conclusion – philosophy has no conclusion. And every answer that has been given by these fellows creates one hundred questions, so simply don't wait for them."

The king said, "Then what am I supposed to do?"

The old man said, "I am a common man, not a learned man, and as far as I can see you should do a commonsense thing: you take your fastest horse and escape from this palace, this palace is dangerous. At least this much is certain – that you should not be here at that moment when death comes. Go as far away as possible."

It was worth considering. The king said, "Okay. There is no other possibility, because these fellows are confusing me even more. So let them discuss and let them decide, and I will escape."

When you have fear, escape seems to be the only door. So he took his fastest horse, a wonderful horse, and he escaped from the palace. When the sun was rising he was out of the town, when the sun was setting he was hundreds of miles away. And when the sun was just going to set he reached a big tree. He thought, "This will be a good place for the night." He came down from his horse and he thanked the horse, saying, "You are just wonderful. You are the only friend who helped me in such a great difficulty. When scholars were of no use, you helped me. At least you have brought me so far away."

While he was saying this and patting the horse, suddenly he saw the same shadow behind him. He trembled and he said, "What! You have come?"

The shadow said, "Yes, I was waiting under this tree for you the whole day. And I was afraid whether your horse would come or not – the place is so far away from your palace. Let me thank your horse, he is really wonderful."

Whatsoever you do, and wherever you escape, you cannot escape death; wherever you reach, death will be waiting for you there. If you are rich you can have a fast horse; if you are poor you will have to walk, but you will reach – you will reach anyway.

Fear is there around the heart, the heart is in the grip of the fear of death. And it spoils everything. You cannot really love. When you are in love, death is there. And love is so deathlike that lovers always become conscious of death. If you have loved anyone you will be aware of it. You may not have noticed, but whenever you love someone the lover is bound to ask, "Will you love me forever?" – the fear of death. "Will you always be with me?" – the fear of death.

When you are deep in love you become more aware, because deep in love you are near the heart, and near the heart is the shadow of death. Every beat of the heart is aware that the next heartbeat may not come. Wherever you move, you cannot feel blissful.

Look at a beautiful flower. The beauty of it grips you, for a moment the mind stops; but suddenly you become aware that the flower is going to die by the evening, and just after the beauty of the flower comes the sadness of death. It is everywhere. You will find it moving with you, moment to moment. How can you be at ease? How can you be at peace? How can you live in bliss? Impossible!

The sun god said, "But if you become aware of the one behind the many, if you become aware of the one in the many...." If this multiverse disappears and the universe appears, you will be at peace – because then you cannot die. The ocean cannot die, the life energy that is waving in you cannot die. The wave will disappear, but the energy will continue in other waves. That's what reincarnation means.

All the religions which have penetrated very deep – Hinduism, Jainism, Buddhism, three religions which have penetrated very deep into the soul of man – they all believe in reincarnation. Mohammedanism, Christianity and Judaism don't believe in reincarnation, but they never worked very hard; they never penetrated the heart of man very deeply. They remained social phenomena, they were more sociopolitical, less religious. The whole history of Islam is sociopolitical, and whenever anybody in the fold of Islam tried to penetrate deeply, he was immediately destroyed and killed.

For example, al-Hillaj Mansoor: he was a man of the same caliber as Buddha, a man who penetrated deeply. When he came to feel that he is Brahman, he is God, he declared it. He said, "Ana'l haq – I am Brahman."

But this appeared blasphemy to Mohammedans, and they immediately killed him. They said, "This is impossible. At the most you can be a worshipper, but you cannot become God. This is too much, this cannot be tolerated – a human being declaring that he is God!"

They killed Mansoor, they killed many Sufis. In Islam only Sufis penetrated deeply. Sufism is the central core of Islam, the essential Islam – but Islam killed them. So just to survive Sufis disappeared. They became a secret society and they compromised. As far as their outward behavior was concerned they compromised with Islam, deep down they remained a very revolutionary sect. But they were not accepted by the society at large; Islam remained a sociopolitical phenomenon.

Christianity also remained a sociopolitical phenomenon. It created kingdoms. Even the pope himself became a king, and he still rules a small kingdom, the Vatican. Eckhart, Boehme and Blake were never accepted, the main current never accepted them – and many were destroyed and killed. Whosoever tried to assert the deepest phenomenon of one's being, the absolute reality, he was never accepted in Christianity. That's why they couldn't penetrate to the phenomenon of reincarnation.

Millions of lives you have had, and if you don't stop in your stupidities you are going to have millions more. If you stop then waves disappear – you become the ocean. And the ocean is at peace, the ocean is always blissful. So it is not a question of how to put your mind at ease, how to relax the mind. No, that won't do. It is a question of how to move deep, so deep that the mind is left behind and you reach the base of your being, the very substantial base of your being, and the mind becomes the surface, the waving surface. Only then is there peace and bliss.

Said the sun god:

Do not see anything except the self and the supreme. This state is known as yoga. Rooted thus in yoga, carry out your deeds.

This is the state of knowing that waves are on the surface and you are the ocean, not the waves; the state of knowing that waves belong to you, but you are not the waves – they are just your clothing, just your body. You are the nameless, infinite ocean. The sun god said, "This is the state of yoga" – one of the most beautiful definitions of yoga.

Knowing oneself as the ocean is yoga. You have met, the meeting has happened. You are no longer separate, you are no longer an island – you have become one with a vast continent of consciousness. This is yoga.

The word yoga means meeting, joining together. The root from which the word yoga comes is the same as for the English word yoke: yoking together, joining together, becoming one. When you feel you are the Brahman, this is the state of yoga.

Rooted thus in yoga, carry out your deeds.

Then there is no need to escape to the forest. The Upanishads were never life-negative, remember this. There is a deep misunderstanding in the West, and it has been created by one of the most sincere men of this age, Albert Schweitzer. He himself was in a misunderstanding and was very confused about Eastern mysticism. He created the idea in the West that the Upanishads are life-negative, not life-affirmative. This is wrong, absolutely wrong. The Upanishads are life-affirming. They don't say, "Move away from life"; they simply say, "Know the deepest life and then act." They don't say, "Stop waving"; they say, "Know that you are the ocean, then go on waving." But then waving becomes a play.

Rooted thus in yoga, carry out your deeds.

These Upanishadic rishis were not lifelong *brahmacharins*, bachelors. They were not: they were married people, they had children, they had their families. They were not in any way negative; they had not renounced life, remember.

The whole thing became confused because of Buddha and Mahavira – they both renounced life. That too is a way, that too is a way to reach the divine, but because of this the whole Hinduism was misunderstood. And they were so significant, they were the most important revolutionaries in India, that even Hindus started thinking in their way. Buddha and Mahavira impressed the country so much; and they renounced life, they were negative. The negative is also a path.

There are two paths, negative and positive, and you have to choose. Either be totally positive, then you transcend; or be totally negative, then you transcend. Either trust life absolutely, then you go beyond life; or mistrust life absolutely, then also you go beyond life. These are the two paths, the two outgoing doors, the positive and negative – because these are the two poles. And remember, you can jump only from a pole, you cannot jump from the middle.

If I am to go out of this room I will have to find a polarity. I cannot jump from the middle of this room, I cannot go out from the middle. There is no way from the middle, I have to find the periphery, and from the periphery I can go out.

These are the two poles: life and death, negative and positive. Either affirm life, then you can jump out; or negate life, then you can jump out. If you affirm life then birth becomes the pole, if you deny life then death becomes the pole. Both Buddha and Mahavira were more interested in death than in birth. But Hinduism is not negative, and the Upanishads are not negative, they are affirmative.

Schweitzer became confused because of Buddha and Mahavira. Not only Schweitzer, even Hindus have become confused, because Buddha's and Mahavira's impact was so deep, and they impressed the whole country so much, that even Hindus had to think about it. And Shankara, one of the greatest Hindus ever born, became almost a Buddhist in the Hindu fold.

Shankara again impressed people very much. For these one thousand years he has been the soul of Hinduism – and he was just a Buddhist. Shankara's enemies, Ramanuja, Nimbark and Vallabh, detected him. They said, "This man is not a Hindu at all; he just appears Hindu. He is a crypto-Buddhist, a hidden Buddhist." And they were right.

Hinduism is totally different from Jainism and Buddhism. The difference, the basic difference, is that Hinduism affirms life. The rishis were not unmarried men, they were householders. They had not renounced, they never renounced anything. You cannot conceive of it. The whole thing has become so distant now, you cannot conceive of these rishis. They were living in life, but living as the ocean, not as the waves. They accepted everything.

Once it happened that King Janak declared that there was going to be a great debate, and whosoever won the debate would get a very big prize. The prize was a thousand beautiful cows with horns of gold, studded with diamonds. These one thousand cows were standing before the palace. All the scholars and pundits came, many people gathered in the hall. Whosoever won would take the cows.

Then came one of the most prominent rishis of that day with his disciples from his gurukul, from his ashram. And remember, those ashrams were not for brahmacharins only, those ashrams were household affairs. The guru lived with his wife and children and his disciples, and his disciples were absorbed into his family. Yajnavalkya came with his disciples, and he said to them, "Take these cows. I will take care of the debate later on" – absolutely affirmative!

These Upanishadic rishis lived life, but from a totally different standpoint, from a totally different center. They said, "Life is good, life is a blessing, and to allow the waves is a game, a beautiful game worth playing. And if God has given you the opportunity, play it to the full – but don't get identified."

Remember, this is a game. Remember, the earth is nothing but a drama, a great drama, and you are nothing more than actors. Remain a witness within and go on acting. There is no need to escape from actions. Even to think in terms of escape shows that you are afraid, and fear cannot lead you anywhere, only love.

And these rishis loved life. They loved everything that life can give; they loved all the blessings – and there are millions of blessings. They never said that life is dukkha, they never said that life is misery. They said that you can make life a misery, but life is not a misery. You can also make a bliss out of it – it is you, not life.

Rooted thus in yoga, carry out your deeds.

The mind of one who is thus rooted in yoga gradually withdraws from all desires, and the seeker feels blissful while engaging himself each day in meritorious acts. He has no interest whatsoever in the contrary efforts of the ignorant. He never betrays the secrets of one to another. He occupies himself solely with lofty deeds.

The mind of one who is thus rooted in yoga gradually withdraws from all desires.

Desires are not to be left; rather you have to be rooted in yoga, then you will withdraw by yourself and the happening will be spontaneous. There is no need to kill desires, there is no need to fight with desires; the only thing is to know your oceanic state, your Brahman state, the one, and then get rooted into it.

The more you are rooted in it, the less and less desires will be there. But you have not renounced them; rather on the contrary, they have left you, because desires become uninterested in one who is rooted in himself. Desires leave him, because now they are not welcome guests. If they come he accepts them, if they come he is not going to destroy them and fight with them – but he is not interested. He has higher blessings with him now, the lower don't attract him. If they come he accepts, if they don't come he never thinks about them. By and by the life energy moves more and more within, withinwards; desires disappear.

Remember this distinction: in Buddhism and Jainism, desires have to be left consciously, effort has to be made to leave them and when you leave them you will be rooted in yourself. In Hinduism it is just the contrary: get rooted in yourself and desires will leave you. Buddha is negative: leave the desires and you will be rooted in yourself. Hinduism is positive: be rooted in yourself and desires will leave you.

It works both ways – it depends on you. If you are a negative type, a person to whom no comes easily, then follow the negative path. There are persons to whom no comes first, even if they want to say yes. If no is easy to you nothing is wrong in it; you are a negative type, that's all. Follow the negative path, say no to life so that you can get rooted in yourself. But if you are a yes type, then no is not your path. Then say yes to life, move with life, get rooted in yourself, and by and by desires will disappear.

And the seeker feels blissful while engaging himself each day in meritorious acts.

Whatsoever such a person does is meritorious, it is *punya*, it is holy, it is sacred. Whatsoever is done by one who is rooted in himself becomes worship, it is meritorious, because now he engages in it just as a play, just as a life-game. He is aware that it is only overflowing energy that moves into acts; he is not interested in doing anything or reaching any goal. His action is not work, his action is play – then the seeker feels blissful.

Whenever you are in play you feel blissful, and if your whole life becomes a play you cannot imagine how blissful you can become. Why do you feel blissful while you play? Even when playing cards you become blissful, the misery disappears. Why? When playing a game – football or hockey or anything – why do you become so blissful? Why do you feel so much joy bubbling in you? What happens?

And side by side with you there may be a professional player; he is not happy. He is not happy because he is just doing work. If you are paid for your card playing you will not be happy, because then you are not interested in the game, you are interested in the salary, and it has become a boredom. You have to do it to get the salary. Then the end is not in it, it is only a means.

This is the difference between work and play: work means the end is not in it, and you are interested in the end. If you can reach the end without this work, you would like to leave it. You have to carry it as a burden, it is a compulsion on you. Somehow you have to finish it and reach the goal.

Play is totally different; the end is in it, it is intrinsic. There is no goal, you are not going anywhere. You are enjoying the very thing. Think about it. A professional player becomes sad. It is something to be carried out, to be finished soon – the sooner the better.

The Upanishadic rishi is just the opposite. Even in profession he is a player; even in profession, in business, in whatsoever he is doing, in whatsoever life has created for him to do, he is a player, he goes on playing. He has no business to do, that's why he is never busy. There is nothing to be done, there is no hurry. If everything is left unfinished there is no worry because it is okay, it was just a play, it ended in the middle – really there was no end to be achieved. This is the attitude of the positive path.

The seeker feels blissful while engaging himself each day in meritorious acts…. He performs only such gentle acts as do not disturb others.

When you are playing there is no need to hurt others, but when you are busy with a business you don't care for others. Rather, you will use whatsoever means are to be used, even if the others are to be destroyed, because it is not a play, it is a serious business. Whosoever comes in your way has to be destroyed and thrown out of the way. In business you are violent, and a mind which is businesslike can never be nonviolent.

That's why I go on saying that Gandhi cannot be nonviolent – he's so businesslike. Even his nonviolence is a business, he is so serious about it. He is not in a play, he is deadly serious. That's why he appealed to us so much: we are all businessmen and he was the supreme, the top. He appealed to us, he had appeal for everybody all over the earth, East or West. He appealed deeply, he appealed to the business mind. He was mathematical, calculating, serious with every penny – not in any way in a play.

He was not a Hindu, he could not be. He was ninety percent a Jaina and ten percent a Christian – negative, businesslike, serious. He was not like Krishna – playful, enjoying, nonserious. Whatsoever happens Krishna is not worried. He is not going to force anything on the course of life. Wherever life leads is the goal – wherever. If life leads to death in the middle of a stream, that is the goal – nowhere to reach.

A nonachieving mind is playful. An achieving mind, always thinking of achieving something, whether in this world or the other, is a business mind.

He performs only such gentle acts as do not disturb others.

When you are playing there is no need to disturb anybody. When you are playful you are nonviolent.

He fears sin, and does not crave any self-indulgence.

But the concept of sin in Hinduism is totally different from that of Christianity. Remember, the word *pap*, sin, has a different connotation. The Upanishads say that which is against the law is sin, just a natural phenomenon. Christianity says that which is disobedience to God is sin. This is absolutely different: disobedience to God.

In Christianity God is something like an aristocrat, something like a dictator; we can paint him just like Hitler or Mussolini. You disobey, and you will suffer and he will punish you. And he is very ferocious in punishment. For small sins, sometimes even when you are innocent, you will be thrown into hell. And Christianity says that it is forever and forever, the hell is eternal. That doesn't seem to be justified. A small sin, falling in love with a woman, and you will suffer forever and forever.

And what did Adam do? – just a small disobedience; something that God prohibited. God said, "You are not to eat the fruit of this tree, the tree of knowledge. You can eat all the fruits available in this garden of Eden, but don't come near this tree."

And it is human to be attracted to something which is prohibited. Adam is so human and lovely, he must have become curious. If he was absolutely stupid, only then could he have followed. Even a little intelligence will say that something is there, otherwise why should God prohibit? If God had prohibited him from eating the snake, then Adam would have eaten the snake and been finished with the Devil. But he prohibited the fruit of the tree of knowledge, and then Adam was expelled from Eden because he disobeyed.

Christianity therefore is conformist; revolutionaries cannot be allowed. Adam was the first revolutionary. And why should God feel so offended for such a small thing? The Christian God cannot be playful. He is serious and ferocious, and he will take revenge. Hinduism cannot conceive of that: God taking revenge on innocent Adam who was just being curious. There was nothing else, he was just curious to know. And the Devil was able to persuade him. The Devil said, "God has prohibited you, because if you eat this fruit you will become God-like, and he is afraid and jealous."

This is the sin in Christianity – disobedience. In Hinduism there is no question of disobedience or obedience. It is a simple natural law; just as water flows downwards, if you follow natural laws you will be happy. There is no one to decide it, it is a simple happening – if you follow natural laws you will be happy. If you don't follow natural laws, you go against them, you will be unhappy. Nobody is taking any revenge, and you are not going to be thrown into eternal hell. If you don't follow, for the time being you will suffer. Immediately you come back to the law the suffering stops.

A simple thing: if you put your hand in the fire you will be burned. No God is deciding, "I prohibit you. Don't put your hand in the fire, otherwise I will take revenge." Nobody is there, it is just the way fire behaves. You have to know that if you put your hand in you will suffer. Don't put the hand in and you don't suffer. And then you can use fire to heat the room, to cook food, and the fire be-comes your help — you can use it. Natural laws can be used if you know them well, flow with them; if you go against you suffer.

Sin is going against a natural law, not against any God. No one is giving you suffering, you are choosing it by moving wrongly. And no one is going to give you bliss, you will choose it by moving rightly. So it is not a question of good and bad, it is a question of right and wrong.

He utters loving and affectionate words. He lives in the company of saints and studies the scriptures. With complete unity of mind, speech and action, he follows them. Seeking to cross the ocean that is the world, he cultivates the above-mentioned ideas. And he is called a beginner, one performing his preliminaries. This is called the first stage.

Remember, all this is just the beginning, just the first step of creating the situation. This is not the end — just the preliminary, just the first step.

5   In Deep Patience

Osho,

Need one be absolutely sure about a guru to become his disciple?

You can never be absolutely sure about a guru, and that is not needed. What is needed is that you should be absolutely sure about yourself. How can you be sure about a master? You exist on two different levels, two different states of mind. Whatsoever you can see, whatsoever you can understand, whatsoever you can interpret, will not be of much use – and there is more possibility of your going wrong than right. But there is no need, so don't be worried about it.

You have to be sure about yourself, about your search, and if you are sure about yourself then you can devote yourself to a master totally. Remember, the totality of surrender is not going to come from the surety about the master; it is going to come from your own surety, your own totalness. The master is bound to remain paradoxical for you unless you yourself become enlightened, because only the same can understand the same.

Only when you have become a buddha will you be able to understand Buddha – never before. When you have become a christ, when Christ is known to you, you can understand; never before. Christ is bound to remain a mystery, and a mystery means paradox. Christ will appear to you as irrational, not because he is irrational but because he is supra-rational, he is beyond reason – and you don't know anything about beyond reason. At the most you can think he is below reason, he is not rational. And the ways of a master are so secret that sometimes he will create a situation in which he will not allow you to be sure about himself, because if you can be absolutely sure about the master then your surrender is meaningless. Then what is the meaning of it? When you are absolutely sure of the master then it is a bargain, then you cannot do anything else other than surrender. When you are uncertain, then surrender is a device; in your uncertainty, hesitation, still you decide. That decision changes you.

The more mysterious a master, the more is the possibility of transformation through surrender. If the master is known to you, just as two plus two makes four, then there is no mystery. Sufi masters particularly will create rumors about themselves, so the new ones who come to them can only enter not because they are sure about the master, but because they are sure about their search – and they are ready to take a risk. Why do you want to be sure about the master? – because you don't want to take the risk. Your mind is a business mind. When a master is something mysterious....

One old woman came from England to see Gurdjieff. She had heard Ouspensky, Gurdjieff's disciple, and Ouspensky was a mathematician, a logician. He was not a master, he was not enlightened, but he was a perfect rationalist and he could explain Gurdjieff better than Gurdjieff himself. Gurdjieff would have remained unknown to the world if there had been no Ouspensky. He was nowhere near Gurdjieff, but he could think in a logical way, express in a logical way. He was professionally a mathematician. Many people were attracted to Ouspensky, and when they were attracted to Ouspensky they would start thinking about going to Gurdjieff – and then they would return frustrated, disappointed.

One old woman became very much impressed by Ouspensky, and then she went to see Gurdjieff. Within just a week she was back, and she told Ouspensky, "I can feel that Gurdjieff is great, but I am not certain whether he is good or bad, whether he is evil, devilish, or a saint. I am not certain about that. He is great – that much is certain. But he may be a great devil, or a great saint – that is not certain." And Gurdjieff behaved in such a way that he would create this impression.

Alan Watts has written about Gurdjieff and has called him a rascal saint – because sometimes he would behave like a rascal, but it was all acting and was done knowingly to avoid all those who would take unnecessary time and energy. It was done to send back those who could only work when they were certain. Only those would be allowed who could work even when they were not certain about the master, but who were certain about themselves.

And to surrender to a Gurdjieff will transform you more than surrendering to Ramana Maharshi, because Ramana Maharshi is so saintly, so simple, that surrender doesn't mean anything. You cannot do otherwise. He is so open – just like a small child – so pure, that surrender will happen. But that surrender is happening because of Ramana Maharshi, not because of you. It is nothing as far as you are concerned. If surrender happens with Gurdjieff, then it has happened *because* of you, because Gurdjieff is in no way going to support it. Rather, he will create all types of hindrances. If still you surrender, that transforms you. So there is no need to be absolutely sure about him – and that is impossible – but you have to be sure about yourself.

Just today one friend came to me and said about himself, "I am just fifty-fifty: fifty percent with you and fifty percent with Subud" – a very good Indonesian technique of meditation. So, "I am fifty-fifty, divided."

I asked him, "What do you mean by fifty-fifty?" and told him one anecdote.

It happened once that Mulla Nasruddin owned a hotel. Then he was arrested and brought to the court of the town, because he was caught mixing horsemeat in chicken cutlets. But he confessed and he said, "I have been committing this crime," and he pleaded guilty.

The magistrate asked, "Nasruddin, will you tell me what the proportion was? How much horsemeat were you mixing into how many chicken cutlets?"

Nasruddin said, very truthfully, "Fifty-fifty."

But the magistrate was not convinced so he asked, "What do you mean by fifty-fifty, Nasruddin?"

Nasruddin said, "It is so obvious. Fifty-fifty means fifty-fifty — one horse to one chicken."

So it is not certain. What do you mean by fifty-fifty? Your mind is confusion, but division will not help, a divided mind will not be of much help. Go to Subud or come to me, but be a hundred percent. And that hundred percentness is needed about *you* – not about me, or about Bapak Subud, or about anybody else. You must be a hundred percent here, then work becomes possible.

What to do? Your mind is cunning – clever, you call it, but it is cunning. It calculates, it cannot take a risk. That's why you have been wandering for so many lives. You were near Buddha, you were near Jesus, you have seen Mohammed – you have seen many masters, but you bypass them just because of your cleverness. Your cleverness is your stupidity. Even with a Buddha you calculate – and what can you calculate? Life is such a mystery; it cannot be explained in terms of logic. And a person like Buddha is so mysterious that whatsoever you come to conclude will be wrong, and by the time you have concluded Buddha will have changed. By the time you have come to a decision, Buddha is not the same – because Buddha is a river, a riverlike phenomenon, flowing. Conclusion will take time, and you will miss.

Religion is for those who are like gamblers, who can take risks. If you are a gambler then something can happen, but if you are a businessman then nothing is possible. Be certain about your search. If you are really in search, then don't be afraid. And I say again: even with a master who is false, pseudo, you are not going to lose anything.

It happened that one of the Tibetan mystics, Marpa, was in search of a master. He reached a master who was not really a master, who was a pseudo-teacher, who was not himself enlightened. Marpa asked him, "What am I supposed to do?"

The pseudo-master said, "You will have to surrender to me. Surrender totally."

Marpa said, "Surrendered! I am surrendered. Now what is to be done?"

Other disciples became jealous, because this Marpa seemed to be a dangerous man: immediately, without arguing, without discussing, he said, "I have surrendered. Now tell me, what is to be done?" He would become the leader, he would become the chief disciple – he had already become it. He had just arrived, and they had been serving the master for many years, and he had superseded them.

They became jealous, and they said to the master, "This is not easy; surrender is such a difficult thing. For many years we have been working, and yet we have not surrendered totally. This man seems to be deceiving. So we must examine whether the surrender is true or not."

The master asked, "How can it be examined and tested?"

So they said, "Tell him to jump from this hill into the valley. If he jumps, then he is surrendered. If he doesn't jump, then he is deceiving." In both ways they were thinking that they were going to be the winners. If he jumped he would be dead; if he didn't jump he would be thrown out of the ashram.

But they didn't know Marpa – he simply jumped. And they were wonderstruck. He jumped – and then he was sitting in the valley! So when they reached him they could not believe it; even the master could not believe that this could happen. So he thought, "It must have been just an accident that he is saved."

He asked Marpa, "How did it happen?"

He said, "I don't know. You must know; I have surrendered to you. Now it is up to you. I don't know what has happened – but a miracle has happened. You have done this!"

The master knew well that he had not done anything – he did not know any a b c – this must have been by accident. So another situation had to be created.

Then they saw a house that was on fire, so they said, "Enter!" Marpa entered immediately. The whole house burned, and they could not know what had happened until the fire disappeared.

Then they went inside. All over the place everything was burned, everything was destroyed and Marpa was sitting in meditation, not even perspiring. So the master asked, "Marpa, how did you do it again?"

He said, "I don't know, master. It is you. And my trust is growing; you are a miracle!"

But it is possible that even an accident can happen a second time, improbabilities are also possible. So they thought, "It has to be tried again, a third time." So they told Marpa to walk on a river. The river was in flood and they said, "Walk on water!" And Marpa walked.

When Marpa was walking and was just in midstream, the master thought, "It seems as if I am doing something, because how can this happen? It must be *my* power." He thought, "If just by surrendering to me Marpa can walk on water, why cannot I walk?" So he started walking – and he was drowned.

No one has ever heard about what happened to that master, but Marpa became enlightened.

So it is not a question of the master, it is a question of your totality. Even with a pseudo-master you can become enlightened. And the reverse is also true: even with an enlightened master you may remain ignorant. Remember, my emphasis is on you. That's why I never say: Don't go to Sai Baba, or: Don't go to Bapak Subud. That is immaterial. Go anywhere. Go totally.

The second question:

Osho,

You often tell stories of persons who went into aloneness in some forest and who became silent and peaceful there. But aloneness seems to make most modern persons anxious and depressed, and it creates a yearning for human companionship. Instead of the patterned mind dropping, we become more acutely aware of it and preoccupied with it. How to overcome this? How can we learn to enjoy long periods of aloneness, and drop the old mind in it?

This is nothing new for the modern mind; this has been always so. Mind cannot exist in aloneness; to be alone means mind will have to commit suicide. Mind becomes anxious – it is a murder. Whenever you go alone, the mind cannot exist in that aloneness.

Mind can exist only in the society; mind is a social phenomenon, others are needed for it. You cannot be angry when alone, or if you become angry you will feel very foolish; you cannot be sad when alone, because there is no excuse; you cannot be violent when alone, because the other is needed; you cannot talk, you cannot go on chattering. You cannot use the mind, the mind cannot function – and when mind cannot function it becomes anxious, worried. It needs functioning, it needs someone to communicate to.

Mind is a social phenomenon, a societal byproduct. And it has always been so. Even when Svetaketu went into the forest, he was anxious, he was worried, he was depressed in the beginning. The difference is not in the mind; the difference is in patience. The mind remains the same, modern or old, but in the old days people were more patient, they could wait. You are not patient –that is the problem. They were not time conscious and you are time conscious.

In the old days in the ancient world, particularly in the East, there was no time consciousness. That's why watches and clocks were not invented in the East. There was more possibility for their invention in China than in India, because they had done many things and it was possible to invent clocks, to measure time, but they were not interested in time. The modern mind is too interested in time. Why? This is a part of the Christian influence on the world. With Christianity and Islam time consciousness entered into the world. There are reasons for it.

In the East it has been believed always that life goes on forever and ever, it is eternal, it is timeless – so there is no hurry; you will be again and again. Millions of times you were here and millions of times you will be again here; there is no hurry. This life is not the last nor the first, it is a long procession, and you are al-ways in the middle – there is no beginning and no end. So there can be no hurry about time; enough time, more than enough, is available.

With Christianity there is only one life – this is the first and the last. Once you die you don't have any time any more; so you have a life span of seventy years at the most. There is so much to do, and so little time with you. That's why in the West there is so much hurry; everyone is running because life is going. Every moment life is becoming less and less. Time is passing, you are dying, and you have so many desires to fulfill and no time to fulfill them, so anxiety is created.

In the East it was totally different. It is said in one of the Tibetan scriptures that even if you have to go in a hurry, go slowly. Even if you have to go in a hurry, go slowly. It is said that if you run you will never reach; if you sit you can reach, but if you run you will miss. An eternal procession, many lives, millions of lives, enough time – patience was possible.

In the West only one life, and every moment life changing into death; nothing is fulfilled, no desire completed, everything incomplete – how can you be patient? How can you wait? Waiting has become impossible. With the idea of one life, and with another idea of linear time, Christianity has created anxiety in the mind; and now Christianity has become a global influence.

Christianity says that time is not moving in a circle, it is moving in a straight line. Nothing is going to be repeated again, so everything is unique. Every event is once and for all, it cannot be repeated. It is not a circle; it is not like a wheel of a cart moving where every spoke will come again, where again and again the same spoke will be repeated.

In the East time is a circular concept, just like seasons moving in a circle. The summer comes and then the summer will come again, and it has been so always and it will be so always. And the Eastern concept is nearer to truth than the Western, because every movement is in a circle. The earth moves in a circle, the sun moves in a circle, the stars move in a circle, the life moves in a circle – every movement is circular. So time cannot be an exception; if time moves at all, it moves in a circle. The linear concept of time is absolutely wrong.

That's why in the East we were never interested in history. We have been interested in myth, but never in history. The West introduced history into the world. That's why Jesus became the center of history, the beginning of the calendar. We go on measuring time with "before Christ," "after Christ." Christ became the center of all history, the first historic person.

Buddha is not historic, Krishna is not at all; you can never be certain whether really Krishna was ever born or not, whether the whole thing was just a story or a history. But the East was never worried about it. They say everything is a story, and it has been told many times and will be told again and again. There is no need to be concerned with facts, because facts are repetitive. It is better to be concerned with the theme, not with the facts – so you may not be able to understand many things.

It is said that before Rama was born, one of the *avatars* of India, Valmiki, wrote his story – before he was born! It is impossible. How can you write the history when the man is not yet born? But Valmiki wrote first, and then Rama had to follow his story, whatsoever he had said. How did it happen? This is mysterious, but not mysterious at all if you look at the Eastern concept of time.

Valmiki says, "I know Rama, because in many ages he has been born before – I know the very theme. So I create the story, because I know the theme, I know the essential. The nonessential I will put in the story."

And Rama must have thought, "Why contradict Valmiki? Why contradict this old man? Follow it." And he followed.

The East lives in myth; myth means a repetitive theme, the essential is always there. In the West myth is meaningless. If you can prove that something is a myth it becomes meaningless. You have to prove that it is history, it has happened in time; you have to be exact about it.

This linear concept of nonrepetitive life creates anxiety, so when you go into silence, alone, you become worried. One thing is: time is wasted. You are not doing anything, you are just sitting. Why are you wasting your life? And this time cannot be regained, because they go on teaching in the West: Time is wealth. It is absolutely wrong, because wealth is created by scarcity, and time is not scarce. The whole economics depends on scarcity: if something is scarce it becomes valuable. Time is not scarce, it is there always. You cannot finish it; it will always be there – so time cannot be economic. It is not scarce; it cannot be wealth.

But we go on teaching, "Time is wealth – don't waste it. Once wasted it never comes again." So if you go into aloneness and then you sit there, you cannot sit there for three years, you cannot sit there for three months, even three days are too much – you have wasted three days.

And what are you doing? The second problem arises – because in the West being is not very valuable, doing is valuable. They ask, "What have you done?" – because the time has to be used in doing something. They say in the West that a vacant mind is the devil's workshop. And you know it, in the mind you also know it, so when you are sitting alone you become afraid. Wasting time, not doing anything, you go on questioning yourself, "What are you doing here? Just sitting? Wasting?" – as if just being is a wastage! You have to do something to prove that you have utilized your time. This is the difference.

In the old ancient days, in the East particularly, just to *be* was enough; there was no need to prove anything else. No one was going to ask, "What have you done?" Your being was enough and accepted. If you were silent, peaceful, blissful, it was okay. That's why in the East we never demanded from sannyasins that they should work – no, no need. And we always thought that sannyasins, those who had left all working, were better than those who were occupied in work.

This cannot be done in the West. If you are not working you are a vagabond, a bum. Hippies are a very new phenomenon. The East has always been hippie-oriented. We have created the greatest hippies of the world – a Buddha, a Mahavira: not doing anything, just sitting and meditating, enjoying their being, just being blissful as they are, not doing anything. But we respected them – they were the supreme, the highest, the most respectable. Buddha was begging, but even kings had to come to bow to his feet.

Once it happened that Buddha was passing through a village, and the chief minister of the king of that locality told the king, "Buddha is coming, so we will have to go to receive him and touch his feet and pay our respects."

The king said, "But is it necessary for a beggar? He is just a beggar, and I am a great king. Why should I go and respect him and bow down to him? If he wants to see me, he can come and take an appointment with me."

The old chief minister, who was a very wise man, immediately gave in his resignation. He said, "If this is the case then I cannot remain here for a single moment."

The king was worried, because this man was much too valuable to be lost, so he said, "But why?"

The old man said, "This is absolutely wrong. You may be a great king, you may become the emperor of the whole earth, but you cannot become greater than Buddha. He has left all kingdoms, and you are still obsessed with wealth, riches, prestige, power. He has left all of them, he has nothing, and only a person who has nothing is the highest, because he doesn't desire. You will have to go and respect him, otherwise take my resignation. I cannot remain in this unholy palace for a single moment." The king had to go.

The East was totally different; a different milieu was there. Being was respect-ed. No one was going to ask, "What have you done?" Everyone was just asking, "What *are* you?" Enough! If you were silent, peaceful, loving; if compassion was there; if you had flowered – enough! Then it was society's duty to help and serve you. No one would say you should work, or you should create something, you should be creative. In the East they thought that to be oneself is the highest creativity, and the presence of such a man was valuable. He could go into silence for years.

Mahavira was in silence for twelve years. He would not speak, he would not go into villages, he would not see anybody. And when he started speaking, somebody asked him, "Why were you not speaking before?"

He said, "Speech becomes valuable only when you have attained silence, otherwise it is futile – not only futile, dangerous also, because you are throwing rubbish into others' heads. So this was my effort: that I would speak only when talking had completely stopped inside. When the inner talk had disappeared, only then would I speak. Then it is not a disease."

And they could wait, because the East believed in reincarnation. They could wait. There are stories that a disciple would come to the master and wait for thirty years, would not ask anything but just wait for the master to ask, "For what have you come?" Thirty years is too much – one life completely wasted – but waiting for thirty years will do the work.

People from the West come to me and they say, "This very evening we are leaving, so give us some key. How can we become silent? But we don't have any time to stay – we must go." They are thinking in terms with which they have become acquainted – instant coffee – so they think there must be some instant meditation, a key I can hand over to them and it is finished. No, there is no key. It is a long effort, it is a deep patience. And the more you are in a hurry, the longer it will take. So remember this: if you are not in any hurry it may happen this very moment. When you are not in a hurry the quality of mind is there, silence is there.

I will tell you one story. Once it happened that two monks were traveling. They crossed a river in a boat, and the ferryman said to them, "Where are you going? If you are going to the city beyond this valley, go slowly."

But the old monk said, "If we go slowly we will never reach, because we have heard that the gates of that city are closed after sunset, and we have just one or two hours at the most, and it is a very long distance. If we go slowly we will never reach, and we will have to wait outside the city. And the outside of the city is dangerous – wild animals and everything – so we will have to make haste."

The ferryman said, "Okay, but this is my experience: those who go slowly, reach."

The other monk listened to it. He was a young man and he thought, "I don't know this part of the country, and this ferryman may be right, so it is better to follow his advice." So he walked slowly, leisurely, as if not going anywhere, not in a hurry, just for a walk.

The old man hurried, started running. He had many scriptures on his back. Then he fell down: tired, carrying weight, old, and in such a hurry, so tense, he fell down. The man who was not in a hurry simply walked and reached.

The ferryman was coming and he came near the old man. He was lying by the side of the road; his leg was broken and blood was oozing out. The ferryman said, "I told you that this has been always so: those who walk slowly reach, those who are in a hurry always manage to stumble somewhere or other. These parts are dangerous. The road is rough and you are an old man. And I had advised you, but you wouldn't listen to me."

This is one of the Korean Zen stories, and this is how it is in life. Go slowly, patiently, not in a hurry, because the goal is not somewhere else – it is within you. When you are not in a hurry you will feel it; when you are in a hurry you cannot feel it because you are so tense. If you are not going anywhere at all, then you can feel it more immediately.

In Japan meditation is called *zazen*. Zazen means simply sitting and not doing anything. So Zen priests, monks, have to sit for six hours a day or even more; the master never gives them anything to do, they have just to sit. They have trained themselves for just sitting, not asking for anything to do, not even a mantra – just sitting.

It is very arduous. It looks easy but is very arduous, because the mind asks for some work, something to be done. And the mind goes on saying, "Why? Why waste time? Why just go on sitting? What is going to happen by just sitting?" But for three years, or even more, the seeker sits. Then, by and by, the mind drops asking. It is useless now, you don't listen to it. It has got fed up with you, so the mind stops asking. By and by, when the mind is not asking, you start realizing a new life force within you which was always there but you were so occupied you couldn't listen to it, you couldn't feel it. Unoccupied, you start feeling it.

Mind has always been creating problems and loneliness. Go in aloneness at least for three months, and decide beforehand that whatsoever happens you are not going to listen to the mind. Decide beforehand that you are ready to waste three months, so there is no need to think again and again that you are wasting time. You have decided that you are going to waste three months, and you are not going to do anything – you will simply sit and wait. A miracle is possible.

Just within these three months, some day suddenly you will become aware of your being. When there is no doing you become aware of being. When there is too much doing you go on forgetting the being which is hidden behind.

The third question:

Osho,

I feel very devoted to you, and since being with you my life has transformed very much. In my heart I feel you are my master. For the first time I feel a contentment with my outer life and my relationships with others, and there is no desire for anything external. But an inner yearning for the ever elusive enlightenment and bliss remains, and I cannot do anything to stop that desire. Is this a barrier? Isn't it likely to remain until the reality is realized, however?

Yes, it is a barrier, because there is no question of any desire, whether for external things or for internal things. Desire is the same, there is no distinction, so don't divide desire, and don't say, "No more are worldly desires within me, but the otherworldly desire is there." The otherworldly desire is as worldly as any worldly desire – desire is worldly. So don't divide, don't play tricks.

Objects of desire are not significant; desiring is significant. You can desire wealth, you can desire God – desiring remains the same, only the object has changed. You can desire a palace here, you can desire a palace in paradise – objects have changed, but the desire remains the same. You can desire anything whatsoever, desire will be the same. Remember this.

And with desire you cannot attain realization. Desire has to be dropped. So what to do? Really there is nothing to do. You have to realize more and more that your desire creates suffering. Now this new desire is creating suffering. Before there were other desires; you have left those desires, so you feel contentment, you feel peaceful with life. Your relationships have become more loving because desires have disappeared from that field.

Now be aware: when there were desires in that field you were not content. You were frustrated, you were filled with jealousy, anger, hatred; relationship was difficult, it was suffering and misery.

Now desire has left that field; that field has become peaceful. So become aware that now you are creating a new suffering: when will this enlightenment happen? And unless it happens you cannot be content. How can you be content unless you become a buddha? So, "When will I become a buddha?"

One Buddhist, Nagarjuna, is reported to have said that the desire to become a buddha is the greatest barrier to becoming a buddha – because unless you stop desiring to become a buddha you will not come to know that you are already a buddha. This desiring dissolves and your buddhahood appears; it is there. So now feel this new misery which is coming into being with the new desire.

Every desire brings misery. There is nothing to be done –simply become aware that every desire brings misery. If you realize this, desires will disappear; internal or external, no desires are needed. When there is no desire you have achieved. Then this very moment is ecstasy; then right here and now you have become the goal. There can be no misery then. But don't make this distinction. Mind is so cunning, it goes on deceiving you. It says, "Okay, if worldly desires create misery, leave them. I will be content with nonworldly desires." So the object changes, but the desiring remains the same.

I will tell you one anecdote. I have heard, it happened in New Delhi that a *netaji*, a great political leader, dragged Mulla Nasruddin to the court. That great leader, the netaji, said to the court, "This man, Mulla Nasruddin, has insulted me in public. He has called me a donkey."

That political leader was a powerful man. The magistrate said to Nasruddin, "This is not good. You will have to be punished."

Nasruddin said, "I was not aware that it is an offense to call a leader a donkey. I was not aware. So forgive me, and I give you my promise that I will never do it again." So he was forgiven, and even the political leader was satisfied.

Then Nasruddin asked the magistrate, "But if I call a donkey netaji, leader, have you any objection?"

The magistrate laughed and he said, "There is no objection – unless the donkey comes to the court, and I hope no donkey will come. If you feel good, and if you like it, you can call any donkey netaji. We don't have any objection to it."

Mulla Nasruddin turned immediately towards the netaji and said, "Netaji, how are you?"

The mind remains the same. It goes on changing objects, but the inner quality persists. So whether you call a leader a donkey, or you call a donkey a leader, it makes no difference – you will have to stop calling.

So a desire for the outer, or a desire for the inner, is just a change of the object – the mind remains the same. Drop it. As you have dropped the outer desire, you can drop the inner also. And you know now that just by dropping the outer you are feeling a deep contentment with yourself. So why carry this new desire? Drop it also.

When you drop all desire, you have become paradise itself. Then you are the heaven, you are the *moksha*. With desires you are destroying it; with desires you are so occupied you cannot be in contact with your own deepest center, your own deepest depth.

The last question:

Osho,

This morning you said that the Upanishadic sages had a positive approach towards life, and that Buddha and Mahavira had a negative approach towards life. Which is Your approach – affirmation or negation of life? Which approach would You have Your disciples take?

I have got no approach – or, both are mine. I don't divide. To me, the positive can also lead to the same goal as the negative, so I don't say that the positive is the only approach, and I don't say that the negative is the only approach. Both are approaches, and both are as good as each other.

My emphasis is not on the approach, my emphasis is on the disciple. So I don't say that you should follow this or that wholesale. I would like you to decide whether you have a negative mind or a positive mind. If you have a positive mind then follow the positive approach; if you have a negative mind then follow the negative approach. And there are both types of people here.

That's why Hinduism cannot be a world religion, Buddhism cannot be a world religion. Up till now there exists no religion which can be a world religion, because every religion chooses one approach. Whatsoever I am saying can be a world-comprehensive thing, because I don't choose any approach. All approaches lead to the same goal. The goal is important, and the disciple who is to travel is important – the path is irrelevant. And both types exist.

Remember, there are males and females, and their number on the earth re-mains almost equal. This is a miracle: biologists cannot explain how it happens that man and woman remain in equal numbers on the earth. And if sometimes the balance is lost, immediately the balance is regained. For example, in a war the balance is lost because more men are killed than women. Immediately after the war more boys are born than girls. How this happens has been a mystery for biology – but the number of men and women remain equal.

The mystery is because of the polarity: man is one pole of life and woman is the other pole of life. If a man is born, immediately a woman is born, because the other pole has to be there; without the other pole this magnet cannot exist. So whenever there are wars and more men are killed, immediately more men will be born. Ordinarily also, more boys are born than girls. The proportion is this: one hundred and fifteen boys are born to one hundred girls, because boys are weaker than girls, and by the time they are sexually mature fifteen boys will have died. So by the age of sexual maturity the number will be equal – fifteen boys will have died.

Girls don't die so easily, they are stronger. And it is a fallacy created by men, male chauvinists, that man is the stronger sex. This is a fallacy, woman is the stronger sex. In every way she is stronger. She is ill less than man, she goes mad less than man, she lives longer than man. The average life-expectancy of women all over the world, in every country, is five years more than men. If men live to be seventy-five, women are going to live to be eighty. And they die less in childhood – fifteen percent less. They are the stronger sex.

And this is how it should be, because they have to do the greatest creativity of this life – give birth. It is such a long suffering, a *tapascharya*, a sadhana, to give birth. Just think, if man had to give birth the world would have disappeared. Just think, for nine months carrying a baby in your stomach. It is impossible to conceive of man doing that and then bringing up the child. No man would be ready for it. He is weak.

Wherever the balance is lost it is immediately regained. Why? – because man and woman are a polarity. There is a myth in India, a Jaina myth, which you may not have heard, and I think it is very probable that sometime it may have been true. In Jaina Puranas, in Jaina mythology, it is said that in the beginning only twins were born, never a single child: twins, one boy and one girl. And they were to be married – brother and sister, twins.

In the beginning, millions of years ago in the past, only twins were born, a boy and a girl. They were the natural wife and husband, and the world was very peaceful. It must have been, because if you could get a natural wife and a natural husband, life would be totally different – because it is always the wrong person that you choose. It is so difficult to choose a right wife and a right husband – almost impossible! How can you choose?

Just think of another thing: if you had to choose the right father and the right mother it would have been impossible. Where to choose and how to choose? And whosoever you had chosen, you would have felt frustrated in the end. But nature chooses for you, so the mother and father are always almost okay; you cannot do anything about it.

The Jaina myth says that wife and husband were born as twins. They were naturally related; they had a harmony, the deep harmony of twins. There was never a conflict between them; they behaved as two bodies and one soul. Jainas say that those were the peaceful days in the world. When that harmony was disturbed everything was disturbed. That's possible, and I think it can become again possible. Science may be helpful in the coming century to create this possibility again – then the pole is born with you. But whether the pole is born with you or not, the pole is born simultaneously somewhere: a boy is born, a girl is born somewhere; a girl is born, a boy is born somewhere.

The same polarity exists between the positive mind and the negative. When-ever there is a positive mind, just by the side of it there is a negative mind. That number is always equal. So in the world, half are always Hindus and half Buddhists – or you can name it in another way, but half are positive persons and half are negative persons.

I don't choose anything. If someone comes to me and says, "Which is right, man or woman?" I will say both are right, because neither can exist separately – their harmony is right. So if you ask me, "Which is right, positive or negative?" I say both are right, because neither can exist without the other – their harmony is right. That's why my statements seem so contradictory, because sometimes I am talking with a positive person; then I have to make totally different statements. Sometimes I am talking to a disciple who is negative; then I have to make absolutely contradictory statements. And when they both meet, they will be confused.

So remember, whenever I say something to you, I have said it to *you*. Don't listen to anybody else; this is personal. Whenever I have said something to you, I have said it to you, and if somebody says that I have said something contradictory to him, don't listen. I may have said it…because to me approaches are not important, persons are important.

I do not have a fixed approach. When a different type of person comes to me, I immediately change my approach. I always adjust to the person, I never try the reverse – I never try to adjust the person to an approach. To me that looks absurd. I don't make readymade clothes for you and then say, "Cut your legs a little because the dress…." I always cut the dress immediately if I feel it doesn't suit you. The dress is wrong, you are never wrong.

Then there are bound to be many contradictions – but I contain contradictions. To me they only appear contradictory; they are joined together just like man and woman, positive and negative, day and night, life and death. Both approaches are mine. That's why I go on talking about Buddha with as much love as I go on talking about Patanjali or Lao Tzu or Jesus or Mahavira or Mohammed.

I contain all.

Remember that – that will help you to be less confused.

6   With the Grace of the Sages

Now follow the traits of seekers of the second stage,

called the stage of thought.

He lives in the care of learned men who explain best what

listening, remembering, right conduct, contemplation –

dharana – and meditation are. Having acquired knowledge of such scriptures as are worth listening to, he efficiently discriminates between what is duty and what is not, and he knows well the division between a word and the thing it symbolizes.

His mind does not suffer from an excess of conceit, pride, greed and attachment, although externally they are apparent to some extent.

He gives up his external impurities as a snake casts off its slough.

Such a seeker acquires the actual

knowledge of all these things with the grace of the scriptures,

the guru, and the sages.

The first stage for the seeker is to create a milieu around himself of the feeling that the ocean is real and waves are just superficial surface phenomena. To live in that oceanic feeling is the first stage. This becomes the soil. Unless this milieu is there, there is no possibility of any growth into the higher realms of being. So remember this: you must be aware more and more of the center, less and less of the surface; more and more aware of the depth, and less and less aware of the circumference. The focus must change from the periphery to the innermost core.

If you continue being involved with the surface you cannot penetrate to the ultimate being, because the ultimate being, Brahman – or you may call it the truth or God or whatsoever you like – the ultimate being is the center of existence. And we exist on the periphery.

This is natural in a way, because whenever you come in contact with something, you come in contact with the periphery, the outermost. This is natural. But don't remain there – move ahead, move further. Leave the periphery be-hind and go deep. With everything – with a rock, with a man, with a tree, with whatsoever – always remember that the surface is the outermost body, and this is not the whole. The whole illusion consists of thinking of the surface as the whole.

The surface belongs to the whole, there is nothing wrong in it; but when you get this impression, this identity that the surface is the whole, then there is no possibility of inner growth because then you have to stay with the surface – the surface has become the whole. Don't allow the surface to become the whole. This is not something which is going against the surface; this is simply going with the truth, with the reality.

The surface will be there. When you have conceived the whole, the surface will be there, but in its right place. Nothing is to be eliminated, only a greater perspective is needed. And when your perspective has become total, everything will be there. This world will be there; whatsoever you have will be there, but in a new harmony, in a new gestalt.

This is something to be understood very deeply, because it happens to persons who are on a religious search that either they get identified with the surface, or they become against it. Then they start thinking that this world is to be negated, the world of the waves has to be denied. Either they think that waves are the ocean, or they move to the opposite pole: they start saying that the waves are illusory, that they are not, that they have to be denied. Both standpoints are wrong. From one wrong polarity, if you jump to the other, the other is bound to be wrong. The truth is somewhere in between, in the middle.

Don't jump from the waves to the ocean, but rather from the waves and the ocean to just in the middle from where you can see both – the ocean and the waves also. Then your life becomes a synthesis, and when your life is a synthesis the music of the divine is created.

The Upanishads are not against the world. They are for Brahman, but they are not against the world. Their Brahman includes everything, the Brahman is inclusive. This is the first state.

Now follow the traits of seekers of the second stage, called the stage of thought.

The first stage is the stage of feeling, feeling that Brahman surrounds you, everywhere is Brahman. And remember, the seeker has to start from the feeling, from the heart, because only the heart can be the base. The heart is the base of your body, and the heart is going to be the base of your divine body also.

If you go to the physiologist he will say, "Yes, there is a heart, but that heart is only physiological, just a pumping system; nothing more is there – no love, no feeling," because he dissects the body and he comes only to know the body and the bodily. But everybody, even that physiologist, when in love will put his hand on his heart. If he is frustrated in his love, then he will feel a deep ache in his heart. He cannot explain it. As a physiologist he will say, "This is illusory," but as a man he also feels the same. And remember, a physiologist is just a specialization, a fragment; man is the whole.

So don't listen to the physiologist, listen to his totality. When he is in love he feels his heart is filled, something has poured into it, he has become heart-full. We don't have such a thing, not even such a word – heartful. We say that a man is healthy, healthful; we say a man is mannerly, mannerful – but we never say a man is heartful, or loveful. These words must be created, because these are existential facts. When you are in love, you are heartful, loveful, overflooded, and of that overflooded feeling the heart is the center.

When you are in love, close your eyes and feel where your feeling has its center. It can never be in the head; it is impossible. It can never be anywhere else – it will be just in the heart. The heart is the base of your body, and it is going to be the base of your higher body also. That's why the Upanishads say that the first stage is of feeling. Thought is not denied, thought has to take its own place – but that is the second stage.

When feeling is there, then thought cannot go wrong. If feeling is not there, thought is bound to go wrong. If you follow thought without feeling, you will become destructive. That's what happened with Hitler, with Mussolini, with Tojo; that's what is happening every day with Mao, with all the dictators – the thought is leading them. The heart has been silenced, or as if cut off from their being; there is only thought, and then thought can be destructive.

Hitler thought that it would be good and a compassionate act if all weaklings were destroyed: no weak person should exist on the earth. It was logical, be-cause these weaklings create problems. These weaklings give birth to more weaklings, they destroy the whole purity of humanity. This is logical – but just logical. If you ask Buddha, he will say that the weakling has to be supported: the strong should serve the weak, and that is his strength; otherwise for what is his strength needed? The stronger the person, the more he will serve the weak – but this comes from the heart. Then service itself becomes the strongest thing in your personality.

But if you think from the mind only, then weaklings have to be destroyed because they are the deterioration; through them humanity will deteriorate, will fall down. The ill have to be destroyed because through them illness will spread more. The mad have to be killed because through them madness will be spread all over the world. This is logical; nothing is wrong in it as a mathematical argument – and that's what Hitler tried to follow. He killed millions of beings.

You cannot argue with him logically; he is exactly right that the weak should be destroyed. But then what is strength? If all the weaklings are destroyed, where will be the strong? And if this logic is continued to its climax, then only one person can exist on the earth – the strongest – because all others will be weaklings in comparison to him. So if you go on destroying the weak, then only one person can exist, not even two. This is the conclusion of the logic. And then what is that one person going to do? And what is the meaning of his life? For whom is he going to exist?

Life has the deepest secret, and that is this: that when you exist for someone you exist for the first time. And if your existence becomes a service to many it becomes richer. When you exist only for yourself you exist uselessly; there is no significance, no meaning. The moment you start existing for someone, your existence becomes meaningful, significant, for the first time. That is the meaning of service. But that service can be based only on the heart; it cannot be based on thought.

But that doesn't mean that the Upanishads deny thinking. They don't deny; they say thought has much to do, but it must follow feeling. The mind must follow heart, only then can it be good. Then it cannot go wrong because the heart will always guide in the right direction. The heart becomes the compass – and the heart has the center of love, and love cannot lead you wrongly.

It happened once, a man came to Saint Augustine and he said, "What should I do? And tell me in short, because I am an illiterate person and I cannot understand great theological things. So just in short, simply, so that I can understand and remember it, just tell me the essence of religion."

Saint Augustine is reported to have said, "Love, and then all else will follow. And don't bother about anything else."

If you love you cannot do wrong. The more you love the more it becomes impossible to do wrong – love cannot go wrong. But *your* love goes wrong. That simply means that your love is not love. Your love even creates hell, misery; you even become destructive to your lover. Move into any family and you will feel the destruction that love has brought: wife and husband continuously fighting, quarreling, trying to dominate each other, trying to possess each other – really trying to destroy the other.

The wife wants the husband just to be a thing, not a person. The husband wants the wife just to be a thing to be possessed; a beautiful thing of course, but a thing, not a person – because a person needs freedom to be, only a thing can be made totally a slave. A person can never be made a slave, and the more you make a slave of him the less he is a person. And this is happening through love! And Augustine says, Buddha says, Jesus says, "Love, and everything will be right. Love, and you will be on the right path." Your love is not love.

The more I try to understand people who are in love, the more I see that their love is just a form of hate. They disguise it, they think it is love, but their thinking cannot be believed, because the results show something else. And a tree is known by its fruits, not by the declaration. The tree may declare, there may be a big sign on the tree, a signboard saying "This is an apple tree," but it is to be known by the fruits. If apples never come the signboard is not worth anything, it is lying. If love gives one the direction towards divineness, then *your* love cannot be called love because it leads into misery.

Oscar Wilde has written in his memoirs, "This has been my problem my whole life: I cannot live without a woman, and I cannot live with a woman. If I live with a woman it creates hell; if I don't live with a woman that creates hunger and starvation and I feel I should have a woman." You cannot live with a woman, and you cannot live without a woman. What is the problem? The problem is that love has to be learned. Love is a creative art; one is not born with the capacity to love, no one is born with the capacity to love. Love is a growth, an achievement, and the finest achievement possible.

It is just like music: no one is born playing an instrument, you have to learn it. And the more complex the instrument, the longer it will take. Someone asked Godowsky, "Now you have become a great master of music, a maestro, do you still practice?"

He said, "Yes, if I don't practice for a single day, I notice things are going wrong. If I don't practice for two days, then experts in my audience notice something is going wrong. And if I don't practice for three days, everybody becomes aware that something is going wrong." Eight hours per day he was practicing when he was a world famous maestro.

And love is the greatest music, and you have to play it upon the most complex instrument – the lover or the beloved. You think you are born with the capacity, so you destroy the instrument. You fall in love with a woman, but you don't know that that woman is the most complex instrument in the world. You are going to destroy, and when the woman is destroyed she becomes chaotic, she becomes chaos – anger and hatred are bound to be there.

Love has to be learned as an art, the greatest art, the art of life. That's why we go on talking about love, but love is the most scarce thing on this earth. It happens only once; millions of people are in love and it happens only once – one in a million becomes capable of love. There are reasons. When a child is born, the child has only self-love. And this is natural: he does not know anybody else, he knows only himself. The child is the most selfish being, the most selfish, self-centered being. He exists for himself, and he imagines that the whole world exists to serve him. And because he is so helpless everybody has to serve him, so he is justified. Whenever he cries the mother runs to give him food, milk, help, warmth, love, and he becomes dictatorial.

Every child becomes dictatorial and he knows that everybody follows. Whatsoever his desire it has to be fulfilled immediately, otherwise he goes mad. He is so helpless, and nothing can be done – we have to serve him. His ego becomes strengthened. The mother, the father, the family, everybody around him helps him, serves him, and he feels that he is the center of the world. And almost always it happens that you never grow out of this childhood nonsense. You remain the center, and you think everybody has to serve you.

How can you love? – because love means the other has become the center. Love is a very great jump: you are not the center, the other has become the center. You have become the shadow. Now the other has the meaning, and just to serve him or her is happiness. But this never happens. The husband is juvenile, the wife is juvenile, and they remain with their childhood concept that I am the center and the other has to serve me. This creates chaos, this creates misery and hell. Love has to be learned; it is a growth. When you can throw your ego, only then can you love.

The Upanishads are not against thought, but they have a preference list – love must be first. And we have done quite the opposite. There is not a single school, college or university where love is taught. Only thought is taught everywhere: schools, colleges, universities – they all exist to train you how to think. Nobody trains you how to feel, how to be more loving. And it is simple: if nobody teaches you mathematics, you are not going to learn it; if nobody teaches you language, you are not going to learn it; and nobody teaches you love, so you have not learned it. But you believe that you are a lover, and in search of the right person who can love you.

I have heard about one man: he was in search of a perfect wife, the ideal woman. Obviously he could never find her. He searched and searched and then became old. Then somebody asked, "For what are you waiting? Now get married! You are just on the verge of death."

The man said, "But I cannot – unless to an ideal woman, a perfect woman."

So the friend asked, "But you have been searching. Could you not find a single woman upon this whole earth?"

He said, "Yes, once I did – but that woman was in search of a perfect husband."

You think you are perfect; you are waiting just for the other perfect person and then everything will be good. This is not going to help; this is impossible. You have learned to think, and that has become the base. That's why your whole personality is upside down.

The second stage is of thought, the first of feeling. What is this stage of thought?

He lives in the care of learned men who explain best what listening, remembering, right conduct, contemplation and meditation are.

Not only logic…. Our schools teach only logic. In many ways they make you argumentative, that's all. The Upanishads say, the first thing: *He lives in the care of learned men.*

In the days of the Upanishads teaching was a very intimate phenomenon, a very personal phenomenon; it was really just like a love affair. So students would move all over the country in search of a master with whom they could feel closeness, intimacy, from whom they could feel care – somebody who cared, who loved, in whose presence they could flower. Sometimes thousands of miles would be traveled to find a master with whom to live. That was the first requirement. Teaching was not so important; the teacher was more important.

Nowadays, particularly in America, they say the student is more important than the teacher. They say "student-oriented education," and they have made their point and the students have heard about it – that they are the center and the teacher is just a servant, there to serve. This is absolute nonsense, because a disciple cannot be the center. He has come to learn, and learning means he has to be receptive, trusting, in deep faith. So if there is so much student unrest all over the world, it is the natural consequence, the logical consequence, of the whole nonsense that has been spread in this century that education should be "student-oriented." Then the teacher becomes just a servant.

In India in the days of the Upanishads the teacher was the center, and the real thing was not what he was teaching; the real thing was what he was. Just his presence was a deep phenomenon; it helped the person to grow. He cared, he loved, and teaching was secondary, teaching followed. That was also not very important. The important thing was to be near a person who was grown-up, who was really an adult. So the way, the method that was followed was really one of the most intricate systems ever developed in the world.

The system was this: that for twenty-five years everybody was to remain celibate, a brahmachari – for twenty-five years, for the first stage of life. Every boy, every girl, was expected to remain celibate for twenty-five years. Not that they were against sex – no, really they were the persons who knew the beauty of sex, and they created a phenomenon where sex could be lived to its utmost, where sex was transformed into samadhi – but they knew the way. Twenty-five years of celibacy would create the energy; you would accumulate energy, enough energy so that sex would become a very deep and penetrating phenomenon.

Now in the West sex has become superficial. It is not more than sneezing – just something to be thrown out of the body, just a type of relief. And it is so: if you don't have enough energy gathered then sex will become superficial, just like sneezing – a relief, not a transforming phenomenon, not an alchemy.

When you had so much energy, when you had waited twenty-five years and your every cell was filled with energy, then they allowed you to move into marriage and love. Then this experience of love was going to be very very deep, intense. The intensity depends on energy. This is the law: intensity depends on energy. If there is no energy there will be no intensity; the more energy, the more intense the phenomenon. And if you had waited for twenty-five years, you would have become a tremendous energy, and even in one sexual experience you could attain to the very highest that is possible through bioenergy.

Then they allowed the man to move into family life. For twenty-five years he was to live an ordinary life: to feel every desire, every thirst, every hunger; to fulfill every desire – at least to try for twenty-five years, with intense force. When the person was fifty, then his children would be coming back from the gurukul, from the house of the master. His children would be coming back, and they would then be about twenty-five.

And this was the rule: when a person had reached fifty, about fifty, and his children were back and were going into marriage, he should again become celibate – because it was thought absurd that a father should be making love in the house when the son was making love. This was thought absurd, this seemed childish, because then the father had not grown beyond it. And how could a son respect a father when he felt that the father was just the same as him? If the son was playing with sex and the father also was playing with sex, how could he think that he had grown up? The moment the son was married the father was ready to move beyond sex. So this stage of twenty-five years was called *vanaprastha* – looking towards the forest. He had not yet gone to the forest, but was now ready to leave, packing.

When the son had reached fifty and was ready to pack to go to the forest, the father would be seventy-five and he would have renounced life. Now he was an old, wise man; he had lived life. And this man would become the teacher. At the age of seventy-five he would move to the forest, he would create a small school around him, he would become the teacher. And this was the thought: that only an old man can be the teacher, because how can one who has not lived life be a teacher? How can one who has not known all – the good and the bad both; one who has not moved through all the ways that life gives you, the right and the wrong both – how can he be a teacher? Only one who has been through desires, who has known the intensity of desires and the foolishness also, who has been into sex and who has gone beyond sex – only such a man can be a teacher, only such a man can teach life.

It was inconceivable that a young man could become a teacher. It was inconceivable. How can he become a teacher? He has not been through life, he is not yet seasoned. One must be with old, wise men, in their care, just near them; such men who can explain what right listening is, right remembering is, right conduct is, right contemplation is, right meditation is. And you cannot explain these things just by reading and studying; only a lived experience can make you capable of teaching.

What is right listening? *Shravan,* right listening, is the base...because when a disciple comes to a master or a student to a teacher, the first thing is to be taught how to listen. Nowdays nobody is teaching how to listen. You go to any school, even in the kindergarten, and they have started lecturing, but no one has ever taught how to listen. Unless you know how to listen, how can you be taught? Sometimes the training for how to listen takes years. Your mind has to be completely silent, only then can you listen. So a master will try to quiet your inner talk, the inner chattering, the constant chattering which is there.

If you are chattering inside, you cannot listen. I am talking here. If you are talking within yourself, how can you listen? Then your mind is just like a radio, and the arrow by which you tune into a station is wavering, or you have caught two stations simultaneously and so everything is a confusion. I am talking here and you are talking within yourself, so there are two stations simultaneously. Everything is in confusion. You cannot learn and you cannot understand – you can only misunderstand. How to listen was the first thing – in ordinary teaching and in spiritual teaching also. How to listen? The first rule is: the inner talk must cease.

It happened, there was one famous Zen monk, Nansen. He lived in a deep forest away from the capital of Japan, Tokyo. One day a professor of the university of Tokyo, a professor of philosophy, came to visit Nansen. He came into the hut and said, "Tell me something about spirituality. Tell me something about the inner self."

Nansen said, "You look tired after traveling so long, there is perspiration on your head, so rest a little, relax a little, and I will prepare tea for you."

So the old Nansen prepared tea, and the professor rested. But the rest was just superficial; inside he couldn't rest. How can a professor rest? Impossible! He goes on talking inside.

I had one professor…I was the only student in his subject. Sometimes if I was late I would see that he had already started, he was already lecturing. And he had told me, "If you want to go out, you can go, but don't disturb me" – and I was the only student! So I used to go out, roam about, and then come back, and he was still lecturing. I was irrelevant.

A professor, and a professor of philosophy at that – insult added to injury…. He rested only bodily, the inner talk continued. But you cannot escape a person like Nansen; he looks inside. So he brought tea, put a cup in the hand of the professor, poured tea, continued pouring, and the tea started flowing into the saucer also. Then the professor became afraid because he was continuing; soon it would start going onto the floor. So he said, "Now stop! Are you mad? Now my cup cannot have any more tea, not a single drop."

Nansen started laughing and he said, "You are so careful about the tea and the cup, and you know well that when the cup is full not a single drop more can be held in it. And you ask me about spirituality, meditation. You are so full inside, not a single drop can enter. So first go out, empty your cup, and then come back. Unless you are empty I am not going to waste my energy pouring into you."

The first thing for right learning, right listening, is to be empty; that was taught. Now education is doing completely the reverse. The first thing is how to fill your mind, and the more your mind is filled the more you are appreciated. Your mind must be clean, pure; inner talk must cease. Only then you can be attentive.

Then right remembering. Remember that only remembering is not enough; you need the opposite capacity of forgetting also. If you go on remembering everything you will go mad. And that is what has happened – you cannot forget. Forgetting is as much needed as remembering. The useless must be thrown out of the mind and forgotten, and only the essential should be remembered.

Right remembering means continuously throwing rubbish out; choosing only the essential, the true, the real, and throwing all that is rubbish. Much rubbish is there. The newspapers are filled with it, the books are filled with it, and everybody goes on pouring his rubbish into you. The first thing for right remembering is: throw the rubbish out, don't fill the mind with rubbish – unnecessary, nonessential.

Shankara has said that if you cannot make the distinction between what is essential and what is nonessential, your mind will become just a wastepaper basket; useless things will be there – and they are. Right remembering means also right forgetting. Be alert, because every single moment millions of facts are being thrown into your mind. Your mind is taking much information from everywhere. That's why you cannot sleep: there is so much excitement in the mind, so many things going on. You cannot remember, because you remember so much that the whole capacity, the whole energy, is lost.

When Alexander came to India he was surprised; he could not believe the capacity of Hindu brahmins for memorizing things. He couldn't believe it, it was almost impossible. It happened that wise men in Greece had told him, "When you come back from India, bring the Vedas, the four scriptures, the supreme-most Indian scriptures. Bring them with you." Only at the last moment when he was returning he remembered, so in a village of Punjab he inquired, "Who has got the Vedas?"

They said, "A brahmin family – but it is impossible, they will not give them to you."

Alexander said, "Don't you worry about that. I will force them, I will kill them – they will have to give."

The brahmins' house was surrounded by the military, and Alexander went to the head of the family, the old man, and said, "I want the four scriptures, the four Vedas, and I will burn the whole house if you say no. You and your four Vedas all will be burned."

The old man said, "There is no need. I will give them to you, but in the morning. And let your military be there, don't be suspicious. I will give them in the morning."

Alexander said, "Why not now?"

He said, "Before giving them I will have to go through a ritual of departure. My family had them for thousands of years, they have become part of our heart, so the whole night we will pray, go through a particular ritual, and in the morning we will present them."

Alexander believed the old man. The military was there and there was no possibility that he could escape. But in the morning when he came a fire was burning and the old man was sitting there reading from the last page of the four books. Alexander waited. The old man read the last page and threw it in the fire. Alexander said, "What are you doing?"

He said, "The four Vedas have gone into the fire, but these are my four sons. They have listened the whole night and they remember. You take them."

Just one listening! Alexander could not believe it. He called other brahmins to check. How could they remember such big books? And they had heard them only once! They repeated verbatim from the first word to the last. Alexander told his wise men, "We don't know anything about what right remembering is. These Hindus have done miracles. How can they remember?"

The secret is that if you are capable of forgetting nonsense, you have so much energy to remember that anything can be remembered – the energy is the same. For example, if you have one hundred percent energy, ninety-nine percent is involved in nonsense. In the old days, a brahmin had one hundred percent of energy available; then he could remember the Vedas. Whatsoever you remember is always more than the four Vedas, so the capacity is there but you have devoted it to nonsense. Right remembering was taught: how to forget the useless, how to choose the essential, and only remember the essential.

Right conduct: how to behave rightly, a right discipline of behavior – because everything helps you grow. When you behave wrongly you are not doing something wrong to others, you are doing wrong to yourself. When you behave wrongly your energy moves into wrong directions. Outwardly, right conduct may seem like something imposed; it is not.

For example, Gurdjieff used to say – in his institute in Paris he had written it on the walls in big letters – one motto: "A person is good who respects his father and mother." In the West particularly this seems absurd. And just this is the definition of a good man, "A person is good who respects his father and mother?"

What was he saying? Remember that life is such that you are bound to hate your father and mother; every boy, every girl, has to hate. This is how it happens naturally, because the father has to say no to many things, the father has to discipline you, the father has even sometimes to be angry with you. He cannot allow you absolute freedom because that would be destructive to you. He has to force discipline, and the ego of the child is hurt; he starts hating.

Every man hates his father unless right conduct is taught from the very beginning; every girl hates her mother unless a right conduct is taught from the very beginning. And if you cannot respect your father, you cannot respect anybody – then the whole possibility of respect is lost. The father is the first point from where respect grows.

If you can respect your father, you will respect many people. If you hate your father, then all father figures will be hated. If you hate your father, you will hate your teacher, because he is also a father figure. If you hate your father, you will hate anybody who is powerful. You cannot love God, because he is the father figure for the whole cosmos.

In the West, first the respect for the father disappeared, and then God was dead. It is not accidental that every religion says, "God, my father, the father of all." It is not accidental, it is meaningful – but it has to grow from your own father. If you respect your father then all father-figures will be respected, and ultimately you can respect the divine.

If you hate your mother then hatred will become the very base of your life, because the first love has to be learned through the mother. You cannot love a wife if you have hated your mother, because the wife is a woman, and one who hates his mother hates women. And the mother will follow you like a dangerous shadow – every time you look at a woman, the mother will be present there. Really, every woman is a mother, essentially a mother. You cannot love a woman if you hate your mother. Really, you cannot love at all.

Gurdjieff was right; this is the definition of a good man – that he respects his father and mother. This is impossible. Remember, this is not easy. It is one of the most impossible things to respect the father and mother; to respect one's parents is one of the impossible things in this world. False respect is not meant, just hypocrisy is not meant, but a real respect. That was taught; that was called right conduct.

Respect and love were taught, many other things were taught. Right conduct means to be always happy, blissful in your behavior, to be refined, gentle, to not hurt anybody in any way – because this then becomes the pattern. Right conduct helps you grow, and it helps you avoid unnecessary problems, unnecessary crises. You create many problems unnecessarily, and in those problems and in solving them you waste energy, time – you waste everything. A small problem can become destructive to your whole life. Right conduct means moving in this world in such a way that there is no conflict with others, no conflict arises; moving in this world in such a way that you don't create unnecessary enemies – the very way you behave creates friendship. This is good for you.

Right contemplation and right meditation....

This will look a little paradoxical, because we think meditation is always right, contemplation is always right. That is not the case; you can contemplate on wrong things. For example, when you are angry you contemplate; really, when you are angry you contemplate more. You become obsessed with one thing and you go on thinking around and around it, near it. Try to think about God; contemplate for one single moment and you have moved away to something else. But think about sex and the contemplation is easy; you can contemplate.

There are people who go on doing that. If you give them a picture or a statue of God they will say, "What will this do? This is just a picture." But give them a pornographic magazine, give them a picture of a nude woman, and they will hide it under the pillow, and when there is no one around they will contemplate. Pornography is contemplation; the mind starts moving around and around a center.

Contemplation means mind moving around a center: not moving in a line, not going from one subject to another, but just sticking to one subject, and the whole energy moving in a circle. When mind moves in a circle around a subject, that subject becomes deep-rooted; whatsoever you contemplate, ultimately you become. Right contemplation means contemplation which will help you to grow beyond desire, which will help you to transcend desire. You contemplate, but wrongly.

This happens with meditation also. You have moments of meditation sometimes. If you are angry and you hit a person, in that moment of hitting all thought stops. You have just become anger; the whole energy is transformed into anger. You are one-pointed, deep in meditation, not a single thought in the mind, no cloud in the mind, the whole mind and energy and body moving in one direction – but that is wrong meditation. Mind has stopped thinking but has become anger – it should become love, it should become compassion.

In sex, meditation happens. A moment comes when you are reaching the climax, a moment comes just before ejaculation or orgasm when mind stops. You become pure energy, bioenergy, just a stream of energy, no-mind. No-mind is meditation. But if you become stuck just in sexual meditation you will not grow. Nothing is wrong in it, but you have to grow beyond it because this sexual meditation depends on the other and anything that depends on the other cannot make you ultimately free; you will remain dependent.

Right meditation means a moment where mind ceases, you have become one energy – but not moving towards the other, not moving in any direction, but simply remaining in yourself. That will become samadhi. Meditation moving towards the other becomes a sexual act; meditation moving nowhere, remaining inside, becomes samadhi. These things are for the second stage.

Having acquired knowledge of such scriptures as are worth listening to, he efficiently discriminates between what is duty and what is not.

This is called *vivek*: discrimination between duty, what is duty, and what is not. In the second stage you have to be continuously alert of what to do and what not to do. If you are not alert you will be in a mess. What to do and what not to do? You have a certain amount of energy. You can waste it in things which are not worth doing, and you can create complexities through doing them.

You talk to someone and then a discussion arises, then the discussion be-comes an angry fight – you are wasting energy. And this will create a pattern; the man will try to take revenge in some other circumstances. You have created a karma, a pattern; now it will follow you. But why move into a discussion unnecessarily? Why create an argument?

I have heard one Chinese Taoist parable. Three Taoists, followers of Lao Tzu, went into a forest to meditate. They decided that they were not going to chatter, discuss anything. One year passed in silence. Then suddenly one day a horseman passed before their cave, so one of the monks said, "What a beautiful white horse!" This was the only utterance in one year.

One year passed again, then the second monk said, "This is not good. You have started an argument. The horse was not white but black!"

Then one year passed again, and the third monk said, "If there is going to be bickering, I am leaving!"

One year had passed, but it had not passed from the mind of the second monk. He was continuously thinking that the horse was black, not white. Then he could not withhold it any more, so he said, "Enough. The horse was black. But I don't want any dispute about it."

Then the third monk must have continued thinking inside that they had disturbed the silence and they were creating a dispute. Then it became so much that he could not control it any more, so after one year he said, "Enough. I am leaving. This is too much. You are creating an argument! We have not come here to decide whether the horse was white or black!"

This is how mind functions. A small trigger and it goes on and on – it may go on for eternity if you don't become aware. Discriminate as to what is to be done, and then you will feel there is a very very small number of duties. You can do them very well. Discriminate as to what is not to be done, and ninety percent of your acts will drop. They are unnecessary, you could have avoided them. Why get entangled? Remain more and more aloof, and do only that which is absolutely necessary. And remember, do it only when it is going to help somebody, otherwise don't do it.

...And he discriminates also between what is the symbol – pada – and what is the thing symbolized – padarth.

This is something to be understood very deeply. Krishnamurti goes on saying that the word god is not God – this is the meaning of this statement. What is a symbol, and what is symbolized? The word god is not God – you can mistake the very word for God – just like the word water is not water. When you are thirsty, I can write in big letters on a paper WATER and give it to you. You cannot drink it. Even if I do it very scientifically and write h2o, it is useless. You will throw it away, you will say, "Keep your science to yourself. I need water, not h2o."

The word water and water are two different things, and one who is in search of truth must remember it constantly, because there is every possibility you may become obsessed with words and symbols and may lose contact with reality.

His mind does not suffer from an excess of conceit, pride, greed and attachment, although externally they are apparent to some extent.

The second stage is not the end. There is bound to be some greed, some pride, some attachment, some anger, but one has to be aware and start dropping them from inside. Outside it may not be possible to drop them immediately, because sometimes they are needed also.

In ordinary life, if you cannot become angry you will lose many things. Sometimes just a show of anger will be helpful, but drop it from inside! It has to be dropped from outside also – but later on, when you don't bother, when nothing makes any difference, when even if you lose something it makes no difference. But remaining in the world, trying for growth, be aware and alert. Don't suffer from these things. These are sufferings.

If you have very deep-rooted pride, conceit, jealousy, you will suffer. No one else is going to suffer for it. You continue it in the mind, you suffer for it. Somebody is laughing and you think he is laughing at you – then you suffer. You are conceited, and you are always in search of something to hurt you. You are like a wound, waiting for somebody to touch you and then you will be hurt.

Whenever you feel hurt, remember that you have a wound. Don't throw the responsibility on the other. Just remember that you have a wound and that man has unknowingly touched your wound. Try to heal this wound and then nobody can hurt you, there is no possibility; nobody can laugh at you. That doesn't mean that nobody will laugh at you – they may laugh, the whole world may laugh, but you can also join in, you can also laugh with them.

He gives up his external impurities as a snake casts off its slough. Such a seeker acquires the actual knowledge of all these things with the grace of the scriptures, the guru, and the sages.

Continuously you have to throw your old skin just like a snake. Every moment it becomes old, and every moment you have to come out of it; then only can you remain alive. Otherwise it always happens that you are almost dead before you die – many years before you die.

It happened once, Mulla Nasruddin came to a police station. He reported that his wife was missing, so they asked him to give some details about his wife – how she looked, how old she was. He said,

"One of her eyes is missing. She cannot hear, both the ears are missing. She is crippled, she cannot walk rightly, one leg is missing." And then he said, "Before I missed her almost ninety percent was missing already!"

Before you die you will have died many years before. Everybody dies a posthumous death. You can prevent this happening only if you die every moment, if you leave the past completely, jump out of it. Dust gathers, memories gather, every moment you become old. Cast off this old skin just like a snake. Come out of it. Be fresh, young again, and live in the moment. Only then will you be able to know what eternal life is. A dead man cannot know it; only a man who is alive to his full capacity can know it.

Such a seeker acquires the actual knowledge of all these things with the grace of the scriptures, the guru, and the sages.

Whatsoever you do will need much visible and invisible help. Sometimes you may not be even aware, but many currents of help are around you, helping you; many sources are just pouring down upon you. You will become aware only in the end when you have achieved. Then you will see that you have to thank the whole universe.

Just think: if Buddha was not there, if he had not happened, if Jesus was not there, if he had not happened, if the Upanishads were never written, if Lao Tzu had not accepted to write down the Tao Te Ching, if there was no Bible, no Koran, no Vedas, where would you have been? You would have been just in the trees, you would have been monkeys. The whole universe has been helping you to grow – known, unknown sources.

You may not be aware, but invisible vibrations are in the atmosphere. Once Buddha is there, the human consciousness can never be the same again. We may forget him completely, we may not even know his name – because many buddhas have been there and we don't know their names, they were never recorded – but they are there, invisible sources helping you. And when you grow to your totality, then you will become aware that thousands and thousands of hands have been helping you.

That's why Hindus depict their God with a thousand hands. And you are such a problem that two hands cannot do – thousands even are not of much help. With the grace of the scriptures, with the grace of the master, the guru, with the grace of all the sages, you will achieve. At the second stage this has to become a deep seed within you – the gratitude to all and everything. Even those who have wronged you have also helped you.

Gratitude at the second stage will help you much. And if you become aware, fully alert about this gratitude, then more help will become available. The more you feel the grace and feel thankful, the more grace becomes available to you.

7   You Become the Offering

Osho,

Contemplating you floods me with a deep ecstasy, and I feel the grace. You say you are not doing anything to create this ecstasy in us, but it is for sure that I also am not doing anything. Then from where is this bliss coming and how is it happening if neither you nor I are doing anything? Is it possible for you to explain more about the mystery of it? What is this phenomenon which we call grace?

It can happen only when neither the disciple nor the master is doing anything; it can happen only in a nondoing, absolute nondoing, because grace is not something you can do anything about. You can simply be receptive, open, that's all. Nothing positively can be done about it. It is already flowing – the whole existence is filled with grace.

You are closed, and the more you do something, the more you will become closed – because every effort gives you a more egocentric feeling; whatsoever you do creates your ego. You feel I am doing something – and whenever you do something you start thinking of the future, of the result. You start expecting.

So two things happen: firstly, whatsoever you do becomes a food for the ego; secondly, whatsoever you do leads you into the future, then you are not here and now. And these both are the barriers. One thing: you must be here and now, and you must not be – you must *not* be – an ego. Then you are open, and whenever you are open the grace is already flowing; it has been flowing forever. If you are not getting it, it is not something that you can get by doing. The more you do, the more it will be impossible for you to get it.

The whole effort of the master is to teach you nondoing, nonaction. Or in other words, the whole effort of the master is to take you back – to teach you how to die, how to throw the ego completely, and how to be in a state of nothingness, a state of nonbeing. Buddha called that state *anatta*, the state of no-self: you are but you are not a self. Then there is no boundary to it, then there is no barrier around you, then all the doors are open – then life can flow, come and go, through you. Grace is not something special that is going to happen to you: grace is the very existence itself, it is grace-filled. The blessing is showering on you.

I will tell you one Buddhist anecdote – it happened in Buddha's time. One of Buddha's great disciples, Manjushree, was sitting under a tree meditating. Then suddenly he became aware that flowers were dropping from the tree, many flowers showering. But he was surprised because it was not the season for the flowers, and just in the morning when he had come there was not a single flower on the tree – so where were these millions of flowers showering all around coming from?

So he looked at the tree. Then he was even more mystified, because they were not coming from the tree, they were showering from the sky. So he asked, "Who is doing this? What is happening?"

A voice was heard, "We are the deities, and we are happy that you have attained, and just to express our happiness we are showering these flowers."

Manjushree said, "What have I attained? I have attained nothing. Rather, on the contrary, I have lost myself. There is no attainment because there is no one who can attain now. This very afternoon I have died."

The voice said, "We are celebrating your death, because your death is the birth of a new life. You have died, Manjushree, but for the first time you are born."

More and more flowers showered. Somebody reported to Buddha, "Some-thing has happened. Manjushree is sitting there and flowers go on showering."

Buddha said, "For the first time Manjushree is not there, that's why flowers are showering. Up till now Manjushree was there; just today he has disappeared. He has attained the state of no-self, anatta – that's why flowers are showering."

These flowers are just symbolic, they indicate grace. This voice is symbolic, no one had said anything. The flowers that were showering there were not those you can see, but invisible flowers. The whole existence celebrates it when you disappear – the whole existence feels blissful. When you are there, you are like a wound – the whole existence suffers with you.

I am trying only one thing – I am not doing anything – to make you filled with bliss. But that cannot be done. Only one thing can be done, and that is to help you to disappear, to help you not to be. And whenever, even for a single moment, you are not there, flowers will start showering. When Manjushree is not there, flowers have always showered.

I am not doing anything, I have never done anything with you. You are doing something. When you also stop, growth happens. When you also drop doing, suddenly the ego disappears. You are not ill; you have become whole and healthy. And whenever you are whole you have become holy.

Both the words come from the same root. The word holy doesn't mean anything more than becoming whole. Whenever you are whole you are holy. And you cannot be whole with the ego, because ego consists of division. Ego creates a split, you divide yourself. When the ego disappears divisions disappear. So the whole effort is how to make you effortless, and the whole doing is how to bring you to a point where doing ceases, is no more.

Grace has been flowing always, that is already the case. It is there right now, flowing around you, but you don't give a door to it. All your windows are closed, all your doors are closed; you are closed, imprisoned in yourself, you don't allow any winds to blow. These meditations we are doing are just to help you to drop all doing.

It is said that once Milarepa, a Tibetan mystic, asked his master, Naropa, "Following you, listening to you, I have dropped everything. But still nothing has happened."

Naropa laughed and said, "Drop this also – that you have dropped everything. Drop this also, don't say it any more, because this again is a clinging: I have dropped everything. But the 'I' has remained, and the dropping itself has been converted into doing. The doer has remained."

One man, a great king, came once to Buddha. In one hand he had brought many flowers; in the other hand he had brought a very rare, valuable diamond. And he had brought both because he thought, "Maybe Buddha will not like the diamond; then I will give these flowers, put these flowers at his feet."

He came, both hands were full; in one hand the great diamond, in the other, flowers. First he tried to put the diamond at Buddha's feet. Buddha said, "Drop it!" He thought, "He has rejected the diamond," so he dropped it on the ground. Then he tried to put the flowers and Buddha said, "Drop it!" so he dropped those flowers also. Then there was nothing to give him as a present, so with both hands joined in *namaskar*, he tried to put his head at Buddha's feet. And Buddha said, "Drop it!" Then he was in a puzzle – what to do? How to drop this head?

Buddha started laughing and he said, "Those things were useless – you can drop the diamond, that is not of any significance; you can drop the flowers, that is not of much significance – unless you drop yourself. And those two droppings, those two orders, were just to prepare you so that you can learn dropping. Now the ultimate has come. Drop yourself!"

And there cannot be anything else before a buddha. What can you give as a present? Flowers, diamonds are meaningless – unless you give yourself, unless you become the offering.

I am not doing anything; you are still doing – that's why there is a problem. Whenever one of you drops doing and becomes just like me, not doing anything, suddenly the happening, suddenly flowers will start showering. When Manjushree disappeared.... Flowers had always been showering there at that tree, only Manjushree could not see them. When he disappeared he could see.

The second question:

Osho,

We can practice right behavior, and behavior according to duty, but then we will be wearing false faces, as we are inwardly, as you say, a madhouse. So should we act as we feel, or act as we ought?

The first thing to be understood: you have to be authentic to yourself – sincere, honest. But that doesn't mean that you have to hurt others through your honesty and sincerity, that doesn't mean that you have to disturb others, that doesn't mean that you have to disturb the rules of the game. All relationships are just rules of the game, and many times you will have to act and wear masks, false faces. The only thing to remember is: don't become the mask. Use it if it is good, and keep the rules, but don't become the mask, don't get identified. Act it, don't get identified with it.

This is a great problem, particularly in the West for the new generation. They have heard too much; they have already been seduced by this idea: be sincere and be honest. This is good, but you don't know how cunning and destructive the mind is. Your mind can find excuses. You can say a truth, not because you love truth so much but just to hurt somebody; you can use it as a weapon. And if you are using it as a weapon it is not truth, it is worse than a lie.

Sometimes you can help somebody through a lie, and sometimes relationship becomes more easy through a lie. Then use it – but don't get identified with it. What I am saying is: Be a good player, learn the rules of the game; don't be too adamant about anything.

It happened:

I came back from the university and my father and my mother were worried; they were worried about me, about what I was going to do. They were worried about my marriage. So my father started sending messages through his friends asking my opinion whether I was ready to get married or not. So I told his friends, "This is between me and my father, don't you come in. Tell my father that he can ask me."

And he was afraid, because I have never said no to him for anything. So he was afraid, he was afraid because I would not say no. Even if I didn't want to be married I would say yes – that was the worry in his mind. Even if I didn't want to get into a householder's life, I would not say no, I would say yes. And that yes would be false. So what to do? He couldn't ask me – he has not asked yet – because he knew well that I would not break any rule. I would have said yes.

Then he tried through my mother. She asked me one night; she came to my bed, sat there, and asked me what I thought about marriage. So I said, "I have not married yet, so I have no experience. You know well, you have the experience, so you tell me. Take fifteen days: think over it, contemplate, and if you feel you have achieved something through it, then just order me. I will follow the order. Don't ask about my opinion – I have none, because I have no experience. You are experienced. If you were again given a chance, would you get married?"

She said, "You are trying to confuse me."

I said, "You take your time, at your own ease. I will wait for two weeks, then you order me. I will just follow…because I don't know."

So for two weeks she was worried. She could not sleep, because she knew if she said to marry I would obey. Then she would be responsible, not I. So after two weeks she said, "I am not going to say anything, because if I look to my own experience, then I would not like you to move into that life. But I cannot say anything now."

So this is how I remained unmarried. Sincerely, authentically, I was not ready to marry, I was not intending it at all. But I could have acted. And nothing is wrong, because every experience helps you to grow. No-marriage helps, marriage also helps; there is not much difference. Everything helps you to grow in its own way.

The one thing to remember is: life is a great complexity. You are not alone here, there are many others related to you. Be sincere unto yourself, never be false there. Know well what you want, and for yourself remain that. But there are others also; don't unnecessarily hurt them. And if you need to wear masks, wear them and enjoy them, but remember, they are not your original face, and be capable of taking them off any moment. Remain the master, don't become the slave; otherwise you can be violent through your sincerity, unnecessarily you can be violent.

I have seen persons who are cruel, violent, aggressive, sadistic – but sincere, very true, authentic. But they are using their authenticity just for their sadism. They want to make others suffer, and their trick is such that you cannot escape them. They are true, so you cannot say, "You are bad." They are good people, they are never bad, so no one can say to them, "You are bad." They are always good, and they do the bad through their good.

Don't do that, and don't take life too seriously. Nothing is wrong in masks also, faces also. Just as in the drama on the stage they use faces and enjoy and the audience also enjoys, why not enjoy them in real life also? It is not more than a drama. But I am not saying for you to be dishonest. Be sincere with yourself, don't get identified. But life is great; there are many around you related in many invisible nets. Don't hurt anybody.

I will tell you one anecdote. It happened, Buddha became enlightened, and then he came back to his town after twelve years. He had escaped one night from his house without even telling his wife that he was leaving. He had gone to her room. She was sleeping with Buddha's child, the only child, who was just a few days old.

Buddha wanted to touch the small child, to feel, to love and embrace, but then he thought, "If the wife is awakened she may start crying and weeping and may create a mess. The whole house will gather, and then it will be difficult to leave." So he simply escaped from the door; he just looked in and escaped like a coward. Then for twelve years he never came back.

After twelve years, when he had become enlightened, he came back. His chief disciple was Ananda. Ananda was his elder cousin-brother, and before he took initiation with Buddha he had asked for a few promises. He took sannyas, he took initiation from Buddha, but he was older than Buddha, "So," he said, "before I take initiation give me some promises as your elder brother, because once I have been initiated you will be the master and I will be the disciple. Then I cannot ask anything. Now I can even order you."

You Become the Offering | 143

These are the rules of the game. So Buddha said, "Okay." He was enlightened, and this unenlightened man was saying, "I am your elder brother." So Buddha said, "Okay. What do you want?"

He said, "Three promises. One: I will always be with you, you cannot send me anywhere else; wherever you go I will be your shadow. Second: even in the night when you sleep in a room I can come in and out – even while you are asleep. No rules will apply to me. And third: even at midnight when you are asleep, if I bring someone, a seeker, you will have to answer his questions."

Buddha said, "Okay. You are my elder brother, so I promise." Then Ananda took initiation, then he become a disciple, and Buddha followed these three things his whole life.

When he came back to his home, he said to Ananda, "Just make one exception, Ananda. My wife Yashodhara has been waiting for twelve years. She is bound to be very angry, and she is a very proud woman. Twelve years is a long time, and I have not been a good husband to her. I escaped from her like a coward, I didn't even tell her. And I know that if I had told her she would have accepted it because she loves me so much, but I couldn't gather the courage.

"Now after twelve years, if you come with me when I go to meet my wife, she will feel even worse. She will think that this is a trick; that I have brought you with me so that she cannot express her mind, her suppressed anger, and the many things of these twelve years. And she will behave in a ladylike way, because she belongs to a very good family, a royal family. She will not even cry, no tears will come to her eyes; she will keep the rules of the game. So please, Ananda, only one exception I ask you, and I will never ask any other exception. You just wait outside."

Ananda said, "Bhante, I think you are enlightened. You are no longer a husband and she is no longer a wife, so why play this game?"

Buddha said, "I am enlightened, she is not. I am no longer a husband, but she is still a wife, and I don't want to hurt her. Let her keep her mind a little while and I will persuade her. I will persuade her to take a jump and become a sannyasin. But give me a chance. I am enlightened, she is not."

So Buddha went inside the palace. Of course, Yashodhara was mad. She started saying things; she was angry, crying, weeping, tears coming down, and Buddha stood there, silent, listening to everything patiently, with deep compassion. When all her anger was out she looked at Buddha; when her tears were no more there in her eyes then she looked at Buddha. Then she realized that this man was no longer a husband and she had been talking to a ghost of her memory. The man who left her was no more there. This was totally a different man.

She surrendered, and she said to Buddha, "Why have you come? You are no longer a husband."

Buddha repeated again, "I may not be a husband, but you are still a wife, and I have come to help you so that you can also transcend this misery, this relationship, this world."

Others are there, consider them, and don't try to be violent through so-called good things. So when it is said, "right conduct," it means right relationship with others. You need not be false. When you can be true without hurting anybody, be true. But if you feel that your truth is going to hurt many and is unnecessary, it can be avoided, then avoid it, because it is not only going to hurt others, it will create patterns of cause, and those causes will return as effects on you, they will become your karmas. Then you will get entangled, and the more entangled you are the more you will have to behave in wrong ways.

Just stop. Just see the situation. If you can be true without hurting anybody, be true. To me, love is greater than truth. Be loving. And if you feel that your truth will be hurtful and violent, it is better to lie than to be true. Wait for the right moment when you can be true, and help the other person to come to such a state where your truth will not hurt him. Don't be in a hurry.

And life is a big drama; don't take it too seriously — because seriousness is also a disease of the mind, seriousness is part of the ego. Be playful, don't be too serious. So sometimes you will have to use masks, because there are children around you and they like masks, they like false faces, and they enjoy. Help them to grow so they can face the real face, they can encounter it. But before they can encounter it, don't create any trouble. Right conduct is just consideration for others.

And look: there is a great difference. You may misunderstand what I am saying. When you lie, you lie for yourself. And I am saying: if you need, and if you feel the need to lie, only lie for the consideration of others. Never lie for yourself, don't use any mask for yourself. But if you feel it is going to help others, it will be good for them, use the mask. And inside remain alert that this is just a game you are acting, this is not real.

Sometimes you may need to be angry to your child, to your son, to your daughter. There are situations when anger helps. If you say something to your child coldly, it is not loving. If you say to your child, "Don't do this," in a cold manner, it is not loving, it is not going to help. When you say, "Don't do this!" to your child in anger, deep anger, it reaches the child, and he feels that you love him, that's why you are angry.

A father who has never been angry with his son has never been loving; anger means that you consider him, you can even be angry. You love him, you feel for him. Sometimes even when you are not feeling angry but you see the need, show the anger, have the face of anger – but remain the master. And if you are the master, then the faces are beautiful, you can use them. But don't become the face; if you become the face you have become the slave. The whole thing is not to get identified. Remain aloof, distant, and capable at any time to put it on and off – the face is just a device. It will be difficult and complex. It is easy to be untrue, it is easy to be true. The most difficult thing is to be the master of yourself to such an extent that if you want to be untrue you can be untrue, and if you want to be true you can be true.

Gurdjieff's disciples have written many books about him, and every disciple describes him in a different way. This is very mysterious, it has never happened with any other person in that way. Sometimes it happened that a person went to see Gurdjieff, then left, and then his friend went to see him. They would report to each other and would both give a different picture.

Gurdjieff was a master of changing faces. It is said that he had become so capable that a person sitting by his right side would feel one thing, and a person sitting by his left side would feel differently. He may have been very loving with his left eye, and that half-face was showing love, and with the other side he may have been angry. And both persons would report to each other outside: "What type of man is this? He was so loving." The other would say, "You are in some illusion...because he was so angry."

That is possible and such a mastery is beautiful. It is said that no one reported Gurdjieff's real face, because he never showed anybody his real face. He was always acting, but helping in a way; in many ways he was helping. He would show you the face that was needed by you for your consideration; he would never show you the face that was not needed by you.

To me, and to the Upanishads also, right conduct means just the right rules of behavior with others. You are not going to be here forever. You cannot change the whole world, you cannot change everybody; you can at the most change yourself. So it is better to change yourself inwardly, and don't try to be in a continuous fight with everybody. Avoid fight – and faces can be helpful. Avoid unnecessary struggle, because that dissipates energy. Preserve your energy to be used for the inner work. And that work is so significant and it needs all your energy that you can give to it, so don't waste it in unnecessary things.

For the outside world remain an actor, and don't think that you are deceiving anybody. If they like deception, that's what they need, that's what should be given to them. If children like toys to play with, you are not deceiving them. Don't give them a real gun; let them play with the toy gun, because they like the toy. And don't think that the toy gun is false; don't think, "I must be true, I must give a real gun to the child. If he needs a gun, then I must give the true thing. How can I give the toy? This is a deception."

But the child needs the toy, there is no deception; he doesn't need the real gun. So just look at the other, at what he needs, and give him that which he needs. Don't give out of your own consideration, give out of consideration for him. Look at him, study and observe him, and behave in such a way that will be helpful to him and will not be unnecessary trouble for you. This is all that is meant by right conduct.

The third question:

Osho,

Though we can be aware of anger and refrain from hurting others with it, inner anger seems to remain in a dormant state, and at times it becomes aroused by outer happenings. It doesn't seem possible to entirely throw it as it is deep-rooted in early, wrong training, and a lifetime of struggle in the world. Isn't the total disappearance of anger simultaneous with enlightenment? Does an enlightened one ever have any anger?

The first thing: if you feel angry and if you think that it is needed for it to be suppressed, suppress it for the time being – because it is useless just to be angry with someone and then create a chain. Then he will be angry and then more anger will be created, and this can continue even for lives. Everything has a continuity of cause and effect; it becomes a chain.

So if you feel anger and you see it is going to be destructive to you and to the other person, smile, have a false face. And move to your room, close the doors, take your pillow and beat it. Write the name of the person on the pillow and do whatsoever you wanted to do with the person. Don't suppress it in the system because that is too dangerous. Anger is poison, and when the body is ready to fight the blood is filled with poison – you have to act it out. If you don't act it out, if you don't go through a catharsis then you will have to suffer for it. It may become a physical disease, it may cripple your body, and it may poison your relationships – because you were not angry, but the anger was there.

Your boss insulted you and you couldn't reply to him, so you will come home and you will find some excuse to get angry with the wife. And you will think that she has done something wrong, but that is just rationalization; you wanted someone who is weaker than you, to whom you can be the boss. You will throw the anger on the wife, and she will wait for the child to come back from the school. Suppressed anger finds outlet towards the weaker person. She will wait for the child to come and she will find something – and you can always find something, there is no problem. She can say, "Why are your clothes dirty?" They have always been dirty; every day he comes with dirty clothes from the school. He is a child, not an old man – he doesn't care about clothes. He can play with the dirt; that is more valuable than those clothes. Then the mother is going to beat the child. And what is the child supposed to do? He will go, take his dog and beat it, or throw his book into the street, or do something that he can do. This way anger goes on moving and moving, it creates ripples, and a single phenomenon becomes multidimensional, unnecessarily.

So I say to you, there is no need to be angry with the person by whom anger has come into you – there is no need. But there is no need to suppress it also. Express it in the vacuum. Have a room in your home, your meditation room, so whatsoever happens, go in that room and do it. And you will enjoy it so much, you cannot imagine; the whole exercise is so beautiful. In the beginning it will look absurd, but soon you will get into it and you will enjoy it. And the pillow is not going to answer, the pillow is not going to create any chain. Rather, on the contrary, the pillow will be very happy that you related with it.

Never suppress, but never create chains – this is the rule. Remember not to suppress, and remember not to create any chain. Once you learn the art you can be free of all these madnesses which come into you, without creating any disturbance in life. Every day catharsis is needed. Life is complex, and many things come into the mind which have to be thrown. That's why I emphasize Dynamic Meditation so much. You don't know what you are doing here. When you get into it you are doing all sorts of things. Somebody is throwing anger, somebody is throwing jealousy, somebody throwing hatred, somebody throwing his sadness, screaming – the whole life of misery is being thrown in it.

Make it a point every day: just as you clean your body every day, clean your mind. This is a bath for the mind. Throw everything, but don't throw upon anybody; that is violence. Throw it into the vacuum. And the vacuum is big enough, the space is big enough. Don't you get worried about what will happen to the pillow, what will happen to the space – nothing is going to happen, all that you throw into it is absorbed. And then it never replies to you, there is no chain created. The act simply ends, no karma is created through it. Do things in such a way that no future is created through them.

Whatsoever has happened to you, relief is needed, you need that it should be thrown out, but don't throw it on persons. If you can remember that, soon you will realize that it was absolute foolishness to throw it on persons when it could be thrown just on a pillow. And the same relaxation is felt – even more, because whenever you throw on a person you will feel repentance in the end. You will feel bad, you will feel that you have not done good; then you will feel that it would have been better if you had not done it. But now nothing can be done, and you cannot undo something which has happened. Whatsoever you do, it is there now, you cannot wash it away. There is no way, because you cannot move to the past; it will remain always there.

That's what Hindus have called the theory of karma: whatsoever you do will remain and will have its influence on your future. A catharsis is necessary, and every day it is necessary unless you have become enlightened, then you don't gather the past. Now you gather, you collect dust. Throw it every day. In the night, every day for one hour, just throw the past, the whole day. Whatsoever has been done to you and you have done to others, or you wanted to do with others...emotions, anger, hate – many things are there – drop them before you go to sleep.

In the West sleep has become a problem, and in the East also it is becoming a problem. And the problem is only this: you don't know how to get rid of the day. It follows you, it continues in the mind, and you cannot stop it. You cannot stop unless you throw it. Whosoever is suffering from insomnia should try this dynamic meditation in the night. Just before going to sleep have an inner bath; throw everything and then go to sleep. You will feel like a child again – innocent, unburdened. Sleep will be totally different, the quality will change. But don't suppress – express. But don't express to persons.

The fourth question:

Osho,

Can love be taught? Can one be schooled in love? Can one without heart learn to have heart?

No one is without heart. You have the heart, but a nonfunctioning heart; it is there, but not functioning. It is there as a seed, it has not grown. Love cannot be taught, but situations can be created where the heart can grow; and when the heart grows love grows. Situations are needed. Love cannot be taught like mathematics. Mathematics can be directly taught, it is informative; love cannot be taught that way, it is not simply information. You have to grow, you have to change – but situations can be created.

In old Eastern universities – Nalanda, Taxila – there were many situations created where love became possible. For example, children were not taught under the roofs, in the rooms; they were always taught under the trees, in the shade of the trees. Have you ever felt any difference? Sit by the side of a concrete wall, and then go out, close your eyes, sit under a tree, your back in contact with the tree, and feel the difference. With a concrete wall you can feel only death just behind you, everything dead – and a dead situation makes *you* dead. Under a living tree in the open, where sunrays are dancing and where flowers are blooming, where the breeze will come and the tree will dance, sitting there under the tree you can feel the vibration of life. The more vibrations of life you feel, the more your heart will start functioning. Play with children and you will feel that you have become younger. One of the secrets of remaining always young is to play with children, because when you play with children you forget that you are old.

There have been many experiments. I was reading about one experiment in an Oxford laboratory. One woman who was eighty years old and almost blind, ninety percent blind, was hypnotized. In hypnosis it was suggested to her that her age was regressing, by and by she was becoming younger, then she was becoming a child again. Then the hypnotist suggested, "Now you are only eight years old" – from eighty to eight. And then the hypnotist said, "Now open your eyes."

She opened her eyes; a book was given to her. It had been impossible for her to read anything, but she simply started reading and she said, "My eyes are so young and fresh." Just the idea that she was now eight years old, not eighty but eight years old, changed the whole pattern of the eyes.

In England there are almost eight hundred people who have gone beyond the age of one hundred. So there was a report: an interviewer went to ask many of these old persons, these centenarians, how they could live so long. Many answers were given, but I liked one the best, and it may be the key. One old man who was one hundred and twenty said, "I am still interested in young girls." That may be the key. If a person of one hundred and twenty is still interested in young girls, he can live long.

It is written in old scriptures that in India, whenever a king became old, it was suggested by the wise men that he should sleep in the night with a young girl on each side. You may be one hundred and twenty, but if a girl of twenty years falls in love with you, you cannot remain one hundred and twenty – immediately something, regression, happens. Play with children and you will be younger; sit with old men, listen to their talk and you will feel you are dead, already dead. Your mind depends on many things; situations help.

Bernard Shaw, in his old age, changed his home from London to a village. He was then ninety, and somebody asked, "Why have you changed to this village? Why have you chosen *this* village?"

He said, "I was walking one day in the cemetery of this village, and there I saw one stone. It was written on that stone, on somebody's stone, that this man was born in 1800 and died in 1900, and it was written that this man died untimely, when he was only one hundred years of age. So," Bernard Shaw said, "this village is good to live in, because people here think that death at one hundred years is untimely death. This is a good milieu for living a long time." He really lived a long time.

Love cannot be taught; you cannot be given a book to read about love. But a situation, a more natural milieu, birds, trees, animals, where you feel life more, will help you to grow into your heart dimension. Persons who love are needed near you, because love is infectious. When a loving person comes near you...you may have been sad before, but when he comes – blissful, loving – suddenly the sadness disappears as if a cloud has moved and the sun has become visible. You feel it. Sit with someone who is sad; within minutes you will feel a sadness gathering in you. We are not like islands, we are joined together, so everyone influences everybody else.

A loving milieu is needed to teach love. In our schools, colleges, universities, there is no loving milieu. The teacher is not related at all. Just because of the traditions of the old days, in India the vice-chancellor is never called the vice-chancellor, he is called *kulapati*, the head of the family. There were ten thousand students in Nalanda, and the head of the family, the vice-chancellor, knew every student by his face and name. He knew everybody – ten thousand students. When someone was ill and when someone was okay, he would go and see. He loved his students, he knew them by name. He was really the "head of the family." Just traditionally in India they still go on calling the vice-chancellor kulapati.

I was in a university, and I asked the kulapati, "What type of kulapati are you? What type of head of the family are you? You don't know even a single student by name – no personal relationships, you are not related at all. You may be an administrator but you are not a head of the family." The teacher has to be a loving father; only through love can love be taught. If you love a child you are teaching love to him.

I was reading a letter somebody wrote to me. The woman who wrote the letter belongs to a theosophical family, very religious. She wrote to me, "When-ever there was any problem in the family, any sadness, any anger, any conflict, my mother would give me a book and she would say, 'Go and look in it.' The Philosophy of Divine Love, or The Art of Love – but nobody loved me ever; they would always give me books to read. So I would read the books, but I never felt what love is."

Love cannot be taught in that way; a milieu has to be created. The teacher, the family, the society, must be loving; only then a child learns how to love. Many experiments have been done. A child can be brought up without the mother, or without the mother's breast. He will grow, he will be healthy, but he will become incapable of love. If the mother has not loved him, if he has not been breastfed, if he has not felt the warmth of his mother's body, if he has not been touched lovingly, he will not be able to love anybody, his sensitivity will never grow.

So I know love cannot be taught, but still I say it has to be taught. And by teaching love I mean create a milieu, an atmosphere where love can grow, where heart can start functioning. And remember, you *are* with a heart, but a nonfunctioning heart. It is there waiting to function, and when it starts functioning you will be totally a different person.

8   The Unwavering Mind

After this the seeker enters the third stage of yoga

which is known as nonattachment. He fixes his mind unwaveringly on the meaning of scriptural words.

He lives in the monasteries, ashrams, of saints well established

in austerities. He occupies himself with the discussion of the

scriptures and sleeps on a rocky bed. Thus it is that he lives his life. Because he has attained peace of mind, the man of good conduct spends his time in the enjoyment of pleasures that come naturally to him from his excursions into the forest.

He remains detached however, from the objects of desires.

Through the ritual of meritorious deeds and the cultivation of right scriptures, he attains that clarity of vision which sees reality.

On completing this stage,

the seeker experiences a glimpse of enlightenment.

The second stage is that of thought – purity of thought, intensity of thought, contemplation, meditation. Thought is energy; it can move through desires to the objects of the world, it can become a bondage. If thought is associated with desire it becomes bondage; if thought is not associated with desire, freed from desire, thought can be used as a vehicle to reach the ultimate liberation.

The way is the same, only the direction changes. When thought moves to objects, to the world, it creates entanglements, it creates slavery, it creates imprisonment. When thought is not moving to objects but starts moving within, the same energy becomes liberation. The second stage is of thought – to make it pure, to become a witness of it.

The third stage is of *vairagya* – nonattachment. Nonattachment is very significant, the concept is very basic to all those who are in search of the truth. Mind has the capacity to get attached to anything, and once the mind gets attached to something the mind itself becomes that thing. When your mind is moving towards a sexual object and you get attached, mind becomes sex; when the mind is moving towards power and you get attached to it, mind becomes power, mind becomes politics.

Mind is just like a mirror: whatsoever you get attached to becomes fixed in the mirror, and then mind behaves like a film of a camera. Then mind is not just a mirror, it has become a film. Then whatsoever comes to it, the mind clings to it. These are the two possibilities, or two aspects of the same possibility. Mind has the capacity to get attached, identified, with anything whatsoever.

In hypnosis this is revealed very clearly. If you have seen any hypnotic experiments...or if you have not seen any, then you can try a few experiments yourself; they will be very revealing. Hypnosis is not difficult, a very simple process. Let someone who is willing to cooperate lie down in a relaxed posture, and tell him to fix his eyes on something – the electric light bulb will do – anything shiny so that the eyes get dazed. Let him concentrate without blinking the eyes. After two or three minutes you will feel that his eyes are becoming vacant, empty, sleepy.

Then you start suggesting. You simply say, "Your eyes are getting very heavy, even if you try you cannot keep them open." And he has to try to keep them open, he has to exert effort to keep them open. Go on suggesting, "Your eyes are getting heavy, heavier, heavier...it is difficult now, you cannot do anything, it is impossible, the eyes are going to close by themselves...no will, no effort of yours can keep them open...." And the person will start feeling as if the eyes have be-come loaded, heavy. He will try, he will make every effort to keep them open, and you go on suggesting the opposite.

After five or six minutes the eyes will close, and the moment the eyes close, the man will start feeling that something is happening which is beyond his control – he cannot keep his own eyes open. Then you go on suggesting, "You are falling into deep sleep, you will become unaware of everything except me." You have to suggest, "Only my voice will be heard, and everything else will become blank." Go on suggesting. After ten minutes the person will be fast asleep, but this sleep is totally different from normal sleep because he is not asleep to you. He is asleep to the whole world, he cannot hear anything; if someone else talks he cannot hear, but if you talk he will hear. His conscious mind has dropped, but his unconscious is linked with you – now he is suggestible.

Now try something, some experiment. You can prick his body with a pin and tell him that there will be no pain, and you can go on pushing in the pin and he will not feel any pain. Then you can believe that he has become suggestible. You can give him an onion to eat and tell him that it is an apple and he will think, "This is very sweet, very tasty. I like it." He is eating onion, but if you have suggested that it is an apple, he will feel that it is an apple. Then he has become more suggestible.

Put a piece of stone, a piece of rock in his hand, and tell him that it is a burning coal. Immediately he will throw it as if his hand has been burned – and it was just a piece of rock, cold, but he will feel it as hot. And not only that, but the spot on his hand, on his skin, will look as if a burning coal has been put there. The skin has burned, it has happened; the body has reacted because the mind accepted the idea.

This is how in India, in Ceylon, in Burma, fakirs, monks, *bhikkus*, have been walking on fire. They just believe so totally that the body has to follow. Remember, the body always follows the mind. If you think that a cold stone is a burning coal and your mind gets attached to the idea, then the body reacts in that way. The reverse is also true. You can put a burning coal on the hand and say that it is a cold piece of rock, and the hand will not get burned.

Whatsoever the attachment, your life follows that. In this world, the Upanishads say, we are behaving as if we are hypnotized; we are in a deep hypnosis. Nobody else has done that, we have hypnotized ourselves. For millions of lives we have been attached to certain objects of desire; they have become fixed. So whenever you see a woman, immediately your body starts working in a sexual way.

Once it happened, I was sitting on the bank of the Ganges with a friend of mine. Suddenly I felt that he was uncomfortable, so I asked, "What is the matter?"

He said, "That woman!"

A woman was taking a bath in the river, and we could see only the back of the woman — long hair, curly hair, a beautiful back — and he was excited, so he said, "Pardon me, excuse me, we will continue our discussion later on. I must go and see, the body seems to be so beautiful."

So he went, and then he came back very frustrated because it was not a woman, it was a *sadhu*, a Hindu monk, a Hindu sannyasin with long hair taking a bath, and the body was beautiful and looked feminine. There was no woman, but the mind got attached, a fixation, and then the whole chemical process in the body started.

Attachment creates the life; a life is created around whatsoever you are attached to. So the Upanishads say it is basic, the third step of sadhana, that the mind should get nonattached; only then this illusory world that you have created around you will disappear. Otherwise, you will remain in a dream.

The world is not a dream, remember. This has been very much misunderstood. In the West it has been very much misunderstood; they think that these Indian mystics have called the world illusory. They have not called the world illusory, they call the world you have created around you illusory. And everybody has created a world around himself that is not the real world, that is just your projection. You have got attached to certain things, then you project your dreams onto the reality. By nonattachment, reality is not going to be destroyed; only your dreams will be destroyed, and reality will be revealed to you as it is. So nonattachment becomes a basic step, very foundational.

Now we will enter the sutra:

After this the seeker enters the third stage of yoga which is known as non-attachment. He fixes his mind unwaveringly on the meaning of scriptural words. He lives in the monasteries, ashrams, of saints well established in austerities. He occupies himself with the discussion of the scriptures and sleeps on a rocky bed.

Everything has to be understood. These are old symbols, they have to be penetrated deeply; they are not literal, they are symbolic.

He fixes his mind unwaveringly....

This is the first thing in nonattachment, because a wavering mind cannot get non-attached. Only a nonwavering mind, *nishkam*, a nonwavering mind, can get nonattached. Why? Look at your mind, observe it: every moment it is wavering. It cannot remain with one object for a single moment, every moment a flux is passing; one thought comes, then another, then another – there is a procession.

You cannot remain with one thought even for a single moment, and if you cannot remain for a single moment with one thought, how can you penetrate it? How can you become aware of its full reality? How can you see the illusion that it creates? You are moving so fast that you cannot observe – observation is impossible. It is just as if you come running into this hall. As soon as you enter from one door you go out from the other. You have just a glimpse, and you cannot know later on whether this hall was real or a dream. You had no time here to know, to penetrate, to analyze, to observe, to be aware.

So fixation of the mind on one content is one of the essential requirements for any seeker – that he should remain with one thought for long periods. Once you can remain with one thought for long periods, you yourself will see that this thought is creating attachment, this thought is creating a world around it, this thought is the basic seed of all illusion. And if you can retain a thought for long periods, you have become the master. Now the mind is not the master and you are not the slave.

And if you can remain with one thought for long periods you can drop it also. You can say to the mind, "Stop!" and the mind stops; you can say to the mind, "Move!" and the mind moves. Now it is not so; you want to stop the process but the mind continues, the mind never listens to you. The mind is the master and you are just following the mind like a shadow. The instrument – mind is just an instrument – has become the soul, and the soul has become the servant. This is the perversion and this is the misery of human beings.

Try to fix your mind on one thing, anything will do. Sit on the ground outside and look at a tree and try to remain with the tree. Whatsoever happens, remain with the tree. The mind will try many waverings, the mind will give you many alternatives to move. The mind will say, "Look! What type of tree is this? What is the name?" Don't listen to it, because even if you have moved to the name you have moved away from the tree. If you start thinking about the tree you have gone away from the tree. Don't think about it, remain with the fact that the tree is.

It will be difficult in the beginning because you are not so alert. You are so sleepy that you will forget completely that you were looking at the tree. A dog will start barking and you will look at the dog; a cloud will come in the sky and you have moved; somebody passes and you have forgotten the tree. But go on, again and again. When you remember again that you have forgotten and fallen asleep, move again to the tree. Do it.

If you go on working, after three or four weeks you will be capable of retaining one content in the mind at least for one minute. And that's a big capacity! That's a big phenomenon! – because you don't know, you think one minute is not much. One minute is too much for the mind, because mind moves within seconds. For not even a full second is your mind on one thing. It is wavering – wavering is mind's nature, it goes on creating waves. And that is the way the attachment is retained.

You love a woman. Even if you love a woman you cannot retain the idea of the woman in your mind. If you look at the woman you will start thinking about her – and you have moved away. You may think about her clothes, you may think about her eyes, you may think about her face and figure, but you have moved away from the woman. Just let the fact remain, don't think about it, because thinking means wavering. To retain a single content means: don't think, just look. Thinking means moving, wavering. Just look – looking means nonwavering.

That is the meaning of concentration, and all the religions of the world have used it in this way or that. Their methods may look different but the essential is this: that the mind has to be trained to retain one thing for longer periods. What will happen? Once you get this capacity nothing is to be done. You can penetrate, anything becomes transparent. The very look, and in that look your energy moving, goes deep.

There are two ways for the mind. One is linear, from one thought to another – a, b, c, d – the mind moves in a line. Mind has energy. When it moves from a to b it dissipates energy, when it moves from b to c again energy is dissipated, when it moves from c to d energy has been dissipated. If you retain only a in the mind and don't allow it to move to b, c, d and so forth and so on, what will happen? The energy that was going to be dissipated in movement will go on hammering on the fact a, and then a new process will start – you will move deeper in the a. Not moving from a to b, but moving from a1 to a2, a3, a4. Now the energy is moving directly, intensely, in one fact. Your eyes will become penetrating.

One sannyasin came to me just yesterday. She is working well, doing well, but just after a meditation I looked deeply into her eyes when she was standing here, and she started trembling and weeping and crying. Then she came to me, crying and weeping, and said, "Why did you look at me so penetratingly? Can't you look at me a little sweetly?" She said, "I became afraid, and I thought that I must be doing something wrong, that's why you were looking so penetratingly."

We have become completely unacquainted with the penetrating eye. We know only superficial, moving eyes from a to b, from b to c – just touching and moving, touching and moving. If somebody looks at you, stares at you deeply, and he is not moving from a to b, b to c, you will become scared – but that is the real look. And you will become scared because his eyes are going deep within you; he is not moving on the surface, he is moving deep, in the depth. You will become scared because you have become unacquainted with it.

Fixation of the mind will give you a penetrating eye. That eye has been known in the occult world as the third eye. When you start moving on a point, not in a line, you gain a force, and that force works. All over the world mesmerists, hypnotists, and other workers in the psychic field have been aware of it for centuries. You can try it. Somebody, a stranger, is walking on the road. You just go behind him and look at the back of his neck. Stare. Immediately he will look back towards you, the energy hits there immediately if you stare.

There is a center at the back of the neck which is very sensitive. Just stare at the center and the person is bound to look back because he will become uneasy, something is entering there. Your eyes are not simply windows to look through, they are energy centers. You are not only absorbing impressions through the eyes, you are throwing energy – but you are not aware. You are not aware because your energy is being dissipated in movement, is waving, wavering from one to two, two to three, three to four – you go on, and every gap takes your energy.

He fixes his mind unwaveringly....

First one has to try to fix this mind unwaveringly on objects, and then *on the meaning of the scriptural words.*

This is a totally different science. You read a book. Reading is linear: from one word you move to another, from another to another – you go on moving in lines. You may not have observed that different countries have different ways of writing. English is written from the left towards the right, because English is a technical language, not very poetic; a male language, not feminine. Urdu, Arabic, are written from the right to the left. They are more poetic, because the left side is poetry and the right side is mathematics – right is male, left is female.

Chinese is written downwards; neither from left to right, nor from right to left, just from up downwards, because Chinese was developed through Confucian ideology, and Confucius says, "The middle is the goal, the middle is golden – the golden mean." So they don't move from left to right, or from right to left; they move from up to down. This is the middle, the mean, neither male nor female.

English is male, Urdu is female – that's why Urdu is so poetic. No language in the world is as poetic as Urdu. In any language of the world you will need hundreds of lines, and then too you will not be able to express a poetic thing. In Urdu just two lines will do and they will stop the heart. It moves from right to left, from male to female – female is the end.

All over the world God has always been conceived of as the father. Only in the East are there a few religions which conceive of God as the mother – but Sufis, Mohammedans, are the only ones who conceive of God as the beloved; not mother, beloved. The feminine is the end. From the male they move to the female, to the feminine, but movement is there.

Chinese moves from up to down, into the depth, so Chinese symbols can express things no other language can express – because every language is linear, and Chinese is in the depth. So if you have read Lao Tzu's Tao Te Ching in translation, you know that every translation differs. If you read ten translations then all the translations will be different; you cannot say who is wrong and who is right, because Chinese carries so much meaning and depth that ten, or even one hundred meanings are possible. In depth more and more meanings are revealed.

In India it is said that a scripture like the Vedas, the Upanishads or the Gita, is not to be read in a linear way. You have to concentrate on each word. Read a word, then don't move; look at the word, close your eyes, and wait for the meaning to be revealed. This is a totally different concept of studying a thing, so Westerners sometimes cannot understand that a person goes on reading the Gita every day for his whole life. This looks absurd. If you have read it once it is finished! Why do you go on reading the Gita every day? Once you have read it, what is the meaning in reading it again?

But Hindus say the Gita is not a linear book. Each word has to be looked at with a fixed mind; in each word you have to penetrate deep – so deep that the word disappears and only silence remains. And the word does not have the meaning, remember – the meaning is hidden in you. The word is just a technical support to help the meaning that is within you to come up. So the word is a mantra, or a yantra, a design which will help you to bring up the meaning which is hidden in your soul.

See the difference. In the West if you read a thing, then the word has a meaning; in the East the word has got no meaning – the meaning is in the reader. The word is just a device to bring the reader to his own inner meaning, to encounter the inner meaning. The word will just provoke you inside so that your inner meaning flowers through it. The word has to be forgotten and the inner meaning has to be carried, but you will have to wait; and mind needs fixation, mind needs concentration, only then the inner meaning can be revealed. So one has to go on reading the same thing every day, but it is not the same because *you* have been changing.

If a boy of fifteen reads the Gita the meaning is going to be boyish, immature, juvenile. Then a man, a young man of thirty reads the Gita – the meaning is going to be different, more romantic. In that meaning sex will be involved, in that meaning love will be projected, in that meaning the youth will project his youth. And then an old man of sixty reads the Gita. He has passed through the ups and downs of life, he has seen misery and glimpses of happiness, he has lived through much. He will see something else in the Gita; in that something else death will be involved, death will be all over the Gita.

And a man of one hundred, to whom even death has become irrelevant, to whom even death has become an accepted fact, not a problem, who is not afraid of death but rather, on the contrary, is just waiting for it so that the imprisonment in the body is broken and the soul can fly – he looks in the Gita and it will be totally different. Now it will transcend life, the meaning will transcend life.

The meaning depends on the state of your mind. So the meaning of a word is not in the dictionary, the meaning of the word is in the reader, and the words are used as devices to bring that meaning up. But if you go on reading fast that will not help. In the West they go on creating more and more techniques for how to read fast, how to finish the book as fast as possible, because time is short. And there are techniques by which you can read very fast; whatsoever your speed right now it can be doubled very easily, and you can even double it again if you work a little harder. And if you are really persistent you can again double that speed.

So if you are reading sixty words per minute, you can read two hundred and forty words per minute if you work hard – but then you will be moving in a linear way. And if you move fast then your unconscious starts reading, the conscious just gives hints. Subliminal reading becomes possible, but then you cannot penetrate.

The question is not to read much, the question is to read very little but to read deep. The depth is significant, because in the depth quality is hidden. If you read fast quantity will be great, but quality will be no more there, it will be mechanical. You will not be imbibing whatsoever you are reading, you will not be changed through whatsoever you are reading; it will just be a memorization.

He fixes his mind unwaveringly on the meaning of the scriptural words.

In Sanskrit every word has multi-meanings. In the West it will be thought that this is not good; a word should mean only one thing, it should have only one meaning. Only then can there be a science of language, only then can the language become technical, scientific. So one word should have only one meaning. But Sanskrit is not a scientific language, it is a religious language. And if the people who spoke Sanskrit claimed that their language is divine it means something. Every word has multi-meanings; no word is fixed, solid, it is liquid, flowing. You can derive many meanings through it – it depends on you. It has many shades, many colors; it is not a dead stone, it is an alive flower.

If you go in the morning it looks different, if you go in the afternoon the same flower looks different, because the whole milieu has changed. When you go in the evening the same flower has a different poetry to it. In the morning it was happy, alive, dancing, filled with so many desires, hopes, dreams, was maybe thinking to conquer the whole world. By the afternoon desires have dropped, much frustration has come, the flower is not hoping so much now, it is a little depressed, a little sad. By the evening life has proved illusory, the flower is on its deathbed, shrunken, closed, no dreams, no hopes.

Sanskrit words are like flowers, they have moods; that's why Sanskrit can be interpreted in millions of ways. The Gita has one thousand interpretations. You cannot conceive of The Bible having one thousand interpretations – impossible! You cannot conceive of the Koran having one thousand interpretations – not a single interpretation exists. The Koran has never been interpreted. There are one thousand interpretations of the Gita, and still they are not enough. Every century will add many more, and while human consciousness is on the earth interpretations will be added forever and ever. The Gita cannot be exhausted, it is impossible to exhaust it, because every word has many meanings.

Sanskrit is liquid, flowing, moody, and this is good because this gives you freedom. The reader has freedom, he is not a slave; the words are not imposed on him, he can play with those words. He can change his moods through those words, and he can change those words through his moods. The Gita is alive, and every alive thing has moods; only dead things have no moods. In that way English is a dead language. It will look paradoxical, because English scholars go on saying that Sanskrit is a dead language because no one speaks it. They are right in a way – because nobody speaks it, it is a dead language, but really modern languages are dead.

No one speaks Sanskrit now, but it is an alive language, the very quality of it is alive; every word has a life of its own and changes, moves, flows, riverlike. Much is possible through the play of Sanskrit words, and they have been arranged in such a way that if you concentrate on them, many worlds of meanings will be revealed to you.

He fixes his mind unwaveringly on the meaning of scriptural words. He lives in the monasteries....

First he fixes on the Vedas, on the old scriptures. These scriptures are not just books. They are not written for any other reason than this: they have been written to reveal a certain deep secret. They are not for you to read and enjoy and throw just like novels; they are to be pondered, contemplated, meditated on. You have to go so deep in them that this going into depth becomes natural to you. And they were not written by persons who were writers, persons not knowing anything but just through their egoistic feeling writing things.

Gurdjieff divides all scriptures into two divisions: one he calls subjective, the other he calls objective. These scriptures – the Vedas, the Upanishads, are objective, not subjective. The whole literature that we are creating is subjective, the writer is throwing his own subjectivity into it. A poet, a modern poet, or a painter, a modern Picasso, or a novelist, a story-writer – they are writing their own minds there. They are not concerned with the person who is going to read, remember, they are more concerned with themselves. This is a catharsis for them. They are mad inside, burdened – they want to express.

You can read a good novel, but don't go to see the novelist; you may be disappointed. You can read a good poem, but don't go to see the poet; you will be disappointed, because the poetry will give you a glimpse of a high realm, it will put you on high, but if you go to see the poet you will find a very ordinary man – you may even be better than him. The man has not changed through his poem, how can the poem change you? The man has not known that height, he may have dreamed it or he may have taken LSD.

One girl came to me just two or three days ago, and she said, "I was in Goa" – she is my sannyasin – and she said, "I took LSD and then I became certain that enlightenment had happened to me, so I threw your mala into the sea, because now there is no need. I changed the dress, because I am now enlightened, so what is the use of orange or the mala or anything?"

This is a sort of madness. Enlightenment is not so cheap. But in the West they are making everything cheap. I go on hearing that there are three week intense enlightenment growth groups – in three weeks you are enlightened!

A poet may have dreamed, may have taken hashish. And scientists say that poets have some difference, some chemical difference from ordinary persons – they have some hashish in their blood, really, so they can imagine more, they can dream more, they can go on dream trips more than others. So they write, but their writing is imaginative, it is not objective. It may help them as a catharsis, that they are unburdened.

But there is another type of literature, totally different, which is objective. These Upanishads were not written for the joy of the writer, they were written for those who were going to read them – they are objective. What they will do to you if you contemplate on them has been planned; every single word has been put there, every single sound has been used. If someone contemplates on it, then the state of the writer will be revealed to him; the same will happen to him if he contemplates. These scriptures are called holy; that's why.

A totally different body of literature exists in the East, a totally different body – not meant to be enjoyed, but meant to be transforming. And when one has penetrated deep into the meaning of the scriptures.... And these scriptures belong to those who have known. It was thought to be a great sin to write something which you have not known. That's why very few books were written in the past.

Now every week ten thousand books are written all over the world – every week, ten thousand. And this goes on and on. Now they are worried, because libraries cannot contain such a growing body of literature, so minibooks have to be created, or microfilms of books have to be created so that they can be contained; otherwise soon there will be more libraries than there are houses. And people don't have shelter, so how can one shelter books? It is becoming almost impossible.

But in the past very few books were written because no one was interested just in writing. Modern authors write because it gives an egoistic feeling that you are an author, everybody knows your name because you have written a book. Your book may be dangerous because it will carry your mind and your germs. If you are ill, then whosoever reads that book will get ill; if you are mad.... Just read Kafka's books or look at Picasso's paintings. Try this method with a Picasso painting – you will go mad. Just fix the mind on a Picasso painting, go on staring at it for the inner meaning. Soon you will feel that insanity is arising within you. Picasso is insane, he is putting his insanity on the painting. That is good for him because he is relieved, but not good for you; it is dangerous.

I have heard an anecdote. Once it happened that one of Picasso's very valuable paintings was stolen, and Picasso was there when the thief came and took the painting, so he had seen the thief. The police asked for particulars, for details of how the thief looked, so he said, "It is difficult to say, but I will paint him."

So he painted a picture. The police caught twenty persons. Of those twenty persons one was a professor, one was a politician, one was a musician – all types of men. And not only that, it is said that many other things were caught – some machines, and finally the Eiffel Tower!...Because you cannot know what Picasso paints, it is difficult to say what the painting says; it says nothing, or it says so much that it is a confusion.

So don't try this method on modern writings, you will go mad. Kafka, Sartre, or paintings of Picasso – don't try this method on them. Only with objective literature can you go deep, because the opposite will be the result. These writings are from those who have known, who have become enlightened, and they have put in these writings their own mind – the mind is hidden there. If you penetrate, the mind will be revealed to you. And only after that...

He lives in the monasteries, ashrams, of saints well established in austerities.

The ashram is an Eastern concept, there is no word to express it in English. "Monastery" is not a good word; ashram is totally different. You have to understand the concept. A monastery is where monks live. There are Christian monasteries – there is no need for an enlightened person to be there; abbots are there, administrators are there. The monastery is like a training school. The abbot need not be enlightened, but he will train you, because they have a curriculum, a course. Christian priests are prepared that way.

I used to visit a Christian theological college. For five years they train the priest there. Everything is conditioned: how much you have to raise your hand when you assert something from The Bible, how you have to make gestures, how loudly you have to speak, and where you have to go slow – everything is trained. They become robotlike and the whole thing is missed.

If you have read about Vivekananda then you will remember this. Vivekananda himself was not an enlightened person, but he impressed America very much – and the reason was not that he was enlightened, the reason was something else. The reason was that he was the only spontaneous person there. All the Christian missionaries, priests, abbots, and big names in Christianity were all disciplined, conditioned, nonspontaneous, robotlike.

So when Vivekananda stood in the American Fair of World Religions, just from the way he stood there, from the way he started, from the first thing when he said, "Brothers and Sisters," the whole audience was happy – because when you say, "Ladies and gentlemen," it is something else. No one had addressed the audience there in that fair in that way. Hundreds of speeches were made, and Vivekananda said, "Brothers and sisters...." Immediately the faces of people sitting there changed. Someone was spontaneous, not formal. And whatsoever he said was not very significant, because he was a Hindu sannyasin, untrained.

A monastery is a training school; an ashram is not a school, an ashram is a family. And an ashram doesn't exist as an institution, cannot exist as an institution. The ashram exists around an enlightened person, that is a basic must. If the enlightened person is not there the ashram disappears; it is the person around whom the ashram can come into being. When the person is dead the ashram has to disappear. If you continue the ashram it becomes a monastery.

For example, Aurobindo is dead and now the Mother is dead – now Pondicherry is a monastery, not an ashram. It will persist as a dead thing, an institute. When Aurobindo was there it was totally different. The person is important, not the institute – institutions are dead. So remember this: a live phenomenon, a master, just by his presence creates a milieu – that milieu is the ashram. And when you move in that milieu you are moving in a family, not in an institute. The master will take care of you in every way, and you will be there in intimate, close proximity.

Eastern ashrams are disappearing, they are becoming monasteries, institutes. The Western mind is so obsessed with institutes that everything is turned into an institute. I was just reading a book on marriage. It begins by saying that marriage is the greatest institute, the greatest institution – but who wants to live in an institute? The ashram is more intimate, more personal.

So every ashram will differ from others, every ashram is going to be unique, because it will depend on the person around whom it has been created. All monasteries will be similar but no two ashrams can be similar, because every ashram has to be individual, unique; it depends on the personality of the master. If you go to a Sufi ashram it will be totally different – much dancing and singing will be there; if you go to a Buddhist ashram, no dancing, no singing, much sitting silently will be there. And both are doing the same, they are leading towards the same goal.

The first thing to remember: an ashram exists with a master; it is his personal influence, his person, the atmosphere, the milieu that he creates through his being. An ashram is his being, and when you enter into an ashram you are not entering into an institution, you are entering a live person, you are becoming part of the soul of the master. Now you will exist as part of the master, he will exist through you. So no forced discipline, but spontaneous happenings will be there.

He lives in the ashrams of saints well established in austerities.

In the third state it is good to move to someone who has known, to live with him. The first two will make you capable, *patra;* the first two will make you worthy of having a master look at you, of a master allowing you to be in intimacy with him. Without the first two no master will look at you; you will not be allowed, he will avoid you, he will create situations so that you will have to leave his ashram. Only after these two states, when you enter the third, will you be allowed, because a master is not going to waste…. He cannot work with you unless you are ready, and unless you show readiness.

One sannyasin goes on writing letters to me. He is here, he has again written a letter to me, a very long letter, saying, "Give me the method so that I can move into my past lives." And he is not capable at all even to live in this life! He will go mad if I give him a method to move into the past lives. Why do you think nature prohibits it? Why does nature create a barrier so that you cannot remember the past lives?

Nature is more wise than you. Nature creates the barrier because even one life is too much; it is a burden. You have to forget many things, and if you continuously remember the past life you will be confused, you will be nowhere, you will not be able to decide what is what. Everything will become vague, cloudy, and the past life will remain on your mind like a burden and it will not allow you to live here and now.

Just think, you are in love with a woman and you remember that in the past life she was your mother! So now what will you do? If you go on making love to her you are making love to your mother, and that will create guilt. Or if you think that she is your mother so you should leave her, that will again create guilt because you love her so much. The whole thing will become very difficult and arduous to carry on. And this is how it is happening: your wife may have been your mother, your husband may have been your son, your friend may have been your enemy, your enemy may have been your friend. You have moved in so many lives, it is very complex. Nature creates a barrier: when you die a curtain falls and you cannot remember.

This man goes on writing to me, "Give me a method." And now he has threatened, "If you don't give me a method I am going to leave sannyas." If you leave sannyas, what is it to me? And if I give you a method and you go mad, then who will be responsible? And you will go mad – you are already mad, just on the brink; any step further, a little more burden on the mind and you will explode.

The ashram, or the master, will accept you only when you are ready, and he will start working only when a certain thing can be done to you, you have come to a certain state; nothing can be done before it. And this should be the attitude of the disciple – that he should not ask. The master knows what is to be done and you have to wait. If you cannot wait you have to leave, because nothing can be done when you are not ripe for it.

The first two stages make you ripe to be accepted by a master.

He occupies himself with the discussion of the scriptures, and sleeps on a rocky bed.

This is actual and symbolic both. In the old ashrams everybody had to sleep on a rocky bed – actually also, because it helps. In yoga, your spine, your backbone, is very important, and not only in yoga but in biology also. Now biologists say man could become man because he started standing erect, his backbone erect. Animals' backbones are parallel to the earth, only man has a backbone which is not parallel to the earth but makes an angle of ninety degrees. This changed the whole being of man, this angle of ninety degrees with the gravitation created the possibility for the mind to develop. Now biologists say that just by standing on two feet the animal became human – because it changes the whole thing. Less blood flows in the head, so the head and the nervous system there can become more delicate and refined. When more blood flows in the head the subtle tissues are broken, they cannot grow.

So don't do too much *shirshasana*. Unless a master suggests it to you don't do shirshasana, because I have never seen a person who has been doing shirshasana who is not stupid. You will become stupid. You will become more healthy of course, because animals are more healthy; so if you are just after health, shirshasana is good, do it forever. You will become healthy like a bull but at the same time stupid also, because when more blood moves into the head delicate tissues are destroyed, and those delicate tissues are needed for intelligence. When man stood erect the possibility developed for more delicate tissues in the head.

You see primitives sleep without pillows, and they will remain primitives if they continue to sleep without pillows, because more blood flows in the night. A more intelligent person will need more pillows. He may not be healthier, but intelligence needs a certain mechanism in the mind, a very delicate mechanism. And mind is very complex; seventy million cells are there, and so delicate, bound to be so delicate, when in such a small head there are seventy million. They are very delicate, very small particles, and when blood flows fast, in great quantity, they are destroyed, they are killed. So biologically, and scientifically also, the spine is the most important thing in man. Your head is nothing but a pole to your spine: you exist as a spine – on one pole is sex, on the other is your mind, and your spine is the bridge.

Yoga worked very much on the spine, because yogis became aware of its significance – that the spine is your life. The angle of ninety degrees will be more exact if your spine is straight, so yogis say that when you sit, sit with a straight spine. They worked out many postures, *asanas*; all their asanas are based on an erect spine, straight. The straighter it is, the more is the possibility to grow in intelligence, awareness.

You may not have observed: if you are listening to me and you are interested your spine will be straight, if you are not interested then you can relax. If you are looking at a movie in a cinema, whenever something interesting comes you will sit straight immediately, because more mind is called for. When the interesting scene has gone you can relax again into your chair.

In the day the spine has to be erect for yogic postures, and in the night also it has to be trained to be more straight. On a rocky bed it is more straight than on a Dunlop mattress. On a rocky bed it is bound to be straight, because the rocky bed is not going to give way for it. If the spine is erect the whole night it will be-come conditioned to being erect, so in the day also, while walking, sitting, it will remain erect. This is good. So this is physiologically, biologically, and in the eyes of yogis, very helpful. But this is only one part of it, the other part is symbolic.

Whenever a person goes through suffering we say he is lying on a rocky bed. And the ashram is going to be a long suffering, because many old habits are to be broken and they are hard; many old patterns are to be broken and they are very fixed. Really you have to be destroyed and created again, and in between there is going to be suffering and chaos. That is the rocky bed.

With a master you will have to move through much suffering. You have got many blocks in the body and the mind; they have to be destroyed, and to destroy a block is painful. Unless those blocks are destroyed you cannot flow, you cannot become spontaneous, your energy cannot rise high, it cannot move from the sex center to the sahasrar, it cannot move to the ultimate center of your being. So many things have to be destroyed and every habit has a big pattern, its own system – it takes time.

If you are ready and you trust your master it will not take so much time, be-cause trusting him you can pass through suffering. If you don't trust, then every suffering becomes a problem, and the mind says, "What are you doing here? Why are you suffering here? Leave this man, go away! You were happy before." You were never happy before, but when suffering starts you will feel that you were happy before.

For the real happiness to happen you will have to throw all suffering, you will have to pass through it – it is part of growth. And when all suffering has been passed through, only then you become capable of bliss; for the first time you can become happy. And there is no other way.

Thus it is that he lives his life. Because he has attained peace of mind, the man of good conduct spends his time in the enjoyment of pleasures that come naturally to him from his excursions into the forest.

This is something very significant. In an ashram, under the guidance of a master, you will have to pass through many sufferings. But you are not to create those sufferings, you are not to be masochistic. Many pleasures will also come. Re-member, this is the type of our mind – that either we are attached to pleasure and then we demand pleasure, or we can even become attached to suffering and then we say we don't want any pleasure. We start having pleasure through suffering, and that is dangerous. That's the masochistic attitude – you can torture yourself and you can enjoy it.

This is a very deep phenomenon in the human psyche, and it has happened because of some association. Every pleasure is with some pain, so if pleasure becomes intense you will feel pain, and the reverse is also true: every pain has its own small pleasure, and if the pain becomes intense you will feel pleasure. Pain and pleasure are not really two things, the difference is only of degree.

You love a woman. To be with her for a few hours is beautiful, to be with her for a few minutes is just heavenly, to be with her for a few seconds you feel you are in nirvana. But to be with her for twenty-four hours becomes difficult, and to be with her continuously for months becomes boring, and if you are to be with her for your whole life you would like to commit suicide. Every pleasure has its pain, and every pain has its pleasure. They are not two. They differ in intensity, degrees, but they don't differ in quality.

And there is another, deeper, association. When you make love.... Love is the most pleasurable thing in the world, naturally – beyond nature there are more pleasures, more blisses, but naturally, biologically, love is the most pleasurable thing. Sex is one of the most pleasant things nature has given to you, but in sex, pain is also involved. When you make love you do many things which give mild pain, but they are good. Even your kiss is a mild pain. You play with each other's body, and in playing with each other's body you create a certain pain also. In the Kama Sutra, Vatsyayana has given many clues and suggestions. He says that when really you love a woman, then you will do many things – biting, penetrating your nails into her body – and she will enjoy it. In other circumstances it would be painful, but associated with love it becomes pleasure. But this can go to an extreme, you can become a de Sade.

From de Sade's name comes the word sadism. De Sade had many devices to torture his beloveds, his mistresses. Nails wouldn't do, so he had thorns; nails wouldn't do, so he had iron instruments to penetrate the body. The blood would ooze and he would whip them. He would always travel with a bag with him; in his bag there were all these things. Whenever he found a woman who was ready to love him he would close the door. First he would beat her, blood would start oozing. He would torture the woman and then he would make love. And you will be surprised: he loved many women, and the women, any women that he loved, would declare later on that after de Sade loved them, nobody else has loved that way. He gave them the greatest pleasure, he really loved them.

Even a torture can be pleasurable, because when you beat a person more energy is thrown all over the body, the whole body becomes sexual. When you beat a person the whole body is excited – and then you make love. From the excitement of torture, suddenly fall in love. It gives a very pleasant sensation...as if first you were hungry, starved, and then came good food – the contrast.

But in every pleasure some torture, some pain, is involved. You can move to the other extreme, you can start giving pain to yourself and can enjoy it. Go to Benares, you will see the monks lying on a bed of thorns. They are enjoying it, it is a sexual pleasure. They have left the pleasure part and retained the pain part.

So in the ashrams you are not to make yourself suffer, not to be a sadist, not to torture yourself. You have to be hard just to break the old habits, but there is no need to seek pain, and if pleasures come by automatically, you are allowed to enjoy them. An ashram is not a torture house; if pleasures come by themselves you are allowed to enjoy them. They are good. You have to be thankful for them.

Because he has attained peace of mind, the man of good conduct spends his time in the enjoyment of pleasures that come naturally to him from his excursions into the forest. He remains detached, however, from the objects of desire.

He remains detached. Pleasures come, moments of enjoyment come; he enjoys them and forgets them. He will not demand them again, he will not say, "Now I cannot live without these pleasures." Whatsoever God gives, one has to be thankful but never demanding. He remains unattached to desire.

Through the ritual of meritorious deeds and the cultivation of right scriptures, he attains that clarity of vision which sees reality. On completing this stage, the seeker experiences a glimpse of enlightenment.

Just a glimpse – not enlightenment. This glimpse is known in Japan as satori. Satori is not samadhi, satori is just a glimpse. You have not reached enlightenment, you have not reached the peak of the hill, but standing in the valley when there are no clouds, when the sky is clear, you can look at the peak with snow caps – but it is very far away still. You cannot see when the sky is clouded, you cannot see when it is night, you cannot see if you are standing at such a point from where it cannot be looked at.

These three steps will bring you to such a viewpoint from where the peak can be glimpsed. These three stages will make your mind clear. The clouds will disappear and the peak will be revealed – but this is a faraway glimpse, this is not enlightenment. At the third stage a glimpse comes, but remember well, don't think that this is enlightenment. And this can happen even through chemical help also. Through LSD, marijuana, or other drugs also this is possible, because drugs can create such a chemical situation within you, they can force such a chemical situation where for a moment clouds disappear; suddenly you are thrown to a point from where the peak can be glimpsed. But this is no attainment, because chemistry cannot become meditation and chemistry cannot give you enlightenment. When you come back from the trip you are the same again. You may remember it, and that memory may disturb you, and that memory may make you an addict. Then you have to take LSD again and again, and the more you take the less will be the possibility of even the glimpse, because the body gets accustomed and then a greater quantity is needed. Then you are on a path which will lead to insanity and nowhere else.

So don't try chemical things. If you have tried them, thank God, and don't try them again. Once you become addicted to chemical help sadhana becomes impossible, because chemicals seem so easy and sadhana seems so difficult. Only sadhana, only spiritual discipline, will help you grow, will give you growth to the point from where the glimpse is not forced but becomes natural. And it is not lost then – any moment you can look, you know from where to look, and the peak will be there. Occupied in your day-to-day activities, any moment you can close your eyes and see the peak and that will become a constant happiness within you, a joy, a continuous joy. Whatsoever you are doing, whatsoever is happening outside, even if you are in misery – for you have built so many jails – you can close your eyes and the peak is there.

After the third stage the glimpse is always available. But the glimpse is not the end – that is only the beginning.

9   The Means is the End

Osho,

Is vairagya, nonattachment, a method, a means, an intermediate stage, or an end in itself?

It is all – because means and ends are not two things. The way and the goal are not two things. The way is just the beginning of the goal, and the goal is just the ending of the way. So please, don't divide, and don't think in terms of the means being different from the end. Means *are* the end. Once you can conceive of this, the quality of your effort will change immediately.

Ordinarily mind is always concerned with the end; means are used, exploited, to reach the end. If you could avoid the means you would like to avoid them; if you could achieve the end directly without any means, if you could reach the goal without the way, without the path, you would like to do so. You would like to reach the goal immediately. The mind divides ends and means; end is meaningful, means are just necessary, they have to be suffered.

This is how the ordinary mind functions, and because of this whatsoever you do becomes a suffering – because you have to pass through the path, you have to use means, methods, and therein is all suffering. Happiness is in the goal, somewhere in the future, not here and now. Here and now will be means and the end will be somewhere else, somewhere in the future, tomorrow – so today will always be a suffering.

And remember, if your today is a suffering your tomorrow cannot be a happiness, because it is born of today, it comes out of this moment. The future comes out of the present, so whatsoever the present the same will remain in the future. If you are suffering now you will suffer then also. If you are suffering here you will find the hell there also – because who will find that heaven which you think is there? You? Your whole attitude creates the suffering.

So those who are on the spiritual path must be aware of this tendency of the mind. Forget the end and look at the means as if they are the end, and enjoy them as if they are the goal. Then the very path becomes blissful, the very journey itself becomes blissful. Every step becomes blissful, because you are not waiting for the bliss, for the next step. And out of this blissful step the next is going to be born – it will be more blissful. The tomorrow will be more blissful if today is blissful, and the bliss will grow.

We are doing meditations. These meditations are means, but they are goals also; so don't try to exploit them, otherwise you will be in a hurry, you will constantly think of how to be finished with them and reach the goal. Then you will never be able to be finished with them and the goal will always remain illusory, always like the horizon, always distant. And the more you move ahead, the goal will also move ahead in the same proportion.

Ends and means are not two things. Don't divide. The end is just the flowering of the means, the end is just the realization of the means. The end is hidden in the means, just like the tree is hidden in the seed. The seed is the tree. Don't look at the seed as if the seed has some secondary importance and the tree is meaningful and significant, and you can avoid the seed. If you avoid the seed the tree will never be there. Take care of the seed, love the seed, give soil to it, prepare the ground, and help the seed to grow. It will become the tree. It is already the tree unmanifest.

So let me say it in this way: means are the unmanifest end, and end is the manifest means. Means are seeds, and ends will be the trees, the flowering – so love the means as the end.

Vairagya is all, nonattachment is all. It is the beginning, it is the middle, it is the end. It is a method, it is an intermediate stage, it is the goal. Desirelessness is the end – but the end must be there in the beginning, only then can it grow. So desirelessness is both the first step and the last also. Of course the quality will differ. In the first step the desirelessness will be with effort, in the inter-mediate stage desirelessness will have become unconscious effort. In the beginning it will be conscious effort, you will have to do it; in the middle it will start happening, it will have become unconscious effort. Effort will be there, but indirect, unconscious. In the end it will be spontaneous, effort will have completely disappeared. But desirelessness is the same. Desirelessness in the beginning is with conscious effort, in the middle is with unconscious effort, in the end is effortless.

Avoid this tendency to divide, to cut things, and see that every phenomenon is a continuity, everything is joined together. Even those things which look opposite are also joined together, they are also polarities. Develop this way of looking at things – that will be very helpful. For those who are really sincerely interested in traveling this inner path, this approach of nondividing is a must.

The second question:

Osho,

Are there really discrete stages on the way to the ultimate happening, as this Upanishad seems to suggest, or does this happening occur suddenly and unexpectedly? Is it a matter of long conscious effort, or of a sudden total surrender to existence?

It is both. You have to make all effort that is possible, that you can do. No stone should be left unturned, no energies should be left unused. You must get totally involved. You are required to work as a unit, only then the flowering, the happening, will become possible. But that doesn't mean that it is an outcome of your effort; just by your effort it is not going to happen. This is a little delicate and you will have to be very penetrating about it, then only will you understand.

The Means Is the End | 181

Look at it in this way. You see a person walking on the street. Suddenly you have a feeling that you remember the face or you feel that you even know the name, and you say it is just on the tip of your tongue, but it is not coming. The more effort you make the more frustrated you feel – it is not coming. But you cannot leave it at that, because you have the feeling that you know this face, you know the name. And there is even this feeling that somewhere, just in the corner of the mind, the name is waiting, you have only to recall it.

You make all effort, you try in every way. You close your eyes, you contemplate, you ponder over it, you try to associate, you go into the past, you start feeling for some key, some clue, but nothing happens. You get frustrated, bored; you leave the whole effort, and you go into the garden and start working, or you start smoking, or you take a cup of tea. Suddenly the name is there, suddenly the memory has come, suddenly you have recognized.

Now two things are happening. One: you are making every effort possible, but it is not coming through the effort. Then you leave all the effort, and then it comes. Effort is needed but is not enough. If you don't make any effort it will not come when you go to the garden or when you take a cup of tea. If you have not made total effort it is not going to come. And if you make just the effort – total even – then too it is not going to come. So total effort is needed, then total relaxation also – then it will bubble up.

Many Nobel prizes have been given for certain discoveries which happened in this way. One Nobel prize winner was working on the inner structure of the human cell, the lymph cell. He was working for years, contemplating, brooding, making many experiments, and nothing was happening, every effort was a failure. After many years of research, effort, failure, one night suddenly he had a dream, and in the dream he saw the structure, the very structure he was looking for, the structure of the human cell, just as if a magnified picture was there. He got up. Immediately he drew the drawing and then he worked on it, and it proved that the dream was true.

But remember, *you* are not going to have this dream, it cannot happen to you. It happened after so many years of effort. The conscious was exhausted. The conscious did everything that could be done and then the conscious was tired, the conscious mind was finished, the conscious accepted the failure. When the conscious is exhausted the unconscious comes into focus and starts working – but it comes only when the conscious is exhausted. If the conscious is still hoping, if the conscious is still trying, then the unconscious will not function. And this is one of the basic laws of the human psyche: that if you want the unconscious to function, exhaust the conscious completely.

Effort will not lead you to enlightenment, but without effort no one has ever achieved it. This may look like a paradox. It is not, it is a simple law.

Buddha tried for six years continuously, and no man has tried as totally as Buddha did. He made every effort possible, he went to every master available. There was not a single master Buddha did not go to. He surrendered to every master, and whatsoever was said he did so perfectly that even the master started feeling jealous. And every master finally had to say to Buddha, "This is all I can teach. And if nothing is happening I cannot blame you, because you are doing everything so perfectly. I am helpless. You will have to move to some other teacher."

This rarely happens because disciples never do everything so perfectly, so the master can always say, "Because you are not doing well, that's why nothing is happening." But Buddha was doing so well, so absolutely well, that no master could say to him, "You are not doing well." So they had to accept defeat. They had to say, "This is all we can teach, and you have done it and nothing is happening, so it is better you move to some other master. You don't belong to me."

Buddha moved for six years, and he followed even absurd techniques when they were taught to him. Somebody said "Fast," so for months he fasted. For six months he was continuously fasting, just taking a very small quantity of food every fifteen days, only twice a month. He became so weak that he was simply a skeleton. All flesh disappeared, he looked like a dead man. He became so weak that he couldn't even walk. He finally became so weak that he would close his eyes to meditate and he would fall down in a fit.

One day he was taking a bath in the river Niranjana, just near Bodhgaya, and he was so weak that he couldn't cross the river. He fell down in the river and he thought that he was going to be drowned; it was the last moment, death had come. He was so weak he couldn't swim. Then suddenly he caught hold of a branch of a tree and remained there. And there for the first time the thought came to his mind, "If I have become so weak that I cannot cross this ordinary small river in summertime when the water has gone completely, when there is no more water and it is very small, just a little stream – if I cannot cross this little stream, how can I cross this big ocean of the world, *bhavasagar?* How can I transcend this world? It seems impossible. I am doing something stupid. What to do?"

He came out of the river in the evening and sat under a tree, which became the bodhi tree, and that evening when the moon was coming up – it was a full moon night – he realized that every effort is useless. He realized that nothing can be achieved, the very idea of achievement is nonsense. He had done everything. He was finished with the world, with the world of desires. He was a king and he had known every desire, he had lived every desire. He was finished with them, there was nothing to be achieved, there was nothing worthwhile. And then for six years he had been trying all austerities, all efforts, all meditations, yoga, everything, and nothing was happening. So he said, "Now there is nothing more except to die. There is nothing to be achieved, and every concept of achievement is nonsense; human desire is but futile."

So he dropped all effort that evening. He sat under the tree, relaxed, with no effort, no goal, nowhere to go, nothing to be achieved, nothing worth achieving. When you are in such a state of mind, mind relaxes – no future, no desire, no goal, nowhere to go, so what to do? He simply sat, he became just like the tree. The whole night he slept, and later on Buddha said that for the first time he really slept that night – because when effort is there it continues in sleep also.

A person who is earning money and who is after money goes on counting even in his dreams, a person who is after power and prestige and politics goes on fighting elections in his dreams. You all know that when you are sitting for an examination in the university or college, in sleep also you go on doing the examination; again and again you are in the examination hall answering questions. So whatsoever effort is there it continues in sleep – and there is always some effort for something or other.

That night there was no effort. Buddha said, "I slept for the first time in millions of lives. That was the first night that I slept." Such a sleep becomes samadhi. And in the morning when he awoke he saw the last star disappear. He looked. His eyes for the first time must have been mirrorlike, with no content, just vacant, empty, nothing to project. The last star was disappearing, and Buddha said, "With that disappearing star I also disappeared. The star was disappearing and I also disappeared" – because the ego can exist only with effort. If you make some effort ego is fed – you are doing something, you are reaching somewhere, you are achieving something. When there is no effort how can you exist?

The last star disappeared, "And," Buddha said, "I also disappeared. And then I looked, the sky was vacant; then I looked within, there was nothing – anatta, no self, there was no one."

It is said Buddha laughed at the whole absurdity. There was no one who could reach. There was no one who could reach the goal, there was no one who could achieve liberation – there was no one at all, no entity. Space was without, space was within. "And," he said, "at that moment of total effortlessness I achieved, I realized." But don't go to relax under a tree, and don't wait for the last star to disappear. And don't wait thinking that with the last star disappearing you will disappear. Those six years must precede. So this is the problem: without effort no one has ever achieved, with only effort no one has ever achieved. With effort coming to a point where it becomes effortlessness, realization has always been possible.

This is what I go on emphasizing for you to do: make as much effort as you can, and don't withhold any energy. Bring your total energy into it so you get exhausted, so the conscious mind cannot make any more effort. When the conscious cannot do anything, suddenly the unconscious reveals. And it reveals only when the conscious has become a total failure, only then it is needed – otherwise it goes on sleeping inside.

It is just like this. Every human body has three layers of energies. The first layer is only for day-to-day work: eating, sleeping, walking to the office, working in the office, coming home, fighting, making love, anger – routine. The first layer. It has not got very much energy, just routine energy.

The second layer is for emergency situations. Unless the first is exhausted the second is not available. You are tired. You have come from the office, the boss has been very insulting. You come home and the wife is very bad-tempered, the children are creating noise, and the whole house is a mess. You feel tired and dead, and suddenly you find that the house has caught fire, it is on fire. Tired-ness disappears immediately. You need not do anything, you don't even have to take a cup of coffee. Tiredness is no more. The house is on fire, and you have got so much energy that you can work the whole night. From where is this energy coming? The first layer is exhausted, and an emergency is there – the second layer becomes available.

And there is a third layer which is the real source, the source of all energy. You may call it the infinite source, the *élan vital*. When the second layer is also exhausted, only then the third becomes available. And when the third is available you are totally different: you have become divine, because now the source is infinite, you cannot exhaust it.

We live on the first layer and only sometimes in emergencies, accidents, in some dangerous situations where life is at stake, does the second become available. The third remains almost unavailable. All the effort in spiritual sadhana, discipline, is to exhaust the first. Then austerities, arduous efforts, are to exhaust the second. When the second is exhausted you fall into the ocean, and it can never be exhausted. And from that source, the original source – you may call it God, or whatsoever you like – from that original source, once a contact is made, you are totally different. This is what liberation means, this is what becoming infinite means, this is what Jesus used to call the kingdom of God.

But remember, you cannot just slip into it, it is not available. You have to exhaust the first layer and the second layer, only then it becomes available. Effort is needed to exhaust these layers, and then effortlessness is needed to enter the original source.

So the first thing to be understood: effort is needed, but effort alone is not enough – effort and then effortlessness, effort plus effortlessness. Effort precedes, and then effortlessness follows. Effortlessness is the peak of effort, it comes only when you have reached the peak. And this is so difficult to conceive that there are many misunderstandings.

In Japan, Zen, which is an offshoot of the Indian *dhyana*, says no effort is need-ed. And it is right. Because of this Zen has become very influential in the West. And the West has created its own Zen writers – they are Zen writers, not Zen masters. And it has much appeal; no effort is needed, you can become enlightened without any effort. So in the West there are many Zen writers, Zen painters, Zen haiku poets – and they are all bogus, because they have taken this idea.

This idea is very appealing, that there is no need of any effort. If there is no need of any effort, then as you are you are a master, you are enlightened, you have become a *siddha*. But then look at the Zen monasteries in Japan. If you read Zen scriptures, there it is written that there is no need of effort. But then go to the Zen monastery and look: for twenty years, thirty years, a seeker has to make all the efforts. Then the moment comes when that scripture becomes applicable – then, no effort.

Effort will lead you to no effort, and this is a basic law. You can understand if you try to observe your own life. For example, if in the day you have been working hard, sleep will be deep in the night. If you have been working hard, exerting hard, then sleep will be good. If you have slept well in the night, then in the morning you will be capable of doing much hard work again. Hard work is against relaxation, it is the opposite. This would be more logical – that you sleep the whole day, rest, and then in the night you fall into deeper sleep because you have been practicing sleep the whole day. This should be the logic – that a man who has been practicing sleep the whole day must sleep better in the night than others who have not been practicing so much.

Mulla Nasruddin once went to his doctor. He had a cold and had been coughing for many days. As he was entering his doctor's office he coughed. The doctor heard and said, "Nasruddin, it sounds better."

Nasruddin said, "Of course it must because I have been practicing for three months."

But logic is not life. If you sleep and rest the whole day you will not be able to rest at all in the night. That's what is happening with rich people in affluent societies. Insomnia is a luxury, not everybody can afford it. To attain insomnia you have to rest for the whole day. If you can afford that much rest, only then is insomnia possible. A poor man cannot afford it. He has to fall in deep sleep, he is helpless. He has been working hard the whole day.

But work is against rest, so it is not logical – but this is the logic of life. Life depends on opposites, life depends on opposite polarities. Logic is linear, life is polar. Logic moves in a line, life moves in a circle. So a person who has been relaxing will not be able to relax in the night, a person who has been working hard the whole day will be able to relax.

Or look at it from another angle. A person who is always loving, never angry, really cannot be loving. Ordinary logic will say that a person can be loving in the morning, loving in the noon, loving in the evening, loving in the night; always loving in summer, always loving in winter – every season, every moment loving. This love is not humanly possible, because the opposite is needed. He must sometimes become angry. That anger relaxes, that anger becomes the valley and then peaks of love can arise again.

If you want only peaks and no valleys, you are mad. Only peaks cannot exist. With every peak at least two valleys will be needed, and only between two valleys is one peak possible. So a person who is always loving is possible only in two ways. One is that he is not human. That means he must be a buddha, who can be always loving. But then his love cannot have any intensity, his love will be very silent. His love will not be like a peak, it will be just plain straight ground.

That's why a buddha's love can only be called compassion, it cannot be called love. There is no passion in it, it is compassion. There can be no intensity in it, because intensity comes from the opposite. A buddha is never angry, so from where can the intensity come?

In ordinary life you have to be angry, then you regain love. In marriage there is no need for the final divorce if every day you can divorce a little. In the morning divorce, in the evening remarriage, then things move beautifully. And if you go on postponing this everyday divorce then finally you will have to break, then separation is a must. Life is polarity, and this applies to everything. Effort plus effortlessness – they are the polar opposites. The ultimate is reached through effort and effortlessness, so don't cling to one – remember both.

Both the parties exist; there are a few persons who go on clinging to the method, effort, and then they go on making effort. Even if nirvana has been reached they cannot be stopped. They will go on breathing, they will say, "We cannot stop. Effort is needed." So even if God is standing before them they will go on doing chaotic breathing; they will not look, they will not look and see what has happened. They are too much attached to the method and the effort.

And then there is the other polar opposite party. They say, "If no effort is needed then why breathe at all?" So they are sitting just waiting for the last star to disappear so that they can become buddhas. Both are wrong. You have to breathe and you have to stop also. You have to make all efforts and then relax also. If these are both possible, only then will you create the rhythm through which every growth becomes possible.

The second thing: "Are there really discrete stages on the way to the ultimate happening, as this Upanishad seems to suggest?"

There are no stages. Life cannot be divided. But without division there is no possibility for you to understand. I call this part of my body my hand; this part of my body my head – but can they be divided? Where my head begins and where it ends – can you draw the line? Nowhere can the line be drawn. Where my legs end, where my hand ends – can you draw a line? No line can be drawn, because inside I am one – my hands, my legs, my head, they are one. But we have to divide to understand. Division is just to help understanding, it is not actual fact.

So this Upanishad is dividing, not because divisions are there, but because you will not be able to understand the whole. The whole will be too much, too complex. The whole will be incomprehensible, and understanding will not be possible. That's why the division into seven stages, and that's why there are so many divisions. You can divide in fourteen, you can divide in seventeen – you can divide into as many as you like. And theologians go on fighting about these divisions. They are workable, utilitarian – not existential.

Just feel your body, close your eyes and feel. Where are the divisions? It is one. But if your eyes are not functioning well you will go to the eye specialist. And you know that eyes are not separate, they are one with the body, so then why go to the eye specialist? You can go to any doctor. The eye specialist has tried to understand eyes...because eyes in themselves are such a big, such a complex phenomenon, that just to understand those eyes medical science has divided the body in parts. There are millions of parts in the body, and as science grows more divisions have to be made. But those divisions are just workable, utilitarian – *you* are not divided.

I have heard one story. Once it happened, one master had two disciples and they both were always competing. Who was the head, who was the chief disciple, was always the competition and the problem. And they were always competing with each other to gain the master's heart.

One summer afternoon the master was tired and was sleeping. The disciples wanted to serve him, to massage his body, so the master said, "Okay. Number one, you take my left side. Number two, you take my right side and massage." The master fell asleep. They drew a line with chalk on his body, because one should not enter into the other's territory.

But it happened the master was not aware that he had been divided. He was fast asleep, and he didn't know that now he was not one, but two. So he moved in his sleep, and put his right leg on his left. The disciple to whom the left leg belonged said, "Take away your right leg. Remove it immediately! You are interfering with my work. This is a transgression!"

But the other said, "I cannot remove it. I have not put it on your leg. And if you have any courage, then remove it yourself and see what happens!"

Now they were standing with two sticks, and they were almost going to beat the master. Suddenly the master became aware that something was wrong, so he asked, "What is happening?"

Both said, "You need not interfere. Remain silent and go to sleep. We will decide by ourselves."

All divisions are workable, life remains one. The path and the goal and the stages, they are just to help you, so don't take them dogmatically and don't take them literally. These seven stages are just to help you, to give you a view of the whole path. When you have understood forget that they are seven. But until you have understood follow the division. When you have understood forget the division – it is one progression, one flow.

And thirdly: "Does this happening occur suddenly and unexpectedly?"

Both things can be said. It cannot be predicted, so it happens suddenly. Nobody can say when it will happen. My own disciples go on asking me, "When? Give the date, the day, the month, the year!" And I have to go on lying to them. I go on saying, "Soon!" Soon doesn't mean anything. And soon is a beautiful word, because I need never change it. Whenever you ask I will say, "Soon!"

The happening is unpredictable because it is so vast a phenomenon. And it is not mechanical, it is not mathematical, so you cannot conclude about it. And it is very mysterious; when it has happened, only then you know that it has happened. So in a sense, because it is unpredictable it is always sudden. Even you don't know when it will happen. Suddenly one day when it has happened you become aware that it has happened. Not even a single moment before will you be aware that this is going to happen. You will become aware only when it has happened already. Then you will feel that you are no more the same, the man who was there has disappeared and a new man is there in his place – somebody new. You are unacquainted, you cannot recognize yourself. There has been a gap, the old continuity has been broken and something new has come into its place.

Even your master cannot predict it. He may become aware that something is going to happen, but he cannot predict it. There are problems – because even the prediction will change the whole situation. This is the problem, even the prediction will change it. If I become aware that something is going to happen to you tomorrow morning, I cannot say it because that will change the whole situation. If I say, "Tomorrow morning this is going to happen," you will become tense and you will start expecting and you will start waiting. You will not be able to sleep in the night. Then the whole thing is finished, then it is not going to happen tomorrow morning.

Even if your master becomes aware...because there are signs that show that something is going to happen. Your master can see that you are pregnant, he can feel, but it is not such a fixed affair that within nine months the child will be born. You may take nine years, you may take nine lives, you may not take even nine days; even nine moments may be enough. It depends, and it depends on such multidimensional things that nothing can be said. And if something is said, the very assertion will change the whole situation. So the master has to wait, just watch and not say anything.

In this sense it is sudden, but in another sense it is not sudden, because you have to make efforts for it, you have to prepare. You have to prepare the ground, you have to open the doors. The guest may come suddenly, but if your doors are closed he may come and go back. So you have to open the doors, you have to clean the house, you have to prepare food for the guest – you have to be ready. You have to watch and wait at the door – any moment the guest can come.

Jesus goes on telling one anecdote many times. Once it happened, a great landlord went on a journey. He told all his slaves and servants, "Be alert constantly. Even in the night the house must be ready because I can come any moment. In the morning, in the afternoon, in the evening, at midnight – any moment I can come, and my house must be ready, waiting for me. So twenty-four hours you have to watch and wait. Don't go to sleep!"

And so the servants had to wait and watch. There was no difference between day and night – the master could come any moment.

Jesus used to say, "Your master also can come any moment – you have to be ready. And if you are ready, your readiness also becomes a factor for his coming soon. If you are completely ready he may come back from midjourney. If your whole being is calling him, inviting him, he may come this very moment."

The happening can happen any moment if you are ready. It is sudden because unpredictable; it is sudden because you cannot plan, calculate; it is sudden because it is not mechanical. But still you have to prepare for it, you have to be ready for it, and you have to do much before it can happen.

It is just as if you sow a seed in the ground. You prepare the ground and sow the seed – the right seed in the right season in a right place – and then wait. The sprouting will be sudden, you cannot determine it. You cannot say that on Mon-day morning the sprout will be there. It may not be, it may be, because millions of factors are working. Now scientists say that even music helps. If somebody is dancing and singing near that ground where you have sown the seed, it may help the seed to sprout quickly. If the moon is rising it will help the seed to sprout soon. If the moon is declining it will take more time.

You may not be aware that full moon night is different from any other night. More children are born on full moon night, more than on any other night. The highest number of children born is on the full moon night, and the lowest number is on the no-moon night. That factor goes on working; the whole constellation goes on working – every star is a factor. Even a beggar sitting there near your house and singing will help. If somebody passes, sad, miserable, the seed is affected; that sadness hinders.

There are millions of factors, unpredictable, complex, mysterious – but still you have to prepare everything. So don't wait for the sudden. "Sudden" doesn't mean that you need not do anything and it will happen any moment, suddenly. You will have to prepare, and then too it will happen suddenly. Your preparation will help, but it cannot plan, it cannot force.

The third question:

Osho,

In the past hypnosis has been tried on me, but I could not be hypnotized. Please explain why many persons are not hypnotizable.

This will be important for you to understand. Ordinarily it is thought that those persons who cannot be hypnotized are powerful. This is absolutely wrong – and I say absolutely. The stronger the person the more easily he is hypnotized. The second wrong conception is that a very intelligent person cannot be hypnotized. That too is absolutely wrong. The more stupid a person the less is the possibility of hypnotizing him. You cannot hypnotize an idiot – impossible. You cannot hypnotize a madman – impossible. The more intelligent a person the more easily he can be hypnotized.

Why? – because hypnosis needs cooperation; the basic factor is cooperation, your cooperation. The idiot cannot understand what you are demanding, what type of cooperation; the madman cannot understand what you are demanding. Only an intelligent person can cooperate, and hypnosis is possible only when you cooperate. So if you are paranoid, schizophrenic, neurotic, you cannot cooperate. If you are very much afraid, a fear complex is there, you cannot cooperate.

A person who can trust can be hypnotized easily. A person who cannot trust anybody cannot be hypnotized – because the person who is hypnotizing is not using any force on you. This is again a wrong conception, the third, that the hypnotist is using some force. No, not at all. The hypnotist has no force to use; the hypnotist is only using *your* force, so you have to cooperate. If you don't cooperate nobody can hypnotize you. And cooperation needs trust, because you will be unconscious and you don't know what this man who is hypnotizing will do to you.

So look, I have been experimenting on many things. A Western woman is more easily hypnotized than an Eastern woman, because the Eastern woman is always afraid of sex. When she is unconscious, who knows what this hypnotist may do? Western women in that sense have become freer, less afraid. They can be hypnotized more easily.

A person who is guilty about something is very difficult to hypnotize, be-cause he is always afraid that when he is unconscious the thing he is hiding may come up. A person who has committed some sin, or thinks he has committed some sin and is hiding it, will be very difficult to hypnotize. Only a simple, innocent person can be hypnotized, because he has nothing to hide. You cannot bring anything out; he has no secrets. If you have secrets and you don't want them to be exposed you cannot trust anybody – because hypnosis means that your unconscious is available to the hypnotist. He can penetrate deep down, he can bring out anything that you are hiding.

So those persons are not hypnotizable who fall into these categories. The less guilty and less afraid, and the more intelligent, trusting and cooperative a person is, the more hypnotizable. So don't think that if you cannot be hypnotized you are something great. You may be simply ill, pathological. If you can be hypnotized you show a quality of trust and you show that you are imaginative. You show that suggestions can catch you and your imagination can work through them. You are an imaginatively creative person.

But remember that unless you cooperate nobody can hypnotize you – nobody. Even if Mesmer comes he cannot hypnotize you if you don't cooperate. Your cooperation is needed, your total willingness is needed. And then too you are not completely in the control of the hypnotist. A part of you remains alert even then, and if the hypnotist is going to force you to do something against yourself you will suddenly come out of hypnosis.

It happened, one of my brothers was serving in an office. He trusts me, and I wanted him to leave that service. But he is such a person that whatsoever the situation he does not like to change it. He was not getting good pay, the office was in every way useless, there was no possibility for creative growth, so I was saying to him, "Leave that office." But he is the type that wants to continue whatsoever is going on with no change. So I hypnotized him.

He trusts me in every way, but that day he was mistrustful, because he was aware that if he was hypnotized I was going to say, "Leave that service!" Every-thing was okay, he followed, but a part of him must have remained aware, alert, in case I suggested that thing. So he followed everything, he didn't even feel the pin. I tested in every way and he was hypnotized completely, there was no possibility that he wasn't. And then I said, "Leave that service!" Immediately he came out of hypnosis and he said, "Don't say that!"

Nothing, even in hypnosis, can be forced on you if you are not willing; even after hypnosis has happened nothing can be forced upon you. So if something can be forced that shows that unconsciously you were willing.

For example, a woman who cannot think of kissing any man other than her lover – if it is suggested to her under hypnosis to kiss somebody else, and if really she does not want to kiss anybody, immediately she will come out of hypnosis. But if she goes and kisses the other person, and then after she has come out of hypnosis you tell her and she says, "What could I do? I was hypnotized," then this is just a trick – unconsciously she wanted to kiss him.

Consciously she is alert and she will say, "No, I cannot touch any other man than my own lover. I belong to one," but this is only conscious – unconsciously she must have been hankering. Only then, in hypnosis, can this be forced; otherwise in hypnosis also this cannot be forced, it is impossible. You have to cooperate with whatsoever the hypnotist forces on you. The moment your cooperation is taken back, immediately hypnosis disappears. So many reasons are possible why a person is not hypnotizable, but don't think of it as a good quality. Become more imaginative, cooperative, trusting, and hypnosis can be helpful.

In the old days, particularly in the East, hypnosis was used in every ashram. The master used it in every way to help you, because consciously you may take years to do a particular thing but in hypnosis, through hypnosis, within seconds it can be done.

Unnecessary effort can be saved. But only masters were allowed to hypnotize. Hypnosis remained a secret science in the East; it was not used publicly because there are possibilities of misusing it.

In the West Mesmer brought hypnosis into the market, and then everything which was associated with it became condemned. But now again the wheel is turning. In the West also universities are studying it; there are scientific projects to study hypnosis, and new research is again bringing hypnosis to the status of a science. It can be used now, it is already used, in hospitals in surgery – because there is no need to give an anesthetic; that is destructive to the body, it unnecessarily harms the body. There is no need, simple hypnosis can make you unconscious. There is no need for chloroform or any poison, any gas, to make you unconscious; only your cooperation is needed. And any operation is possible under hypnosis. Even if it takes hours, even if many hours are needed, hypnosis is enough, no anesthetic is needed.

Many hospitals have started using it. Childbirth can be made absolutely painless; not only that, it can easily be made pleasurable, ecstatic, under hypnosis. The mother just has to cooperate and trust, and then she can be hypnotized and it can be suggested that there will be no pain when the child comes out of the womb, but rather on the contrary there will be intense pleasure. And it is possible that the woman, the mother giving birth, can have such a deep orgasm through birth that no sexual orgasm can be any comparison to it – because the same mechanism is involved. The same mechanism which gives the sexual orgasm, the bliss that comes through sex, is involved, and involved more totally. The child passes through the same passage.

Once the woman feels – and the suggestion is there – that this is going to be a very ecstatic feeling, she will achieve a peak. And I think that in the past women used to achieve that peak; they have lost that capacity. Not only lost – birth has become painful. This is again a suggestion.

You can see: the more civilized a society, the more pain in childbirth; the less civilized a society, the less pain. In India there are many primitives who don't know any pain in childbirth, no pain at all. And there are some tribes on the earth even today in Tibet and in other interior parts of Mongolia, where women go simply mad in ecstasy when the child is born. And that may be the reason why every woman deeply longs to be a mother. No man longs to be a father, he wants to be a husband; no woman simply longs to be a wife, she wants to be a mother. That's a basic difference.

I think the reason is that in the old days, in very ancient days, women used to achieve the supreme pleasure of their life through childbirth. That has remained in their unconscious still – they want to be a mother. A father is just a formality. You don't achieve anything through becoming a father; you don't give any birth, you are just a spectator. So the father is just a social convention. The mother is a natural phenomenon. The father can be discarded any day, it is just institutional; the mother is a natural phenomenon.

Every woman longs to be a mother, only then does she feel fulfilled. This feeling must be based on some ecstasy that was there in the beginning and which women have lost. It is just a suggestion that childbirth is painful, but through centuries it has gone deep. It can be changed.

Many illnesses can simply disappear through hypnosis because really they don't exist, they are just in your mind. Fifty percent of illnesses are just in the mind, they don't have any organic existence. They can simply disappear. There is no need for any medicine, any injection or any "pathies" to be worked on you, because then those medicines poison you, your body goes toxic, and then you suffer. You suffer less from your illnesses, more from your medicines. And there are so many doctors that you can escape death but you cannot escape the doctors – they will kill you in the end. Whatsoever you do they will kill you. Fifty percent of diseases can simply disappear from the earth.

Hypnosis is a great force, but with every force there is danger – it can be misused. But just because a force can be misused you need not go against it...because anything can be misused, and if it can be misused that shows it can be used also. So become more vulnerable, become more suggestible, become more available to hypnosis. That means you will become more intelligent, more cooperative, more trusting.

10   Sublime is the
Spontaneous

There are two kinds of nonattachment:

the ordinary and the sublime.

That attitude of nonattachment to the objects of desire in which the seeker knows that he is neither the doer nor the enjoyer,

neither the restrained nor the restrainer, is called ordinary

nonattachment. He knows that whatever faces him in this life

is the result of the deeds of his past life.

Whether in pleasure or in pain, he can do nothing.

Indulgence is but a disease and affluence of all kinds a storehouse of adversity. Every union leads inevitably to separation.

The ignorant suffer the maladies of mental anxiety.

All material things are perishable, because time is constantly

devouring them. Through the understanding of scriptural precepts, one's faith in material things is uprooted

and one's mind freed of them.

This is called ordinary nonattachment.

When thoughts like: "I am not the doer, my past deeds are the doers, or God himself is the doer," cease to worry the seeker,

a state of silence, equilibrium and peace is attained.

This is called sublime nonattachment.

On the path, in the search, every step has two sides: the beginning of the step, and the conclusion. The beginning will always be with conscious effort, it is bound to be so. A struggle will be there, constant need to be alert will be there. Sometimes you will fall, sometimes you will fall asleep, sometimes you will forget, sometimes you will go astray. Again and again you will have to remember, come back to the path. Again and again you will have to make more intense effort to be conscious.

So the beginning of every step will be struggle. There will be ups and there will be downs. Sometimes you will feel very miserable, frustrated; whenever the contact with the method is lost, whenever you have gone astray, frustration will happen, you will feel depressed, sad, lost. There will be moments of intense happiness also. Whenever you regain the control again, whenever even for moments you become the master, whenever even for small glimpses you become capable, you will feel intense joy spreading all over your being.

Peaks and valleys will be there. They will disappear only when the conscious effort has disappeared, when the method is no more a method, when the method has become your very consciousness, when you need not remember it, when you can completely forget it and it still grows, continuous, flows, when you need not maintain it, when you need not even think of it – and then it becomes spontaneous, *sahaj*. This is the end aspect of every step. Remember this: through constant practice a moment comes when you can drop the practice completely, and unless you can drop the practice you have not attained.

Taoist masters have used many dimensions: poetry, painting, and many other crafts have been used as training grounds. Painting has been used for centuries in China and Japan. Taoist painting has a principle, and that principle is that first one should become proficient in painting, in the technique of painting – it takes many years – and then for a few years one has to drop painting completely. One has to forget that one is a painter; throw the brushes, colors, inks, and just drop from the mind that one has learned something. For a few years one has to be completely away from painting. When the thought has dropped, then again the master says, "Now you start." Now this man is not a technician. He knows the technique but he is not a technician, because there is no need to be aware of the technique. Now he can paint like a small child. The effort has ceased, to paint has become effortless. Only then master-teachers are born.

I remember one story I would like to tell you. It happened once in Burma that a great temple was to be built, and the main door had to be something unique on the earth. So many painters, Zen masters, Taoist masters, were asked, and the one who was the greatest was invited to design the door. That great master had a habit that whenever he would paint something, design something, his chief disciple would sit by his side, and whenever he would complete the design he would ask the chief disciple whether it was okay. If the disciple said no he would throw the design and he would again work on it. Unless the disciple said, "Right, this is the thing," he would go on.

Designing this main gate of the temple became a problem, because the chief disciple continued to say no. The master painted at least one hundred designs. Many months passed. He would work for weeks, and when the design was complete he would look at the disciple who was sitting beside him. The disciple would shake his head and he would say, "No," and the master would put aside the design and start again. He was also worried, "What is going to happen? When will this design be complete?" – and he had been doing hard work such as he had never done in his life.

Then one day it happened. The ink with which he was painting was almost finished, so he told the disciple to go out of the house and prepare more ink. The disciple went out to prepare the ink, and when he came back he started dancing in ecstasy and he said, "Now this is the thing! But why couldn't you paint it before?"

The master said, "Now I know. I was also worried, what was happening? Now I know, your presence was the disturbance. In your presence I remained the technician. I was aware that I was doing something, effort was there; I was conscious of the effort, and I was thinking, expecting, that this time you would say yes. That was the disturbance. I could not be spontaneous. When you went out I could forget you, and when I could forget you I could forget myself also."...Because the self is the reaction to the other. If the other is in your consciousness you will remain the ego. They both drop simultaneously; when the other has disappeared, the ego has disappeared.

"And when I was not," the master said, "the painting flowed by itself. This design I have not done. All those hundred designs you rejected were my doings. This design is through Tao, through nature; it has dropped from the cosmos itself. I was just a vehicle. I could forget and become a vehicle."

When you can forget the method, the effort, the self, the other, when everything has been dropped and you have become simply a flow of energy, spontaneous, then really something is attained – not before. And look at the difference in the Eastern and Western attitudes about painting, and about everything else also. In the West you have to make conscious effort and bring the effort to a peak. You become a technician and the other part is missing. In the East you have to become a technician, and then drop that whole technicality and become again innocent, simple, as if you were never trained.

Once somebody asked Winston Churchill, one of the greatest orators the West has produced, "Don't you get afraid of the audience? Thousands of people staring at you – don't you get afraid, scared? Don't you get a little fear inside?"

Churchill said, "This has been my constant practice: that whenever I stand to speak I look at the audience and I think, 'So many fools!' The moment this thought comes to my mind I am okay, then I don't worry."

Somebody asked the same question of a Zen master, Rinzai: "You speak to thousands, don't you ever get worried about it? Don't you ever get scared? Don't you ever get an inner trembling? – because so many persons are present, judging, observing, looking at you."

Rinzai said, "Whenever I look at people I say, 'I am sitting there also. Only I am in this hall.' Then there is no problem. I am alone, these people are also me."

This is the Eastern and Western difference. Churchill represents the West: if others are fools then you are okay, then the ego is strengthened. You don't worry about them, because who are they? – nobodies. And Rinzai says: The other is not. They are just me, my forms. I am alone. I am the speaker and I am also the audience. Then what is the fear?"

In your bathroom when you are alone you can be a good singer – everybody is, almost everybody. And bring the same man out of the bathroom, let him stand here, and the moment he sees you he is no more capable of singing – even humming becomes impossible. The fear grips the throat; he is not alone, the others are there, they will judge. The moment the other is there fear has entered. But the same man was humming beautifully, singing beautifully in the bathroom – nobody was there.

The same happens when you can see in the other your own self. Then the whole earth is your bathroom; you can sing, you can dance. The other is no more there, there is nobody to judge. Through these eyes you are looking, and through others' eyes also you are looking. Then it becomes a cosmic play of one energy in many forms. But the ultimate of any method is to become methodless, the ultimate of every technique is to become nontechnical, innocent. All effort is only to attain an effortless spontaneity.

There are two kinds of nonattachment: the ordinary and the sublime.

The ordinary is the first aspect of vairagya, nonattachment. The sublime is the spontaneous, the end; the other aspect of the same when things have be-come spontaneous.

That attitude of nonattachment to the objects of desire in which the seeker knows that he is neither the doer nor the enjoyer, neither the restrained nor the restrainer, is called ordinary nonattachment.

The emphasis is on the word *knows*. He has to maintain that, he has to remember it: "I am not the doer. I am just a witness. Whatsoever happens I am not involved. I am an outsider, just a spectator." But this has to be remembered, this has to be maintained. This point must not be lost. And it is very difficult to remember it constantly. To remember even for a few minutes is difficult, be-cause for many many lives you have been the doer, constantly you have been the enjoyer.

When you are eating you are the eater, when you are walking you are the walker, when you are listening you are the listener. You have never made any effort to remember that while doing anything you are not the doer but the witness. While eating, try it. The food is going into the body, not into you. It cannot go into you, there is no way, because you are the consciousness and the food cannot enter consciousness. It will go into the body, it will become the blood and the bone, whatsoever the body needs, but *you* remain a witness.

So while sitting at your table eating your food, don't be the eater. You have never been the eater; this is just an old habit, an old conditioning. Look at the eater, the body, and the eaten, the food, and you be the third. You just witness, you just hover above, you just look from a distance. Stand aloof and see your body eating, the food being eaten, and don't get involved in it. But you can maintain it only for a few seconds – again you will become the eater. It has been such a long, long conditioning; it will take time to break it.

You are walking on the street. Don't be the walker, just watch the body walking. For a few seconds you may remember; again you will forget and you will enter in the body and become the walker. But even if for a few seconds you can maintain it, you can remember that you are not the walker, then those few seconds will become satori-like, those few seconds will be weightless, those few seconds will be of a joy such as you have never known. And if this can happen for a few seconds, why not for ever?

Somebody is insulting you – it will be more difficult than with walking or eating to remember that you are the witness. One Indian mystic, Ram Teerth, went to America in the beginning of this century. He never used the word 'I', he would always use the name Ram. If he was hungry he would say, "Ram is hungry." It looked unfamiliar and strange. If there was a headache he would say, "Ram has a headache."

One day it happened that a few people insulted him. He came back laughing and his disciples asked, "Why are you laughing?"

So he said, "Ram was insulted very much, and I enjoyed. I was standing out of Ram and looking. Ram was in much difficulty; much inconvenience, discomfort, was there in Ram."

You become an object of your own consciousness. This is coming out of the body, out of the ego, out of the mind. This is difficult not because it is unnatural, this is difficult only because of a long conditioning. You may have observed that small babies in the beginning never say 'I'; they say, "Baby is hungry." They seem to be witnessing the phenomenon. But we train them to use the 'I' because it's not good to say, "Baby is hungry," or "Baby wants to play." We train them to use the 'I'.

'I' is not existential, 'I' is a social entity; it has to be created. It is just like language: it is needed because if people go on speaking like babies or like Ram Teerth, if like Ram Teerth people go on saying their names, it will be very difficult to say whether they are talking about themselves or about somebody else. It will create confusion. If you say, "I am hungry," immediately it is meant that *you* are hungry. If you say, "Ram is hungry," if people know that you are Ram then it's okay; otherwise they will think somebody else is hungry, not you. And if everybody uses it, it will create confusion.

It is a social convenience to use the 'I'; but this social convenience becomes truth, it becomes the center of your being, a false thing. The 'I' never existed, can never exist. But just because of social utility the child is trained, the consciousness becomes fixed around a center which is just utilitarian, not existential – and then you live in an illusion. And the whole life of a person who has not come to know that there is no ego will be false, because it is based on a false foundation.

To be a witness means to drop the 'I'. The moment you can drop the 'I', immediately you become the witness. Then there is nothing else to do, you can only be the witness. This 'I' creates the problem. Hence the emphasis of all religions to become egoless, to be egoless, to be humble, not to be proud, not to be conceited about it. Even if you have to use it, use it as a symbol. You have to use it, but use it knowingly – knowing that this is just a social convenience.

That attitude of nonattachment to the objects of desire in which the seeker knows that he is neither the doer nor the enjoyer, neither the restrained nor the restrainer, is called ordinary nonattachment.

When you become capable of remembering that you are the witness, this is the first stage of nonattachment.

He knows that whatever faces him in this life is the result of the deeds of his past life.

Try to see that whatsoever action is there, it is not arising out of you but rather arising out of the chain of actions you have done in the past. Try to understand this distinction clearly. Whenever you do something – if somebody insults you, you think that the reaction is arising from you. That is wrong. It is arising not from you but from the chain of your mind which has come from the past. You have been trained in the past that this is an insulting word.

I will tell you one anecdote. Kahlil Gibran writes somewhere that one man came to Lebanon. He was not a Lebanese, he didn't know the language of the country; he was totally a stranger. The moment he entered Lebanon he saw a very big palatial building, many people coming in and out, so he also entered to see what was going on there. It was a big hotel, but he thought, "It seems the king has given a party – so many distinguished guests coming out, going in, and everybody is being served." And, as the human mind works, he thought, "It may be that because I have come to Lebanon, just for my reception, in my honor, the king is doing something."

The moment he entered he was received by the manager, he was placed at a table and food was served. He enjoyed it and he was very happy, he had never been so happy in his life. And then when he had finished his food, drink, and everything, he started thanking them. But they could not understand his language and he could not understand their language. They were placing a bill before him – it was a hotel – but he couldn't understand. He thought, "They are giving in writing, 'It was so good of you to accept the invitation. You have honored us.'" So he took the bill, put it in his pocket, and thanked them again.

Then the manager became disturbed: either he was insane, because he was talking in such strange sounds they couldn't understand, or he was a rascal just trying to deceive. So he was brought to the owner of the hotel. The man thought, "Now they are bringing me to the chief minister or the prime minister of the country." He again started thanking them. It was no use, so he was brought to the court.

When he entered the palatial building of the court, bigger than the hotel, he thought, "Now this is the palace of the king, and he himself is going to receive me in person." Again he started bowing down and thanking, and the magistrate thought, "This man is either mad or a perfect rascal," so he punished him. And it was the punishment of that country in such cases that the man should be forced to sit on a donkey backwards, and a plaque should be hung around his neck on which it was written: "This man has committed the crime of deception, and everybody should be aware."

He was painted black, and he enjoyed it very much because he thought, "A strange country, with strange manners, but they are paying every attention to me." Naked he was placed on a donkey, a plaque was hung around his neck. He enjoyed it. Then the donkey started moving all over town just to make the whole town aware that this man was a criminal. And a crowd, children and many cripples followed, and he enjoyed. He thought, "These people are just following in my honor." The children were enjoying it and he was also very happy and joyful, but only one sadness was in his heart: "Nobody knows what is happening to me in my country. I wish they could become aware of how I have been received. And they will not believe me when I go back, they will say that I am just inventing stories."

Then suddenly he saw a man in the crowd who belonged to his country. He was very happy and he said, "Look how beautifully they have received me! This is not only in my honor, but my country is honored." But the other man who knew the language of this country, Lebanon, simply disappeared in the crowd, hiding his face, because he knew what was happening. This was not an honor. And the man on the donkey thought, "Jealousy, nothing else. This man is jealous. They have honored me and they have not honored him."

You have a mind trained through many lives. Things come out of that, not out of you. You have a long chain of actions; whenever a new act is born in you it comes out of that chain. It is a new link in that chain; it is born out of that chain, not out of you. When somebody insults you, you get angry. That anger comes from your past angers, not from you.

This difference has to be noted, because it will help you to become a witness. And that is what is meant by living moment-to-moment – that is the moment. Don't allow the chain of the past to react. Put aside the chain and let your consciousness function directly. Don't be influenced by the past, respond here and now, directly. The whole life will be different if you can act out of the present moment. But all your actions are almost always out of the past, never out of the present. And action that is born out of the present is nonbinding, an action that is born out of the past chain is a new link in your bondage. But first one has to become aware.

When you get angry just look: from where is that anger coming? from you or just from your past memories? You have been insulted before, you have been angry before – that memory is there waiting, that memory works like a wound. Again something happens and that memory starts functioning, that memory creates the same reaction again. If you watch and observe for twenty-four hours you will see that you are just a mechanical robot, you are functioning out of memories, out of the past. The past is dead, and the dead is so weighty on you that your life is crushed under it. Look at the chain. This sutra says:

He knows that whatever faces him in this life is the result of the deeds of his past life.

Not only that his reactions come from his past memories, but others' actions in connection with him are also part of his past actions.

It happened, Buddha became enlightened and one of his cousins, Devadatta, tried to poison him, tried to kill him, in many ways tried to murder him. He was always a failure, fortunately. Somebody asked Buddha, "Why don't you do something about it? This man is constantly trying in many ways to kill you."

Once he brought a mad elephant and left the elephant near Buddha. The elephant was mad, in a rage. The elephant came running, but suddenly just near Buddha it stopped, bowed down and closed its eyes as if it was meditating. So somebody asked, "Why don't you do something about this man? And why is he doing such things?"

Buddha said, "Because of my past actions. I must have hurt him in the past. He is simply reacting out of that chain. It is not his doing, I must have done some wrong to him in the past. And I must have done something good to this elephant in the past, otherwise there was no possibility…. And I should remain now a witness. If I do something again in connection with Devadatta, then again a chain will be created. So let him be finished with my past deeds – but I am not going to create a new karma for the future."

When someone insults you, the attitude of a witness, of a person who is practicing nonattachment, is this: "I must have insulted him before in some past life somewhere, because nothing is born without a cause. The cause must be there, this is only the effect. So I must wait and take it, accept it as part of my destiny and be finished with it, because if I do something again a new future is created and the chain continues."

Someone insults you. If you answer in any way then the account is not closed, it remains open. If you don't respond then the account is closed. And this is the difference between the Eastern attitude and Christianity. Even very beautiful things sometimes can be basically wrong. Jesus says, "If someone hits you on one cheek, give him the other." This is a beautiful saying, and one of the most beautiful sayings ever uttered in the world. But ask an Eastern buddha. He will say, "Don't do even that. When someone hits you, remain as you were before he hit you. Don't change, don't do anything, because even giving him the other cheek is a response – a good response, a beautiful response, but a response – and you are creating karma again."

Nietzsche somewhere criticizes Jesus for this. He says, "If I hit Jesus on one cheek and he gives me the other, I will hit even harder on the other, because this man is insulting me, he is treating me like an insect. He is not giving me the same status as him." Nietzsche says, "It would be better if Jesus hits me back, because then he is behaving with me on equal terms. If he gives me the other cheek he is trying to play the god and he is insulting me."

That's possible. You can insult a person just by becoming superior – not that Jesus means it, but you can do it. And just trying to become superior will be more insulting, and the other person will feel more hurt than if you had given him a good slap. The Eastern attitude is to not do anything in any way, to remain as if nothing has happened. Somebody hits you, you remain as if nothing has happened. And this hit has come not from this person but from your past deed. So accept it – it is your own doing, he has not done anything – and remain as if nothing has happened. Don't hit him back and don't give him the other cheek, because both will create a new chain. Be finished with it, so the account is closed with this man at least. And this way you close the accounts with all.

When all the accounts are closed you need not be reborn. This is the philosophy of going beyond life and death. Then you need not be reborn again; you simply disappear from this phenomenal world, from this bodily, physical world. Then you exist as cosmos, not as individuals. Jesus' saying is beautiful, very moral. But Buddha's attitude is spiritual, not only moral: not to do anything, because whatsoever you do creates future, and one has to stop creating future.

He knows that whatever faces him in this life is the result of the deeds of his past life. Whether in pleasure or in pain, he can do nothing.

If you think you can do something you can never become a witness; if you think you can do something you will remain a doer. This has to be very deeply realized – that nothing can be done. Only then can the witness arise.

Life has to be observed, and if you observe life you will come to feel that nothing can be done. Everything is happening. You are born – what have you done about it? It has not been any choice, you have not chosen to be born. You are black or white – you have not chosen to be black or white, it has happened. You are man or woman, intelligent or stupid – it has happened, you have not done anything about it. You will die, you will disappear from this body, you will be born in another. Look at all this as a happening, not as a doing on your part. If you feel that you are doing something you can never become a witness.

The modern mind finds it very difficult to become a witness, because the modern mind thinks he can do something, the modern mind thinks he has willpower, the modern mind thinks that it is in its hands to change things and destiny. The modern mind goes on insisting to children, "You are the master of your destiny." This is foolish. You cannot do anything, and whenever you feel that you are doing something you are under a wrong impression.

It happened once, under a tree many stones were piled. A building was soon going to be constructed and those stones were piled there for that building, to fill in the foundations. One small boy was passing, and as small boys do, he took a stone and threw it in the sky. The stone was rising upwards…. It is very difficult for stones even to imagine that they can go upwards, they always go downwards. Just because of gravitation stones always go downwards, they cannot go up-wards. But every stone must be dreaming somehow or other to go upwards. In their dreams stones must be flying, because dreams are fulfillments of those things which we cannot do. They are substitutes.

So all those stones must have dreamed somewhere, sometime, about flying. And this stone must have dreamed that some day he would fly, he would be-come a bird – and suddenly it happened. He was thrown, but he thought, "I am rising." He looked downwards. Other stones, his brothers and sisters, were lying down, so he said, "Look! What are you doing there? Can't you fly? I have done a miracle! I am flying, and I am going to the sky to see moons and stars!"

The other stones felt very jealous, but they couldn't do anything so they thought, "This stone must be unique, an avatar, a reincarnated superior being. We cannot fly. This stone must be a Krishna, a Buddha, a Christ. He has miraculous power; he is flying" – and this is the greatest miracle for a stone.

They felt jealous, they wept over their destiny, they were sad, but they couldn't do anything. Then they started feeling – because this is how mind goes on consoling – "Okay, you are one of us. You belong to us, to this pile, to this nation, to this race. We are happy that one of our brothers is flying."

But then the moment came when the momentum of that small boy's throw was lost, the energy finished and the stone started falling back. For a moment he felt dizzy, for a moment he felt, "What is happening?" and he couldn't control it. But suddenly, as everybody rationalizes, he rationalized, "It is enough for the first day. I have gone too far, and I must go back now to my home." Then he thought, "I am feeling homesick. It is better now to go back, to rest a little. I am tired. I must go back to my brothers and sisters, to my community, and tell them what beautiful phenomena I have seen – the sky, infinite sky, and such vast space, stars, moons – so near. This has been a cosmic event, an historical event; it should be written for the generations to come, for them to remember that one of us had flown once into the sky, had become just like a bird. The dreams are fulfilled."

He started falling back. When he came just near the pile he said, "I am coming back. Don't look so sad. I will not leave you, I will never leave you. The world is beautiful, but nothing is like home." And he fell down.

And this is the story of your whole life. You are thrown, existence throws you. Then for certain moments you enjoy – life, flying, beauty, love, youth – but this is happening. It is happening just like breath coming in and going out. You are not doing anything, everything is a happening. Once you understand this ego disappears, because ego exists only with the idea that you can *do*. To realize that nothing can be done is the highest point for the spiritual seeker to begin with, the climax of understanding. After that is transformation.

And if you cannot do anything, then when someone insults you,

you can remain a witness – because what can be done? You can look at what is happening, you can be detached. A pain comes, a suffering happens – what can you do? You can be a witness. Pleasure comes, you are happy – what can you do? It has happened. It is happening just like night and day, morning and evening.

Watch your mind. There are moments of sadness, and immediately after them moments of pleasure, then again moments of sadness. When you are sad you are just on the brink of being happy, when you are happy you are just on the brink of being sad. This goes on revolving. And you have not done anything really, you are just like that stone. He takes a happening for a doing – that is fallacious. When you fall in love what have you done? Can you do anything to fall in love? Can you fall in love consciously? Try it and then you will see the impossibility; you cannot do anything. And if you have fallen in love, you cannot stop that falling.

There are foolishnesses which belong to youth and there are foolishnesses which belong to old age. This is the foolishness of the youth: he thinks, "I am doing something when I am in love." So he thinks, "This is something of my doing." It is a happening. And this is the foolishness of old age: old people go on saying, "Don't fall in love. Stop yourself, control yourself" – as if love can be controlled. But the whole society exists around the ego – control, doing, not happening. If you can look at life as a happening, witnessing comes easily.

Whether in pleasure or in pain, he can do nothing. Indulgence is but a disease and affluence of all kinds a storehouse of adversity.

This is not condemnation, this is just giving you a hint that the opposite is hidden. When you are in pleasure, pain is there hidden, will come soon.

Indulgence is but a disease and affluence of all kinds a storehouse of adversity.

It is not a condemnation, this is simply the fact. But you go on forgetting. When you are happy you forget that you were ever sad before, you forget that sadness will follow again. When you are sad you forget that you were ever happy before, and you forget that happiness will follow again. You are in a moving circle, in a moving wheel. That's why in the East life is called a wheel, just a wheel – moving. Every spoke will come up and every spoke will go down and will again come up. You may not be able to connect – that's your misery. If you can connect you can see.

Go into loneliness for at least twenty-one days and then watch. There is nobody who can make you happy or unhappy, there is nobody who can make you angry, pleased, or anything. You are alone there. Have a diary and watch and note down every mood that comes to you. Then for the first time you will be-come aware that there is no need for anybody to make you angry – you become angry by yourself. There is no need for anybody to make you sad – there are moments when you suddenly feel sad. And there is no need for anybody to make you happy – there are sudden glimpses when you *are* happy.

And if you can watch for twenty-one days and go on noting down, you will see a wheel emerging. And this wheel is so subtle, that's why you are not aware and you never connect it. If you watch deeply you can even say that one mood is passing and you can say what will follow, which spoke is going to come. If you have observed basically, deeply, you can predict your moods. Then you can say, "On Monday morning I will be angry."

Much research is going on in Soviet Russia about moods, and they say a calendar can be made for every person. On Mondays he will be angry; on Saturdays, in the morning, he will be happy; on Tuesdays, in the evening, he will feel sexual. If you observe yourself you can also approximately fix a routine, a wheel of your life. And then many things become possible. Russian psychologists have suggested that if this can be done – and this *can* be done – then family life will become more easy, because you can look at your wife's calendar and your wife can look at your calendar. Then there is no need to get angry about anything, this is how things are going to happen.

You know that on Tuesdays the wife is going to be terrible, so you accept it. You know from the very beginning that it is going to be on that day, so from the morning you can remain a witness, you need not get involved in it; it is your wife's inner work. Two beings moving side by side need not get concerned with the other's spokes.

And when she is unhappy, sad, it is just foolish to get angry about it, because you create more sadness through it. The day when your wife is unhappy it is better to help her in every way, because she is ill. It is just like menses, a periodical thing.

Now in Czechoslovakia one research has proved that not only women have their menses, periods, but men also; every twenty-eight days they become depressed for three, four days. And it *should* be so, because man cannot be anything else than a wheel; if woman is a wheel man must be a wheel. And there are some secretions in the blood in man also: every twenty-eight days, after four weeks, they pass through a menstrual period, for four or five days they are sad.

With every menses every woman becomes depressed, violent, angry, and her intelligence goes low. It is now a proven fact that girls in menses should not go to sit for examinations because they unnecessarily lose much. Their IQ is low when they are in menses, and unnecessarily they lose much. They should not be forced to go to the examination when they are having a period, they cannot compete rightly. They are angry, disturbed, the whole system is a chaos inside. But there is no rule yet.

In the East it has been one of the traditions that whenever a woman is in her period she should not make any contact with anybody. She should move into a lonely room and remain closed and meditating for four days, because if she is out mixing with people she will create unnecessary bad karmas and they will create chains. She should not touch food, because she is in such a chaos that the food becomes poisonous.

Now scientifically also it is proved that when a woman is in menses, if she takes a flower in her hand the flower immediately becomes sad. Subtle vibrations, chaotic vibrations, affect it. A woman in menses should not be in contact with people, it is better if she simply meditates and rests. Such periods are with men also, but they are more subtle. The body secretes some hormones in the bloodstream.

This calendar can be maintained. You can observe your life for two or three months impartially, and then you can know that you are moving in a wheel and others are only excuses; you impose upon them. You get sad when you are alone also, but if you are with someone you think the other is making you sad. And man and woman are not different, cannot be. They are not two different species, they are one species, and everything has a positive-negative relationship.

Man ejaculates in intercourse; women don't ejaculate, but a subtle ejaculation happens in the bloodstream, subtle hormones are released in the bloodstream, because women are passive. But as far as childbirth is concerned they are positive and man is passive. That's why menses with woman is positive – ejaculation happens, blood comes out of the body. In man ejaculation happens but it moves into the bloodstream, hormones are released. Man is born out of man and woman, woman is born out of man and woman – in every individual both are there.

I remember, once Mulla Nasruddin's wife said to him, "Nasruddin, I wonder...sometimes I get very puzzled. Sometimes you look so manly, so powerful and strong, and sometimes so effeminate, so feminine. What is the matter?"

So Nasruddin brooded, contemplated, and then he said, "It must be hereditary, because half of my parents were men and half were women."

But everyone is bisexual; no one belongs to one sex, and cannot belong to one sex. Half of you is man and half of you is woman. So the difference is only of which part is visible. You may be man only because the male part is visible on the surface and the female part is hidden behind; you are a woman if the female part is visible on the surface and the male part is hidden behind.

That's why if a woman gets ferocious she will be more ferocious than a man, because then she simply comes out of her surface, and what is hidden is the man. Ordinarily when a woman is angry she is not so angry as a man, not so aggressive as man, but if she is really angry then a man is nothing compared to her. A man can be more loving than a woman. He is not ordinarily so, but if he is then no woman can be compared with him, because then the hidden part comes out. And man has not used the hidden part; it is fresh, alive – more alive than woman. So if a man is really in love he is more loving than any woman, because then his hidden woman which is fresh, unused, comes out. And when a woman is angry, filled with hatred, no man can be compared, because the hidden, fresh aggression comes out.

And this happens in life: as people grow old, men become more effeminate and women become more manly. That's why old women are very dangerous; the stories about mother-in-laws are not just inventions. They *are* dangerous, be-cause now the female part has been used so much that it has dissipated and the male part has come in. Sometimes women may grow mustaches when they are old. Their voice will become manly, it will not be so feminine, fine; it will become coarse, because one part has been used. And by the time menopause happens, when the menses have stopped, the female part is dropping, the surface is dropping and the inner part is working more and more. Old men become effeminate, their coarseness is lost.

So this is a rare phenomenon: if they have really lived silently, beautifully, then old men become more beautiful than old women. When young a woman is just wonderful, very beautiful; everything, every curve of her being is beautiful. Old women become coarse, the beauty is lost. Old men become more beautiful than they were when they were young. Look at Mahatma Gandhi's pictures: when he was young he was ugly, the older he grew the more beautiful. Only when he was in the last stage of his life was he beautiful. This happens because man becomes more effeminate, more curves come into his being and corners become soft. This is not to condemn.

Every union leads inevitably to separation.

Every union leads to separation, every marriage is a preparation for divorce.

The ignorant suffer the maladies of mental anxiety.

The ignorant suffer because of ignorance – because they cannot see this polarity. If they can see that every union is going to become a separation they will neither be happy about the union nor unhappy about the separation. And if you are not happy about the marriage and not happy about the divorce you have transcended both. Then a relationship grows which cannot be called marriage and cannot be called divorce. That relationship can be eternal.

But marriage implies divorce, union implies separation, birth implies death. So be aware of the opposite, that will help you to become a witness. It will lessen your happiness, it will lessen your misery also. And a moment will come when happiness and misery will become the same. When they become the same you have transcended.

And this is the way they can become the same: when happiness comes, search for the hidden unhappiness somewhere in it. You will find it. When unhappiness comes, search for the happiness hiding somewhere – you will find it. And then you know that happiness and unhappiness are not two things but two aspects of the same coin. And don't believe too much in the aspect that is visible, because the invisible will become visible, it is only a question of time.

All material things are perishable, because time is constantly devouring them. Through the understanding of scriptural precepts, one's faith in material things is uprooted and one's mind freed of them. This is called ordinary nonattachment.

This is through effort, understanding. With mind you can achieve this ordinary nonattachment. But this is not the goal, this is just the beginning.

When thoughts like: "I am not the doer, my past deeds are the doers, or God himself is the doer..."

Even such thoughts drop. These were the base of the first, these thoughts were the base of the ordinary nonattachment. When even they:

...cease to worry the seeker, a stage of silence, equilibrium and peace is attained. This is called sublime nonattachment.

...Because to constantly think, "I am not the doer," shows that you believe you *are* the doer; otherwise why go on constantly saying "I am not the doer"?

Once it happened, one Hindu sannyasin, a traditional monk, stayed with me for a few days. Every day in the morning, in the *brahmamuhurt*, just before the sunrise, he would sit and repeat constantly, "I am not the body, I am the soul supreme. I am not the body...."

So I heard him doing it, saying that for many days, and then I said, "If you really know that you are not the body, why repeat it? If you really know you are the supreme self, then who are you convincing every morning? That shows you don't know. You are just trying to convince yourself that you are not the body, but you know you *are* the body; that's why the need to convince."

Remember this: the mind works in this way. Whenever you try to convince yourself of something the contrary is the case. If a person tries too much to say, "I love you," know well that something is wrong. If a person tries to say too much about anything, that shows that the contrary exists within; he is trying to convince himself, not you. Whenever a husband feels guilty that he has looked at another woman, or has been friendly, or was attracted, then he comes home and that day he will be more loving to the wife. He will bring ice cream or something. So whenever the husband brings ice cream beware – because now he is not trying to convince you, he is trying to convince himself that he loves his wife more than anybody else.

Whenever mind becomes aware that something has gone wrong, that wrong has to be put right. The first effort for nonattachment is such effort. You go on insisting to yourself, "I am not the body, I am not the doer," but you know well that you *are* the doer, you *are* the body. But this will help. One day you will become aware of both these polarities: that you are insisting that you are not, and still you believe that you are the body. Then both drop, you simply remain silent, you don't say anything. Neither do you say, "I am the doer," nor do you say, "I am the witness." You simply drop this whole nonsense. You allow things as they are. You don't say anything, you don't make any statement. Then *silence, equilibrium, and peace are attained* – when you don't make any statement.

Somebody asked Buddha, "Are you the body or are you the soul?" Buddha remained silent. The man insisted, and Buddha said, "Don't force me, because whatsoever statement I make will be wrong. If I say I am the body, it is wrong, because I am not. If I say I am not the body, that too shows that somehow I am attached to the body, otherwise why this denial? Why this botheration to say that I am not the body? So I will not make any statement. If you can understand, look at me, at what I am."

When you simply are – without any statement, without any idea, without any theory, without any concept...when you simply are, when you have become a tree, a rock, you exist, that's all. And you allow existence to flow from you, within you. You don't create any resistance, you don't say, "I am this," because every statement will be a definition, and every statement will make you finite.

But this will not happen immediately and directly, remember. You cannot drop unless you have made the first effort. So first try, "I am the witness." And bring it to such intensity that in that intensity you become aware that even this is futile. Then drop it and be yourself.

It happened once, Mulla Nasruddin went to England. His English was not very good, just like me – that is not much. He had a very beautiful dog, but very ferocious. So he put a plaque on the door, and instead of writing "Beware of the dog," he wrote "Be aware of the dog." That is wrong English – but wrongly he did a right thing, because the whole emphasis is changed. When you say "Beware of the dog," emphasis is on the dog. When you say "Be aware of the dog," the emphasis is on you. And this English word beware is beautiful. Make it two, be plus aware.

Be plus aware is the first step. In the second step, awareness also has disappeared. Simply be. Don't be even aware, because that will create an effort. Simply be. When you are in that state of being – not doing anything, not even witnessing, because that too is a subtle doing....

A state of silence, equilibrium, and peace is attained.

This is called sublime nonattachment.

11   One in the Many

Osho,

If everything is simply happening, then can there be any ultimate purpose to it all, or is life just an accident? Can it be said that life is evolving towards some ultimate goal?

It is very difficult, particularly for the Western mind, to understand that life is purposeless. And it is beautiful that it is purposeless. If it is purposeful then the whole thing becomes absurd – then who will decide the purpose? Then some God has to be conceived who decides the purpose, and then human beings become just puppets; then no freedom is possible. And if there is some purpose then life becomes businesslike, it cannot be ecstatic.

The West has been thinking in terms of purpose, but the East has been thinking in terms of purposelessness. The East says life is not a business, it is a play. And a play has no purpose really, it is nonpurposeful. Or you can say play is its own purpose, to play is enough. Life is not reaching towards some goal, life itself is the goal. It is not evolving towards some ultimate; this very moment, here and now, life is ultimate.

Life as it is, is accepted in the East. It is not moving towards some end, be-cause if there is some end who will decide the end and why? If God decides it, then you can ask the same question about God: "What is the purpose of creating a world with purpose?" or, "Why should he create a purposive world?" or even more deeply, "What is the purpose of God's existence?"

Maybe life has a purpose and God decides the purpose, but then God's existence has to be questioned – why he exists – and that way the question is simply pushed one step ahead. Then God becomes purposeless, or you have to create another God to decide the purpose of this God. Then you will be in a regress ad infinitum, then there is no end to it. Somewhere deep down you will have to come to the conclusion that this phenomenon is purposeless; otherwise there is no end.

So why go from the world to the God? Why not say that life itself is purposeless? The whole game of logicians, theologians, is stupid in a way. They say, "God created the world, because how could the world come into existence if there was no one who created it?" But the question can be asked, "Who created the God?" – and then they fall on their own. They say, "God is uncreated." If God can exist without being created, why can't this life itself exist without being created? If you accept that something is possible without being created, then what is the trouble? Then why think about a God who created the world?

The East says God is not the creator, God is the creation. Nobody has created it, it is there. It has been so always, it will be so always – sometimes manifest, sometimes unmanifest; sometimes visible, sometimes invisible. It goes on moving in a periodical rhythm, in a circle. But existence itself is uncreated and it has no goal.

Then think about it in other ways also. Firstly, if there is a goal why hasn't it been achieved yet? The existence has been existing timelessly, millions and millions of light-years it has existed, and the goal has not been reached yet. When will it be reached? If so many millions and millions of light-years have passed and the goal is nowhere to be seen, when will it be reached? Secondly, if some day the goal is reached, what will happen to existence? Will it disappear? When the purpose is fulfilled, then what? Conceive of a moment somewhere in the future when the purpose is fulfilled: for what will existence exist then? Then it will be purposeless for it to exist.

The reality is this: that it is already always purposeless. There is no goal towards which the existence is moving. It is moving, but not towards any goal. It has a value, but the value is not in the end, the value is intrinsic.

You love someone. Have you asked the question, "For what purpose does love exist?" The mind, a calculating mind, is bound to ask, "Why love? What is the purpose?" If you can answer then one thing is certain – that you are not in love. If you can show the purpose then love is not there, it is a business, it is a bargain. But lovers will always say there is no purpose to it. To be in love is the goal. The goal is not somewhere else; it is intrinsic, it is in the very phenomenon of love. The goal is already achieved. When you are happy have you asked, "What is the purpose of being happy?" Can there be any purpose to being happy? When you are happy you never ask because the question is absurd. Happiness is itself the goal, there is no purpose to it.

Life is like love, life is like happiness. Life is existence – no goal. And once you can understand this your ways of living will change totally, because if there is no purpose in life itself there is no need to create a purpose for your individual life also – no need. Because of individual purposes you become tense, something has to be achieved. Then an achieving mind is created which is always trying to achieve something or other. And whenever something is achieved again the mind asks, "Now what? What is to be achieved now?" It cannot remain with itself, it has to go on achieving.

This achieving mind will never be blissful, it will always be tense. And whenever something is achieved the achieving mind will feel frustrated, because now new goals have to be invented. This is happening in America. Many of the goals of the past century have been achieved, so America is in a deep frustration. All the goals of the founding fathers who created America and the American constitution are almost achieved. In America the society has become affluent for the first time in the whole history of mankind. Almost everybody is rich. The poor man in America is a rich man here in India.

The goals have almost been achieved – now what to do? Society has become affluent: food is there, shelter is there, everybody has got a car, radio, refrigerator, TV – now what to do? A deep frustration is felt, some other goals are needed. And there seem to be no goals. Instead of one car you can have two cars – a two-car garage has become the goal – or you can have two houses, but that will be achieved within ten years. Whatsoever the goal it can be achieved. Then the achieving mind feels frustrated. What to do now? It again needs a goal, and you have to invent a goal.

So the whole of American business now depends on inventing goals. Give people goals – that's what advertisements and the whole business of advertising is doing. Create goals, seduce people: "Now this is the goal! You must have this, otherwise life is purposeless!" They start running, because they have an achieving mind. But where does it lead? It leads into more and more neurosis.

Only a nonachieving mind can be at peace. But a nonachieving mind is possible only with the background of a cosmic purposelessness. If the whole existence is purposeless then there is no need for you to be purposeful. Then you can play, you can sing and dance, you can enjoy, you can love and live, and there is no need to create any goal. Here and now, this very moment, the ultimate is present. If you are available the ultimate can enter you. But you are not available here; your mind is somewhere in the future, in some goal.

Life has got no purpose and this is the beauty of it. If there was some purpose life would have been mean – just futile. It is not a business, it is a play. In India we have been calling it leela. Leela means a cosmic play...as if God is playing. Energy overflowing, not for some purpose, just enjoying itself; just a small child playing – for what purpose? Running after butterflies, collecting colored stones on the beach, dancing under the sun, running under the trees, collecting flowers – for what purpose? Ask a child. He will look at you as if you are a fool. There is no need for purpose.

Your mind has been corrupted. Universities, colleges, education, society, have corrupted you. They have made it a conditioning deep down within you that unless something has a purpose it is useless – so everything must have a purpose. A child playing has no purpose. At the most, if the child could explain he would say, "Because I feel good. Running, I feel more alive. Collecting flowers, I enjoy, it is ecstatic." But there is no purpose. The very act in itself is beautiful, ecstatic. To be alive is enough, there is no need for any purpose.

Why ask for anything else? Can't you be satisfied just by being alive? It is such a phenomenon. Just think of yourself being a stone. You could have been, because many are still stones. You must have been somewhere in the past, sometime, a stone. Think of yourself being a tree. You must have been somewhere a tree, a bird, an animal, an insect. And then think of yourself being a man – conscious, alert, the peak, the climax of all possibilities. And you are not content with it. You need a purpose, otherwise life is useless.

Your mind has been corrupted by economists, mathematicians, theologians. They have corrupted your mind, because they all talk about purpose. They say, "Do something if something is achieved through it. Don't do anything which leads nowhere." But I tell you that the more you can enjoy things which are useless, the happier you will be. The more you can enjoy things which are purposeless, the more innocent and blissful you will be.

When you don't need any purpose you simply celebrate your being. You feel gratitude just that you are, just that you breathe. It is such a blessing that you can breathe, that you are alert, conscious, alive, aflame. Is it not enough? Do you need something to achieve so that you can feel good, so that you can feel valued, so that you can feel life is justified? What more can you achieve than what you are? What more can be added to your life? What more can you add to it? Nothing can be added, and the effort will destroy you – the effort to add something.

But for many centuries all over the world they have been teaching every child to be purposive. "Don't waste your time! Don't waste your life!" And what do they mean? They mean, "Transform your life into a bank balance. When you die you must die rich. That is the purpose."

Here in the East – particularly the mystics we are talking about, the Upanishads – they say, "Live richly." In the West they say, "Die a rich man." And these are totally different things. If you want to live richly you have to live here and now, not a single moment is to be lost. If you want to achieve something, you will die a rich man – but you will live a poor man, your life will be poor.

Look at rich people: their life is absolutely poor, because they are wasting it transforming it into bank balances, changing their life into money, into big houses, big cars. Their whole effort is that life has to be changed for some things. When they die you can count their things.

Buddha became a beggar. He was born a king, he became a beggar. Why? Just to live richly...because he came to understand that there are two ways to live: one is to die richly, the other is to live richly. And any man who has any understanding will choose to live richly, because dying a rich man doesn't mean anything; you simply wasted yourself for nothing. But this is possible only if you can conceive that the whole existence is purposeless; it is a cosmic play, a continuous beautiful game, a beautiful hide-and-seek – not leading anywhere. Nowhere is the goal.

If this is the background, then you need not be worried about individual purposes, evolution, progress. This word progress is the basic disease of the modern age. What is the need? All that can be enjoyed is available, all that you need to be happy is here and now. But you create conditions and you say that unless these conditions are fulfilled you cannot be happy. You say, "These conditions must be fulfilled first: this type of house, this type of clothes, this type of car, this type of wife, this type of husband. All these conditions have to be fulfilled first, then I can be happy." As if by being happy you are going to oblige the whole universe.

And who is going to fulfill your conditions? Who is worried? But you will try for those conditions, and the effort is going to be so long that they can never be fulfilled really, because whenever something is fulfilled, by the time it is fulfilled the goal has shifted.

One of my friends was contesting an election, a political election, so he came to me for blessing. I said, "I will not give the blessing because I am not your enemy, I am a friend. I can only bless that you may not get elected, because that will be the first step towards madness." But he wouldn't listen to me. He was elected, he became a member. Next year he came again for my blessing and he said, "Now I am trying to be a deputy minister."

I asked him, "You were saying that if you could become a member of parliament you would be very happy, but I don't see that you are happy. You are more depressed and more sad than you ever were before."

He said, "Now this is the only problem: I am worried. There is much competition. Only if I can become a deputy minister will everything be okay."

He became a deputy minister. When I was passing through the capital he came to see me again and he said, "I think you were right, because now the problem is how to become the minister. And I think this is the goal. I am not going to change it. Once I become the minister it is finished."

He has become the minister now, and he came to me a few days ago and he said, "Just one blessing more. I must become chief minister." And he is getting more and more worried, more and more puzzled, because more problems have to be faced, more competition, more ugly politics. And he is a good man, not a bad man.

I told him, "Unless you become the suprememost God you are not going to be satisfied." But he cannot look back and cannot understand the logic of the mind, the logic of the achieving mind. It can never be satisfied, the way it behaves creates more and more discontent. The more you have the more discontent you will feel, because more arenas become open for you in which to compete, to achieve. A poor man is more satisfied because he cannot think that he can achieve much. Once he starts achieving something he thinks more is possible. The more you achieve the more becomes possible, and it goes on and on forever.

A meditator needs a nonachieving mind, but a nonachieving mind is possible only if you can be content with purposelessness. Just try to understand the whole cosmic play and be a part in it. Don't be serious, because a play can never be serious. And even if the play needs you to be serious, be playfully serious, don't be really serious. Then this very moment becomes rich. Then this very moment you can move into the ultimate.

The ultimate is not in the future, it is the present, hidden here and now. So don't ask about purpose – there is none, and I say it is beautiful that there is none. If there was purpose then your God would be just a managing director or a big business man, an industrialist, or something like that.

Jesus says…. Somebody asked him, "Who will be able to enter into the kingdom of your God?"

Jesus said, "Those who are like small children." This is the secret. What is the meaning of being a small child? The meaning is that the child is never businesslike, he is always playful.

If you can become playful you have become a child again, and only children can enter into the kingdom of God, nobody else, because children can play without asking where it is leading. They can make houses of sand without asking whether they are going to be permanent. Can somebody live in them? Will they be able to resist the wind that is blowing? They know that within minutes they will disappear. But they are very serious when they are playing. They can even fight for their sandhouses or houses of cards. They are very serious when they are creating. They are enjoying. And they are not fools, they know that these houses are just cardhouses and everything is make-believe.

Why waste time in thinking in terms of business? Why not live more and more playfully, nonseriously, ecstatically? Ecstasy is not something which you can achieve by some efforts, ecstasy is a way of living. Moment to moment you have to be ecstatic, simple things have to be enjoyed. And life gives millions of opportunities to enjoy. You will miss them if you are purposive.

If you are not purposive, every moment you will have so many opportunities to be ecstatic. A flower, a lonely flower in the garden…you can dance if you are nonpurposive. The first star in the evening…you can sing if you are nonpurposive. A beautiful face…you can see the divine in it if you are nonpurposive. All around the divine is happening, the ultimate is showering. But you will be able to see it only if you are nonpurposive and playful.

The second question:

Osho,

It is felt by many in the West and elsewhere that the peak of love is reached only between an 'I' and a 'thou'. If I and thou are both dropped, can love still exist? Can love exist without relationship?

Love, life, light – these three I's are the most mysterious. And the mystery is this – that you cannot understand them logically. If you are illogical you can penetrate them; if you are simply logical you cannot understand, because the whole phenomenon depends on a paradox. Try to understand.

When you love someone, two are needed: I and thou. Without two how can love be possible? If you are alone how can you relate, how can you love? If you are alone there can be no love. Love is possible only when there are two, this is the base. But if they remain two love is again impossible. If they continue to be two then again love is impossible. Two are needed for love to exist, and then there is a second need – that the two must merge and become one. This is the paradox.

'I' and 'thou' is a basic requirement for love to exist but this is only the base. The temple can come only when these two merge into one. And the mystery is that somehow you remain two and somehow you become one. This is illogical. Two lovers are two and still one. They have found a bridge somewhere where I disappears, thou disappears; where a unity is formed, a harmony comes into being. Two are needed to create that harmony, but two are needed to dissolve into it.

It is just like this: a river flows, two banks are needed. A river cannot flow with only one bank, it is impossible; the river cannot exist. Two banks are needed for the river to flow. But if you look a little deeper those two banks are joined together just below the river. If they are not joined then also the river cannot exist, it will simply drop into the abyss. Two banks, apparently two on the surface, are one deep down.

Love exists like a river between two persons who on the surface remain two, but deep down have become one. That's why I say it is paradoxical. Two are needed just to be dissolved into one. So love is a deep alchemy and very delicate. If you really become one, love will disappear, the river cannot flow. If you really remain two, love will disappear, because there can be no river in an abyss if the two banks are really separate. So lovers create a game in which on the surface they remain two and deep down they become one.

Sometimes they fight also, sometimes they are angry also, sometimes in every way they separate – but this is only on the surface. Their separation is just to get married again, their fight is just to create love again. They go a little away from each other just to come and meet again, and the meeting after the separation is beautiful. They fight to love again. They are intimate enemies. Their enmity is a play, they enjoy it.

If there is really love you can enjoy the fight. If there is no love, only then the fight becomes a problem; otherwise you can enjoy, it is a game. It creates hunger. If you have ever loved, then you know that love always reaches peaks after you have been fighting. Fight – you create the separation, and with separation the hunger arises, you feel starved; the other is needed more. You fall in love again, then there is a more intense meeting. To create that intensity the two should remain two, and at the same time, simultaneously, they should become one.

In India we have pictured Shiva as Ardhanarishwar – half-man, half-woman. That is the only symbol of its type all over the world. Shiva – half is man, half is woman; half Shiva and half Parvati, his consort. Half the body is of man and half of woman: Ardhanarishwar, half-man, half-woman. That is the symbol. Lovers join together but on the surface they remain two. Shiva is one, the body is two – half comes from Parvati, half he contributes. The body is two, on the surface the banks are two; in the depth the souls have mingled and become one.

Or look at it in this way: the room is dark, you bring two lamps into it, two candles into it. Those two candles remain two, but their light has mingled and become one. You cannot separate the light; you cannot say, "This light belongs to this candle and that light belongs to that candle." Light has mingled and become one. The spirit is like light, the body is the candle.

Two lovers are only two bodies, but not two souls. This is very difficult to achieve. That's why love is one of the most difficult things to achieve, and if even for moments you can achieve it is worth it. If even only for moments in your whole life, if even for moments you can achieve this oneness with someone, this oneness will become the door for the divine. Love achieved becomes the door for the divine, because then you can feel how this universe exists in the many and remains one.

But this can come only through experience – if you love a person and you feel that you are two and still one. And this should not be just a thought but an experience. You can think, but thinking is of no use. This must be an experience: how the bodies have remained two and the inner beings have merged, melted into each other – the light has become one.

Once experienced, then the whole philosophy of the Upanishads becomes exactly clear, absolutely clear. The many are just the surface; behind each individual is hidden the nonindividual, behind each part is hidden the whole. And if two can exist as two on the surface, why not many? If two can remain two and still one, why can't many remain many and still one? One in the many is the message of the Upanishads. And this will remain only theoretical if you have never been in love.

But people go on confusing love with sex. Sex may be part of love, but sex is not love. Sex is just a physical, biological attraction, and in sex you remain two. In sex you are not concerned with the other, you are concerned with yourself. You are simply exploiting the other, you are simply using the other for some biological satisfaction of your own, and the other is using you. That's why sexual partners never feel any deep intimacy. They are using the other. The other is not a person, the other is not a thou; the other is just an it, a thing you can use, and the other is using you. Deep down it is mutual masturbation and nothing else. The other is used as a device. It is not love, because you don't care for the other.

Love is totally different. It is not using the other, it is caring for the other, it is just being happy in the other. It is not your happiness that you derive from the other; if the other is happy you are happy, and the other's happiness becomes your happiness. If the other is healthy you feel healthy. If the other is dancing you feel a dance inside. If the other is smiling the smile penetrates you and becomes your smile.

Love is the happiness of the other; sex is happiness of your own, the other has to be used. In love the other's happiness has become even more significant than your own. Lovers are each other's servants, sex partners are each other's exploiters.

Sex *can* exist in the milieu of love, but then it has a different quality; it is not sexual at all. Then it is one of the many ways of merging into each other. One of the many – not the only, not the sole, not the supreme. Many are the ways to merge into each other. Two lovers can sit silently with each other and the silence can become the merger. Really only lovers can sit silently.

Wives and husbands cannot sit silently, because silence becomes boredom. So they go on talking about something or other. They go on talking even nonsense, rubbish, rot, just to avoid the other. Their talk is to avoid the other, because if there is no talk the other's presence will be felt, and the other's presence is boredom. They are bored with each other so they go on talking. They go on giving each other news of the neighborhood, what was in the newspaper, what was on the radio, what was on the TV, what was in the film. They go on talking and chattering just to create a screen, a smokescreen, so the other is not felt. Lovers never like to chatter. Whenever lovers are together they will remain silent, because in silence merging is possible.

Lovers can merge in many ways. Both can enjoy a certain thing, and that enjoyment becomes a merger. Two lovers can meditate on a flower and enjoy the flower – then the flower becomes the merger. Both enjoying the same thing, both feeling ecstatic about the same thing, they merge. Sex is only one of the ways. Two lovers can enjoy poetry, a haiku, two lovers can enjoy painting, two lovers can just go for a walk and enjoy the walk together. The only thing necessary is togetherness. Whatsoever the act, if they can be together they can merge.

Sex is one of the ways of being together, bodily together. And I say not the supreme, because it depends.... If you are a very gross person, then sex seems to be the supreme. If you are a refined person, if you have a high intelligence, then you can merge in anything. If you know higher realms of happiness, simply listening to music you can move into a deeper ecstasy than sex. Or simply sitting near a waterfall and the sound of the waterfall, and in that sound you both can merge. You are no more there; only the water falling and the sound, and that can become a higher peak of orgasm than can ever be attained through sex. Sex is for the gross. That is only one of the many ways in which lovers can merge and forget their I and thou and become one.

And unless you transcend sex and find out other ways, sooner or later you will be fed up with your lover, because sex will become repetitive, it will become mechanical. And then you will start looking for another partner, because the new attracts. Unless your partner remains constantly new you will get fed up. And it is very difficult; if you have only one way of enjoying each other's togetherness, it is bound to become a routine. If you have so many ways to be together, only then can your togetherness remain fresh, alive, young, and always new.

Lovers are never old. Husbands and wives are always old; they may be married only for one day but they are old – one day old. The mystery has gone, the newness disappeared. Lovers are always young. They may have been together for seventy years but they are still young, the freshness is there. And this is possible only if sex is one of the ways of being together, not the only way. Then you can find millions of ways of being together, and you enjoy that togetherness. That togetherness is felt as oneness.

If two can exist as one, then many can exist as one. Love becomes the door for meditation, prayer. That is the meaning when Jesus goes on insisting that love is God – because love becomes the door, the opening towards the divine.

So to conclude, love is a relationship and yet not a relationship. Love exists between two, that's why you can call it a relationship. And still, if love exists at all it is not a relationship, because the two must disappear and become one. Hence I call it one of the basic paradoxes, one of the basic mysteries which logic cannot reveal.

If you ask logic and mathematics, they will say that if there are two they will remain two, they cannot become one. If they become one, then they cannot remain two. This is simple Aristotelian logic: one is one, two are two, and if you say that two have become one, then they cannot remain two. And this is the problem – that love is both two and one simultaneously. If you are too much logic-obsessed, love is not for you. But even an Aristotle falls in love, because logic is one thing, but nobody is ready to lose love for logic. Even an Aristotle falls in love, and even an Aristotle knows that there are points where mathematics is transcended – two become one and yet remain two.

This has been one of the problems for theologians all over the world, and they have discussed it for many centuries. No conclusion has been reached, because no conclusion *can* be reached through logic. Not only with lovers – the same is the problem with God. Whether the devotee becomes one or remains separate – the same problem. A *bhakta*, a devotee – whether he remains ultimately separate from his god or becomes one, the same problem.

Mohammedans insist that he remains separate, because if he becomes one then love cannot exist. When you have become one, who is going to love and whom? So Mohammedans pray, "Let me be separate so that I can love you. Let there be a gap so that devotees can be in prayer and love." Hindus have said that the devotee becomes one with the divine, but then it's a problem: if the devotee becomes one with the divine, then where is the devotion? where can the devotion exist? And if the devotee becomes the divine he becomes equal, so God is not higher than the devotee.

My attitude is this: just as it happens in love, it happens with the divine. You remain separate and yet you become one. You remain separate on the surface, in the depths you have become one. The devotee becomes the god and still re-mains the devotee. But then it is illogical. You can refute me very easily, you can argue against it very easily, but if you have loved you will understand.

And if you have not loved yet then don't waste a single moment – be in love immediately, because life cannot give you a higher peak than love. And if you cannot achieve a natural peak that life offers to you, you cannot be capable, worthy, of achieving any other peaks which are not ordinarily available. Meditation is a higher peak than love. If you cannot love, are incapable of love, meditation is not for you.

It happened once, a man came to Ramanuja. Ramanuja was a mystic, a devotee mystic, a very unique person – a philosopher and yet a lover, a devotee. It rarely happens – a very acute mind, a very penetrating mind, but with a very overflowing heart. A man came and asked Ramanuja, "Show me the way to-wards the divine. How can I attain the God?"

So Ramanuja asked, "First let me ask a question. Have you ever loved anybody?"

The devotee must have been a really religious person. He said, "What are you talking about? Love? I am a celibate. I avoid women just as one should avoid diseases. I don't look at them, I close my eyes."

Ramanuja said, "Still, think a little. Move into the past, find out. Somewhere in your heart, has there ever been any flickering – even a small one – of love?"

The man said, "But I have come here to learn prayer, not to learn love. Teach me how to pray. You are talking about worldly things and I have heard that you are a great mystic saint. I have come here just to be led into the divine, not to talk about worldly things!"

Ramanuja is reported to have said...he even became very sad, and said to the man, "Then I cannot help you. If you have no experience of love then there is no possibility for any experience of prayer. So first go into the world and love, and when you have loved and you are enriched through it, then come to me – because only a lover can understand what prayer is. If you don't know anything illogical through experience, you cannot understand. And love is prayer given by nature easily – you cannot attain even that. Prayer is love not given so easily, it is achieved only when you reach higher peaks of totality. Much effort is needed to achieve it. For love no effort is needed; it is available, it is flowing. You are resisting it."

The same is the problem, and the problem arises because of our logical minds. Aristotle says, "a is a, b is b, and a cannot be b." This is a simple logical process. If you ask the mystics, they say, "a is a, b is b but a also can be b, and b also can be a." Life is not divided into solid blocks. Life is a flow, it transcends blocks. It moves from one pole to the other. Love is a relationship and yet not a relationship.

The third question:

Osho,

Can one be absorbed in doing something – for instance, these dynamic meditation techniques – with absolute total intensity, and at the same time remain a witness who is separate, apart?

The same is the problem in many forms. You think that a witness is something apart, separate. It is not. Your intensity, your wholeness, is your witness. So when you are witnessing and doing something you are not two – the doer is the witness.

For example, you are dancing here in kirtan. You are dancing: the dancer and the witness are not two, there is no separation. The separation is only in language. The dancer *is* the witness. And if the dancer is not the witness then you cannot be total in the dance, because the witness will need some energy and you will have to divide yourself. A part will remain a witness and the remaining will move in the dance. It cannot be total, it will be divided. And this is not what is meant, because really this is the state of a schizophrenic patient – divided, split. It is pathological. If you become two you are ill. You must remain one. You must move totally into the dance, and your totality will become the witness. It is not going to be something set apart, your wholeness is aware. This happens.

So don't try to divide yourself. While dancing become the dance. Just remain alert; don't fall asleep, don't be unconscious. You are not under a drug, you are alert, fully alert. But this alertness is not a part standing aloof; it is your totality, it is your whole being.

But this is again the same thing as whether two lovers are two or one. Only on the surface are they two, deep inside they are one. Only in language will you appear two, the dancer and the witness, but deep down you are the one. The whole dancer is alert. Then only peace, equilibrium, silence, will happen to you. If you are divided there will be tension, and that tension will not allow you to be totally here and now, to merge into existence.

So remember that, don't try to divide. Become the dancer and still be aware. This happens. This I am saying through my experience. This I am saying through many others' experience who have been working with me. This will happen to you also. This may have happened to many already. But remember this: don't get split. Remain one and yet aware.

12   Only Knowing Remains

The first stage, to which contentment and bliss

impart sweetness, springs from the innermost recesses of the seeker's heart,
as if nectar has issued forth from the heart of the earth.

At the inception of this stage the innermost recess

becomes a field for the coming of the other stages.

Afterwards the seeker attains the second and third stages.

Of the three, the third is the highest, because on its attainment all

the modifications of will come to an end.

One who practices the three stages finds his ignorance dead,

and on entering the fourth stage

he sees everything, everywhere, equally.

At that moment he is so strongly embedded in the experience of

nonduality – advaita – that the experience itself disappears.

Thus, on attaining the fourth stage

the seeker finds the world as illusory as a dream.

So while the first three stages are called waking ones,

the fourth is dreaming.

The fourth stage. The first is that of the oceanic feeling that Brahman exists everywhere – oneness. The one alone exists, the many are just its forms. They are not really divided, they only appear divided; deep down they are one.

The second stage is that of *vichar* – thought, contemplation and meditation – where mind has to be disciplined to become one-pointed, because it can disappear only when it has become one-pointed, when the flux has stopped; that is, when you can remain with one thought as long as you wish. You have become the master then, and unless you are the master of the mind, the mind cannot disappear, it cannot cease to be; you cannot order it out of existence.

If you cannot order thoughts to stop, how can you order the whole mind to go out of existence? So in the second stage one has to drop thoughts by and by, and retain only one thought. When you have become capable of dropping thoughts, one day you can drop the mind itself, the whole thought process. When the thought process is dropped you cannot exist as an ego. You exist as consciousness but not as mind; you are there but not as an I. We say "I am." When mind drops, the I drops; you remain a pure amness. Existence is there, rather, more abundant, more rich, more beautiful, but without the ego. There is no one who can say I, only amness exists.

In the third stage, vairagya, nonattachment, you have to become alert – first of the objects of desire, the body, the world – and continuously practice and discipline yourself to become a witness. You are not the doer. Your karmas may be the doers, God may be the doer, fate, or anything, but *you* are not the doer. You have to remain a witness, just a seer, an onlooker. And then this has also to be dropped. The idea that "I am the witness" is also a sort of doing. Then non-attachment becomes complete, perfect. The third stage, this Upanishad says, is the highest of the three. Now we will discuss the fourth.

The fourth is the state of *advaita,* nonduality. This word advaita has to be understood before we enter the sutra. This word is very meaningful. Advaita means literally nonduality, not two. They could have said one, but the Upanishads never use the word one; they say nonduality, not two. And this is very significant, because if you say one the two is implied, it becomes a positive statement. If you say there is only one you are asserting something positive.

How can the one exist without the other? One cannot exist without the other. You cannot conceive of the figure one without other figures – two, three, four, five. Many mathematicians have worked it out, particularly Leibniz in the West. He has tried to drop the nine digits, figures. Instead of nine he uses only two: one and two. In his calculations, three, four, five, six, seven, eight and nine are dropped, because he said it is just superstition to continue using ten figures. Why continue using ten figures?

You may not have observed: ten figures exist in mathematics not by any planning, but just because we have ten fingers. The primitives used to count on the fingers, so ten became the basic figure and it has been taken all over the world. These ten figures, this basis of all arithmetic, was produced in India. That's why even today in all languages the words that denote these ten figures are basically Sanskrit: two is *dwi,* three is *tri,* four is *chaturth,* five is *panch,* six is *shashta,* seven is *sapta*, eight is *ashta,* nine is *nava.* These are basic roots.

These ten counting figures, these ten digits, Leibniz says are useless. And science must try to work with the minimum, so he tried to minimize the digits. But he could not minimize more than two, he had to stop at two. So in Leibniz's system there is one, two, and then comes ten; three means ten, four means eleven, and so on, so forth. But he had to at least concede two, because just one cannot be conceived. You cannot use only one digit, at least two are needed – the minimum requirement. The moment you say one the two is implied, be-cause one can exist only by the side of two. So the Upanishads never say that the Brahman is one, the truth is one; rather they use a negative term, they say he is not two. So one is implied but not directly asserted.

Secondly, about the total we cannot assert anything positive, we cannot say what it is. At the most we can say what it is not, we can negate. We cannot say directly, because once we say anything directly it becomes defining, it becomes a limitation. If you say one, then you have limited; then a boundary has been drawn, then it cannot be infinite. When you simply say it is not two there is no boundary – the implication is infinite.

The Upanishads say that the divine can be defined only by negatives, so they go on negating. They say, "This is not Brahman, that is not Brahman." And they never say directly, they never assert directly. You cannot point to the Brahman with a finger because your finger will become a limitation. Then Brahman will be where your finger is pointing and nowhere else. You can point to the Brahman only with a closed fist so you are not pointing anywhere – or, everywhere.

This negativity created many confusions, particularly in the West, because when for the first time the West came upon the Upanishads in the last century and they were translated – first in German, then in English, and then French and other languages – it was a very baffling thought, because The Bible defines God positively. Jews, Christians, Mohammedans define God very positively, they say what he *is*. Hinduism defines God totally negatively, they say what he is not.

In the West this looked not very religious, because you cannot worship a negativity. You can worship only something positive, you can love only something positive, you can devote yourself only to something positive. How can you devote yourself to something which is simply a denial, a negativity, a *neti neti,* neither this nor that? You cannot make an idol of a negative Brahman. How can you make an idol of a negative Brahman?

That's why Hindus conceived their highest conception of Brahman as *shivalinga*. And people go on thinking that shivalinga is just a phallic symbol. It is not just a phallic symbol, that is just one of its implications. Shivalinga is a symbol of zero, *shunya,* the negative. Shivalinga doesn't define any image. There is no image on it – no face, no eyes, nothing; just a zero, not even one. And the zero can be infinite. Zero has no boundaries; it begins nowhere, it ends nowhere.

How can you worship a zero? How can you pray to a zero? But Hindus have totally a different conception. They say prayer is not really an address to God, because you cannot address anything to him. Where will you address him? – he is nowhere or everywhere. So prayer is not really some address; rather, on the contrary, prayer is your inner mutation. Hindus say you cannot pray, but you can be in a prayerful mood. So prayer is not something you can do, prayer is something you can only *be*.

And prayer is not for God, prayer is for you. You pray and through prayer you change. Nobody is listening to your prayer and nobody is going to help you, nobody is going to follow your prayer but just by praying your heart changes. Through prayer, if authentic, you become different – your assertion changes you.

In the south there is one old temple. If you go in the temple there is no deity; the place for the deity is vacant, empty. If you ask the priest, "Where is the deity? Whom to worship? And this is a temple – to whom does this temple belong? Who is the deity of this temple?" the priest will tell you, "This is the tradition of this temple – that we don't have any deity. The whole temple is the deity. You cannot look for the deity in a particular direction. He is everywhere – that's why the place is vacant."

The whole universe is Brahman. And this is such a vast phenomenon that positive terms will only make it finite; hence negativity – it is one of the highest conceptions possible. And this negativity reached its most logical extreme in Buddha. He would not even negate. He said, "Even if you negate, indirectly you assert, and every assertion is blasphemy."

Jews could have understood this. They have no name for God. Yahweh is not a name, it is just a symbol; or it means "the nameless." And in the old Jewish world before Jesus, the name was not to be asserted by everybody. Only the chief priest in the temple of Solomon was allowed once a year to assert the name. So once a year all the Jews would gather together at the great temple of Solomon, and the highest priest would assert the name, Yahweh. And it is not a name, the very word means the nameless.

Nobody was allowed to assert the name, because how can the finite assert the infinite? And whatsoever you say will be wrong because you are wrong. Whatsoever you say belongs to you, it comes through you, you are present in it. So unless you had become so empty that you were no more you were not allowed to assert the name. The highest priest was the man who had become just an emptiness, and to assert the name, for the whole year he would remain silent. He would prepare, he would become totally empty, no thought was allowed in the mind. For one year he would wait, prepare, become empty, become a nonentity, a nobody. When the right moment came he would stand just like an emptiness. The man was not there, there was nobody. The mind was not there. And then he would assert, Yahweh.

This tradition stopped because it became more and more difficult to find persons who could become nonentities, who could become nothingness, who could become anatta, nonbeing – who could destroy themselves so completely that God could assert through them, who could become just like a passage, just like a flute, empty, so that God could sing through it.

Buddha went to the very extreme. If you asked him about God he would remain totally silent. Once it happened: Ananda, his chief disciple, was sitting with Buddha, and a man came, a very cultured, refined philosopher, a great brahmin, and he asked, "Bhante, tell me something about the ultimate."

Buddha looked at him, remained silent, then closed his eyes. Ananda became disturbed, because this man was very useful. This brahmin had a great following, thousands followed him; if he was converted then thousands would become Buddhists. And Buddha remained silent, he didn't answer him. The man, the brahmin, bowed down, thanked Buddha and went away.

The moment he left Ananda asked, "What are you doing? You have missed a great opportunity. This man is no ordinary man. Thousands follow him, he is a great scholar. Thousands worship him, his word is significant. If he becomes a Buddhist, if he follows you, many will follow automatically – and you didn't answer him!"

Buddha said, "For a good horse even the shadow of a whip is enough. The shadow of the whip is enough, you need not beat him. He is converted."

Ananda was not convinced, but next day he saw the man coming with all his followers, his disciples; thousands followed, great scholars. He had a big ashram and they were all coming. Ananda couldn't believe his eyes. What was happening? – and Buddha had not answered the man. So again in the night he asked, "What has happened? You have done a miracle. I was there. You remained completely silent; not only silent, you closed your eyes. I thought this was insulting. The man had come with so much inquiry and you were rejecting him."

Buddha said, "This is the subtlest answer. He knows that nothing can be said about the ultimate. Had I said anything the man would have gone, because the very saying would have shown that my ultimate is not ultimate – it could be defined, something could be said about it. Nothing can be said. And that's why I even closed my eyes – because, who knows, he may have thought that I was saying something through my eyes. So I became completely silent, closed my eyes – this was my answer. And for a good horse even the shadow of the whip is enough. You need not beat him."

The Upanishads are negative about the Brahman. That's why they say "the nondual," that which is not two. Now we will enter the sutra:

The first stage, to which contentment and bliss impart sweetness, springs from the innermost recesses of the seeker's heart.

As I said to you, the first is the feeling, the first is the heart. The first stage be-longs to the heart and only the heart can know contentment and bliss. If you are in contact with your heart you will know contentment and bliss, just like sweet springs flowing towards you, filling you, overflooding you. But we don't have the contact with the heart. The heart is beating, but we don't have the contact.

You will have to understand it, because just by having a heart, don't go on thinking that you are in contact with it. You are not in contact with many things in your body, you are just carrying your body. Contact means a deep sensitivity. You may not even feel your body. It happens that only when you are ill do you feel your body. There is a headache, then you feel the head; without the head-ache there is no contact with the head. There is pain in the leg, you become aware of the leg. You become aware only when something goes wrong.

If everything is okay you remain completely unaware, and really, that is the moment when contact can be made – when everything is okay – because when something goes wrong then that contact is made with illness, with something that has gone wrong and the well-being is no more there. You have the head right now, then the headache comes and you make the contact. The contact is made not with the head but with the headache. With the head contact is possible only when there is no headache and the head is filled with a well-being. But we have almost lost the capacity. We don't have any contact when we are okay. So our contact is just an emergency measure. There is a headache: some repair is needed, some medicine is needed, something has to be done, so you make the contact and do something.

Try to make contact with your body when everything is good. Just lie down on the grass, close the eyes, and feel the sensation that is going on within, the well-being that is bubbling. Lie down in a river. The water is touching the body and every cell is being cooled. Feel inside how that coolness enters cell by cell, goes deep into the body. The body is a great phenomenon, one of the miracles of nature.

Sit in the sun. Let the sunrays penetrate the body. Feel the warmth as it moves within, as it goes deeper, as it touches your blood cells and reaches to the very bones. And sun is life, the very source. So with closed eyes just feel what is happening. Remain alert, watch and enjoy. By and by you will become aware of a very subtle harmony, a very beautiful music continuously going on inside. Then you have the contact with the body; otherwise you carry a dead body.

It is just like this: a person who loves his car has a different type of contact and relationship with the car than a person who doesn't. A person who doesn't love his car goes on driving it and he treats it as a mechanism, but a person who loves his car will become aware of even the smallest change in the mood of the car, the finest change of sound. Something is changing in the car and suddenly he will become aware of it. No one else has heard it; the passengers are sitting there, they have not heard it. But a slight change in the sound of the engine, any clicking, any change, and the person who loves his car will become aware of it. He has a deep contact. He is not only driving, the car is not just a mechanism; rather he has spread himself into the car and he has allowed the car to enter him.

Your body can be used as a mechanism, then you need not be very sensitive about it. And the body goes on saying many things you never hear because you don't have any contact….

In Russia a new research has been going on for thirty years. Now they have concluded many things. One result which is very revealing is this: that when-ever a disease happens, for six months continuously before it happens the body goes on giving signals to you. Six months is such a long time! A disease is going to happen in 1975; in the middle of 1974 the body will start giving you signals – but you don't hear, you don't understand, you don't know. When the disease has happened already, only then will you become aware. Or even then you may not be aware – your doctor first becomes aware that you have some deep trouble inside.

The person who has been doing this research for thirty years has now made films and cameras which can detect a disease before it actually happens. He says that the disease can be treated, and the patient will never become aware of whether it existed or not. If a cancer is going to happen next year it can be treated right now. There are no physical indications, but just in the body electricity things are changing – not in the body, in the body electricity, in the bioenergy, things are changing. First they will change in the bioenergy and then they will descend to the physical.

If they can be treated in the bioenergy layer then they will never come to the physical body. Because of this research it will become possible in the coming century that no one need be ill, there will be no more need to go to the hospital. Before the disease actually comes to the body it can be treated, but it has to be detected by a mechanical device. You cannot detect it, and you are there living in the body. There is no contact.

You may have heard many stories that Hindu sannyasins, rishis, Zen monks, Buddhist bhikkus, declare their death before it happens. And you may be surprised to know that that declaration is always made six months before it happens – never more, always six months before. Many saints have declared that they are going to die, but just six months before. It is not accidental, those six months are meaningful. Before the physical body dies the bioenergy starts dying, and a person who is in deep contact with his bioenergy knows that now the energy has started shrinking. Life means spreading, death means shrinking. He feels that the life energy is shrinking; he declares that he will be dead within six months. Zen monks are known to have even chosen how to die – because they know.

It happened once: one Zen monk was to die, so he asked his disciples, "Suggest to me how to die, in what posture." That man was a little eccentric, a little crazy, a mad old man but very beautiful.

His disciples started laughing; they thought that he may have been joking because he was always joking. So somebody suggested, "How about dying standing in the corner of the temple?"

The man said, "But I have heard a story that in the past one monk has died standing, so that won't be good. Suggest something unique."

So somebody said, "Die while just walking in the garden."

He said, "I have heard that somebody in China once died walking."

Then someone suggested a really unique idea: "Stand in *shirshasana*, headstand, and die." Nobody has ever died standing on his head, it is very difficult to die standing on the head. Even to sleep standing on the head is impossible, death is too difficult. Even to sleep is impossible and death is a great sleep. It is impossible – even ordinary sleep is impossible.

The man accepted the idea. He enjoyed it. He said, "This is good."

They thought that he was just joking, but he stood in shirshasana. They became afraid: What is he doing? And what to do now? And they thought he was almost dead. It was weird – a dead person standing in shirshasana. They became scared, so somebody suggested, "He has a sister in the nearby monastery who is a great nun. Go and fetch her. She is the elder sister of this man and may do something with him. She knows him well."

The sister came. It is said that she came and said, "Ikkyu" – Ikkyu was the name of the monk – "don't be foolish! This is no way to die."

Ikkyu laughed, jumped from his shirshasana, and said, "Okay, so what is the right way?"

She said, "Sit in *padmasana*, Buddha posture, and die. This is no way to die. You have always been a foolish man – everybody will laugh."

So it is said he sat in padmasana and died, and the sister left. A beautiful man. But how could he decide that he was going to die? And even to choose the posture! The bioenergy started shrinking, he could feel it – but this feeling comes only when you have a deep contact not only with the surface of the body but with the roots.

So first try to be more and more sensitive about your body. Listen to it; it goes on saying many things, and you are so head-oriented you never listen to it. Whenever there is a conflict between your mind and body, your body is almost always going to be right more than your mind, because the body is natural, your mind is societal; the body belongs to this vast nature, and your mind belongs to your society, your particular society, age, time. Body has deep roots in existence, mind is just wavering on the surface. But you always listen to the mind, you never listen to the body. Because of this long habit contact is lost.

You have the heart, and heart is the root, but you don't have any contact. First start having contact with the body. Soon you will become aware that the whole body vibrates around the center of the heart just as the whole solar system moves around the sun. Hindus have called the heart the sun of the body. The whole body is a solar system and moves around the heart. You became alive when the heart started beating, you will die when the heart stops beating. The heart remains the solar center of your body. Become alert to it. But you can be-come alert, by and by, only if you become alert to the whole body.

While hungry, why not meditate a little? – there is no hurry. While hungry just close your eyes and meditate on the hunger, on how the body is feeling. You may have lost contact, because our hunger is less bodily, more mental. You eat every day at one o'clock. You look at the watch; it is one – so then you feel hunger. And the clock may not be right. If somebody says, "That clock has stopped at midnight. It is not functioning. It is only eleven o'clock," the hunger disappears. This hunger is false, this hunger is just habitual, because the mind creates it, not the body. Mind says, "One o'clock – you are hungry." You have to be hungry. You have always been hungry at one o'clock, so you are hungry.

Our hunger is almost ninety-nine percent habitual. Go on a fast for a few days to feel real hunger, and you will be surprised. For the first three or four days you will feel very hungry. On the fourth or fifth day you will not feel so hungry. This is illogical, because as the fast grows you should feel more and more hungry. But after the third day you will feel less hungry, and after the seventh day you may completely forget hunger. After the eleventh day almost everybody forgets hunger completely and the body feels absolutely okay. Why? And if you continue the fast.... Those who have done much work on fasting say that only after the twenty-first day will real hunger happen again.

So it means that for three days your mind was insisting that you were hungry because you had not taken food, but it was not hunger. Within three days the mind gets fed up with telling you; you are not listening, you are so indifferent. On the fourth day the mind doesn't say anything, the body doesn't feel hunger. For three weeks you will not feel hunger, because you have accumulated so much fat – that fat will do. You will feel hunger only after the third week. And this is for normal bodies. If you have too much fat accumulated you may not feel hungry even after the third week. And there is a possibility to accumulate enough fat to live on for three months, ninety days. When the body is finished with the accumulated fat, then for the first time real hunger will be felt. But it will be difficult. You can try with thirst, that will be easy. For one day don't take water, and wait. Don't drink out of habit, just wait and see what thirst means, what thirst would mean if you were in a desert.

Lawrence of Arabia has written in his memoirs: "For the first time in my life, when I was once lost in the desert, I became aware of what thirst is – because before that there was no need. Whenever my mind said, 'Now you are thirsty,' I took water. In the desert, lost, no water with me and no way to find an oasis, for the first time I became thirsty. And that thirst was something wonderful – the whole of the body, every cell, asking for water. It became a phenomenon."

If you take water in that type of thirst, it will give you a contentment that you cannot know just by drinking through habit.

So I say to you that Mahavira, and people like Mahavira, have known the real taste of food. You cannot know it...because for three months Mahavira would fast, then he would go begging. And he would go begging only when the body would say so, not the mind. When the body would say, "Now I am exhausted completely," and the hunger gripped the whole body and every cell of it asked, then he would go begging. He would not listen to the mind. He must have tasted food as no one has ever tasted on this earth. But Jainas think completely differently; they think that he was taste-less, they think that he had no taste. My feeling is, only he knew what taste is, and he knew it with his whole body, his whole being.

You know only by your tongue, and that tongue is very deceptive. That tongue has been serving the mind so long it is no more serving the body. The tongue can deceive you, it has become a slave of the mind. It can go on saying, "Go on eating. It is very beautiful." It is not serving the body any more, otherwise the tongue would say, "Stop!" The tongue would say, "Whatsoever you are eating is useless. Don't eat!" Even the tongues of cows and buffaloes are more body-rooted than your tongue. You cannot force a buffalo to eat any type of grass – she chooses. You cannot force your dog to eat when he is ill – he will immediately go out, eat some grass and vomit. He is more in contact with his body.

First one has to become deeply aware of this phenomenon of the body. A revival of the body, a resurrection, is needed – you are carrying a dead body. Then only will you feel, by and by, that the whole body with all its desires, thirsts and hungers, is revolving around the heart. Then the beating heart is not only a mechanism, it is the beating life, it is the very pulsation of life. That pulsation gives contentment and bliss.

Contentment and bliss impart sweetness.

Your whole being becomes sweet, a sweetness surrounds you, it becomes your aura. Whenever a person is in contact with his heart you will immediately fall in love with him. Immediately, the moment you see him, you will fall in love with him. You don't know why. He has a sweetness around him. That sweetness your mind may not be able to detect, but your heart detects it immediately. He has an aura. The moment you come into his aura you are intoxicated. You feel a longing for him, you feel an attraction, a magnetic force working. You may not be consciously aware of what is happening; you may simply say, "I don't know why I am attracted," but this is the reason. A person who lives in his heart has a milieu around him of sweetness – sweetness flows around him. You are flooded with it whenever you are in contact with that person.

Buddha, Jesus, attracted millions of people, and the reason is that they lived in the heart; otherwise it was impossible. What Buddha demanded was impossible. Thousands of people left their homes, became beggars with him, moved with him in all types of sufferings, austerities, and enjoyed it. This is a miracle. And those who left their homes were rich, affluent people, because India knew the golden age in the time of Buddha. It was at its highest peak of richness. Just as America is today, India was at that moment. At that moment the West was just wild; no civilization existed really. The West was totally uncivilized at the time of Buddha, and India was at its golden peak.

Buddha attracted millions of people who were rich, living in comfort, and they moved and became beggars. What filled them, what attracted them, what was the cause? Even they couldn't explain what the cause was. This is the cause: whenever a person of heart is there, a person who lives in his heart, he imparts around him vibrations of sweetness. Just being in his presence, being near him, you feel a sudden joy for no visible cause. He is not giving you anything, he is not giving you any physical comfort. On the contrary, he may lead you into physical uncomfort; through him you may have to pass through many sufferings – but you will enjoy those sufferings.

Buddha was dying, and Ananda, his disciple, was weeping. So Buddha said, "Why are you weeping?"

Ananda said, "With you I can move on this earth, millions of times I can be reborn and it will not be a suffering. I can suffer everything. Just if you are there, then this *sansar*, which you call *dukkha*, suffering, is no more suffering – but without you even nirvana will not be blissful."

Such a sweetness surrounded Buddha, such a sweetness surrounded Jesus, such a sweetness surrounded Saint Francis, such a sweetness surrounds all those who have lived through the heart. Their charisma is that they live in their heart.

Jesus was not a very learned man, he was just a villager; he remained a carpenter's son. He was talking in people's ways, ordinary parables. If someone gives you Jesus' parables, his statements, without saying that these belong to Jesus, you will throw the book, you will never read it again. But he influenced people, impressed so much, that Christianity became the greatest religion of the world. Half the earth belongs now to Christianity, to a carpenter's son who was not educated, not cultured. What is this mystery? How did it happen? He was not a man of knowledge, he was not like Bertrand Russell. Bertrand Russell could have easily defeated him in any argument. It is not difficult to conceive of that. Jesus could be defeated easily.

It happened in India in just the last century. Ramakrishna, Vivekananda's master, was here. He was a man of heart, completely uneducated, not in any way proficient in the scriptures. He had no logic, no arguing force, could not convince anybody. It happened that one of the greatest scholars ever born in India, Keshavchandra Sen, went to see Ramakrishna. He was a great scholar, very logical, rational, argumentative, so many people followed just to see what would happen, because everybody knew – it was decided – that Ramakrishna would be defeated immediately. Nobody could argue with Keshavchandra.

Ramakrishna's disciples were very scared. They also knew that this Keshavchandra was going to be difficult, and once Keshavchandra defeated Ramakrishna – and he could defeat him on any point, there was no question about it – then that defeat would spread all over the country. So what to do? How to protect Ramakrishna? They started thinking. They were so worried they couldn't sleep for days. Whenever they said anything to Ramakrishna he laughed and he said, "Let him come. I am waiting."

Then that day came. The whole ashram was sad. Keshavchandra came, very proud, very egoistic. And he had reason to be proud and egoistic; he was one of the finest intellects, a genius. And many of his followers came; professors of the universities, pundits, scholars, men who knew the Vedas – there was a big, big crowd of many renowned persons. Keshavchandra started the argument. "Does God exist?"

So Ramakrishna said, "You say whatsoever you want to say."

Keshavchandra started criticizing, saying that there is no God, but by and by he became very uncomfortable, because whenever he would give an argument against God, Ramakrishna would laugh and enjoy so much that there was no argument. And he would say, "Right! Absolutely right!" He was not refuting, he was not going against, so the whole thing became nonsense because you can defeat a person only when he argues. The very effort to win was futile because there was no one to defeat. Then by and by he became sad, and the whole thing looked useless. Then he asked Ramakrishna, "Why do you go on saying 'Yes'? I am saying God is no more!" Keshavchandra thought, "He is so foolish, he cannot understand what I am saying."

Ramakrishna said only one thing: "I was never so convinced that God is before I saw you, but the moment I saw you I was absolutely convinced that God is."

Keshavchandra asked, "Why?"

Ramakrishna said, "How could such a beautiful mind exist without God? Such a refined intellect. You convince me that God is! I am a poor man, uneducated; such a mind like me can exist even without God, but such a mind like you? – impossible!"

Keshavchandra had to touch his feet and say, "You have defeated me!" He became a lifelong devotee of Ramakrishna.

What was the miracle? What was the charisma? A person living in the heart. Keshavchandra is reported to have said to his followers, "This man is dangerous, don't go near him. He has converted me, not saying anything, just being present there, laughing, enjoying. And he filled me with such sweetness as I have never known. Just in his presence I have felt the first ecstasy of my life, the peak experience. The unknown has touched me."

The first stage, to which contentment and bliss impart sweetness, springs from the innermost recesses of the seeker's heart, as if nectar has issued forth from the heart of the earth. At the inception of this stage the innermost recess becomes a field for the coming of the other stages. Afterwards the seeker attains the second and third stages. Of the three, the third is the highest, because on its attainment all the modifications of will come to an end.

All the modifications of will come to an end. The third is the highest. And the reason? Let it penetrate deep in your heart. The third is the highest. Why? – because all the modifications of will come to an end. Your will is the cause of your ego. You think you can do something, you think you will do something, you think you have got willpower, you think that there is a possibility for you to struggle with existence and win. Will means the attitude to fight, the attitude to conquer, the attitude to struggle. Will is the force of violence in you.

Bertrand Russell has written about "the conquest of nature." This is impossible to conceive in the East. Lao Tzu cannot use these words, conquest of nature, because who will conquer nature? You are nature. Who will conquer nature? You are not separate from it. But the West has lived for these twenty centuries with this wrong concept – the conquest of nature. We have to defeat nature, to destroy it, to cripple it, to force it to follow us. You cannot win, this whole struggle is nonsense, because you are nature. There is no division. The East says, "Follow nature, become nature. Leave the will. The will is the cause of misery. The will is the door to hell."

The third is thought to be highest, because when you leave all desires there is no need for the will – because will is needed to fulfill desires. You have desires, you need will. There are many books in the West, and particularly in America, which go on teaching willpower. And they are sold in millions, they are best-sellers, because everybody thinks that he has to conquer and create willpower. People even come to me, to such a person who is absolutely against will, and they say, "Help us. How can we have more willpower?"

Will is your impotence. Because of will you are defeated, because you are doing something absolutely absurd, something which cannot happen. When you leave will, only then will you be powerful. When there is no will you have become potent. Omnipotent also you can become when there is no will, because then you are one with the universe, then the whole universe is your power.

With the will you are a fragment fighting with the whole existence, with such a small quantity of energy. And that energy is also given by the universe. The universe is so playful that it even allows you to fight with it, it gives you the energy. The universe gives you the breath, the universe gives you the life, and enjoys your fighting. It is just as a father enjoys fighting with a child and challenges the child to fight. The child starts fighting and the father falls down and helps the child to win. This is a game for the father. The child may be serious, may get mad; he will think, "I have conquered."

In the West this childishness has become the source of many miseries: Hiroshima, Nagasaki, the two world wars, were because of this will. Science should not be any more the conquest of nature. Science must now become the way towards nature – surrender to nature, not conquest of nature. And unless science becomes Taoist – surrender to nature – science is going to eliminate the whole of humanity from this earth. This planet will be destroyed by science. And science can destroy only because science has become associated with this absurd notion of conquest.

Man has willpower. Every will is against nature, your will is against nature. When you can say totally, "Not mine, but your will should be done" – "your" means the divine, the totality, the wholeness – for the first time you become powerful. But this power doesn't belong to you, you are just a passage. This power belongs to the cosmos.

The third is the highest, because all the modifications of will come to an end. Not only the will but the modifications – because will can get modified. We saw that the Upanishad divides desirelessness, nonattachment, in two parts. First, when you make effort to be nonattached – that too is a modification of the will. You struggle, you control, you detach yourself, you make all the efforts to remain a witness. Those efforts to remain a witness belong to your will, so really that is not real nonattachment, just a rehearsal; not real, just a training ground.

Nonattachment will become real only in the second stage, when even this struggle to be a witness has dropped; when even the idea that "I am a witness" has dropped, when there is no more conflict between you and existence. No more any conflict, you simply flow with it.

Lao Tzu is reported to have said, "I struggled hard but I was defeated again and again, fortunately." He says, "Fortunately I was defeated again and again. No effort succeeded, and then I realized – against whom am I fighting? Against myself I am fighting, against the greater part of my own being I am fighting. It is as if my hand is fighting against my body, and the hand belongs to the body. It can fight, but the hand has the energy through the body." Lao Tzu says, "When I realized that I am part of this cosmos, that I am not separate – the cosmos breathes in me, lives in me, and I am fighting it – then the fight dropped. Then I became like a dead leaf."

Why like a dead leaf? – because the dead leaf has no will of her own. The wind comes, takes the dead leaf; the dead leaf goes with the wind. The wind is going north, the dead leaf doesn't say, "I want to go to the south." The dead leaf goes to the north. Then the wind changes its course, starts flowing towards the south. The dead leaf doesn't say, "You are contradictory. First you were going to the north, now you are going to the south. Now I want to go to the north." No, that leaf doesn't say anything. She moves to south, she moves to north, and if the wind stops she falls down on the ground and rests. She doesn't say, "This was not the right time for me to rest." When the wind raises her into the sky the dead leaf doesn't say, "I am the peak of existence." When she falls to the ground she is not frustrated. A dead leaf simply has no will of her own. "Thy will be done." She moves with the wind, wheresoever it leads. She has got no goal, she has no purpose of her own.

Lao Tzu says, "When I became like a dead leaf, then everything was achieved. Then there was nothing to be achieved any more. Then all bliss became mine."

All the modifications of will come to an end. One who practices the three stages finds his ignorance dead, and on entering the fourth stage he sees everything, everywhere, equally.

Two things: *One who practices these three stages finds his ignorance dead*. Your ignorance cannot become dead by accumulating knowledge. You can accumulate all the knowledge available in the world, you can become an *Encyclopaedia Britannica*, but that won't help. You can become a walking encyclopedia, but your ignorance will not be dead through that. Rather, on the contrary, your ignorance will become hidden, secret; it will move to the deep recesses of the heart. So on the surface you will be knowledgeable and deep down you will remain ignorant. This is what has happened, and all the universities go on helping this.

Your ignorance is never dead; it is alive, working. And just on the surface you are decorated, you are a painted being. Your knowledge is painted just on the surface and deep down you remain ignorant. The knowledge, real knowledge, can happen only when the ignorance is dead. Before that, knowledge will remain information – borrowed, not yours, not authentic – it has not happened to you. It is not a lived experience, but only words, verbal, scriptural.

And ignorance can become dead only when you practice these first three stages, because ignorance is a mode of life, not a question of information. It is a way of life, a wrong way of life, that creates ignorance. It is not just a question of memory, of how much you know, or how much you don't know – that is not the point. That's why Ramakrishna can become wise and Keshavchandra remains ignorant. Jesus became enlightened and Pontius Pilate remained ignorant. He was more cultured than Jesus, more educated; he had all the education that was possible. He was the governor-general, the viceroy, he knew whatsoever could be known through books. And in the last moment before Jesus was sent to the cross he asked him a very philosophical question.

Nietzsche wrote about Pontius Pilate, because Nietzsche was always against Jesus. When he became mad in the end – and he was bound to become mad because his whole way of life, the whole style was madness – he started signing his signature as "Anti-Christ, Friedrich Nietzsche." He would never sign his signature without writing before it "Anti-Christ." He was absolutely against Jesus. He says that only Pontius Pilate was the man who knew, and Jesus was simply an ignorant carpenter's son. And the reason that he proposes is that in the last moment before Jesus went to the cross, Pontius Pilate asked him, "What is truth?" This is one of the most significant philosophical questions which has always been asked, and philosophers enjoy answering it – but nobody has answered yet. To Nietzsche Jesus looks foolish. He writes that when Pontius Pilate asked Jesus, "What is truth?" he was asking precisely the peak question, the sole question, the ultimate question, the base of all philosophy, the base of all inquiry – and Jesus remained silent.

Nietzsche says that was because in the first place Jesus would not have understood what Pontius Pilate meant, and secondly, he could not answer because he didn't know what truth is. He was ignorant, that's why he remained silent. And I say to you, he remained silent because he knew, and he knew well that this question can never be answered verbally.

Pontius Pilate was foolish – educated, well-educated, but foolish – because this question cannot be asked in such a way, and it cannot be answered when a person is going to be hanged. For the answer to this question Pontius Pilate would have had to live with Jesus for years, because the whole life has to be transformed, only then can the answer be given. Or the transformed life itself becomes the answer, there is no need to give it.

Jesus remained silent, that shows he was a wise man. Had he given any answer, to me he would have proved that he was ignorant. Even Jesus' followers became a little uncomfortable, because they thought that had he answered Pontius Pilate, and had Pilate been convinced that his answer was true there would have been no crucifixion. But crucifixion is better than answering a foolish question with a foolish answer. Crucifixion is always better than that. And Jesus chose crucifixion rather than answering this foolish question…because such questions need a mutation in life; you have to work upon yourself.

Truth is not something which can be handed over to you. You will have to raise your consciousness, you will have to come to the climax of your being. Only from there the glimpse becomes possible.

And when you die completely to your ego truth is revealed, never before. It is not a philosophical inquiry, it is a religious transformation.

One who practices the three stages finds his ignorance dead, and on entering the fourth stage he sees everything, everywhere, equally. At that moment he is so strongly embedded in the experience of nonduality – advaita – that the experience itself disappears.

This is a very subtle and delicate point. Let it go deep in your heart. He is so embedded in the fourth stage.... After the three stages the fourth follows automatically. The three have to be practiced, the three have to be deeply rooted in your being through your effort – the fourth happens. Suddenly you become aware that there is nonduality, only one exists – one being, one existence.

He is so strongly embedded in the experience of advaita – nonduality – that the experience itself disappears.

...Because for experience to exist, duality is needed. So the Upanishads say you cannot experience God. If you experience God, then the God remains separate and you remain separate, because only the other can be experienced. Experience divides. This is the deepest message of all the Upanishads: "experience divides," because whenever you say experience it means there are three things: the experiencer, the experienced, and the relationship between the two, the experience.

The Upanishads say that God cannot be known, because knowledge divides the knower, the known and the knowledge. If really you have become one, how can you experience? So even the experience disappears. The Upanishads say a person who claims he has experienced the divine is false, his claim proves that he is false. A knower cannot claim, one who has really experienced the divine cannot claim, because the very experience disappears. Buddha says again and again, "Don't ask me what I have experienced. If I say anything then I am not true. Rather come near me, and you also go through the experience."

One man came, Maulangputta, and he asked Buddha serious questions. Buddha said, "You wait for one year and then I will give you the answers. And for one year you have to follow me, whatsoever I say, with no argument, no discussion. Put your reason aside. For one year be with me and experience, and after one year has elapsed you can ask all your questions, bring all your reason back, and then I will answer you."

While Buddha was saying this and Maulangputta was being convinced, one sannyasin, one bhikku of Buddha, Sariputta, who was sitting under a tree, started laughing. Maulangputta became uncomfortable. He asked Sariputta, "Why are you laughing? What is wrong?"

Sariputta said, "Don't be deceived. This man is a deceiver – he deceived me the same way. Now I cannot ask, so he need not answer. If you want to ask at all, ask now. After one year it will be too late!"

Then one year passed, and Maulangputta waited, meditated, became more and more silent, and started realizing why Sariputta was laughing – because the questions were disappearing. One year passed and then he started hiding, because if he met Buddha he would say, "Now where are the questions?"

But Buddha remembered. Exactly on the day when he had come one year be-fore, exactly on that day as he was hiding behind ten thousand monks, Buddha said, "Where is Maulangputta? He must come now, the time has come. Bring your reason and bring all your questions. I am prepared to answer."

Maulangputta stood, and said, "You are really a deceiver. That Sariputta was right – because now I have no questions!"

Buddha says, "Experience – and you cannot even claim that you have experienced."…Because who will experience? There is no other. Who will experience whom? Even the experience itself disappears. There is nothing like God-experience; it is only in the minds of the ignorant. The knowers know that God disappears and the I disappears, the duality disappears. Knowing is there, but the knower is not and the known is not.

Because of this Mahavira has used a beautiful word. He calls it *kaivalya gyan;* he calls it, "Only knowing remains" – only knowing, neither the known nor the knower. You disappear, the God you were seeking disappears, because really the God you were seeking was created by you. It was your ignorance that was seeking. Your God was part of your ignorance. It is bound to be. How can you seek the real God? You don't know it.

You project your God through your ignorance, you seek it. All your heavens are part of your ignorance. All your truths are part of your ignorance. You seek them and then your ignorance disappears. When your ignorance disappears where will those gods remain who were created by your ignorance? They will also disappear.

It happened: when Rinzai became enlightened he asked for a cup of tea. His disciples said, "This seems to be profane."

And he said, "The whole thing was foolishness: the seeking, the seeker, the sought. The whole thing was foolishness. You just give me a cup of tea! None existed. The seeker was false, the sought was false, so of course the seeking was false. It was a cosmic joke."

That's why I say there is no purpose – God is joking with you. The moment you can understand the joke you are enlightened. Then the whole thing be-comes a play, even the experience disappears.

Thus, on attaining the fourth stage the seeker finds the world as illusory as a dream. So while the first three stages are called waking ones, the fourth is dreaming.

When the fourth stage is attained, when even God disappears, when the God-seeker, the worshipper disappears, this whole world becomes like a dream. Not that it is not there – it is there, but like a dream; it has no substantiality in it. It is a mental phenomenon, it is a thought process. You enjoy it, you live in it, but you know that this is all a dream.

This is the Hindu concept of the world, they say it is a dream in the mind of God. It is just as when you dream in the night; when you dream you can create a reality in the dream, and you never suspect that this is a dream and you are the creator. The beauty is this – that you are the creator, you are the projector, and you cannot suspect that it is just a dream. Hindus say that as there are private dreams, individual dreams, this is the collective dream – God dreaming the world. You are a dream object in the God's dream. We take dreams to be real, and Hindus say the reality is a dream.

I will tell you one anecdote.

Once it happened, Mulla Nasruddin was fast asleep with his wife in bed. The wife started dreaming; she had a very beautiful dream. One charming young man was making love to her, and she was enjoying it very much. She was old, ugly, and he was a very charming young prince and she was enjoying it.

Suddenly in the dream, when she was enjoying the lovemaking, Mulla Nasruddin entered from the roof – in the dream. She became afraid. She became so afraid and disturbed that she said loudly, "My God, my husband!" She said it so loudly that Mulla heard it and jumped out of the window. He thought he was sleeping with some other woman.

Our dreams are realities for us.
For the Upanishads, our reality is just a dream.

13   When the Coin
        Disappears

Osho,

Some mystics have been very introverted and silent. In your own case, you appear to be moving both introvertedly and extrovertedly without any difficulty. Please explain how this is possible.

The mind goes on dividing on every level of being. Wherever the mind looks immediately it divides; division, to divide, is the nature of the mind. So we say above and below, we say up and down, we say this world and the other world, we say life and death, we say in and out, extroversion and introversion – but all these divisions are of the mind. The below is part of the above, the beginning of the above; up is nothing but the extension of down. Life and death are not two, but the same energy arising is life, the same energy dissolving is death. Out and in are not two, the division is only mental.

But we exist extrovertedly, we exist outside. The ordinary man exists outside, he never goes in. He moves further and further out, because desires can be fulfilled only in the outside; some object is needed to fulfill them. The object can be found in the outside, there is no object within – there is only subjectivity, there is only you. You need something to fulfill desires, so you move in the world. The out is created because desires are moving outwardly.

Then a moment comes in everyone's life when you get frustrated with this whole business – desires, the search for them, the objects – and you come to realize that the whole thing is futile. Then the other extreme arises in the mind: "Don't go out, go in!" Then you simply reverse the whole process. Before you were going out, now you start going in; before you were for the out, now you have become against it.

This type of mind which has become against the world, the out, is just the same man, the same mind, standing on its head. You are standing on your feet, he is standing on his head, but he is the same man, there is no difference. The difference comes into being only when you are not moving at all, neither out nor in, when the division between out and in has dropped.

And this can drop only when you are not. If you are, then you are bound to divide the within and the without. When the ego disappears, which is within? Where is within then? It was around your ego. If ego has disappeared, then where is within and where is without? They were in relation to your ego. When the ego has disappeared, out and in disappear – then there is no introversion and no extroversion. Man exists as extrovert or introvert, but when you transcend the ego you have transcended the man. Then you simply exist – the within and without have become one, the boundaries have disappeared.

Just as we are sitting inside this room...if these walls disappear, then what will be the inside and what will be the outside? Then the inside will become the outside and the outside will become the inside. In actuality, even now this very moment, is the space outside and the space within really divided? Can you divide it? You can create walls but you cannot divide it, you cannot cut space. And you can use the inside only because of the doors; otherwise you cannot use the inside. And from the door it continues to be the same, from the door the inside and the outside are one.

Lao Tzu uses this symbol very much. He goes on saying that the room is valuable not because of the walls but because of the doors. The room has value not because of the walls but because of the doors – and doors mean no division between outside and inside.

Doors are the link, you can come in and you can go out. But if you destroy the walls then the division disappears, when the ego drops the division disappears.

So Jung's psychology will be meaningless when the ego has disappeared. Jung divides mind into two, the extrovert mind and the introvert mind – but this is a division of the mind, not of consciousness. Consciousness is just like space, mind is just the walls. But you can use mind only because mind has a few doors, and through those doors the within moves into the without and the without goes on moving into the within.

A mystic is a person whose mind has disappeared, he has attained to no-mind. So if a mystic insists that "I am against the world," he is not a mystic really; he still belongs to the world, because he still carries the same division.

I will tell you an anecdote.

It happened once two Zen monks were returning to their monastery. The evening was near, the sun was just going to set, and they came upon a small stream. When they were just going to cross the stream they saw a very beautiful young girl there. One monk who was old, traditional, orthodox, immediately closed his eyes because it is not good to see a woman – desire may arise, lust may come in, passion may happen. Just to avoid he closed his eyes and moved into the stream.

The other monk who was a young man, newly ordained, not well trained in the orthodoxy of the sect, asked the girl, "Why are you standing here? The sun is going to set, soon it will be night, and this place is lonely."

The girl said, "I am afraid to go into the stream. Can't you help me a little? Can't you give me your hand?"

The monk said, "The stream is deep. It will be better if you come and sit on my shoulders and I will carry you."

The other monk, the old monk, reached the other shore and then he looked back: what was happening? And when he saw that the girl was sitting on the monk's shoulders he became very disturbed. His mind was revolving fast: "This is sin!" He himself also felt guilty, because he was older, senior; he should have told the other young monk to avoid the situation. This is sin and he would have to report it to the abbot.

The young monk crossed the stream, left the girl there, and started going towards the monastery. The monastery must have been one or two miles away. They walked. The old monk was so angry that he couldn't speak. They walked in silence. Then they reached the door of the monastery, and when they were crossing the door the old monk stopped and said, "You have done wrong! It is prohibited! You should not have done this!"

The young monk was surprised. He said, "What? What are you saying? What have I done? I have remained completely silent. I have not even said a single word."

The old monk said, "I am not talking about these two miles you have walked with me, I am talking about that beautiful young girl you were carrying in the stream."

The young man said, "But I dropped the girl there and it seems you are still carrying her."

If a mystic is really a mystic he cannot carry any division. He cannot say, "That is outside and this is inside," because only ego can divide; ego is the boundary. Only mind can divide, no-mind cannot divide. Nothing is outside and nothing is in – the whole existence is advaita, one, nondual. Divisibility is not possible – it is oneness, it is a harmony, no boundaries exist. But if somebody goes on condemning....

There are monks, millions of monks all over the world in Hindu monasteries, in Christian monasteries, in Buddhist monasteries, who are afraid of the outside and who go on condemning it. That shows they are really interested, still interested in the outside; otherwise, why condemn? They have a deep unconscious lust for it, otherwise why condemn? Their condemnation shows they have some deep greed for it. When the greed really disappears how can there be condemnation? How can you hate the world? The hate is possible if love is somewhere hidden behind. Love and hate are not two things, love-hate is the phenomenon; they are two aspects of the same coin. You can change the aspects, from love you can come to hate. When you were in love with the world hate was hidden be-hind; now you hate the world, love is hidden behind – the other aspect remains.

A real mystic is one for whom the coin has disappeared; there is no hate, no love – no hate-love relationship. He simply exists without dividing. And there is no difficulty in it. If you try to make a harmony between the two then there will be difficulty, if you try somehow to synthesize then there will be difficulty. You cannot synthesize. This has been tried.

Reading the Upanishad you may come to realize, intellectually of course, that the out and the in are one, within and without are the same. If you realize intellectually then you will start trying to make a synthesis of the division. In the first place division is wrong; in the second place, to try to synthesize is doubly wrong, because synthesis means that you still think they are divided and somehow they have to be joined. Then it is very difficult and your synthesis will remain superficial, deep down the division will exist. You can only whitewash it, that's all – you cannot do much.

But it is very simple if you disappear. Then there is no need to synthesize. When *you* disappear they are simply one – there is no need to synthesize, there is no need to join them together. They were never apart. They have always been joined, they have always been one. It was you, because of you the division existed.

Many people try many types of synthesis. In India this last century, many people have tried to synthesize all religions, the divisions of religions. Gandhi made much effort to synthesize Christianity, Hinduism, and Mohammedanism, but the whole effort was a failure. It was bound to be a failure, because in the first place he believed in the division – that they are separate – and then he tried a synthesis. The foundation was that they are separate and they have to be joined together, so at the most he could create a hodgepodge thing – not very meaningful, not alive. The real synthesis happens only when you can see there are no divisions. Not that you synthesize – simply you see there are no divisions. There is no need to join them together, they have never been apart.

A mystic is one who has disappeared. Through his disappearance all divisions simply disappear. And I say all divisions, absolutely all divisions. He cannot divide between the good and the bad, he cannot divide between God and the Devil, he cannot divide between hell and heaven – simply he cannot divide. It is not only a question of in and out, because that's very simple. We can think, "Okay, maybe in and out are the same" – but heaven and hell? Devil and God?

You may not be aware that the English word devil comes from the same root as the word divine. Both come from the Sanskrit root; the Sanskrit root is *dev*. Dev means god, divine, *devata*. From dev comes the English word divine, and from dev comes the English word devil. Both are divine. Both are one. Good and bad…. Very difficult to conceive, because the mind persists. How can one think that the bad is also good and the good is also bad?

Look. For a moment try to look into the nondivided reality of things. Can you think of any man who is good if there exists no man who is bad? Can you think of Buddha, Krishna, Christ, without there existing a Hitler, Mussolini, Stalin, Napoleon, Alexander? You cannot conceive of it. A Buddha cannot exist without there being someone who is a Genghis Khan, a Tamerlane. Tamerlane is also impossible, cannot exist, if there exists no Buddha. Just look in your society: the sinner cannot exist without the saint and the saint cannot exist without the sinner – they are joined together.

Many people come from the West and ask me, "In India there have been so many saints, but the whole society seems to be of sinners. Why this paradox?" This is not a paradox, this is a simple, obvious fact; this must be so because saints can exist only amidst sinners. They are not two – the more saints, the more sinners. If you want sinners to disappear you will have to destroy saints first; when saints disappear sinners disappear.

Lao Tzu says in Tao Te Ching that when the world was really religious there were no saints. When there were saints immediately sinners appeared. So the saint cannot exist without the sinner. That means they are joined together somehow, they are part of one reality. Make one disappear and the other will disappear automatically.

It is just like hot and cold; make hot disappear completely and cold will disappear, because cold is nothing but a degree of hot. Make cold disappear completely and hot will disappear, because the difference is only of degrees, the quality is the same. And saints and sinners are just like hot and cold, they are degrees on the same thermometer. Destroy one, the other is destroyed immediately – they exist as polarities. People go on asking, "If God is good then why is there evil in this world?" God cannot exist without the evil, the evil is because God is. The light cannot exist without darkness, neither can the darkness exist without light.

For Christianity this has been such a big problem that for twenty centuries Christian theologians have been continuously working on this one problem: why does evil exist if God is good? They have not solved it, and they will never be able to solve it because they cannot see the simple reality that good and bad are two degrees of the same phenomenon. So they have to divide. They say, "All good belongs to God, and all bad belongs to the Devil."

And from where does this Devil come? If the Devil comes from God himself then why so much fuss about it? He belongs to God. If the Devil is a separate source from God then two Gods exist in this world, and then there is no necessity that the good God will win. The whole situation seems to be otherwise. If the Devil is also a separate source there is every possibility that he will win – because he is winning ninety-nine percent of the time every day! If they are separate sources then it is better to worship the Devil, because you are on the losing side if you go on worshipping God.

So Christian theologians cannot say that the Devil is a separate source; they say that the Devil was also an angel of God, but then he disobeyed. They go on shifting the problem. Then from where does this disobedience come? If it comes from the Devil himself then he becomes a separate source. Or if God himself suggests it to him then it becomes a play, a game.

When I was saying last night that life is a game, a play, and God is playing this whole cosmic joke, one friend immediately wrote a letter saying that it cannot be conceived that Jesus being crucified is just God's play. The crucifixion of Jesus cannot be conceived of as just God's play, it must have some purpose.

The question is not whether any particular thing has some purpose or not, the question is whether the whole has a purpose or not. You are here. You had a purpose in coming here, that I know; without purpose you would not be here. Jesus may have had a purpose, or you may think that he had a purpose. Christians may think that he had a purpose – salvation was the purpose, to liberate humanity from the sin that Adam committed was the purpose. But this is your thinking. If Jesus is enlightened he cannot have any purpose, because purpose belongs to ignorance. He can only be in a play. And if he also thinks that whatsoever he is doing is very serious, purposive, then he belongs to the same business mind as you.

And the whole, the cosmos, cannot have any purpose, because purpose means something outside. There is nothing outside the whole. And whenever we think that God must have some purpose we are talking in deep absurdities, because if God has any purpose, he is omnipotent so he can do it immediately. Why waste so much time? If he has only this purpose – that man should reach heaven – he can simply order, "Go to heaven!"...because when he can say, "Let there be light," and there is light; when he can say, "Let there be the world," and the world is there, then why can't he say, "Let there be only heaven," so that everybody is in heaven? Then why this whole nonsense of Adam committing sin, then Jesus helping people? Why this nonsense?

Purpose is absurd in terms of the total. Purpose may exist for individual egos because egos cannot exist without purpose, but for the cosmic there is no ego. It cannot be anything else than a cosmic play. Even Jesus' crucifixion is a play. That's why Jesus can go to the crucifixion so easily, not disturbed, as if it is just a drama, as if he is just acting a role. The man of knowledge is just an actor enacting a role. What is going to be the result is not his concern. Whatsoever the result, everything is good. There is neither good nor bad, there is neither in nor out, there is neither beginning nor end – but this happens only when you have disappeared.

You can misunderstand me. I am not saying to go and do evil because there is no difference. I am not saying to go and kill somebody because it is just a drama. And if you are really thinking of killing someone, then when you are sent to jail or killed, murdered by the court, then you will have to enjoy it – it is a game. If you are ready to accept the whole, then you can go and kill. But then don't complain – because in a game, in a play, complaining is useless.

To understand this intellect alone will not be of much help. It can only prepare the ground. Unless your being is transformed you cannot see this unity, you cannot see this vast unity of polar opposites. They exist together, they disappear together. Gurdjieff used to say an apparently very absurd thing, but deep down a reality. He used to say that everything remains in the same quantity always, the proportion remains the same. The same proportion always remains between saints and sinners. That cannot be disturbed, otherwise the world will lose balance. The same proportion exists between ignorant people and people who are wise – that cannot be disturbed.

Now modern psychology also has discovered a few facts which are relevant. One of them is this: five percent of people, only five percent, are intelligent, talented, genius, and five percent of people are idiotic, stupid – exactly the same proportion. On one polarity five percent with intelligence, on another polarity five percent with complete absence of intelligence. And then there are other grades, and every grade has a proportionate grade on the other side. You can divide the whole world. It is like two polarities balancing each other; whenever something grows more, immediately the balance has to be regained.

It is just like a walker, a tightrope walker. The tightrope walker has a trick, a balancing trick. Whenever he feels that he is losing balance and is leaning towards the left and will fall down, immediately he moves to the right. When he feels that he has moved too much to the right and will fall down, he again moves to the left. Walking on the rope, continuously he goes on moving from left to right, from right to left, regaining balance by the opposite.

The same happens in existence, the proportion remains almost the same. Whenever there is born a very saintly person, immediately a sinner is born somewhere. Whenever a wise man is born, immediately one idiot has to balance him, otherwise the world would disappear immediately. Whenever you do a good act, know well that somewhere someone will have to do a bad act to balance you. So don't get too proud that you have done some good acts, because by doing them you have created the other also. Someone has to balance you because you unbalanced the world. Whenever you do a bad act someone is bound to become a saint because of you.

I am not saying to do this or that. The Upanishads are not concerned with your doing, they are concerned with your understanding – that you understand well that the world exists in duality, and if you go on dividing you will remain a part of ignorance. Don't divide; transcend division and look at the world as one vast expanse. Once you know that the two are not two, the opposites are not opposites, you cannot be tense, because tension is possible only when you choose. When you say, "This must be and that must not be," when you say, "This is good and that is bad," you are creating anguish for yourself. You will create tension, you will create a conflict within the mind; expectations, hopes, frustrations – all will follow. Once you can understand that no choice is needed because everything is the same, suddenly all anguish disappears. And then you have a tranquility, a peace, a bliss, that can exist only when divisions have disappeared.

The second question:

Osho,

If one experiences or understands inwardly the deep feeling of becoming as a dry leaf to be moved only by the existence itself, then how can one push oneself to breathe or jump or do anything at all but lie flat on the earth and dissolve?

First, to experience and to understand are two different things. If you experience this there is no need to ask the question – just lie down flat on the ground and dissolve. Why ask the question? This is an act, you are doing something. No dry leaf has ever asked. But the very question shows that intellectually you understand, but you have not experienced any such thing – and intellectual understanding is not understanding at all. Intellectual understanding is just appearance of understanding, it is not understanding.

Why do I say this? I will read the sentence, you will feel why. "If one experiences or understands...." You cannot use the "or" because they are not the same thing – either you experience or you don't experience. First thing, intellectual understanding is not equal to experience. "...Or understands inwardly the deep feeling of becoming as a dry leaf to be moved only by the existence itself, then how can one push oneself to breathe or jump or do anything at all but lie flat on the earth and dissolve?"

You will have to do that also – to lie flat. You will have to do that also – to lie flat on the earth. And if you can do that, why can't you push, jump and breathe?

I will tell you one anecdote.

It happened, one Zen monk, Dogen, used to tell his disciples, "Unless you die, you will not be reborn."

So one stupid disciple – and there are always many – thought, "If this is the key, then I must try it." So one day he came and did just as you have said. He must have lain with closed eyes, flat out in front of the door of the master, just in the morning when the master was expected to come out for the morning prayer. The master opened the door and found that his disciple was lying there not breathing, as if dead. The master Dogen said, "Okay, doing well."

So the disciple opened one eye just to see the expression on the master's face, and Dogen said, "Stupid! Dead men don't open their eyes!"

You will have to do that also – to lie flat on the ground – but that will be your doing. And these breathing exercises are to help you so that it can happen and is not your doing. All these techniques of meditation are to help you to come to this realization when suddenly you feel that it is happening – you have fallen on the ground, dissolving. But that should not be something done on your part, you cannot do it. If it is a doing the whole point is lost. It must be a spontaneous happening.

And right now whatsoever you do will not be spontaneous, whatsoever you are doing you have to make effort. And I know that you have to make effort for breathing, for catharsis, for the mantra

Hoo – and you have to bring all effort possible. These efforts are not going to become your enlightenment, because enlightenment is never achieved through effort, but these efforts will help you; they will bring you to a point where you can become effortless. And when you become effortless, enlightenment is always there. You can stop them, but just by stopping them nothing will happen. Continue them, and do them as totally as possible because then you will come to realize sooner that nothing can be achieved through effort.

Nothing can be achieved through effort – you have to realize this. I can say this, but this will not be of much help. I know well that just by breathing fast you are not going to enter into nirvana. I know it well. And just by crying and dancing no one has ever entered there. Even if their door is open they will close it, if they see that you are coming doing Dynamic Meditation they will close the door. This I know well.

I have heard, one Christian missionary was giving a sermon to some middle-school students, small boys and girls. After the sermon he asked, "Those who want to go to heaven should raise their hands."

So all the boys except one raised their hands. Only one boy, someone called Johnny, remained silent.

The missionary asked, "Don't you want to go to heaven?"

Johnny said, "Not with this bunch!"

So if you go doing Dynamic Meditation even I cannot enter with you, it is impossible. But I know that Dynamic Meditation is not the end, it is just to prepare you so that you can drop automatically. It is to exhaust you and your ego; it is to exhaust your mind, your body; it is to exhaust your individuality. And when your individuality is exhausted completely you will drop on the ground like a dry leaf. But not like Dogen's disciple – if he could have done Dynamic Meditation the whole story would have been different. Then there would have been no need to lie down on the ground, he would have fallen on the ground.

And if you have to lie down, that shows only that you are withholding yourself, you are not really exhausted. If you simply move totally in whatsoever I am saying to do you will get exhausted.

You have a certain amount of energy, a limited amount of energy – that energy can be exhausted. Once exhausted you will become a dry leaf, a dead leaf.

When you cannot do anything only then can nondoing happen. While you can do something, nondoing is not possible.

The third question:

Osho,

Does returning to the heart center mean becoming more passionate? Is the heart also the source of passion? Can a man who is authentically centered at the heart be called passionate?

Heart is not the center of passion; rather, heart is the center of compassion. And the man who lives in the heart cannot be called passionate, but can be called compassionate. Passion comes from the sex center, all passion comes from the sex center. You can join the sex center and the heart, but from the heart only love flows, not passion.

Love is a very silent flow, nonaggressive, almost passive; it is a very silent breeze. Sex is passion, violence, aggression, with force, with strong energy – it attacks. The heart and the sex center can join together, then love becomes passionate. If heart is not joined with the sex center then love becomes compassionate. Then love is there in its total purity and only then, when there is no passion in it, is love pure. It is silent, passive, nonaggressive. You can invite it but it will not knock at your door. It will not even ask to be invited. You can persuade it to come, it can become your guest, but it will not come uninvited.

Love cannot rape, and sex always rapes in many ways. Even when legally it is not a rape, sex is rape. You may persuade the other person legally, in the way the society allows, but in the mind rape remains the center. You are just thinking to rape the other person, you are aggressive, and all that you do before it is just a foreplay, just to achieve the end. That's why, when two persons get married, foreplay disappears.

When the Coin Disappears | 277

When you meet a girl or a boy for the first time, there is much foreplay! Before you enter into a sex relationship you have to go on playing, so that the sex doesn't look like a rape, but that is on the mind, that is in the mind. In your mind you are constantly thinking of the end, and everything is just persuasion, seduction, just to make the whole thing appear loving. But the more you become intimate with the girl or the boy, the less foreplay is there; if you get married, no foreplay. Then sex becomes just direct, something to be done and finished with.

Look at this. If two persons are really in love, then not only foreplay but afterplay also will be there. If two persons are not in love then sex will happen and they will go to sleep, there will be no afterplay. Foreplay will not even be there, and afterplay is impossible, because what is the use? The thing has happened, the end has been achieved. Rape is in the mind.

The sex center knows only rape, it is the center of aggression. That's why the military doesn't allow sex for soldiers, because if they have sex relationships they cannot be good fighters. The aggression moves through the sex center. If sex is allowed and a soldier is living with his wife or with his beloved, he will not feel like fighting on the battleground.

This is one of the reasons why American soldiers are defeated everywhere: their girls follow them. They cannot be aggressive because the center of aggression is sex. If sex is allowed, aggression flows out of you and then you don't feel like fighting. So the soldiers have to be prohibited from sex, they must suppress their sex; then the whole sex becomes aggression. Then rather than entering a woman's body they can enter anybody's body with a bullet. But it is the same thing – the entry. Your bullets, your knives, your guns, are just phallic symbols – to enter the other's body, to destroy.

The coaches of athletes who go to the Olympics tell them, "Don't have sex at least for two weeks before," because if you have sex you will not be a good runner. From where will you get the aggression to fight and run and compete? All religions all over the world – almost all, I will say, because only one wonderful sect, Tantra, is an exception – all religions all over the world have told their monks to be celibate, because they think that religion is also a sort of struggle. You have to fight with yourself, so retain the aggressive energy and fight with yourself.

Sex can easily become violence because it is passion, it is rape. Love, the heart center or the love center, is totally different. It is nonviolent, it is passive, not even active. It can come to you like a very silent perfume, and that too when you invite. That's why persons like Buddha or Jesus, they have much love, but we cannot feel their love, because we can feel love only when it is too violent. We have become addicted to violence. And Buddha's love is so silent. It showers on us but we cannot feel it, we have become so insensitive. Only when someone attacks do we start feeling.

The heart center is not the center of passion, but is the center of compassion. And compassion is absolutely different from passion, just the opposite. It is non-aggressive energy, moving without any noise, but you have to become very sensitive to feel it. So only very sensitive persons can become attracted to Buddha, because only very sensitive persons can feel that some love is flowing from him. If you are asking for strong doses of passion, then Buddha will just look dead; nothing is coming out of him.

Remember this: passion has to be transformed into compassion, only then will you move from the sex center to the heart center. Now even your heart has to follow your sex center, which is the higher following the lower. Then your sex center will follow the love center, the heart center – the lower following the higher. And this should be the order of your being – always the lower following the higher. Then the lower becomes totally different, the quality changes.

When sex follows love, sex becomes beautiful, a grace, a blessing. When love follows sex, love becomes ugly, a destructive force; you destroy each other through your love. All the courts of the world are filled with persons who have been in love and now are destructive to each other. Fifty percent of marriages break down completely, and the other fifty percent are continued somehow, not for love, but for other reasons – for children, for society, for family, for prestige, for money, for other reasons, but not for love. Fifty percent break down completely.

Love has become so destructive because it is following a lower center. Re-member, this should be the law within you: always remember that the lower should follow the higher, then everything is beautiful and a blessing. Nothing is to be denied, there is no need to deny anything; only let the higher lead, because following the higher the lower changes its quality. And if the higher has to follow the lower everything becomes ugly.

The fourth question:

Osho,

Did Mulla Nasruddin become enlightened?

He must have – because if he is not enlightened then nobody can be.

Mulla Nasruddin is a Sufi figure, one of the oldest figures of Sufi anecdotes, and he shows whatsoever I have been saying here: that the world is a cosmic joke – he represents that. He is a very serious joker, and if you can penetrate him and understand him, then many mysteries will be revealed to you.

Mulla Nasruddin illustrates that the world is not a tragedy but a comedy. And the world is a place where if you can learn how to laugh you have learned everything. If your prayer cannot become a deep laughter which comes from all over your being, if your prayer is sad and if you cannot joke with your god, then you are not really religious.

Christians, Jews and Mohammedans are very serious about their god; Hindus are not, they have joked a lot. And that shows how much they believe – because when you cannot joke with your god you don't believe in him. You feel that through your humor, your joke, he will be insulted. Your belief is shallow, it is not deep enough. Hindus say that the trust is so much that they can laugh; the trust is so much that just by laughing it cannot be broken.

One Buddhist, Bodhidharma, one of the greatest followers of Buddha, used to say to his disciples, "Whenever you take the name of Buddha immediately rinse out your mouth, because this name is dangerous and it makes the mouth impure." Another Buddhist monk, Bokuju, used to tell his disciples, "While meditating, if this fellow Gautam Buddha comes in kill him immediately, because once you allow him then he will cling to you and it will be difficult to be alone."

And they were great followers, they loved Buddha – but they could laugh. Why? The love was so intimate, so close, that there was no danger that something might be taken wrongly. But Christians have always been afraid, so immediately anything becomes blasphemy – anything. They cannot take anything humorously, and if you cannot take anything humorously, if you cannot laugh at yourself, at your god, then you are ill, you are not at home, and your god is something to be feared.

In English we have a word, God-fearing, for religious people. A God-fearing person can never be religious, because if you fear God you cannot love him. Love and fear cannot exist together. With fear, hate can exist, love cannot; with fear, anger can exist, love cannot; with fear you can bow down but you cannot surrender; with fear there can be a relationship between a slave and a master but there cannot be a love relationship. Hindus, Buddhists have a totally different attitude, and that attitude is different because they think the whole existence is a cosmic play, you can be playful.

Sufis are very playful; they created Mulla Nasruddin. And Mulla Nasruddin is an alive figure, you can go on adding to him – I go on adding. If some day he meets me there is bound to be difficulty, because I go on creating around him. To me he is a constantly alive figure, in many ways symbolic – symbolic of human stupidity. But he knows it and he laughs at it, and whenever he behaves like a stupid man he is just joking at you, at human beings at large.

And he is subtle enough. He will not hit you directly, he hits himself; but if you can penetrate him then you can look at the reality. And sometimes even great scriptures cannot go as deep as a joke can go, because the joke directly touches the heart. A scripture goes into the head, into the intellect; a joke directly touches the heart. Immediately something explodes within you and be-comes your smile and your laughter.

Nasruddin must have attained enlightenment, or he is already an enlightened figure, there is no need to attain. I go on using him just to give you a feeling that to me religion is not serious. So I go on mixing Mulla Nasruddin with Mahavira – which is impossible, poles apart. I go on mixing Mulla Nasruddin with the Upanishads, because he gives a sweetness to the whole serious thing. And nothing is serious, nothing should be serious.

To me, to laugh wholeheartedly is the greatest celebration that can happen to a man – to laugh wholeheartedly, to become the laughter. Then no meditation is needed, it is enough.

I will take one or two anecdotes from Nasruddin.

Once it happened that Nasruddin and his friend Sheikh Abdullah lost their way in a forest. They tried and tried to find their way but then evening came, the night was descending, so they had to wait for the whole night under a tree. It was dangerous ground, there were many wild animals, and they had to keep awake because any moment they could be killed.

They tried every way to keep awake, but Mulla was tired, yawning, feeling sleepy, so he said to Sheikh Abdullah, "Invent something, because I am feeling sleepy and it seems impossible now to stay awake. The whole day we were traveling, and I am tired."

Sheikh Abdullah asked, "What should I do?"

Nasruddin said, "We should play a game, a game of guessing. You describe a film actress – just become the film actress and describe – and I will guess who this film actress is. Then I will do the same and you guess."

Even Abdullah became interested, it seemed to be a good game. So Abdullah said, "Okay." He contemplated and then he said, "My eyes are like Noor Jahan, my nose is like Cleopatra, my lips like Marilyn Monroe," and so on and so forth.

Mulla Nasruddin became very excited, his blood pressure rose high. Even in the dark you could have seen his eyes, they became so fiery. And then when Sheikh Abdullah said, "Now the measurements of my body – thirty-six, twenty-four, thirty-six." Nasruddin jumped over to Sheikh Abdullah. Sheikh Abdullah said, "Wait, guess!"

Nasruddin said, "Who is bothered about guessing? I don't care who you are. Quick! Kiss me!"

The human mind is such – imagination, desire, passion, projection. You project, you imagine, and then you become the victim. And this is not a joke, this is reality – and this is about *you*.

Enough for today.

14   The Motionless Flame of a Lamp

On the attainment of the fifth state, the mind of the seeker ceases, like clouds in an autumn sky, and only truth remains.

In this state, worldly desires do not arise at all.

During this state all thoughts of division in the seeker are stilled

and he remains rooted in nonduality.

On the disappearance of the feeling of division, the fifth stage, known as the sushuptapad – sleeping –

draws the enlightened seeker into its nature.

He is perpetually introverted and looks tired and sleepy,

even though externally he continues his everyday activities.

On the accomplishment of this stage, the desire-free seeker enters the sixth one. Both truth and untruth, both egoism and egolessness and all sorts of mentation cease to exist in this state,

and rooted in pure nonduality, the seeker is free from fear.

As the entanglements of his heart dissolve, so all his doubts drop. This is the moment when he is completely emptied of all thought. Without attaining nirvana, he is in a nirvana-like state and becomes free while yet dwelling in the body.

This state is like that of the motionless flame of a lamp.

And then comes the seventh stage.

The first three stages belong to the part of your mind which is called will. The first three belong to the realm of effort. You have to do them, they will not happen on their own; and unless you have done them the other states will not follow.

After the third stage everything becomes spontaneous. There is a sequence: one after another things will happen, but you will not be doing them. The only thing to remember for the other stages after the third is to allow them to happen. The first three you have to force to happen, they will not happen by themselves. After the third you have to allow them to happen, if you don't allow they will not happen.

So the first three belong to the positive effort and the remaining belong to the negative effort. Let it be understood well what I mean by positive effort and negative effort. By positive effort is meant: you have to do something, only then will something happen. By negative effort is meant: you are only to allow, you have to remain passive, not doing anything, open, receptive, that's all, and things will happen. For example, the sun is rising outside. You can close your doors. If the doors are closed you can leave them closed. The sun will be outside, the sunrays will be outside, but you will remain in darkness. Negative effort means let your doors be open, that's all. But you have to open the doors, that is positive effort in the beginning. Open the doors, then you have not to do anything else. The sun will rise, the light will enter. And as the sun rises more and more, more and more light will come to your room. The darkness will disappear.

You cannot bring the sunrays inside, you cannot put them in a bucket and bring them inside. You cannot force the sunrays to come in. No positive effort is needed, only to open the doors you have to be positive, that's all. Then the sun by itself will fill the room. If you are open, passive, receptive like a womb, nothing can then prevent the light from entering. Or in other words, the first three steps are male, and the remaining steps are female. In the first three steps you have to be aggressive, masculine; in the remaining steps you have to be female, feminine, passive, receptive. That's why I say that in the negative steps you have to be just a womb to receive.

Have you observed it? No woman can rape a man, so all over the world, in no law book is there any law against it. No woman can rape a man because her whole sexuality is receptive, she cannot be aggressive. But a man can rape a woman, even if she is not willing she can be raped. If a man is not willing he cannot be raped, you cannot do anything, rape is impossible, because male energy moves outward, female energy simply waits inward – just waits.

That's why no woman worth the name will be aggressive in love. She will not initiate any love affair. She will not say, "I love you." She will just wait for you to say that you love her. And if a woman says in the beginning that she loves you and you have not initiated it, escape from her; that woman is dangerous, you will suffer for it. That woman is not really feminine; she is aggressive, unwomanly. She will wait. She will seduce you, but her ways of seduction will be passive, indirect. She will not hit you directly on the head, she will not say anything. So in the end no man can say, "You persuaded me into this love affair." No man can say that. The woman will always say, "You dragged me into this affair, you initiated me, so you are responsible," because she can wait, she can be patient, she can be only receptive. And that is natural.

The first steps are male, the last steps are female. Then there are a few things implied. The first three steps will be difficult for women, they will have to make more effort for them. The first three steps will be easy for men. The last steps will be easy for women and they will be difficult for men. This will be the difference in sadhana. The first three steps will come easily to a man. There is no problem because they suit his nature, he can be aggressive easily. The first three steps will be difficult for a woman; she will have to exert force, she will get tired easily. But if she can wait for the fourth then the whole wheel turns. The last steps will be very easy for a woman – she can wait, she can be receptive. Negative effort just suits her nature.

Nobody is at any advantage and nobody is at any disadvantage. The whole – half is male, half is female. So remember this: if you are a woman the first three steps are going to be a little difficult. Knowing it well, make all efforts. If you are a man then remember that after the third difficulty will arise for you, because it is difficult for a man to be in a let-go. He can do something, that's easy. But to not do anything, to just remain waiting, is difficult. But if the first three steps have been done well that difficulty will not be so difficult, it will dissolve by and by.

Now the sutra. Before we enter it one thing more: that after the third the fourth will follow, you are not to drag it. After the fourth the fifth will follow, after the fifth the sixth will follow, after the sixth the seventh will follow. They will come automatically. Once your life energy starts moving things will happen automatically.

That's why it is said that samadhi, the last, the seventh step, happens by the grace of God. That's true in a way, because you will not be making any effort for it. Suddenly one day you will feel yourself filled with grace – suddenly, not knowing any visible cause. So sometimes samadhi has happened in such moments that one was not even aware, one could not even imagine that samadhi would happen in such a state.

One Zen nun, an old woman, was coming one night from the well carrying two pails of water on her shoulder on a bamboo pole. The full moon was in the sky. As she was walking towards her hut, towards the monastery, suddenly the bamboo broke. The two earthen pots fell down on the ground, were broken, shattered to pieces, the water flowed out – and the woman became enlightened. She started to sing and dance.

In the morning the people of the monastery found her still dancing, singing. She was transformed, metamorphosed – a completely different being. They asked, "What happened?"

She said, "When those two pots fell down, shattered, the water flowed out – the moon in the water disappeared. The moon was in the sky, it was reflecting in the water of the pots. The pots fell down, water spread, the moon in the water disappeared – and then I looked at the real moon and I was enlightened."

What is she saying? Just when those two earthen pots fell down on the ground...she must have been waiting for long, all effort had been done. She must have been growing by and by, spontaneously. And when growth comes spontaneously you cannot be very much aware of it, it goes on and on. It is just as when a child becomes a young man, he never knows when he became a young man. A young man becomes old, he cannot draw the line when he be-came old. It is happening so spontaneously moment to moment, it is happening always all the time, there is no demarcation. So after the third things will flow. Your master may become aware, you will not be aware. You will become aware only when the seventh has happened.

The pots fell down on the ground, shattered, water spread out, and the moon disappeared. The falling of those pots triggered it, the sound, the shattering of earthen pots. Suddenly...as if the body disappeared, because the body is earth-en. The water flowed out because there was now nothing to hold it together. The soul is the water. The body broken, the water spread out, became one with the cosmos. There was nothing to hold it in. And then the ego disappeared – which is a reflection of the real moon, of the real God. Only God can say 'I'. We go on saying 'I' – that is just a reflection.

Water in the earthen pot reflects the moon.

Consciousness in an earthen body reflects the divine, becomes 'I'.

But such an ordinary situation – the shattering of two earthen pots – became the cause of enlightenment. But it is not a cause, because you can break as many pots as you like and it will not happen, so it is not a cause. A cause means something which can produce the effect, so it is not a cause, it has not caused it – it was already happening. It was as if the woman was asleep and suddenly the sound of the breaking of the pots awoke her, she became aware. What has happened? Then she must have looked at the pots and at herself. Suddenly there was no body, no pots, no ego; everything had disappeared. Then the energy was dancing, not that woman; that was the metamorphosis, that was the transformation.

In the morning when the monastery found her she was no more the same. So they asked her, "Where has the old woman gone?" It has become one of the oldest Zen sayings to ask a person who has been transformed, "Where has the old woman gone?" or, "Where has the old man disappeared to?"...Because now there is only energy with no will of its own, dancing. The dance is not willed, it is spontaneous.

In many situations enlightenment has happened, sometimes very ordinary situations. It is told of Nanak that he was serving in an ordinary store, just selling things to people, the whole day weighing, measuring things and selling them to people. One day – he must have been growing inwardly, he was not aware of it – he was weighing something and giving it to a man. He counted: one, two, three, four, five...and then he came to thirteen. Thirteen in Hindi is *tera*. Tera means thou, thine. The word for thirteen in Hindi is *tera*. Tera has two meanings: one – thirteen; another – thine.

Suddenly when he said "Tera," he forgot the shop, he forgot the weighing, he forgot the counting, he forgot that tera means thirteen; suddenly he became aware that tera means thine. Then he went on weighing, but never the fourteen came again. He would weigh something that he was selling and would say, "Tera, tera, tera."

Evening came. The owner of the shop was informed that Nanak had gone mad; he was not proceeding further, he had become obsessed with tera. The owner came and he looked. He must have been a man who knew scriptures, who knew something about mysticism. He bowed down to Nanak, because his whole face was transformed, he was no more the same man. And after that moment everything became God's; Nanak was not now his own, he was God's. The whole existence was God's.

He left the shop, became a monk, a wandering monk with a follower, Mardana, who would play on an instrument and Nanak would sing the glory of the lord. And then Nanak moved all over the country and even outside the country. He went even to Mecca, everywhere – but the song remained the same: "Thine, tera – everything is yours, nothing is mine."

It happened just in an ordinary shop. It can happen anywhere, no bodhi tree is needed. It was accidental that Buddha was sitting under the tree and Nanak was sitting in that shop, it was accidental. It can happen anywhere because every spot on the earth is his, and every spot on the earth is sacred. Wherever you are, if you have done the right effort then things will grow, and one day – the happening. And that happening is going to be grace, because you cannot say, "I have done it." You were not doing anything at all. That's why so much insistence that the ultimate happens through grace, it is a gift of God. It is nothing which you have produced.

But remember, you have still been doing something which is negative: you were not creating hindrances. If you create hindrances even God's grace cannot be available to you. There is a reason for it. As I told you, love cannot be aggressive, and grace is the suprememost love – the love that existence has for you. It cannot be aggressive, it cannot even knock at your door. If the doors remain closed the grace will simply wait there for millions of your lives. If the doors remain closed the grace will not knock, because knocking is aggression. Unless you open the doors on your own the grace will not enter. It is not aggressive, it has no sex center in it. It can wait infinitely.

One thing you have to do: don't create hindrances after the third. And once the fourth has happened these stages will follow. They follow just as a river flows to the sea. Once it has started, once it has crossed mountains – because in the mountains there will be a little struggle, effort, resistance; the rocks, the valleys, the mountains…. Once the river has followed the mountains, has crossed them and has come to the flat land, then there is no problem, things flow easily. It will reach one day to the ocean.

The three stages for your river are as if in the mountains, then from the fourth you are on plain ground, you can flow. Sooner or later the ocean will be there and you will fall down into it. And the whole course is now going to be spontaneous, you have just to flow and not do anything. And for flowing one need not do anything, flowing is not something to do.

You enter a river: if you want to swim, then you will have to do something. But if you just want to flow with the river you need not do anything, you have simply to allow the river to take you – no resistance. That's why a miracle happens. A live man may be drowned, but no river can drown a dead man, no river is so powerful it can drown a dead man. And any man who is live, alive, can be drowned by a small river also. The dead man must know some secret which alive men don't know.

The alive man fights with the river. The river is not drowning him; through his own fight he gets exhausted, he becomes tired, dissipates energy, becomes impotent – through his own fight, unnecessary fight. The river is not fighting him, he is fighting the river and wants to swim upstream. Every one of you wants to swim upstream, because only when you fight with the river and swim upstream is ego created. Then you feel you are winning, you are becoming victorious. The swimming upstream creates the ego.

One day you are bound to get tired of it, and then the river will drown you because then you will have no energy left. But a dead man knows a secret. He cannot fight, he is dead; he cannot flow upstream. He simply allows the river to take him anywhere it wants. Not he, but the river now wills. No river can drown him. He can move, he can become the flow.

After the third stage you have to become like a dead man, that is the negative effort. That's what is meant by old Indian scriptures when they say that the guru, the master, is like death, he will kill you. Only when you are dead will the grace become possible to you. So all the efforts you are making here are just to become available to me so I can kill you. I have to be a murderer, because unless you are dead grace will not be possible for you, you cannot receive it.

Dead men flow. They are spontaneous because they have no will of their own. After the third stage you should be like dead men. Then these stages follow:

On the attainment of the fifth stage –

the fourth is advaita, the feeling of nonduality –

the mind of the seeker ceases, like clouds in an autumn sky, and only truth remains.

The fourth is advaita, nonduality, when you can see that only oneness exists, clouds start disappearing, only the sky remains. Clouds are there because you divide, because duality is there. Your mind is clouded, many clouds float there, because you cannot see the one sky hidden behind the clouds. You are too obsessed with the clouds, with the contents.

One psychologist was conducting an experiment. He came into his class, fifty students were present there. On the big blackboard in the classroom he pasted a white paper of just the same size as the blackboard. On that white paper there was a simple small black dot, the only thing; otherwise the whole paper was white, clean, clear. There was just a small dot, difficult even to see.

And then he asked the students, "What do you see here?" So they stared, and everybody had to write what he was seeing. And the fifty students, with not even one exception, all wrote that they saw a small black dot. Nobody saw that big white sheet, just a small dot. Nobody saw, nobody wrote that they saw a big white sheet. Everybody saw the small black dot.

We see the clouds, not the sky. The background is always missed, and that background is the real, the big, the wide and the vital and the vast. Whenever you look in the sky you see a small cloud floating there, you never see the sky! The emphasis has to change, the focus has to change – from the black dot to the white sheet, from the cloud to the sky. When you look inside the mind you always see small thoughts. They are nothing compared to your consciousness; your consciousness is vast, but you always see small dots floating there.

When nonduality comes to you dots will disappear and the background will become clear. And once you can see the white sheet, once your mind is focused on the white sheet, that small dot will disappear, because if you are focused on the small black dot you cannot see the white sheet so big. Focusing on the black dot the big white sheet disappears. So why shouldn't it be otherwise? – when you focus on the white sheet the black dot disappears. When you can see the sky clouds disappear. When you can see the consciousness thoughts disappear.

On the attainment of the fifth stage the mind of the seeker ceases, like clouds in an autumn sky, and only truth remains.

The sky is the truth, the vagabond clouds are not true. They are not eternal, they are momentary phenomena, they come and go. Remember, this is the definition of the Upanishads, the definition of truth: that which remains always. The real is not true if the real moves and changes. Upanishads have a particular definition of truth: truth is that which always remains, and untruth is that which comes and goes.

The untruth can exist, but it is momentary, it is dreamlike. Why do you call dreams untrue? They exist, they have their existence, their reality; in the dream you believe in them, but in the morning when you have awakened you say they were dreams, untrue, unreal. Why? They were there, so why do you call them unreal? You must be following unknowingly the definition of the Upanishads – because they are no more. They were, but are no more. There was a moment when they were not, then there was a moment when they were, now there is again a moment when they are not, and between two nonexistences how is existence possible? That existence which exists between two nonexistences must be unreal, dreamlike.

One day you were not here on this earth, in this body. If your name is Ram, then Ram didn't exist before your birth. Then, after your death, Ram will not exist again. So two nonexistences on two poles, and between is your existence, the Ram. It is dreamlike. If there is something which existed before your birth and will exist after your death, the Upanishads call that the truth.

They say, "Find the eternal, the nonchanging. Unless you come to that which has always been, will always be, consider all else dreaming." They say, "Clouds are dreams. Not that they are unreal – they are real, they are there, you can see them, but they are dreams, because they were not and they will not be again. And when they were not the sky was, when they are the sky is, when they will not be again the sky will be. So the sky remains, the space remains, and everything appears in it and disappears.

This world of appearance and disappearance is called maya – the illusion, the dream. The background which remains always constant, continuous, eternally there, which never changes – which *cannot* change – that is the truth.

Your life is also divided by the Upanishads into two parts: one that changes and one that remains permanent, eternal – eternally permanent. That which changes is your body, that which changes is your mind, and that which never changes is your soul. Your body and mind are like clouds, your soul is like the sky. At the attainment of the fifth stage clouds disappear; your body, your mind, clouds in the sky...and all that is impermanent disappears, and the permanent is revealed...and only truth remains.

In this state, worldly desires do not arise at all.

...Because worldly desires can arise only for the clouds, for the objects, for the impermanent; you cannot desire that which is always. There is no need to desire it, it is always there. You can desire only that which will not be there. The more impermanent the more you are attracted towards it. The sooner it flies into nonexistence the more your obsession with it.

All beauty appeals, because it is the most impermanent thing in existence. A flower has an appeal, not the rock just lying down there beside the flower. You will never see the rock, you will see the flower, because the flower is impermanent. In the morning it is there, by the afternoon it will be no more – or at the most by the evening it will disperse, fall down, dissolve. The flower attracts you, not the rock.

You may have heard about Zen gardens, which are called rock gardens. They don't make flower gardens in Zen monasteries, they make rock gardens. They say, "Flowers disappear, they are not true; rocks remain." That is just symbolic. So Zen gardens are really unique in the world; nowhere else do such gardens exist. In their gardens only sand and rock is allowed, no flowers. Vast grounds with sand and rocks, and a Zen disciple has to sit there just to meditate on rocks, not on flowers. It is just symbolic.

You never see the rocks, you always see the flower, because your mind is concerned with the impermanent. And you become more concerned because it is going to dissolve soon; before it dissolves, possess it. Possession arises in the mind. Beauty disperses, is impermanent; possess it before it disperses. That's why there is so much possessiveness in human relationship and so much misery in it – because you are aware that this is something which is not going to last forever. It is moving: the young woman is becoming old, the young man is becoming old; every moment death is coming in and you are afraid, the fear is there. You want to possess and indulge more and more so that you have tasted it before death appears.

At the fifth stage only truth remains. *Worldly desires do not arise at all* – because they arise only for the impermanent. The world means the impermanent: power, prestige, beauty, wealth, fame – all are impermanent. You may be a president today and next day a beggar on the street and no one looking at you. Have you observed? – this is happening every moment.

Where is Doctor Radhakrishnan now, do you know? He was the president. Then his photograph was in every newspaper. Now he lives in Madras. Nobody knows about him, nobody reports what he says. He must be wiser than when he was a president, he has lived more; whatsoever he says is now more significant – but nobody reports it. The newspapers will report only when he dies, and that too in a corner and that too only because he is an ex-president, not because he is Radhakrishnan. Fame is flowerlike; power, prestige, flowerlike.

I was reading Voltaire's life. He was so famous, so loved by people, by the masses, that it was impossible for him to go to Paris, because whenever he would go such a great crowd would gather to receive him that he was almost crushed many times by the crowd. A big police force had to be maintained whenever he came. And there was a superstition in those days in France that if you could get a piece of the clothing of a famous man like Voltaire, it was worth preserving, it helped you. So whenever he would go to Paris he would reach his home almost naked because people would snatch his clothes. His body would be scratched.

Then suddenly the fame disappeared, people forgot him completely; he would go to the station and there would be no one even to receive him. And when he died only four persons followed him to the cemetery – three men and one dog. But these things attract the mind, and the more impermanent the more the attraction – because if you are not in a hurry you may lose.

At the fifth stage *worldly desires do not arise at all* – because now your focus has changed, your emphasis changed. Your gestalt has moved from the foreground to the background, your gestalt has changed from the content to the container. Now you don't look at the clouds, you look at the sky. And the sky is so vast, so infinite, that your clouds don't mean anything now. Whether they are there or not, they are not – they have no significance.

During this state all thoughts of division in the seeker are stilled, and he remains rooted in nonduality. On the disappearance of the feeling of division, the fifth stage, known as the sushuptapad – sleeping – draws the enlightened seeker into its nature. He is perpetually introverted and looks tired and sleepy, even though externally he continues his everyday activities.

The Upanishads say there are four stages or four steps of human consciousness. First, the waking state of consciousness. Just now you are in the waking state of consciousness. The second, the dreaming state of consciousness, when you dream in the night. The third, the sleeping state of consciousness, when you don't dream, simply sleep, deep sleep. These three are known to you. Then the fourth, when all these three have disappeared and you have transcended them. This fourth is simply called *turiya;* turiya means the fourth.

The first three, which need your will and effort, belong to the waking consciousness. The fourth and fifth belong to your sleeping consciousness, to your dreaming consciousness. The sixth belongs to your sleeping consciousness. And the seventh will belong to the turiya, the transcendental state of consciousness.

On the disappearance of the feeling of division, the fifth stage, known as the sushuptapad, draws the enlightened seeker into its nature.

In deep sleep mind disappears, because there is not even dreaming, no content. In deep sleep you have fallen back again into your nature. That's why deep sleep refreshes you. In the morning you feel alive again, rejuvenated, young, vital, because in deep sleep you had fallen again to your original nature. You were no more an ego, you were no more a mind – you were just part of nature. While you are deep asleep you are just like a tree or a rock, you are no more an individual. You have become part of the ocean, of course unknowingly, unconsciously.

If this can happen knowingly, consciously, *sushupti,* deep sleep, becomes samadhi, becomes ecstasy. In sushupti, deep sleep, you touch the same point which Buddha touches, which Ramakrishna, Ramana, Eckhart or Jesus touch. But they go to that point conscious, you go to that point unconscious. You move into your nature but you are not aware of what is happening. They also move to the same nature, but they are aware. That is the only difference between sleep and samadhi; otherwise they are the same.

Alert, conscious, aware, you move into yourself, you are enlightened. Unconscious you move every night, but that doesn't make you enlightened. You give yourself to nature. Tired of your ego, tired of your day-to-day activities, the routine, tired of your personality, you fall into a sleep. Nature reabsorbs you, recreates you, gives you back your vitality in the morning.

So if a person is ill, very ill, the physicians will try first to give him deep sleep, because nothing will help, no medicine can help if you are not falling back to your nature. If an ill person can go into deep sleep, even without medicine he will become healthy. So the first effort of the physician is to help you to fall into deep sleep, because nature spontaneously rejuvenates.

On the disappearance of the feeling of division, the fifth stage, known as the sushuptapad – sleeping – draws the enlightened seeker into its nature. He is perpetually introverted – in this stage, the seeker will remain perpetually introverted – and looks tired and sleepy, even though externally he continues his everyday activities.

If you go to Sufi monasteries you will see there many persons very sleepy, as if someone has hypnotized them. They will look like zombies – as if they are walking in sleep, working in sleep, following orders in sleep. And monasteries were created because of such things.

A person who is in the fifth stage will have many difficulties in the world because he will move sleepily. He is constantly deep in his nature, as if fast asleep. He will have to make effort to be awake. He will be introverted, he will not be interested in the outside world. He would like more and more time to move inwards. You will be able to see from his eyes also; they will be droopy, tired. He doesn't want to look out, he wants to look in. His face will show the same state as that of a hypnotized medium. The face will be relaxed, as if he can fall any moment into sleep. He will become just like a child again.

The child in the mother's womb sleeps twenty-four hours a day for nine months; never awakens, just sleeps, goes on sleeping for nine months. Those nine months are needed, because if a child awakens then the growth will be hindered. In those nine months of deep sleep his whole body is created. Nature is working. The waking consciousness will create disturbance in nature, so the child sleeps completely.

Then the child is born and after his birth he sleeps less and less. Twenty-four hours he was sleeping in the womb; out of the womb he will sleep twenty-three hours, then twenty-two hours, then twenty hours, then eighteen hours. His sleep will come to eight hours only when he has become sexually mature – that is at fourteen, fifteen, sixteen, somewhere around there. Then his sleep will remain fixed because now the body has grown up completely, biologically. He can reproduce, he can now himself give birth to a child, he is sexually mature. Now there is no work left to do in the body; the body has stopped working, no new creation is going on. Eight hours sleep will do.

Then as he becomes old, after fifty, there is less and less sleep. Old men cannot sleep; four hours, three hours, then two hours, then even one hour will be too much, they will not be able to sleep. If you can understand this then when you get old you will not be worried. There is no need now for more sleep. And if you can understand this then you will not force small children to be awake when they feel sleepy.

Every family tortures children, because you want them to behave like you. If you get up early in the morning, at five, you would like your children also to get up in *brahmamuhurt*. You are foolish. That is destructive to children, they need more sleep. You can drag them and they cannot do anything because they are helpless. Sleepy they will get up. You can force them to sit and read. Sleepy they will somehow do it. You force small children, and then when you become old and when they become old, they will think that if they cannot sleep for eight hours then something is wrong. Nothing is wrong. An old man doesn't need...there is no new work in the body. Sleep will be less and less.

When this fifth stage happens the seeker will become again like a small child. He will feel sleepy, he will need more sleep, he will be more introverted. His eyes will like to be closed more than open, because he is not interested in looking outside, and a new work has started in his being again. Now he is again a child. Something new, phenomenal, is happening now; alchemically a new being is created again. He himself has become the womb now. He will feel more sleepy.

Monasteries were needed for such people, because in the world people will not tolerate you in this stage. They will say, "You have become lazy! Go to the doctor, take some activizers. This is not good." You will look dead and dull, your shining face will become dull. People will think you are ill or that somebody has hypnotized you. You will look like a zombie. Monasteries were needed for the fifth stage, really. The first three can be done in the world, but after the fourth you will need.... And in the fifth you will certainly need a monastery where people understand you.

Meher Baba used to sleep for forty-eight hours, sixty hours when he was in the fifth stage. Ramakrishna would fall asleep for weeks and he had to be taken care of, he had to be fed milk while he was asleep. The body was to be taken care of. Very loving friends, disciples who would care, were needed to help him. For two weeks he would remain as if in a coma. He became so introverted that it was impossible to open the eyes. The whole energy was moving inwards. If he had been left alone he would have died.

Monasteries will be needed for such people, masters will be needed for such people, because they have again become children.

Somebody has to mother them. The monastery becomes your mother, and there people know what is happening, where you are and what you need. In this stage only milk can be fed; nothing else will be good for the body, because the man has again become a child. Anything solid will disturb him, just milk will be enough.

He has to be taken care of just like a child. He will be asleep and you need not disturb him, because the more he remains in this state the sooner the sixth will follow. If you disturb him then he will remain in the fifth, and he will feel just as you feel if something awakens you in the morning suddenly – an alarm clock, or something else – the whole day you feel depressed. If the sleep is disturbed, ordinary sleep, the whole day you will feel disturbed, frustrated, angry, irritated – anything will create the irritation – and you don't know what has happened. It is because you were taken forcibly from your nature; when you were deep in it, suddenly you were called. An alarm is dangerous, because you have to come suddenly to the surface.

People who understand will not disturb anybody's sleep, one must come out of it gradually. But this is for ordinary sleep. When the person is in the fifth state then it is a very deep sleep – you don't know about it. It is falling to the original nature so deeply that it is very difficult to be pulled out. Nobody should disturb. That's why monasteries were made deep in the hills, forests, where nobody would come. Nobody would disturb anybody unnecessarily, and only a few people would be there who knew.

Sometimes a seeker will remain for months at a time in sleep, and then very loving care is needed, no disturbance. He is being created again. And this can happen continuously even for nine months, just as it happens in the womb. And when the seeker comes out of it he will be totally new. A new child is born, the old man is no more. He will be completely, totally fresh. You look into his eyes and they will have a depth, an abysslike depth. You cannot find the bottom. You can go in and in and in and there is no end to it.

This is what Jesus says: "Unless you become like children again, you will not enter into the kingdom of my God." The fifth stage will make you again a child.

He is perpetually introverted and looks tired and sleepy, even though externally he continues his everyday activities.

He can continue but he will look like a robot. He will go to the bath, take his bath; he will go to the kitchen, eat his food. He will do, but you can see that he is doing as if walking in sleep, somnambulistic.

On the accomplishment of this stage, the desire-free seeker enters the sixth one.

All desires disappear in the fifth. He becomes totally introverted: no extroversion, no outgoing energy. Desire-free, then the seeker enters the sixth one.

Both truth and untruth, both egoism and egolessness, and all sorts of mentations cease to exist in this state, and rooted in pure nonduality, the seeker is free from fear.

Remember, in the fifth untruth disappears, truth remains. In the sixth even truth disappears. In the fifth clouds disappear, the sky remains. In the sixth the sky also disappears — because you cannot continue to remember the sky without the clouds. And when there is no untruth how can you remember the truth? The duality is needed. When there is no black how can you remember the white?

Think, if the whole earth was populated by white men and there were no colored people, nobody would have been called white. Because of black people, colored people, a few people are white. Or think, if the whole earth was populated by Negroes, Negroid people, black, nobody would have been black. The contrast is needed. Only in contrast can the thing continue to be remembered. When untruth has disappeared how can you carry truth any more? How can you remember that it is truth? It has to be dropped, it will drop automatically. But first untruth drops, then truth is forgotten, it ceases. And when truth also drops you have reached something, not before it.

The sixth is the door, the real door, to the infinity. The sixth is the door, the real door, to the ultimate. Lao Tzu says — and whatsoever he says belongs to the sixth and seventh — he says, "If you are good you are still bad. If you feel that you are a saint you are still a sinner.

If you look in the mirror and feel you are beautiful you have ugliness in you"…because when a person is really beautiful he cannot remember that he is beautiful, only ugliness can remember. When a person is really good he cannot feel he is good, because first the bad disappears, then the good also. No divisions.

In the sixth…truth and untruth, both egoism and egolessness, and all sorts of mentations cease.

Ego disappears in the fifth, because ego is a cloud, it is part of the world of the clouds. It is just like a rainbow in the clouds – false, dreamlike. When you be-come aware of the soul you are not an egoist; you become egoless, you become humble. But Lao Tzu says that if you are still humble the ego exists somewhere; otherwise, how can you feel that you are a humble person?

Go to somebody who is humble, watch him, and you will feel that his ego is very subtle, that's all. He goes on saying, "I am a humble person." He insists that he is humble. His humbleness has now become his ego and pride, and if you say, "No, you are not," he will be angry. If you say, "I have seen a more humble person in your town," he will say, "This is impossible. I am the most humble, the humblest." But "I am" remains. Now the 'I' claims humbleness, before it was claiming something else.

I have heard: Once it happened that a great king went to a mosque to pray. It was a religious day for the Mohammedans so he was praying. It was dark, just in the morning when there was no one there, and he was saying to God, "Allah, O my God, I am nobody, just dust on your feet."

When he was saying this, suddenly he became alert that somebody else was also in the dark mosque, in another corner, and was saying the same thing: "Allah, my God, I am nobody, just dust on your feet."

The king was irritated. He said, "Who is saying in front of me that he is no-body? When I am saying I am nobody, who else is claiming here that *he* is nobody?" Even nobodiness….

And then the morning dawned and the king looked; the man who was claiming was a beggar. So the king said, "Remember, when a king is saying that he is nobody, nobody else can claim that – and you being just a beggar!" So even nobodiness can become part of the ego.

In the sixth stage ego disappears, egolessness also. Then there will be problems. If egolessness disappears then you will have difficulty in interpreting. A real sage is without the ego and without humility. If humility is there the sage is not real, not yet real. He has not reached the sixth stage, he has not reached the door.

But then you will be in a difficulty, because you always think that humility is the quality. If you go to a buddha you will not see any humility in him. You will not see any ego either, but you will not see any humility also. And this disappearance of humility may make it seem to you that he is not humble. Buddha says, "The Vedas are of no use, scriptures are to be thrown." If you go to him it will look as if he is not humble. He is saying that scriptures are of no use, the Vedas are to be thrown – he looks very egoistic. He is not, but he is not humble either. So whatsoever he is saying is neither related to ego nor related to egolessness. That will be the problem.

Look at Jesus, he was not a humble person at all. He was not an egoist, but not humble either. That created the problem, that led him to the cross. He was not humble at all. And now many psychologists say that he was neurotic, and they have a point. Many psychologists say that he was an egomaniac; they have a point. If psychologists study Buddha and Mahavira they will conclude the same things – but they have not studied them. They should have been studied very minutely.

So they say he was an egomaniac. Why? You can find reasons – because he was not humble. He used to say, "I am God," or "I am the son of God. I and my father in heaven are one." To the egoist mind this will appear like ego. And no-body can say that this man is humble who claims that he and God are one, or who claims that he is the son of God. It looks like a claim to us; to Jesus this was a simple fact.

And he was not claiming that you are not the son of God: claiming that he is the son of God, he claimed for you all. It is Christianity which claimed the wrong thing; Christianity started to claim that he is the *only* son of God. That is absurd, that is egomania. But Jesus was saying a simple fact: if the whole creation is out of God, the whole creation is the son, God is the father. He was saying a simple fact with no ego in it, but this disturbed people. They thought a sage must be humble. He used to say, "I am the king of the Jews." This has been said many times, but to people who were more wise than Jews. Jews were offended that this man who was just a beggar on the street, no more – just a vagabond, just an old hippie – that this man claimed, "I am the king of the Jews." But he was not claiming anything, he was in a state of mind where there is no ego. Kingship comes into being, but that is not ego. And that kingship doesn't belong to any worldly affairs, it is not a claim to rule anybody. That kingship is just felt as an inner nature.

Ram Teerth, an Indian mystic of this century, used to call himself Emperor Ram. He was a beggar, but nobody took offense in India because we have known so many beggars saying that, and we know that that happens: a moment comes when a person becomes an emperor without any kingdom. Really, a person be-comes an emperor only when there is no kingdom.

He went to America, and the American president invited him to visit. The American president felt uncomfortable because Ram Teerth always used to say "Emperor Ram." Even while talking he would say, "Emperor Ram says this." So the president humbly asked, "I cannot understand this. You don't seem to have any kingdom, why do you claim that you are an emperor?"

Ram Teerth said, "That's why I claim – because I have nothing to lose, no-body can defeat me. My kingdom is of the eternal, you cannot take it from me. Your kingdom can be taken, your presidency can be destroyed. Nobody can destroy me, I have nothing to lose. I am an emperor because I have no desires."

If you have desires you are a beggar. So there are two types of beggars, poor beggars and rich beggars. When Jesus said, "I am the king of the Jews," he was saying this. But people got offended. They said, "This is too much. This man cannot be tolerated – he must be crucified, he must be killed." But Jesus was a humble man, humble in this sense, that even humbleness was not there – egoless, egolessness was not there – truly humble. But then one starts saying facts. And you live in a world of ego, you interpret because of your egos. So people thought, "This man is claiming something – that he is the son of God, he is the king of the Jews – and he is nothing, just a beggar, a vagabond!"

In India nobody would have taken any offense. India has seen so many Jesuses, nobody would have taken offense. In India every sannyasin is called *swami;* swami means the master, the king. We call a man swami; swami means the lord. When he leaves everything, when he doesn't claim anything, when he has nothing, then he becomes swami, then he becomes the lord. Jesus was claiming something Indian in a country which was not India; that became the problem.

...And all sorts of mentations cease in this state, and rooted in pure non-duality, the seeker is free from fear.

Fear can exist only if the other is there. If you are alone, there can be no fear – the other creates the fear. You are sitting in a room alone, then somebody looks in through the window. Fear has come in. If you know the person well then less fear; if the person is absolutely a stranger then more fear, because then he is more other. If the person speaks your language then less fear, because he is somehow related. But if the person doesn't speak your language then more fear. If the person is a Christian and you are also a Christian then less fear. But if the person is a pagan then more fear.

If the person is totally other – doesn't belong to your country, doesn't belong to your language group, doesn't belong to your religion, doesn't belong to your race – more fear is created. The more the other is other, the more you become afraid. But whatsoever the other may be, howsoever near, the fear continues. The husband is afraid of the wife, the wife is afraid of the husband. They are close but the fear remains. Sartre says that the other is hell....

Sartre has a very beautiful story to tell. Somewhere in one of his dramas called "No Exit" a person suddenly awakens and finds himself in hell. So he looks around for the usual, traditional concept of hell – fire burning, oil boiling, sinners being thrown in it – but there is nothing. It is one air-conditioned room, but without any exit, you cannot go out. And he is not alone, there are three other people also.

They live in the room. Every desire is fulfilled immediately. That too is contrary, against the traditional concept of hell – that you will have your desires fulfilled. You will be thirsty, water will be flowing, but you will not be allowed to drink – that is the traditional concept. Desire will be there, the possibility to fulfill it will be there just in front of you, and you will not be allowed. But every desire is fulfilled immediately. Somebody comes in – from where nobody knows because there is no door – and brings food, drink, everything. And these four persons, one old lady, one young girl, another young man, and this person who has awakened, live together.

For one or two days they gossip – from where they have come, inquiries, introductions – but then they have finished. And there are no more newspapers, nothing, so they cannot continue. They have even repeated many times the same things. Then they get fed up – and nobody can go out. You cannot put the light off, there is no switch. So they sit, they eat, they sleep. Even while sleeping they know that three persons are there, they are not alone. So all become torturers – all the other three for each one. For each one the three are always present.

Then suddenly it is revealed to the man that this is hell. It becomes so impossible to live there, just the presence of the other three becomes so heavy that they want to commit suicide, but there is no way. They ask the person who brings the food. The person says, "In hell you cannot commit suicide. That much freedom is not allowed here – you can only live."

So they ask, "How many years do we have to live?"

And the man says, "Hell is eternal. You will have to live here forever and forever and forever."

Just think! Sartre says the other is hell – and this is a more dangerous hell than all the theologians combined have invented ever, because you can tolerate other things. If you are burned or thrown into boiling water or oil, or you cannot drink, you can tolerate it because still something is going on. And you are not alone, many are being thrown in the same suffering. You can even enjoy it, by and by you can get accustomed to it. But just living in a closed room with no exit, with a few people forever and forever, will be hell.

Your life is a suffering because the other is everywhere. You cannot destroy the other. You try to do it – the husband tries to destroy the wife so that the wife becomes a thing and the other is not felt. You may not have observed – you do it. Your servant enters the room, you don't take any notice. If you are reading the newspaper you go on reading as if no one has entered. You have forced the man, the servant, to be a thing, just a utility. You don't take any notice. It will be difficult to take notice because the other will bubble up.

Servants are forgotten as if they are not, and they are taught to behave in such a way as if they are not: to not make any noise, to not bump here and there, to just move silently, absently. A good servant is one who is not a person but a thing, a mechanism. We try this. We try with children: they should not create a noise, they should not jump, they should not play, they must behave, they must be obedient. All these teachings are just to force them not to be persons but things.

The husband tries the same with the wife, the wife tries the same with the husband, and we create hell for each other. The other cannot be destroyed; he remains a person, howsoever forced. Just look in the eyes of your servant and he remains a person. The "thing-ness" is just a surface, just a device to avoid you, just a device not to disturb you because he has to serve you, that's all. He cannot exist without it so he has compromised – but he remains a person.

That's why masters will not talk to servants, will not laugh with them, will not make any personal relationship, because once you laugh with a servant he is no more a thing. The person has come out. Then he will start behaving like a friend. You have to be strict. But when you are strict with a servant not only is he reduced to a thing, you are also reduced to a thing, because you cannot be open, you cannot be free. Not only is he confined, you are also confined. Whenever you create a prison for somebody else it is also a prison for yourself. Whenever you possess something you are also possessed – and then you suffer.

So what to do? How to kill the other? It is impossible. And you cannot exist without the other. If you can kill…. That's what a Hitler tries to do – kill. But even then the others are there. Hitler wouldn't allow any woman to sleep in his room in the night. Even his mistresses were not allowed to sleep in his room, he would remain alone. He was afraid of the other. He didn't get married his whole life. He got married only on the day when it was absolutely certain that Germany was defeated and everything was destroyed and he had to commit suicide. The same day he married and committed suicide – both within three hours.

First he got married, then he committed suicide with his mistress who had become his wife. The mistress had been continuously saying, "Marry me," but he would not marry because once you marry a person they come close and the other remains always there. He got married only when it was certain that within hours he would be committing suicide – then there was no fear of the other. But even if you are alone in the room like a Hitler, all around the room there are persons who are guarding. They are there, even in your sleep you know they are there.

The world remains around you, because you cannot exist alone. So what is the way to get out of this hell that the other creates? The Upanishads say, "You disappear!" When *you* are no more, the other is no more. You create the other by being yourself. The more the ego, the more the other will be there. The other is a creation, a by-product of the ego. And then, when you are no more and the whole has become one, the other and 'I' are not divided, there is no fear. *The seeker is free from fear.* And you cannot be free from fear in any other way.

Many people come to me to ask how to get rid of fear. You cannot. They say, "Would it be helpful if we pray to God?" No, it will not be helpful because of the other; the God will be the other now and you will be afraid of him. You will be constantly in fear whether you have been praying rightly or wrongly, whether God is happy with you or not. You will be in fear again.

If the other is there fear will remain. And the other can disappear only when you are not.

As the entanglements of his heart dissolve, so all his doubts drop.

Remember this. One man came to me just a few days ago. He had a long list of doubts, he had noted them down, and he told me, "Unless all these, my doubts, are dissolved, unless you answer all these I cannot meditate, I cannot become a sannyasin, I cannot surrender – so first these doubts. What do you think, can they be answered?"

I said to him, "I will not look at your list. You just close it and go. If I answer one doubt, I will say something and your doubting mind will create more doubts about what I have said." Doubts cannot be answered, they can only be dropped, because doubts are not significant, the doubting mind is significant. And you can focus the doubting mind on anything, you can go on.... Doubts arise in your mind just as leaves arise in a tree: the old fall, the new take their place. And you can go on cutting leaves but the tree will think you are pruning, so you cut one and four leaves will come out.

This Upanishad says that only at the stage – this stage, the sixth – when all the entanglements of the heart, all the confusions of the mind, the mentation itself drops, then all doubts drop, never before. Only at the sixth stage a man be-comes doubtless, never before. You can trust before it, but you have to trust with doubts; the doubts remain by the side. They will always remain unless you reach the sixth. All that you can do is push them aside, don't pay much attention to them. Nothing can be done. They cannot be answered, you cannot be satisfied. And you cannot drop them before the sixth.

Then what should be done? You can just put them aside in the corner. Let them be there but don't pay much attention to them, be indifferent to them. Buddha has said, "Be indifferent to your doubts and wait, and go on doing whatsoever is possible." A state of mind comes when doubts disappear, when suddenly at the sixth stage you look – the doubts are not there in your consciousness, they have gone. They go with the change of your consciousness, not with answers.

This is the moment when he is completely emptied of all thought. Without attaining nirvana, he is in a nirvana-like state, and becomes free while yet dwelling in the body. This state is like that of the motionless flame of a lamp. And then comes the seventh stage.

Without attaining nirvana, he is in a nirvana-like state.

The sixth state is not nirvana. He is still in the body, the mind has disappeared but the body is there. He has still to live, he has still to fulfill his karmas, he has to pay his debts, he has to finish all the accounts, close all the accounts that he has opened in many lives – but his mind has gone. The body will go when the time is ripe, when all the accounts are closed – then he will reach nirvana. But *he is in a nirvana-like state,* it is just close to nirvana.

You are not exactly in the garden but just sitting by the side of it. You can feel the coolness, the cool air comes to you. You can smell the scent coming from the flowers. You can feel, it is showering on you, but you are standing outside. Soon you will enter. You are just at the gate but still not in it. That's why the sixth state is called nirvana-like, but not nirvana.

This state is like that of the motionless flame of a lamp.

No movement, no wavering, all mentation has ceased, all thoughts stopped. You are unwavering, the consciousness is *nishkam,* without any wavering, like a flame with no wind. In a closed room where no breeze is coming, the flame of a lamp or a candle will become static, there will be no movement. Your consciousness in the sixth becomes a motionless flame.

And then comes the seventh stage....

15   God Seeks You

Osho,

I feel lost in you without reason or direction. Questions and desires fall in confusion before you. Overpowered by senseless faith and love, listlessly I wait, feeling like a fool. Are there differences between blind faith, love and surrender?

There is a state when you certainly feel like a fool, but this is the beginning of wisdom. Only fools think they are wise, and those who are wise become wise when they start thinking that they are fools. The moment you can feel that you are a fool wisdom has dawned upon you. Now you will change, now there will be transformation, now the possibilities open infinitely...because this is part of the foolish mind – not to realize the foolishness. And this is the beginning of a wise mind – to realize one's ignorance, foolishness.

So this is good news that you realize that you are a fool, this is something worth attaining. The ego cannot exist now. The ego always exists with knowledgeability, one goes on feeling one knows without knowing.

It is reported that the oracle of Delphi declared Socrates the wisest man on the earth. So a few people, disciples of Socrates, came to him and said, "Socrates, be happy. The oracle has declared that you are the wisest man on the earth."

Socrates laughed and said, "Go back. There must have been some mistake. How can I be the wisest man? – because I know only one thing, that I don't know anything, I am ignorant. So there has been some mistake. You go back and tell the oracle."

They went back to the oracle and said, "Socrates himself has denied it, so there must be something erroneous. He says he is not wise, he says he realizes only one thing – that he is absolutely ignorant, he knows nothing. He claims only this much knowledge, that he knows nothing."

The oracle said, "That's why I have declared that he is the wisest man, that is the reason – because only the wisest can say that he does not know anything."

Fools always claim knowledge. Only then, only there through their claim, can they hide their stupidity. So be happy if you feel that you are a fool and you can see your foolishness. The one who can see his foolishness has become separate from it; now foolishness exists apart. It is there but you are separate; you can witness it, you are not identified with it now. Consciously alert, everybody will see that he is a fool.

Secondly, there is no difference between blind faith, love and surrender – be-cause all differences belong to the intellect, all distinctions belong to the intellect. The heart knows no distinctions. Whether you call it blind faith or you call it surrender or you call it love depends on your intellect. The heart doesn't know any distinction, the heart knows only the feelings – the feeling is the same.

When do you call a faith blind? When? When the intellect says that this faith is wrong then the intellect calls it blind. When the intellect feels that some faith is justified by reason, then the intellect says that this faith is right. But does faith need any justification from reason? Is reason in any way the authority to know what is right and what is wrong in the world of feeling?

Always rationalists have said that the believers are blind – always. But have you known any believer who was not blind? People who were following Jesus were blind – everybody condemned them. Those who were following Buddha were blind, rationalists condemned them. Rationalists have always been saying that faith is blind. This is just a trick of logic to say that that faith is right which is not blind – but there is no such faith.

The very word faith means that where there are no grounds to believe, you believe. If there are grounds then there is no need for faith. For example, you don't believe that the earth exists. Is it not a fact? There is no need for faith. The earth exists: this is a fact, justified, rational; faith is not needed. Faith comes only when the reason cannot justify but the heart feels it. And reason is not the totality, reason is not the total life and existence. There are things which go beyond reason, which reason cannot comprehend but which the heart feels.

There are only two ways: either you deny the heart or you deny reason. When reason and heart are in conflict, these are the two alternatives: either you follow reason and say to the heart that it is blind, and unless something is justified, proved, you are not going to believe.... But do you know, whenever something is rationalized, proved, there is no need to believe.

Marx, the founder of communism, used to say, "I will not believe in God unless God is proved in a scientific laboratory." But he knew it well, so he added, "Don't try to prove God in a scientific way, because once you prove God in a scientific way, in a scientific laboratory, there will be no need to believe." Do you believe in chemistry or physics? There is no need. Only the unproved needs faith; the heart feels that it is there but reason cannot prove it.

I have loved very few sentences in my life – very few, rare, they can be counted on one's fingers. One of these few sentences is one from Tertullian, one Christian mystic. He said, "I believe in God because God is absurd, because God cannot be believed, is impossible to prove. That's why I believe."...Because if it is possible to prove there is no need to believe, then there are facts. The heart can feel and lead you. The reason will say heart is blind because reason thinks that only he has eyes, but the heart has its own eyes. When you love a person, love is always blind. Have you seen any love with eyes? A person who goes on following reason will never be in love.

It happened to Immanuel Kant, one of the greatest German thinkers. He was a complete rationalist. One woman loved Immanuel Kant and proposed marriage to him. He said, "Wait, because first I will have to think pro and con – whether marriage can lead to happiness or not. And unless I decide rationally I cannot take any step."

So he thought and thought and brooded and contemplated, and he wrote at least one thousand pages for and against. And then he concluded that both the sides seemed to be almost equal, and a decision was difficult. So he went to find the woman to tell her that a decision was difficult and she would have to wait a little longer, but when he went there he found that she was already married and the mother of three children. Immanuel Kant remained unmarried; such a man cannot be in love. And this is the rationalist mind, one of the keenest minds – logical, logical to the very extreme – but if you start deciding with the mind, love cannot happen.

To reason, love is blind and for the heart, reason is foolish. For the heart reason is foolish, stupid; it may be useful as far as the market is concerned, but is not useful as far as life is concerned. So those who live in reason live in the market and all that transcends the market, is greater than the market, is beyond them. They never realize it, they never have a glimpse; that rainbow never arises in their lives, it goes beyond. They live in the mundane, the trivial. No poetry ever happens to them, no singing ever descends in their hearts, no dance is possible for them – ecstasy is not for them.

So it doesn't matter what you call it – blind faith, love or surrender – call it whatsoever you like. Remember only one thing: it should arise from your feeling, and it cannot arise from your mind. And don't force your mind to be the leader, don't force reason to be the leader, because through mind you may be-come more powerful but you will be less happy. Through mind you may attain much wealth but you will remain poor within. Through mind you may rule thousands of people but you will not be a master like Buddha or Jesus – inside you will remain a slave.

This has to be chosen: if you want more power, more money, more prestige, follow reason; if you want more happiness, more bliss, more silence, more peace, more God, more ecstasy, then don't listen to reason, follow the heart. They are two different dimensions and don't try to confuse them. Decide well, and then follow one path. Can you be satisfied just by reason? Can only logic make you happy? Logic is simply dead, dry; one cannot live by logic alone. As Jesus says one cannot live by bread alone, I say one cannot live by logic alone. But you can try, and in that effort you will lose all that is life, all that is of worth, and all that can be felt as a blessing and beatitude.

"Overpowered by senseless faith and love, listlessly I wait." Nothing else can be done but there is no need to wait listlessly – you can wait ecstatically. This listlessness will come because reason goes on interfering. Reason goes on saying, "What foolishness are you doing? What are you doing here? Why are you waiting and wasting time?" That reason creates the listlessness, otherwise waiting can become a joy. The most joyous thing possible is waiting – hope throbbing, heart beating for the unknown, and you wait in silence with infinite patience.

If you can wait with joy there will not be much need to wait for long, if you cannot wait with joy you may have to wait for many lives – because the divine can happen to you only when your waiting is ecstatic, filled with joy. Just look at a woman waiting for her lover: she has faith, she has ecstasy – the eyes and the infinite patience and the happiness. Wait like a lover, only then is your waiting meaningful. Don't wait listlessly, because if you are so listless your lover may come but will not find you worthy to be with. Only your joy can become the invitation. Wait blissfully, ecstatically, and then I say to you that you will not need more waiting. There will be no need, it can happen this very moment.

If your joy is total this very moment there is no need to wait. The divine will descend in you – you have fulfilled the condition. And this I call the condition: waiting with infinite patience, but ecstatically. This is the condition. Fulfill this and a single moment will not be lost.

It is said in old Egyptian books that whenever the disciple is ready the master appears. Whenever, wherever the disciple is ready the master appears. There is no need for the disciple to seek the master, it is always the master who seeks the disciple. Even if you go to the master, it is always the master who seeks you, who finds you.

The same is true for the divine happening: whenever you are

ready it happens – God seeks you. He has always been seeking you. He has been following you, he has been waiting for you. Whenever you are ready the seed will sprout, the bud will become the flower. But getting ready means waiting – waiting is the only prayer you can do. But if you don't believe you cannot wait. Only faith can wait. Reason always insists on things happening immediately. Heart can wait, there is no urgency for the heart.

Try to understand this: time exists only for reason. For the heart there is no time, heart exists in timelessness. Only for reason is there time. So mind goes on insisting on haste, hurry, urgency, and mind is always tense. Time is going, flowing, life is becoming less and less every moment. Things should happen instantly – that is the insistence of reason. But the heart knows no time, there are no clocks for the heart. Heart exists timelessly, that's why the heart can wait – the heart can wait infinitely.

If you love, if you have faith, if you trust, then there is no hurry, and then there is no need to wait listlessly. Why not dance while waiting? Why waste this time in listlessness? Why not dance? It will be better when your lover comes if your lover finds you dancing. It will be a good meeting, it will be the right moment.

The second question:

Osho,

If even fifty percent of all persons should become enlightened, does it mean that fifty percent will have to immediately become idiots? The polar opposite theory doesn't seem to give much hope to more than five percent.

You misunderstood – but that is always more possible than to understand. Your mind moves immediately to the wrong conclusion, and you cannot help it, that's how you have trained your mind. In all these talks I have been telling you that enlightenment means going beyond the polar opposites. So there is no state against enlightenment, it means transcending the division. We have been saying again and again that mind is enlightened only when it transcends division.

If fifty percent of persons are intelligent, then fifty percent will be foolish; if five percent are geniuses, then five percent will be idiots. But a genius is not enlightened – he is as unenlightened as the idiot, there is no difference. He may be an Einstein, he may have won Nobel prizes, but that doesn't make any difference. Just by winning a Nobel prize you don't become enlightened. A genius is as far away from enlightenment as an idiot. An idiot can also jump into enlightenment just as a genius can jump into it.

Intelligence and stupidity are polar opposites. To enlightenment there is no polar opposite – it is transcendence of both. So there exists no state which is against enlightenment. Have you ever heard of anyone who is just the polar opposite to Buddha or Jesus? There is no one. The whole Vedanta, the whole of Upanishads' teaching, the very doctrine is this: that when you transcend duality you attain a totally new dimension, nothing exists against it.

In Sanskrit we have three terms: *dukkha* which means pain, suffering, misery; *sukkha* which means happiness, pleasure, joy; and *ananda* which can be translated as bliss. Happiness is against misery, they are polar opposites. Bliss is not against anything, there is no state which is against bliss. If you are happy you will become miserable, if you are miserable you will become happy. You can move, this duality is there. But if you are blissful you cannot move anywhere – duality has disappeared. Against ananda, against bliss, there exists no state.

Enlightenment is not against ignorance, it is against ignorance and knowledge both. It is beyond, not against. So a person who knows more is not enlightened, and a person who knows less is not unenlightened because he knows less. Wherever you are you can take the jump into enlightenment. So sometimes very uneducated people have also jumped, not very intelligent people have also jumped. The jump is needed.

And sometimes it happens that a person who is not educated much is more courageous and can take the jump more easily than a person who knows too much. Just because he knows too much he becomes too afraid of taking risks, because he is so clever he becomes cunning also – cleverness creates cunningness. He becomes calculative, and on the path of the divine you cannot calculate. Only gamblers, only those who can jump without calculating, only those who can take risks, only they can enter.

So this question is just through your misunderstanding. In the world balance exists, but when you transcend the world you also transcend this polar balance. You go beyond the two, you become one.

The third question:

Osho,

Does laughter belong to every stage?

This is worth considering, significant. The first thing to understand is that, except man, no animal is capable of laughter. Laughter shows a very high peak. If you go out on a street and you see a buffalo laughing you will be scared to death, and if you report it nobody is going to believe that it happened. It is impossible.

Why can't animals laugh? Why can't trees laugh? There is a very deep causality to the laughter; only that animal can laugh which can get bored. Animals and trees are not bored. Boredom and laughter – this is the polar duality, these are the polar opposites. Man is the only animal who is bored; boredom is the symbol of humanity. Look at dogs and cats – they are never bored. Man seems to be deep in boredom. Why are they not bored? Why does only man suffer boredom? And the higher your intelligence the more you will be bored, a lower intelligence is not bored so much. That's why primitives are more happy.

You will find more happy people in a primitive society than in a civilized society; even a Bertrand Russell becomes jealous. When Bertrand Russell for the first time came in contact with some primitive tribes he started feeling jealous because they were so happy – not bored at all. Life was a blessing. They were poor, starved, almost naked; in every way they had nothing, but they were not bored with life. In Bombay, in New York, in London, everybody is bored – more intelligent, more civilized, more boredom.

So the secret can be understood: the more you can think, the more you will be bored, because through thinking you can compare – past, future, present. Through thinking you can hope, through thinking you can ask, "What is the meaning of it?" And the moment a person asks, "What is the meaning of it?" boredom will enter, because really there is no meaning in anything. If you ask the question, "What is the meaning of it?" you will feel meaninglessness. And when meaninglessness is felt you will be bored. Animals are not bored, trees are not bored, rocks are not bored. They never ask, "What is the meaning of life, what is the purpose of life?" They never ask so they never feel it is meaningless. As they are they accept it, as life is it is accepted. There is no boredom.

Man feels bored, laughter is the antidote. You cannot live without laughter, because you can kill your boredom only through laughter. You cannot find a single joke in primitive societies, they don't have any jokes. Jews have the largest number of jokes, they are the most highly bored people on the earth. But they must be so, because they win more Nobel prizes than any other community. The whole last century almost all the great names are Jews: Freud, Einstein, Marx – Jews. And look at the list of Nobel prizewinners – almost half the Nobel prizes go to the Jews. They have the largest number of jokes.

And this may be the reason why all over the world Jews are hated – because everybody feels jealous of them. Wherever they are they will always win any type of competition, so everybody feels jealous of them, the whole world is united against them, feels hate for them. When you cannot compete with someone hate is the result. And they have the most beautiful jokes on the earth. Why? They must be feeling very bored; they have to create jokes – a joke is the antidote to feeling bored. Laughter is needed to exist, otherwise you will commit suicide.

Now try to understand the mechanism of laughter, how it happens. If I tell a joke, why do you laugh? What happens? What is the inner mechanism? If I tell a joke, expectation is created, you start expecting. Your mind starts searching for what the end is going to be, and you cannot conceive the end. A joke moves in two dimensions: first it moves in a logical dimension, you can conceive it. If the joke goes on being logical to the very end there will be no laughter. Suddenly the joke takes a turn and becomes illogical, something which you could not conceive. And when the joke takes a turn and the result becomes illogical, the expectation, the tension that was created in you, suddenly explodes. You relax, laughter comes out of you.

Laughter is a relaxation, but a tension is needed. A story creates expectation, tension. You start feeling that now the crescendo, now the crescendo will come, something is going to happen. Your backbone is straight like a yogi, you have no more thoughts in the mind; the whole being is just waiting, all the energy moving towards the conclusion. And all that you could conceive is not going to happen.

Suddenly something happens which the mind could not conceive; something absurd happens, something illogical, irrational. The end is such a turn that it was impossible for logic to think about it. You explode. The whole energy that has become a pillar inside suddenly relaxes. Laughter comes out of you through this relaxation. Man is bored, hence he needs laughter. The more bored he is, the more and more laughter he will need, otherwise he cannot exist.

Thirdly, it has also to be understood about laughter that it is of three types. One, when you laugh *at* someone. This is the meanest, the lowliest, very ordinary and vulgar – when you laugh at somebody else's cost. This is violent, aggressive, insulting. Deep down there is a revenge.

Secondly, when you laugh at yourself. This is worth achieving, this is cultured, and the man who can laugh at himself is valuable. He has risen above vulgarity, he has risen above low instincts – hatred, aggression, violence.

And thirdly, the highest laughter, which is not about anybody – neither the other nor oneself. The third is just cosmic, you laugh at the whole situation as it is. The whole situation as it is, is absurd – no purpose in the future, no beginning in the beginning. The whole situation of existence is such that if you can see the whole – such a great vastness, an infinite vastness, moving to no fixed purpose, moving to no goal; so much going on without leading anywhere;

nobody in the past to create it, nobody in the end to finish it; a whole cosmos, and moving so beautifully, so systematically, so rationally — if you can see this whole cosmos, then a laughter arises.

I have heard about three monks. No name is mentioned, because they never told their names to anybody, they never answered anything. So in China they are only known simply as "the three laughing monks."

They did only one thing: they would enter a village, stand in the marketplace, and start laughing. Suddenly people would become aware and they would laugh with their whole being. Then others would also get the infection, and then a crowd would gather, and just looking at them the whole crowd would start laughing. What is happening? Then the whole town would get involved, and they would move to another town. They were loved very much. That was their only sermon, the only message — that laugh. And they would not teach, they would simply create the situation.

Then it happened they became famous all over the country — the three laughing monks. The whole of China loved them, respected them. Nobody had preached that way — that life must be just a laughter and nothing else. And they were not laughing at anybody in particular, but simply laughing as if they had understood the cosmic joke. They spread so much joy all over China without using a single word. People would ask their names but they would simply laugh, so that became their name, the three laughing monks.

Then they became old, and in one village one of the three monks died. The whole village was very expectant, filled with expectations, because now at least when one of them had died they must weep. This would be something worth seeing, because no one could even conceive of these people weeping.

The whole village gathered. The two monks were standing by the side of the corpse of the third and laughing such a belly laugh. So the villagers asked, "At least explain this!"

So for the first time they spoke, and they said, "We are laughing because this man has won. We were always wondering who would die first, and this man has defeated us. We are laughing at our defeat, at his victory. He lived with us for many years, and we laughed together and we enjoyed each other's togetherness, presence. There can be no other way of giving him the last send-off, we can only laugh."

The whole village was sad, but when the dead monk's body was put on the funeral pyre, then the village realized that not only were these two joking – the third who was dead was also laughing...because the third man who was dead had told his companions, "Don't change my dress!" It was conventional that when a man died they changed the dress and gave a bath to the body, so he had said, "Don't give me a bath because I have never been unclean. So much laughter has been in my life that no impurity can accumulate near me, can even come to me. I have not gathered any dust, laughter is always young and fresh. So don't give me a bath and don't change my clothes."

So just to pay him respect they had not changed his clothes. And when the body was put on the fire, suddenly they became aware that he had hidden many things under his clothes and those things started...Chinese fireworks! So the whole village laughed, and those two said, "You rascal! You have died, but again you have defeated us. Your laughter is the last."

There is a cosmic laughter when the whole joke of this cosmos is understood. That is the highest, only a buddha can laugh like that. These three monks must have been three buddhas. But if you can laugh the second, that too is worth trying. Avoid the first – don't laugh at anyone's cost, that is ugly and violent. If you want to laugh, laugh at yourself.

That's why Mulla Nasruddin in every one of his jokes and stories always proves himself the stupid man in it, never anybody else. He always laughs at himself and allows you to laugh at him. He never puts anybody else in the situation of being foolish. Sufis say that Mulla Nasruddin is the wise fool. Learn at least that much – the second laughter.

If you can learn the second, the third will not be far ahead, soon you will reach the third. Leave the first laughter, that is degrading. But almost ninety-nine percent of the time you laugh the first one. Much courage is needed to laugh at oneself, much confidence is needed to laugh at oneself. For the spiritual seeker, even laughter should become a part of sadhana. Remember not to laugh the first laughter, remember to laugh the second – and remember to reach the third.

The fourth question:

Osho,

Can there be moments of effortlessness while a seeker is engaged in the first three stages? Is effort completely lacking in the second four stages? Does there come a point at which both effort and effortlessness must cease?

First, there can be moments of effortlessness even while making effort. If you are total in your effort there will be glimpses of effortlessness. Suddenly effort will have disappeared for a moment, there will be a gap. If you are aware and look deep in the gap you will see. Just doing meditation here, I feel many of you achieve for a single moment effortlessness. You may not be aware, but try to be aware. While doing, a moment comes when you feel you are not doing it – as if it is happening.

You may have started it as a doing. When you start taking deep, fast chaotic breaths, of course, it is a fact that you start it. But have you observed that sometimes the breathing takes you, the mastery has changed? Now the breathing is going by itself, it has taken over. When you start the second stage, in the beginning there is effort to allow madness; even sometimes to imitate, to force, to do something because everybody else is doing. But you can watch: a moment comes to many, to at least ninety percent of people here, when the madness has taken over. You are not doing it, rather it is doing you. You are not the doer, it is moving by itself – then it is effortless. And when it is moving by itself it is beautiful, only then is the catharsis happening. When you are doing it is not catharsis, you are only starting it. When the madness has taken over and is on its own and the movement is going automatically, then it is catharsis – now the repressed energies are working. You may have started laughter in catharsis. Then a point comes when you feel that laughter is going by itself. You can watch it, it will continue. No need to do it, it is happening.

Sometimes fear grips at that moment, because then you feel you have gone insane. Up to that moment you are making effort, you are the master and you are not afraid. You know that you can stop it, you know that it is within your control, you are doing it. Fear enters whenever you feel that it has become automatic. You get scared, because now you see it may not stop, it may continue. Then what are you going to do? And if you become afraid you again start doing. And that's why you cannot watch effortless moments.

There is one day left (*of the meditation camp);* watch and don't get afraid, because that is the *right* moment – when the catharsis is starting to happen, when you become scared. When things are coming out, immediately you close yourself and make all efforts again to do something. With the doing the mind is at ease; with the happening the mind is afraid, and effortlessness will mean happening. But don't be afraid, because any happening can be stopped – if you have started it, it can be stopped. So don't get afraid.

That's why my insistence that when I say "Stop!" stop completely – because if you cannot stop when I say stop it can be dangerous. I don't want you to be-come mad, rather I want you to become saner through throwing madness out. You must remain in control. But don't try, there is no need. If you have started it, this is the law: if you have started, you are deep inside in control. Don't get scared, allow it to happen. Any moment it can be stopped.

That's why after the third stage I always insist that when I say stop, when you hear the word stop, you stop, because that will make you the master and you will remain the master. Even while catharsis is happening you know that at any time you can push the button off. Once you become aware that the button can be put on and off you will never be afraid.

Madness is there within everyone and the more you hide it the more you are vulnerable, the more you can go mad any moment. And if you go mad then you will not be the master. If you never started it then you cannot stop it. You can only stop that which you have started. If you have not started it you cannot stop it.

So don't go on suppressing, because a quantity can be tolerated but there comes a moment when the quantity reaches the climax, the evaporating point –one hundred degrees. Then you start boiling and evaporating. Many persons who were just like you a day before are in madhouses now. You can be there any day. If you don't allow catharsis you are all prone to go mad, because civilization is such, the situation is such, that everybody accumulates madness. You have to throw it every day to remain clean and pure, to retain the clarity of mind and vision.

But if you know the law that if you start a thing you can stop it, then you can start anything and you can stop. Be the master in the starting, you will be the master in the end also. But if a thing starts by itself then you cannot stop it, then you don't know where the button is to turn on and off.

And secondly, "Is effort completely lacking in the second four stages?"

Yes. In the first three effort is there, in the last four there is no effort. And if you make effort you will not grow in them. As without effort you will not grow in the first three, with effort you will not grow in the last four. Effort is helpful in the first three, effort is a hindrance in the last four. So one has to learn effort and then one has to learn to drop effort, because there are things for which effort cannot be made.

For example, you sow some seeds, some flower seeds; effort is needed because the seeds are to be sown. You choose the soil, you give water, sunrays, fertilizers; you arrange everything, you do everything. Effort is needed. But then the seeds sprout, you need not pull them to make them grow faster. You need not pull them, if you pull them they will die. Effort is not needed.

And when buds come to your plant, don't try to open them and make them flower. You will kill the whole thing. And if you open unripe buds those flowers will be ugly, there will be no fragrance and they will look artificial. You can do everything to help the plant but you need not make any positive effort to open the flowers. They will open by themselves. And when they open by themselves they will be ripe, they will be ready to express themselves. Their fragrance, their beauty, their ecstasy will come out.

The same is the case in spiritual discipline. The first three stages are just to make the ground ready – seeds sown, every condition prepared – and the four end ones are just the flowering stages, they come by themselves. Don't interfere with them by your effort, and don't do anything positively. You simply wait and you will see that your inner consciousness is growing every moment.

And thirdly, "Does there come a point at which both effort and effortlessness must cease?"

Yes. Effort is positive, effortlessness is negative. The first three stages are effort, the second three stages are effortless, and the seventh, the last, is neither. It is neither effort nor effortless, it is neither positive nor negative – it is the transcendence. The seventh is the transcendence. We will try to understand that tomorrow morning. The seventh is the transcendence. Nothing is needed – neither effort nor awareness not to make effort. Both have to be dropped.

The last question:

Osho,

What is moment-to-moment understanding in relationship?

A difficult question – because unless you learn to live moment to moment you cannot understand it. As we live, we live out of the past. If someone insults you, you immediately react. That reaction comes from your past experiences. It is not from you, it is from the chain of your experiences.

If someone is loving towards you, you become loving – that loving may be from the past experiences. So living moment to moment and understanding moment to moment in relationship comes only if you become aware of the past chain and don't allow it to function. And always respond in the present, not through the past.

For example, someone insults you. Many people have insulted you in the past; there has come a wound in your heart, through all the insults a wound is created. This insult will also hit the wound, and then you will react. That reaction will not be justified because this man is not creating the wound. And if the wound is touched, the pain is not created by his insult really. It has been created by many insults and the reaction is accumulated; it is not justified.

That's why it happens that if you react the other always feels, "Why are you reacting so much? I have not said anything." You also know it: you are not aware that you have said something to someone which has become a hurt in him and he reacts. And you say, "You have misunderstood me, because I have not said anything to insult you. Why are you reacting? Are you mad?" But you don't know. He has a wound, and when you hit the wound the whole pain comes towards you. The wound may have been created by many people – unknown, known, not remembered – but the whole wound is poured on this person. This is not justified.

So what will it be to respond immediately? It will be first to put aside the past. Look at this man with alertness so that the past doesn't cloud you. Look at whatsoever he has said, dissect it, analyze it, in the light of the present. And it will be better if you can wait a little and meditate on it.

It happened once, one woman wrote a letter to an American author, Dale Carnegie. Dale Carnegie had delivered a lecture on the radio on Abraham Lincoln, and he had mentioned many wrong dates in it. The woman was a lover of Abraham Lincoln, so she wrote a very angry letter saying, "If you don't know the ABC of Abraham Lincoln's life you should not go on the radio. And this is insulting. If you are not well informed, then first get informed and then start lecturing."

Dale Carnegie was a man of fame, had written many bestsellers; he got offended, he was very angry. So he wrote a letter immediately in the same tone, the same anger, the same irritation. But it was late and the servant had gone, so he left the letter on the table. In the morning he would post it.

In the morning, when he was putting it in the envelope, he just looked once more at it. He felt, "This is too much. The woman has not written like this, she doesn't deserve so much anger from me." And in a way he felt she was right also. So he tore up the letter and wrote another which was totally different. There was no anger, no irritation in it, rather the attitude of thanking her for making him aware of some mistakes and he felt obliged. But then he thought, "If in twelve hours so much can change, there is no hurry. I can wait for a few more days."

So he tried one experiment. He left the letter again on the table. By the evening he again read it and he wanted to change a few words again. For seven days he continued, and on the seventh day it became a love letter. And Dale Carnegie relates that that woman proved one of the best friends that he had ever had in his life. What would have happened if the servant had not gone and the letter had been posted? He would have created an enemy.

When Gurdjieff's father was dying he told Gurdjieff, "Only one message I want to give you – and remember it!" Gurdjieff was very small, just nine years of age, and the father said, "I am not rich so I have nothing to give to you, only one advice which my father gave to me when he was dying. And this is the message: that if you get angry, don't answer immediately, wait twenty-four hours. Then do whatsoever you like. Even if you want for to kill the man, go and kill – but after twenty-four hours."

And Gurdjieff says, "In my whole life anger has not created any problem for me, because I have to wait twenty-four hours and then the whole thing seems foolish. And sometimes even the person who created anger seems to be right, so I go and thank him. Through anger I have not created a single enemy, and through anger there has been no complexity in my life."

So alertness is needed in moment-to-moment relationship. Alertness is needed. Be alert! Don't allow your past to come in between you and the person to whom you are relating. It will take time to become aware because the past is so swift, it enters so immediately, there is no time gap. Somebody says something and the past has entered, you have interpreted through the past. So move a little slowly. Look at the person, wait, absorb whatsoever has happened to you, meditate, and then respond in the present. Once you become efficient, once you know this key, you have one of the keys which can allow you to enter into the mystery, into the mysteries of other persons.

Every person is carrying such a mysterious being but the being is closed to you. Every person can become the door for the divine, any ordinary person is extraordinary. Just behind the surface the mysterious is hidden, but you need a key to open it. And that key is moment-to-moment alert response. Not reaction – response. Reaction is always dead; you do something because he has done something. Response is totally different.

I will tell you one anecdote.

Buddha was passing through a village. The people of that village were against him, against his philosophy, so they gathered around him to insult him. They used ugly words, vulgar words. Buddha listened. Ananda, Buddha's disciple who was with him, got very angry, but he couldn't say anything because Buddha was listening so silently, so patiently, rather as if he was enjoying the whole thing. Then even the crowd became a little frustrated because he was not getting irritated and it seemed he was enjoying.

Buddha said, "Now, if you are finished, I should move – because I have to reach the other village soon. They must be waiting just as you were waiting for me. If you have not told me all the things that you thought to tell me, I will be coming back within a few days, then you can finish it."

Somebody from the crowd said, "But we have been insulting you, we have insulted you. Won't you react? Won't you say something?"

Buddha said, "That is difficult. If you want me to react, then you are too late. You should have come at least ten years ago, because then I used to react. But I am now no longer so foolish. I see that you are angry, that's why you are insulting me. I see your anger, the fire burning in your mind. I feel compassion for you. This is my response – I feel compassion for you. Unnecessarily you are troubled.

"Even if I am wrong, why should you get so irritated? That is not your business. If I am wrong I am going to hell, you will not go with me. If I am wrong I will suffer for it, you will not suffer for it. But it seems you love me so much and you think about me and consider me so much that you are so angry, irritated. You have left your work in the fields and you have come just to say a few things to me. I am thankful."

Just when he was leaving he said, "One thing more I would like to say to you. In the other village I left behind, a great crowd just like you had come, there and they had brought many sweets just as a present for me, a gift from the village. But I told them that I don't take sweets. They took the sweets back. I ask you, what will they do with those sweets?"

So somebody from the crowd said, "What will they do? It is easy, there is no need to answer. They will distribute that in the village and will enjoy."

So Buddha said, "Now what will you do? You have brought only insults and I say I don't take them. What will you do? I feel so sorry for you. You can insult me, that is up to you. But I don't take it, that is up to me – whether I take it or not." Buddha said, "I don't take unnecessary things, useless things. I don't get unnecessarily burdened. I feel compassion for you."

This is response. If a person is angry and you are present there, not with your past, you will feel always compassion. Reaction becomes anger, response always is compassion. You will see through the person. It will become transparent that he is angry, he is suffering, he is in misery, he is ill.

When someone is in fever you don't start beating him and asking, "Why are you having a fever? Why is your body hot? Why have you got a temperature?" You serve the man, you help him to come out of it. And when somebody is angry he is also having a temperature, he is in a fever, he is feverish. Why get so angry about it? He is in a mental disease, which is more dangerous than any bodily disease and more fatal. So if the wife is angry the husband will feel compassion, he will try in every way to help her to be out of it. This is just mad – that she is angry and you also get angry. This is just mad, insane. You will look at the person, you will feel the misery she is in or he is in, and you will help.

But if the past comes in then everything goes wrong. And it can happen only if you go deep in meditation, otherwise it cannot happen. Just intellectual understanding won't help. If you go deep in meditation your wounds will be thrown, a catharsis will happen. You become more and more clear inside, clarity is attained, you become like a mirror. You don't have any wounds really, so no one can hit them. Then you can look at the person, then you can respond.

Response is always good, reaction is always bad. Response is always beautiful, reaction is always ugly. Avoid reactions and allow responses. Reaction is from the past, response is here and now.

16   The Art of Dying

In this seventh stage, the state of videhamukti,

liberation while living in the body is achieved. This stage is totally silent

and cannot be communicated in words.

It is the end of all stages, where all the processes of yoga come to their

conclusion. In this stage, all activities – worldly, bodily and scriptural –
cease. The whole universe in the form of the world – viswa,

intelligence – prajna, and radiance – tejas, is just aum.

There is no division here between speech and the speaker.

If however any such division remains, the state has not been attained.

The first sound 'a' of aum, stands for the world,

the second 'u' for radiance and the third 'm' for intelligence.

Before entering samadhi, the seeker should contemplate on aum most
strenuously, and subsequently he should surrender everything, from gross to subtle
to the conscious self. Taking the conscious self as his own self,

he should consolidate this feeling: I am eternal, pure, enlightened, free,
existential, incomparable, the most blissful Vasudeva and Pranava himself.

Since the whole visible world comprising a beginning, a middle and an end, is
sorrow-stricken, he must renounce everything

and merge into the supreme. He should feel that he is blissful,

taintless, without ignorance, without appearance,

inexpressible in words, and that he is Brahman,

the essence of knowledge.

This is the Upanishadic mystery.

Thus ends the Akshya Upanishad.

The first three stages are just like the waking state of the mind, the surface of your personality – just a fragment, the part where waves exist. The fourth and the fifth stages are deeper than the surface. They are like the dream state of the mind, where for the first time you are no longer in contact with the outer world. The outer world has ceased to be, you live only in your dreams. You enter subjectivity. The objects have disappeared, only the subject has remained.

The sixth stage is still deeper, just like the dreamless sleep – the third state of mind – where even dreams cease to be. Objects have disappeared, now subjects also disappear. The world is no more, even the reflections of the world in the mind are no more. You are fast asleep with no disturbance, not a single ripple. These are the three stages of the mind, and parallel stages to these the seeker has to pass through on the spiritual path also.

The seventh is like the fourth. The Upanishads have not given it any name, because no name can be given to it. The first is waking, the second dreaming, the third sleep – but the fourth has been left simply as the fourth, without giving it any name. It is symbolic. The Upanishads call it turiya. The word turiya means simply the fourth, it doesn't say anything more. It is nameless because it cannot be defined. Words cannot express it, it can only be indicated. Even that indication has to be negative. It can be experienced but not formulated in concepts, hence it is called the fourth. The seventh stage of the seeker's consciousness is like the fourth stage of the mind.

Before we enter into the seventh stage and try to penetrate its mysteries, a few things will help to create the base for the understanding of something which is the most difficult to understand. First, the six are stages, but the seventh is really not a stage. It is called a stage because there is no other way to call it, but the seventh is not a stage. The six are stages, the seventh you are. The seventh is not a stage, it is your very nature; it is you, your being.

For example, you were a child once; childhood was a stage. You were not childhood, you passed through childhood. It was a station, a stage, a phase, but you were not identified with it. If you were the childhood itself then there would have been no possibility of becoming a youth. Who would have become a youth? The child could not have become a youth, the child would have remained the child. But you were not the child. You passed through childhood, you became a youth. Then youth is again a stage, you are not one with it. If you are one with it you could not have been a child and you cannot grow old. You will pass through it also, it is a phase.

So this is the definition of a stage: you come into it, you pass through it, you go beyond it – but you are not it. Then you will become old, that too is a stage. You will pass into death. Birth is a stage, death is a stage. One who passes through all these stages.... The being, the life force, the energy that you are, the consciousness that you are – that one is not a stage because you can never pass through it, you can never go beyond it. That is not a stage, that is your very nature; that you are. So the seventh is not a stage. It is called a stage because there is no other way of talking about it. Six are stages, the seventh is the one who passes through these stages. The seventh is your very nature. This is the first thing.

The second thing, all the six can be described, they have a defined nature. You enter into them, they have a beginning; you pass through them, they have a middle; you finish with them, they have an end – they can be defined. Anything which has a beginning, a middle and an end can be defined, but you – you are indefinable. You don't have any beginning, you don't have any middle, you don't have any end. You never begin, you will never end. You are the eternal. The life energy that exists in you has always been in existence, will always be so. There was never a time when you were not, and there will never be a time when you will not be. You will always be, you are nontemporal.

The temporal can be defined through time. The nontemporal cannot be defined, it is timeless. Just as you are nontemporal you are nonspatial also. You exist in this space you call your body, but you have existed in many spaces. Buddha says he remembers his past lives. He says, "Sometime in my past lives I was an elephant." So then he existed in the space called elephant. He relates a beautiful story about the elephant and how the elephant could become a buddha.

Once it happened that this elephant who was Buddha in a past life was living in a forest and the forest caught fire, the forest was on fire. It was a very terrible fire. The whole forest was burning and all the animals and birds were escaping from the forest. This elephant was also running. The forest was very big, and from running and the heat all around and the fire he got tired. Just then he saw a tree which was not yet on fire. There was shade there, so he rested just for a single minute under the shade of the tree.

After he had rested, the moment came when he wanted to move. He raised one leg. When he raised his leg a small hare, a white hare, who was also tired from running, came under his foot just to rest there. So this elephant thought, "If I put my foot on the earth this hare will be killed." So he waited. He thought, "When this hare leaves, when he has rested, then I will move."

But the hare would not move. The hare thought, "It is beautiful to be under the shade of the elephant, and there is no danger when the elephant is there, and the surrounding trees have not yet caught fire." So he waited.

The hare did not move and, tired from standing on three legs, many times the elephant thought, "Crush this hare and move." But then an idea came to his mind: "As I love my life this hare also loves his life. If I am escaping for my life and I am afraid of death, this hare is also afraid of death."

So he waited and died waiting there, because the fire came nearer and nearer and the tree caught fire. He waited for the hare and the hare would not move, so the elephant died standing on three legs. Buddha said, "Because of that awareness I was born as a man. The elephant changed into another being – man." And he goes on relating many stories about his past.

You have also been in many spaces, many types of bodies – sometimes a tree, sometimes a bird, sometimes an animal. Hindus say that there are eight hundred and forty million types of existence, lives, and a man is born only when he has passed through eight hundred and forty million spaces. In the beginning Westerners used to laugh about this – such a great number! There seemed no possibility that eight hundred and forty million life forms exist. But now biologists say that this is almost the exact number, almost exactly this many species exist. And this is a miracle! How could Hindus fall upon this number?...because they had no biological research, they had known no Darwin, no Huxley. They must have come to this number through some other way. They say that they have come to this number through those who have remembered their past lives – Buddhas, Mahaviras, who could remember all the past lives.

Eight hundred and forty million is a very big number. And that's why Hindus say that once you are born a man, don't waste this life, because it is so precious, you have struggled for it for so long, for millions of lives you have waited for it. And for what are you wasting it – food, drink, sex? Eight hundred and forty million lives spent waiting for this life, and then wasting this life in futile things!

You were in many spaces, so you are not confined to space. If you can be an elephant, then a tiger, then a bird flying in the sky, then a small ant, and then you can be a man, that means that no space contains you. You can pass through many types of bodies, but you are bodiless. If you are bodiless, if consciousness is a bodiless phenomenon, then you are nonspatial. And these two things, time and space, are very very insignificant.

Physicists say that existence consists of two elements: time and space. And Einstein turned even these two into one. He said that these are not two. So he used to call it spatiotime – one word, not two. He used to say that there is not space and time, there is only spacetime, and space is nothing but the fourth dimension of time. Hindus say that you are neither in space nor in time; you pass through them but you are not them, you may be in them but you are not them. You pass through them, you go beyond; you enter, you come out. Space and time is your temporal abode, it is not you – hence transcendence is possible, you can go beyond both.

Somebody asked Jesus, "Tell us something about your kingdom of God, something special which will be there, some main characteristic."

Jesus answered in a very strange way, he said a very strange thing. He said, "There shall be time no longer." Hindus have always been saying that – but not only about time. They say there will be time no longer, there will be space no longer, because time and space are really not two things, they are one.

And this you can feel even in deep meditation. The deeper you move the less time will be. You are not aware of how much time has passed – as if time is just on the surface. The more inwards you move, the further and further away time goes. Then a moment comes when there is no time. And the same happens to space: the more inward you move the more you go on forgetting where you are. When you move more inward then you forget whether you are confined in a body or not. When you reach to the innermost center there is no time and no space, you simply exist without any boundary of time or space. Because you are not confined in any way you cannot be defined. Things which are limited and confined can be defined. So the seventh stage, or the seventh no-stage, is indefinable.

The third thing. About the six there is not much mystery, reason can understand them; they are rational in a way, you can argue about them. The seventh is total mystery, absolute mystery. We must understand what mystery is, because this Upanishad ends on the word mystery. What is a mystery? The mystery is that phenomenon which exists but has no cause to exist, the mystery is a phenomenon which is there but is paradoxical, contradictory, the mystery is that phenomenon which is not only unknown but *unknowable*.

340 | Vedanta: Seven Steps to Samadhi

Remember three words: the known, the unknown and the unknowable. The known is that which human mind has come to know – science is the known. The second phenomenon is that of the unknown. The unknown is that which will be known sooner or later, it cannot remain unknown forever. The unknown is the phenomenon philosophy is concerned with – it goes on thinking about the unknown and how to make it known.

The known is science, it has already been known. So science is really the past, the accumulated knowledge, the condensed knowledge, the essential knowledge that human mind has come to know. That's why science is so certain and there is no poetry in science. Science is simply history, the past, the whole past. You may not have observed the fact that science is a dead thing, just the past accumulated. You destroy the past and science will disappear. If there are no more libraries, if suddenly all the libraries are destroyed, science will disappear. It is accumulated past, it is history, the known, but it is dead.

The second phenomenon is the unknown, which will be known sooner or later. Philosophy is concerned with the unknown, with how to make it known. So philosophy is nothing but a vanguard to science, just the pilot car moving ahead. That's why philosophy goes on being reduced to less and less every day – because more and more unknown becomes known, it becomes part of science, and philosophy becomes less and less. In the days of Aristotle philosophy was a vast phenomenon, now it is not so vast. Every day philosophy is becoming less and less because more and more philosophy is becoming science.

And then there is the third phenomenon, the unknowable. Religion is concerned with that. Unknowable means that which cannot be known whatsoever you do; it can never become science, it can never be reduced to history. That is the meaning of mystery, that which cannot be reduced to history, that which cannot become known, it always remains unknowable. It is not unknown, be-cause the moment you say it is unknown it can be known some day – more refined instruments, more technological devices and it will be known. It is not unknown, it is unknowable.

Science says there is nothing like the unknowable, that's why science denies religion. Science says there are only two things, the known and the unknown. And the unknown is that which is possible to know again some day – maybe somewhere in the future – but potentially it can be known. So science believes there is no real mystery, only known facts and unknown facts, and a day will come when science has known everything. This is the presumption of the scientific approach, that somewhere in the future – it may take time, but conceivably, somewhere, a day will come when everything is known and there is no mystery. That is the basic point, the basic conflict between religion and science.

And philosophy also believes that there is no mystery, so philosophy is just a servant, a maidservant to science. That's why philosophers have become secondary to scientists in this century; they are not very important, their departments in the universities are no longer important. Science has taken the place of importance and they have retreated – they exist just in the back rooms of science. They also say there is nothing unknowable. It is unknown, but we will do something – logic, analysis, speculation, experiments – and it will be known.

Religion says that the substratum of existence is unknowable. Whatsoever you do is irrelevant; it will remain unknowable, it cannot be reduced to history. Why? Religion has a point, and that point is: How can a part know the whole? Man is just a part, how can the part know the whole? Man is just a by-product of this existence, just a throbbing of this existence. How can this throbbing know the whole? Your heart throbs, beats; how can the beats of the heart know you, the whole?

The part cannot know the whole, and the whole is vast, really infinite. You cannot conceive of any end to the universe, there can be no boundary to it – or can there be? Can you conceive of any boundary to existence? How will you conceive the boundary? – because a boundary needs two. Your house has a boundary because of your neighbor, the earth has a boundary because of space. The other is needed for the boundary. If there is only one it cannot be bounded, because who will bound it?

The existence is one; then it cannot be bounded, there can be no boundary. If you stand on the boundary what will you see? If you can see anything beyond, this is not the boundary. Even if you can see emptiness ahead then that emptiness is there. Can you conceive of a point in existence where a scientist can stand and there is nothing? But Hindus say that even nothing is something. If you can say that there is nothing then space exists, you will have to move ahead. There cannot come a point where you can say, "Existence ends here!" It cannot end, it cannot have any boundary. The whole is infinite. And you can know something which is finite, you cannot know the infinite. The mystery will remain.

Secondly, man is part, he is not apart from existence. You cannot kiss your own lips – or can you? You will need somebody else's lips to kiss, you cannot kiss your own. Man is part of this whole. To know this whole you will need to be apart, you will have to be separate; the knower must be separate from the known, only then knowledge is possible. The knower is not separate. The existence flows in you, you are just a wave. The existence trees in the trees, it waves in the waves, it mans in you. As it trees the earth, so it mans the earth. 'Manning', if I can coin a new word, manning is just like waving; it is a process. You are not apart from it, not separate.

You cannot kiss your own lips, religion says, hence the mystery. And the more science progresses the more religion is proved right. A few days before Einstein died he asserted, "When I started my journey on the scientific path I was certain that the universe can be known, but now I am not so certain. On the contrary, my uncertainty has been growing every day, and I feel that it is impossible to know the existence in its totality. It is a mystery."

Edison, another top scientist, a great name, said in his last letters to his friends, "I thought in the beginning that the world consists of matter, there is no mind. But the more I penetrate into the secrets the more I feel that the universe is more like thought than like thing. It is more like the mind, less like matter. It is more mysterious."

And that has been the feeling of all individual scientists – not of science, but individual scientists. Science as a body remains adamant, goes on saying that there can be no mystery, and if there is it is only a question of time and we will dissolve it. So the effort of science is to demystify the universe. That may be one of the reasons why people are so unhappy today. That may be one of the basic reasons why people are so bored, that may be one of the basic reasons why people are feeling so meaningless – because without mystery there can be no meaning in life.

If everything is explained then everything is explained away, if everything is known then there is nothing worthwhile, if everything becomes just factual you are finished with it. Just go to a biologist and ask him what love is, or go to a chemist and ask him what love is. He will explain to you the whole mystery, he will talk of hormones, secretions of certain chemicals in the body, and he will say, "You are just a fool! Love is nothing. It is just a question of certain chemicals flowing in the bloodstream."

He can explain everything about love, and when he explains everything about love then all your Kalidases and Shakespeares and Byrons will look stupid – because he can *explain*. But this same man who is explaining will fall in love. He will sit with a woman under the sky and then start talking poetry. This is the mystery. Life remains alive for mystery. And it is a good sign that even a scientist can fall in love, and a few great scientists sometimes even write poetry. This is a good sign. Man can still survive – there is a possibility, we can hope; otherwise, everything explained, poetry dies.

This age is very nonpoetic. Even poets write things which are facts, not mysteries; they talk about mundane things in their poetry. The poetry that has been created in this age is not very poetic, it is more prose than poetry. There is no music in it, because music can come only through mystery. Something unknowable throbs around you; you become part of that unknown mystery, you dissolve into it, become a drop in the ocean.

That's why children are so happy, old men so unhappy. The reason is that the old man knows more – he has explained many things, more facts are known to him – and children are ignorant, more mystery is around them. That's why even in old age you go on thinking that childhood was the golden period, the real paradise.

Why is childhood so paradise-like? – because the child exists in mystery. Everything is mysterious – even the shade of a tree moving with the sun is so mysterious, so poetic. An ordinary flower, maybe a grass flower, is so mysterious because the whole life is expressed through it. A breeze blowing in the tree and creating rhythmic sounds, echoes in the valley, reflections in the water…. Everything is mysterious for a child, nothing is known. He is happy. Remember this, your happiness will be in the same proportion as your mystery – less mystery, less happiness; more mystery, more happiness.

This Upanishad ends with the word mystery. Make that word mystery a secret in your heart, and try to live in such a way that nothing is reduced to facts and even facts become just doors for more mysteries. And unless you can turn facts into mysteries you will not become religious. So I can conclude, a scientist goes on reducing mystery to facts, and a religious man goes on changing facts into mysteries.

The world was happier when it was religious. It was less affluent, it was poorer, food was scarce, wealth was not there; everything was just poor, poverty existed – but people were happier…because you cannot live by bread alone. They lived through mystery. Everything they saw they treated as poetry of life. All these Upanishads are written in poetry. If life can appear to you not like prose but like poetry, a song, a bird in flight always towards the unknown…only then will religious consciousness dawn upon you.

Now we will enter the sutra.

In the seventh stage, the state of videhamukti, liberation while living in the body is achieved.

The Upanishads divide liberation in two. One, liberation while you are in the body. That is called *videhamukti*, liberation while in the body. And then the ultimate liberation when this body dissolves and you no longer enter into another body, you remain bodiless. So liberation with the body and bodiless liberation. Buddhists have used two words: nirvana, and *mahanirvana*. Nirvana means liberation in the body, and mahanirvana means liberation from the body also –

freed from all embodiments, bodiless consciousness. Then you have become cosmos.

The seventh stage is of videhamukti. You are living in the body, but living in the body you are no longer the body; the body has become just an abode, a house or your clothes. You are no longer attached to it in any way. You use it, you live in it, you take care of it, but you are no longer concerned, no longer afraid that if the body dies you will die. Now you know you are deathless; only the body can die, never you. You are not identified with the body, that is the liberation – videhamukti.

This stage is totally silent and cannot be communicated in words.

A person who exists in this stage remains inwardly totally silent. There is no inner talk, he never talks with himself. Really, to talk with oneself is a sort of in-sanity. If you see a man sitting outside alone talking you will think he is mad. But you are also doing the same, only less loudly. He is a little more daring, that's all. You also go on talking within; continuously the inner talk is there, not for a single moment do you stop. Your mind is a marketplace – so many voices, crowded – and it goes on and on and on. And look, observe what goes on there: just futile things, absurd, senseless, with no rhyme or reason. You are just flooded.

In the seventh stage the inner world becomes totally liberated from inner talk, everything is silent within. You can talk, but only with someone else, not with yourself. In that stage Buddha speaks, but he never speaks with himself. Buddha speaks to others, but that speech is qualitatively different from yours. Look! Whenever you are talking with others, then too the other is just an excuse – you continue your inner talk. Observe people talking. When you are talking with someone else you are not really talking with someone else, you go on talking within. You just catch some words from the other, and then you hang your inner talk on those words and continue.

One psychologist was watching two madmen from a window, and he was surprised at their behavior. Those two madmen were both professors – professors are always prone to go mad because they are experts at talking. But he was surprised not because they were talking, he was surprised for some other reason. Both were mad, but whenever one was talking the other would remain silent as if he was listening. When the first one would stop the other would start, and the first one would remain silent as if listening. And the second mystery was this, their talk was not connected at all. The first was talking about one thing and the other was talking about something else which was totally irrelevant, which had no connection at all. They were moving parallel, not meeting anywhere.

So the psychologist went and said to them, "I have observed many madmen, and I have seen that when they talk they don't talk with the other, they simply talk with themselves. That is okay. But I have never seen them remaining silent while the other is talking. So why do you remain silent while the other is talking?"

The professors said, "Just old habit. Just old habit, just to be gentlemanly. When he is talking it is unmannerly to start talking, so we have to force ourselves. When he stops then I can talk and then he has to keep silence. And this is a mutual understanding."

But this is all that is happening amongst you. This is just from mutual understanding and old habit that you keep silent when the other is talking. But you are not silent, you are just waiting for the opportunity, and when he stops you start. Only one thing you will do which those madmen were not doing because they were more frank, and that is that you will catch some word from the other's talk and through that word you will hang your inner talk and you will proceed.

Look at two persons discussing anything, they are never talking about the same thing. Ninety-nine percent of debates and discussions are just mad; people are not talking about the same thing, they are not using the words in the same way, they are not communicating at all. Just look at a wife and husband talking, they are not communicating at all. The husband is saying something and he goes on saying, "You are not understanding me." And the wife goes on saying something else, and she also says, "You are not understanding me, you don't understand what I am saying."

Nobody understands anybody. You cannot understand, because understanding can flower only in inner silence, it cannot flower while you are talking in words. So you are not listening to the other at all. The mind cannot do two things simultaneously – you can listen to yourself or the other. Communication has become such a great problem, everybody feels that one cannot relate. What is the problem? Why can't you relate with the other? – because you are relating with yourself.

A man who has attained the seventh stage is silent inwardly. He can listen, he can communicate, he can relate, he can answer. In India this was taken as a basic condition: one should not start preaching unless one has attained the inner silence...because if somebody starts teaching, advising, and his inner talk has not stopped, he is going to create more mischief in the world which is already there. He will be destrusctive. He cannot help anybody, he is not interested really in helping anybody. He is not interested in giving advice, he is interested only in bringing his inner talk out in the name of giving advice. He is throwing his rubbish on others, he is using you, your mind. He is too burdened, he shares only his burden with you. He may feel a little relief, but for his relief he has created much mischief all around.

Political leaders, social reformers, so-called revolutionaries, they all belong to this category. They go on throwing rubbish on more and more people. And if you go on insisting and telling people something, it is possible they may start believing, because belief is created by constant repetition.

Adolf Hitler writes in his autobiography Mein Kampf that there is no difference between the truth and a lie; the difference is only of repetition. Repeat a lie constantly and it becomes a truth. And this is a proven thing, he himself proved it through his life. He constantly repeated certain things and they became true – and to a country which is one of the most intelligent in the world, Germany. Hitler befooled the Germans. Then remember it, Hitler-type people can befool any country; if Hitler can befool the Germans, then no country is safe.

Germany was the country of the professors, scholars, great scholars, great professors, logicians, philosophers – Kant, Hegel, Schiller, Marx, Feuerbach – the country of the best minds, but a Hitler, just a madman, could befool them. Madmen can befool you very easily, because they are obsessed with their ideas, they go on repeating. They won't listen to you, they are fanatic; they are not worried about what you will think, they will go on repeating, and through repetition it becomes a suggestion, a hypnosis. If somebody goes on repeating you are bound to believe it. Psychologists say that if you go on repeating others will believe, and by repeating constantly in the end you will also believe that it is true.

I have heard one anecdote.

Mulla Nasruddin died and immediately he proceeded towards heaven. He knocked on the door and the man on the gate said to him, "Who are you, and what has been your business there in the world? – because we have a quota, just like the Rotary Club."

Nasruddin said, "I was a journalist. You will have to allow me, otherwise I am going to report it and that will create bad news."

And journalists have become a power, so the man, the watchman, said, "Wait, let me inquire." Then he said, "It is difficult because we have a quota – only twelve journalists can be allowed in heaven and they are already there. And even they are useless because newsprint paper is not available. Moreover, nobody is interested in gossiping in heaven; even if you print a newspaper nobody purchases it. Nobody reads them, so even those who are here are unemployed. It is better," he suggested, "you go to hell. Journalism flourishes there like anything, everybody reads newspapers. Many newspapers are published with great circulation, and there are gossips and stories and news – real news happens there."

You must have heard Bernard Shaw's definition of news. He says, "When a dog bites a man it is not news, but when a man bites a dog it is news."

"So real news happens in hell. You go there, Nasruddin!"

But Nasruddin insisted. He said, "No! I want to be here. You will have to find some way."

So the man suggested, "I will allow you in for twenty-four hours. Go in and spread the news in heaven that a big new newspaper is going to be published soon in hell and editors are needed. You may be able to persuade some other journalists to go. They are unemployed and bored, so if they go, if even one man goes, I will allow you."

Nasruddin said, "Okay!"

For twenty-four hours he was creating the rumor. To whomsoever he met he said, "If you don't feel good here, go. Many posts are vacant, a great newspaper is going to be started soon. Readers are waiting for it, the whole of hell is expectant about it. Editors are needed, sub-editors are needed, news reporters are needed!"

He told the story in such an honest, sincere way that by the evening when he came to the door to ask the watchman if anybody had gone to hell, the watchman immediately closed the door and said, "Don't move out! All twelve have left!"

Nasruddin said, "Open the door. If all twelve have left then there is something in the rumor. I can't wait here, I want to go to hell!"

The watchman said, "What are you saying? You created it!"

Nasruddin said, "It doesn't matter. If twelve persons are convinced it means there must be truth in it, and I don't want to be here!"

If you go on repeating a lie you will end up believing it. Constant repetition becomes hypnotic. In India it has been one of the basic laws that one should not start teaching people unless one becomes inwardly totally silent. When dreams have stopped, only then should one start advising anybody. If you still have dreams don't advise anybody, because you are still in a state of dreaming. Your advice is of no use, you will create more mischief and misery for others. If somebody follows your advice he will be in danger.

Fortunately nobody follows anybody's advice. They say that advice is the thing which everybody gives wholeheartedly, without any cause, but which no-body takes. It is good, fortunate, that nobody takes anybody's advice, otherwise the world would be in more misery, because the advisor – not the advice, but the advisor – is significant.

This stage is totally silent.

And because it is totally silent it cannot be communicated in words. It can be indicated; that is all that can be done, and that is what this sutra is going to do.

It is the end of all stages, where all the processes of yoga have come to their conclusion. In this stage all activities – worldly, bodily, scriptural – cease.

In this stage there is no activity – activity as action, by effort. The person who has achieved the seventh stage leaves all activities. That doesn't mean that he will not do anything, but now he will be spontaneous. He will not be active, he will be spontaneous. He will move like a wind. Whatsoever happens will happen; whatsoever doesn't happen, he will not think about it happening. He will become a flow. Now he will not force anything. That's the meaning that he will not be active.

Buddha was active. After he attained enlightenment, for forty years he was active, but that activity was not activity, he was spontaneous. He moved, but with no conscious effort on his part, as if the existence was moving him, he had become just a passage, a passive vehicle. If life wanted to move through him it would move, if it didn't want it was okay. He had no mind to do anything. Many things would happen, and really only in such a state do many things happen that are wonderful, that are mysterious.

When you are not the doer, then you become capable of receiving existence. This is what is meant by Jesus' saying, "Not I, but he, lives in me. My father lives in me." Jesus is a vehicle, Mahavira is a vehicle, Krishna is a vehicle – just passages. The total can move through them, they don't create any hindrance, they don't change in any way. They have no will of their own, no mind of their own.

The whole universe in the form of the world – viswa, intelligence – prajna, and radiance – tejas, is just aum.

In this seventh stage of consciousness the person has really dissolved and become the whole universe, he has become Aum. This word aum is very symbolic. First, this word aum consists of three sounds: a, u, m. These three sounds are the basic sounds, all the sounds are created out of them. All the languages, all the words, are created out of these three sounds: a, u, m. And this is not a myth, now phonetics agrees that these are the basic root sounds. And the word aum is meaningless, it is simply a combination of all the three basic sounds.

Hindus say that aum is the sound of existence, and then it divides in three: a, u, m, and then the three become many. From one, three; from three, many and millions. Now even science agrees that there is only one energy in existence; that one energy is divided in three. You may call it electron, proton and neutron; you may call it a, u, m; you may call it the Christian trinity: God, the Son, the Holy Ghost; you may call it the Hindu *trimurti:* Shiva, Brahma, Vishnu – whatsoever the name, the name is irrelevant, but one thing is certain: one becomes three, and then three becomes many. And if you want to move backwards to the one, move from the many to three and then let the three combine – it will become one. Aum is a way, it is a mantra, a path, to combine all the sounds in three, to first reduce all the sounds to three – and then aum becomes the door for the one.

And this has been the experience of all the mystics all over the world, not only Hindus. They all have the same experience. They may have interpreted it differently. Mohammedans, Christians, and Jews end their prayers with amen. Hindu mystics say it is the same, aum. They interpreted differently, because the sound can be interpreted in many ways. You are traveling in a train and you can interpret the sound of the train in many ways; you can even feel that there is a song going on, because the interpretation is yours – sound is not creating the interpretation, the mind is creating the interpretation. Hindus say it is like aum; Christians, Jews, and Mohammedans have felt it as aumen, or amen.

English has three or four words which are mysterious for linguists. They are omnipotent, omnipresent, omniscient, and such words. They cannot reduce them to any logical order. What does omnipotent mean? And from where does omni come? It comes from the Hindu word aum. What does omniscient mean? From where does the word omni come? Linguists have no way to explain it, these words have remained unexplained in English. But if you can understand aum then those words become clear, because aum is the symbol of the universe for Hindus. So omnipotent means one who knows all, one who is all-powerful; omnipresent means one who is everywhere present – present in the aum, seeing the aum, powerful like the aum.

If you enter deeper meditation soon you will realize that a sound is continuously happening there. It is the sound of existence itself, the humming sound of existence itself. And if you listen without interpreting it, if you don't force any interpretation on it, if you simply listen and watch and observe, sooner or later you will realize it is aum vibrating inside.

In this stage all activities…cease. The whole universe in the form of the world – viswa, intelligence – prajna, and radiance – tejas, is just aum.

In this stage only aum exists – the sound, the ultimate sound. Or you can call it the soundless sound, the uncreated sound.

There is no division here between speech and the speaker.

This has to be understood. You speak but there is always you, the speaker, and that which you speak. You walk, there is always the division: the walker, you, and the walk, the activity. You eat, there is always the division: the eater, you, and the activity. You can fast but the division will remain: you, the faster, and the activity, fasting. The activity and the active agent remain two, a division exists.

At this stage, the seventh, this division also disappears. The walker is the walk, the observer is the observed, the speaker is the speech – life becomes a process undivided. If you ask a question of the person who is in the seventh stage he never thinks about it, because there is no thinker. You ask the question, he responds. That response is not a thinking one, the response is just like a valley responding, a valley echoing. You sing a song in the valley and the whole valley echoes it. The valley doesn't think that this sound is beautiful and should be echoed in such and such a way.

A buddha is a valley. You throw a question, the valley echoes. There is no-body who can think, there is nobody who can plan, there is nobody who can choose – really there is nobody now. It is emptiness, *shunyata*, it is a void. There is a valley; the valley responds. The speaker and the speech are one, the mover and the movement are one. This inner division falls immediately.

This exists because of the ego. Who thinks when somebody asks a question? Who thinks inside you? The ego. You have to give the right answer, or an answer which will be appreciated. But why are you worried about it? If you are the right person the right answer will flower through you. You are worried because you are not the right person. You have to force an answer, you have to create it, manufacture it somehow through the memory. You have to choose, combine, look at the person, at what type of person he is, and then it is a whole process of planning, choosing and thinking, but you are not spontaneous.

If you are a valley, if you have reached the seventh stage and the ego has disappeared, who will choose? The answer will flow. It will flow from the total person, not from the ego. Because of your ego you cannot be spontaneous – because you are always afraid you may not look good, you may not be appreciated. Your ego is exhibitionist. The speech and the speaker become one because there is no exhibitionist ego. Buddha responds with his totality; whatsoever the response, he is not concerned really.

If however, any such division remains, the state has not been attained.

So this is the criterion: if you feel any division inside, then know well this state has not been attained.

The first sound 'a' of aum, stands for the world – the universe; *the second 'u' for radiance* – life, élan vital; *and the third 'm' for intelligence* – consciousness, awareness. *Before entering samadhi* – that is, ultimate ecstasy, the final ecstasy....

This path has to be remembered well, it will be very helpful. This is the last advice of this Upanishad, the final. And only Hindus and Tibetans have used this advice for millions of years. This is their last secret.

Before entering samadhi – that is, death with consciousness.... Samadhi means death with consciousness, dying fully alert. You have died many times but it was not samadhi, it was simple death, because whenever you died you were unconscious. Before death happens you are unconscious, it is just a surgical procedure. Because death will be so painful for you, you cannot be allowed to be conscious – just as a surgeon gives you anesthetic, chloroform, before he operates on you, and then his operation is just nothing.

Death's operation is so big because the whole being has to be taken out of your body with which it has become so attached, identified. It is not simply removing a bone, it is removing the whole body from you. So nature has a process: before you die you fall unconscious, fast asleep, you are no longer in your senses, and then your being can be removed. This is not samadhi.

And remember, if a person dies in unconsciousness he is born in unconsciousness, because the birth, the coming birth, will be the same, the same quality. If in this life you die unconsciously, in the next life you will be born unconscious in a womb. If you can die consciously then you can be born consciously. And if you can die with total awareness, the whole being alert, not a single part unconscious, then you will not be born at all. Then there is no need, then you can simply discard this body and become bodiless.

Before entering samadhi – that is, conscious, alert, aware of death.... And only the person who has attained the seventh stage can enter it. He will be born no more, he will be out of the wheel of existence.

...The seeker should contemplate on aum most strenuously, and subsequently he should surrender everything, from gross to subtle to the conscious self. Taking the conscious self as his own self, he should consolidate this feeling: I am eternal, pure, enlightened, free, existential, incomparable, the most blissful Vasudeva and Pranava himself – I am the Brahman.

Before entering death the seeker should try this.

Many things. First, before you enter death ordinarily you cling to the body, you don't want to give it up. That is the ordinary reaction of the mind, to cling. Death is snatching everything and you cling, you start a fight with death. In this fight you will be defeated. This sutra says: Give up consciously. From the gross to the subtle to the self, give up everything. Just say to death, "Take it. This is not me. Take this body, take this mind, take this self, this ego. I am not this."

Don't cling, let your life be a gift to death. Don't create any fight and resistance. If you create fight you will become unconscious and you will miss an opportunity again. Give up. Give death whatsoever you have – from the gross to the subtle to the very self, go on giving. Don't create any resistance. This is the foundational thing. Don't create resistance, don't fight with death. What will happen? If you can give up knowingly, consciously, blissfully, you will not fall unconscious, there is no need. Your clinging creates the problem.

It happened just at the beginning of this century, the king of Benares was to undergo an appendix operation. He was a very religious man, a very saintly man, and he said, "I have never taken anything to make me unconscious and I would not like to do that. So please, if you can operate, then operate on me when I am fully conscious. I will not take any anesthetic, chloroform, or any type of thing which can make me unconscious."

The doctors were worried, and the case was serious. The appendix had to be removed soon, otherwise the man would die. And he was adamant. He said, "I can die, that is not much of a problem – but I don't want to be unconscious." He must have been thinking of this sutra, he must have known about this secret, that one should never die unconsciously. Death is not the problem, unconsciousness is the problem.

So he said, "It is okay. If you cannot operate then let me be as I am. I will die but I will die consciously. You give me chloroform, and if I die in the operation then who will be responsible? Can you take the responsibility? Can you give me a guarantee that I will not die through this operation?"

Nobody could give such a guarantee. The case was serious and there was a possibility that he might die in the operation. So the doctors agreed, because there was no other alternative. They said, "Let us try, there is no risk. The man is going to die within hours, so take the risk. Let us try, let him remain conscious."

So no anesthetic was given. That was the first operation of this type in the whole history. And it was miraculous, because the king remained conscious. It was a long operation, almost two hours, and the whole stomach was opened and the appendix removed. The surgeons could not believe that the man was conscious, that he remained conscious. They asked him later on how it happened.

He said, "There is no secret about it. I was not resisting. I said, 'Okay death, take everything – this appendix, this body, this whatsoever I have been calling me – take everything. I am ready. There is no resistance.'"

If there is no resistance there is no problem. Resistance creates conflict, conflict creates problem. So at the moment of death the seeker should contemplate on aum. He should feel himself as the aum, the universe, the very life, the very existence, the very awareness. And subsequently he should surrender everything – *from gross to subtle*. And this is not only for the seeker, even an enlightened person who has achieved the seventh has to surrender.

It is reported of Buddha that he told his disciples one day just in the morning, "This evening I am going to surrender my body back to nature, so if you have to ask anything you can ask. This is the last day."

They were very worried, depressed, sad; they started weeping and crying. And Buddha said, "Don't waste time. If you have to ask anything this is the last day. In the evening when the sun is setting I will surrender my body. I have used so many bodies and I have never thanked nature before. This is the last, now I will never move in a body again. This is the last house I have been living in, this is my last residence, so I have to thank nature and give the body back. It served many purposes, it led me really to this enlightenment. It was a means, and was a good means. It helped me in every way. So I have to thank nature and surrender the whole abode back, because it is a gift from nature and I must surrender it consciously. So there is no time...."

But nobody asked any question, they were not in the mood to ask. They were sad and they said, "You have said everything and we have not followed, so just give us your blessing that we may follow whatsoever you have said."

Then by the evening Buddha retired. He went behind a tree to surrender. And it is said that a man named Subhadra who lived in a nearby town came running – there are many Subhadras always. He came running in the evening when Buddha had retired and he said, "I have some questions to ask."

Buddha's disciples said, "It is too late now, we cannot disturb him now. This is not good. You could have come before. Buddha passed through your village many times, at least ten times in his life, and we have never seen you come to him."

The man said, "Every time Buddha was passing through my village there was something or other which prevented me. Sometimes my wife was ill, sometimes there was too much of a crowd in my shop, too many customers; sometimes I was ill, sometimes there was some other urgent thing to be done, sometimes there was some marriage going on – so I went on postponing. But now I have heard that he is going to die. There is no time to postpone now, and I must ask him. So allow me."

They prevented him. They said, "It is impossible."

Buddha came back from his retirement and he said, "Let it not be written in history that while I was still alive somebody came and knocked at my door and went away empty-handed. Let him ask."

Then he again retired. First he surrendered his body. It is reported that when he surrendered his body there was a radiance around the body as if the body had become energy and was moving into the cosmos – a conscious surrender. Then he surrendered his mind. It is said a fragrance spread, went on spreading. A buddha's mind is a fragrance, the condensed fragrance of such a great and pure and innocent life, it was felt. Then he surrendered his self. These three things surrendered, he died. This was *mahaparinirvana, mahasamadhi.* But it was a conscious surrender, death was given back everything that nature had given. This man will never be back again. Only such a conscious surrender can become samadhi, the ultimate samadhi.

Even if you have not attained the seventh stage, wherever you are, at any stage, when death approaches you try to be conscious, surrendering. Don't fight with death. If you fight with death, death will conquer. If you don't fight with death there is no possibility of conquering.

This is the way with death, to be in a let-go. And this has been done even by buddhas who have attained the seventh stage. So try it. For you it will be an effort, but worth doing. Even if you fail it is good to do, because doing it many times you will succeed. And once you succeed with death fear disappears, surrender becomes easy.

This is the difficulty with surrender. Many people come to me – one girl was here just the other day and she said, "I feel very sad because everybody else seems to be surrendered to you, trusting, in deep faith. I cannot surrender. Meditation is good, I feel good, but I cannot surrender."

What is the problem in surrendering? Surrender is a death, you are afraid of dying. Whenever you think of surrender you feel, "Then I am no more, then I dissolve," and you want to persist.

If you can surrender in death you can surrender in love, you can surrender in trust, you can surrender in faith. And the reverse is also true, vice-versa is also true; if you can surrender in love, surrender in faith, you will be able to surrender in death. Surrender is the same, the same phenomenon – and surrender is the key.

Learn to surrender in death, and if you cannot surrender in death you cannot surrender in life also. Those who are afraid of death are always afraid of life. They miss everything.

And subsequently he should surrender everything, from gross to subtle to the conscious self. Taking the conscious self as his own self, he should consolidate this feeling: I am eternal....

While dying, or while in deep meditation, which is a sort of death, or while making love, which is a sort of death – wherever you feel a surrender, think:

I am the eternal, the pure, enlightened, free, existential, incomparable, the most blissful Vasudeva and Pranava himself – God himself.

It will be a thought for you, because you have not attained the seventh stage. But if you attain the seventh these will be spontaneous feelings, not thoughts. Then you will not do them, they will happen to you. This is the difference: for a seeker who is yet below the fourth stage, this will be an effort; for a seeker who has gone beyond the third, this will be a spontaneous feeling. He will feel this way – that he is God, he is Brahma himself, Vasudeva.

Since the whole visible world, comprising a beginning, a middle, and an end, is sorrow-stricken, he must renounce everything and merge into the supreme. He should feel that he is blissful, taintless, without ignorance, without appearance, inexpressible in words, and that he is Brahman, the essence of knowledge. This is the Upanishadic mystery.

Thus ends the Akshya Upanishad.

What is the Upanishadic mystery? The art of dying is the Upanishadic mystery. And one who knows how to die knows how to live. One who knows how to surrender conquers the whole.

17   Valleys and Peaks

Osho,

Many times I feel so merged in you that it is as if I have died and only you are. But this feeling doesn't remain constant, and always the ego returns. This happens whenever I have to again communicate with others or return to activity. Why doesn't the ego remain dead?

If you make it a goal – egolessness – then you will always remain with the ego. Don't make it a goal, because all goals belong to the ego. If you think that you should remain egoless, who is this "you" who should remain egoless? This is the ego. So the first thing, don't make it a goal. Any goal will feed the ego – even the goal of egolessness.

When you are egoless enjoy it; when you feel the ego again, be alert – but don't expect the contrary. If you start expecting you will be more entangled with the same thing. Whenever egolessness is there enjoy it, feel grateful, thank God, and when the ego comes again, be alert. Soon more and more egolessness will happen to you, less and less ego will return. And the moment will come when ego will disappear, but don't make it a goal. All goals belong to the ego.

Secondly, don't expect anything, because when you start expecting you have moved from the here and now into the future. When you start expecting something you have started to bring your memory, your past, into the present. This very moment you feel egoless – it is okay. Then it goes, the ego comes. You want to repeat the past again – you must be egoless. You project the past in the future and you miss the present.

And remember, egolessness is possible only if you are here and now. If you move into the past, if you move into the future, the ego will persist. So don't ask for any constancy because constancy means you want to continue the past into the future. Remain with the moment and don't expect anything. The ego will drop by itself, no other effort is needed. If the ego has moved it means you are not in the present. So don't fight with the ego, simply move into the present and ego will drop. And this is what is happening.

You say: "Many times I feel so merged in you that it is as if I have died and only you are."

I am here and I am now. I have no past and no future. If you really relate with me you relate with my nowness and hereness, because there is no other thing with which to relate. If you feel a love, a trust, flowing towards me, that love and trust can flow only in the present. That's why you feel you have died. It is not because of me that your ego is dying, it is because you have moved with me in the present. Then your past is forgotten, your future is no more. You are here, totally here.

So don't think that it is something that I am doing to you, it is something that you are doing to yourself – I am just the excuse. Try to understand this because otherwise it will become a clinging. The same can happen anywhere. Remember the secret. If you love me, if you listen to me deeply, if you are here present with me, receptive, open, you are in the present. That's why for a few seconds the ego will disappear. Then you are not. If you can be in the present anywhere, *you* will not be.

You can be only either in the past or in the future – you cannot be in the present. Just think about it, how can you be in the present? There is no need. The past accumulates, becomes crystallized, and you feel 'I'. Then the past projects in the future and says, "This should be, this should not be. I desire this, I don't desire that." This is your past desiring – all the bad experiences you don't want to repeat and all the good trips you want to repeat in the future. This is past asking for something in the future – and you are missing the present, which is the only existence.

Past is no more, it is already dead; future is not yet, it is yet unborn. Both are not. And ego can exist only in nonexistence, it is the most false thing possible. The present moment is, it is the only is-ness; nothing else exists. If you relate with the present you cannot exist as an ego, because the present is the real and the real never creates anything false. Out of the real nothing false is created; only out of the false, false comes.

So it can happen…it may be happening to you that for a few moments you disappear. While listening to me, while just sitting with me, you disappear. But I am not doing anything to you. If you think I am doing something then you will cling to me, you will become attached to me; a new attachment will be formed. And then through that attachment you will ask again and again for the same.

Just try to understand the basic law. Then move into the forest, sit under a tree, and be in the here-and-now. Then be with your friends, remain silent, and remain in the here-and-now. Listen to music, forget the past, forget the future, and be here and now. And if you can be in the present anywhere, suddenly the ego will not be found. And if you ask that this should happen again, ego has come again, because now you are asking for the future, planning for the future. This is the mechanism.

"But this feeling does not remain constant, and always the ego returns." It will remain constant only when you don't ask that it should remain constant. It will happen again and again every moment, it will be continued, but don't ask for its constancy. Rather, enjoy it moment to moment and don't project it. It will arise again and again every moment, but remember, it is never the old, it is always the new arising, every moment being born again and again. It is not the past continuing, it is the new being born every moment.

"This happens whenever I again have to communicate with others or return to activity." Why does it happen when you communicate with others? Really you don't communicate, that's why. If you communicate it will not happen. While you are here with me, this is a communication. You relate with me, you become silent, you drop your past. You listen so attentively that thinking stops. This is communication.

When you communicate with somebody else you are not communicating, you are just throwing out your inner talk. You are thinking of many things. You may be saying something and thinking something else, meaning something else, doing something else. You are many while you communicate with others – then the ego enters.

In activity also the ego can enter because you become the doer. While I am speaking you are not doing anything at all, you are simply here listening. Listening is not a doing, listening is passive, it is a non-act. You need not do anything; you simply be there and it will happen. If you do something you won't be able to listen, if you go on doing something you will only appear to be listening but you won't be listening. When you don't do anything, listening happens. It is a passive thing. You need not do anything to create this capacity, it is always there.

But when you return to activity the ego can return, because again the doer has come. So what is to be done? When you return to activity remain the witness and don't become the doer. Go on doing things but remain the witness. Or if it is difficult then just leave everything to the divine and say that the divine is doing everything, you are just a vehicle, a passage, an agent. That's what Krishna says to Arjuna in the Gita: "You leave everything to me, surrender everything to me. You become just a medium and let things happen. Don't you be the doer, God is the doer."

Or if you cannot think of any God then there is another technique, and that is destiny or fate, that everything that is happening is destined. You are not doing it, it was bound to be so, it was going to happen, it was predestined. These are simple things, but you feel these simple things are difficult because they have become difficult in this age.

In the past these simple techniques helped millions to attain silence, peace, egolessness, because they could trust. Fate, or what Sufis call kismet, helped millions...because then simply you say, "I am not the doer. The whole existence has predetermined everything in me and I am just following." This is the whole secret of astrology.

Astrology is not a science but a technique of religion. If a person can believe that things are settled already and one cannot change anything, then the doer cannot arise. But simple faith is needed for that.

If you feel this is difficult – and this *is* difficult for the modern mind – then only one thing remains, and that is, be alert and move again and again to the present. No faith, no God is needed. But then the path is very arduous because every moment you will have to pull yourself back to the present. It is such an old habit to move ahead, it has become such a fixation that you will have to constantly struggle.

Remember not to move in the past and not to move in the future. Then every moment egolessness will arise, it will become a continuous flow. And the more egoless you are the more moments of egolessness, the more glimpses in the divine. The more you are the less the divine is for you, the less you are the more the divine.

The second question:

Osho,

A number of times I have felt in the past that I had reached a state of effortlessness. It lasted for some time, for days or even weeks, but then I fell back from it. Why does this falling back happen? Can anything be done to prevent it?

Whenever it happens again don't get miserable about it – let it happen and accept it. This is difficult. Whenever happiness happens you accept it, whenever you feel blissful you never ask any questions about it. You never ask, "Why has it happened?" You accept it. But whenever misery comes, whenever unhappiness comes, whenever you are in pain and anguish, immediately you ask, "Why has it happened?" Behave equally to both, have the same attitude to both.

There are two possibilities: one, do the same with unhappiness as you have done with your happiness, or do the same with your happiness as you are doing with your unhappiness. Either accept both or reject both, and then you will have a transformation. If you can accept both, when misery comes accept it as part of life, suddenly the nature of the misery is transformed. Through acceptance the quality has changed – because nobody can accept misery. If you accept it you have changed it, it is no more misery – because we can accept only happiness. Or if you can understand the deeper meaning of it, this is the meaning: whatsoever you accept becomes happiness, and whatsoever you reject becomes pain, misery, unhappiness.

Nothing is happiness, nothing is unhappiness, outside you – it is your rejection and acceptance. Try it. And you know, many times this has happened to you unknowingly. You love a person, you are happy. You accept the person, there is happiness. And then a moment comes when you reject the same person. The person is the same; *you* don't love him, *you* don't accept him. The person is creating unhappiness now, and the same person was creating happiness before. The same object can give you happiness and unhappiness. So the object seems to be irrelevant. It depends on you, on whether you accept or reject.

A person who can accept both misery and happiness equally will transcend, or a person who can reject both will transcend. And these are the two ways, the most fundamental ways of transformation. One is to accept everything – this is the positive path Hindus have been following. The Upanishads belong to this path, accept everything. Then there is the negative path, reject everything. Buddhists, Jainas have been following that, that is the negative path.

But both do the same thing. If you reject happiness you can never be unhappy, if you accept unhappiness you can never be unhappy. How can you make a man unhappy if he accepts it? How can you make a man unhappy if he rejects happiness? You cannot make him unhappy. The problem arises because you divide. You say this is happiness and that is unhappiness. And division is in your mind – reality is not divided. In reality unhappiness becomes happiness, happiness becomes unhappiness. They are flowing.

It is just like peaks and valleys: if a peak is there a valley is bound to be there. And the valley and peak are not against each other, they are part of one phenomenon. If you reject the valley and you accept the peak you will be miserable, because wherever a peak is the valley will be. And the higher the peak the deeper will be the valley. So if you love Everest then you will have to love deep valleys also. Happiness is like a peak and unhappiness is like a valley.

Go to the sea and meditate on the waves. The wave rises high, but just be-hind it there is a gap, a valley. Each wave is followed by a valley. The higher the wave the deeper will be the valley just following it. This is what happiness and unhappiness are – waves. Whenever you reach a high peak of happiness, immediately unhappiness will follow. You have to accept that this is how life is. If you say, "I will accept only peaks and not valleys," you are just behaving stupidly. Then you are going to be miserable.

It has been happening in every camp. People do so much towards meditation, acceptance, happiness, and they achieve small, high peaks. Then they go back, and then suddenly the valley comes in. They feel very miserable after the camp.

Somebody has asked a question:

Osho,

Why don't you carry on Your camps at least for three months, or six months?

Because of this...because if I keep a camp continuing for three months you will reach Everest and then back home you will simply go mad with misery. And you will have to go back – and if it is difficult after nine days it will be impossible after three months. This is good, and part of the training, that you accept both the peak and the valley. Go home and accept the valley also.

The real thing is to learn acceptance. And if you accept the valley then the valley is also very mysterious and beautiful. It has its own splendor. Even anguish has its own beauty if you accept it, even sadness has its own depth. Not only laughter is beautiful; sadness has its own beauty, a depth which no laughter can carry. Sadness has its own poetry, its own rhythm. If you allow me the expression, sadness has its own ecstasy. But one has to accept, only then one will be able to know.

The light is good, but darkness has its own mystery. You may be afraid but that is because of you, not because of darkness. Darkness has its own silence, its own silky expanse, its own infinity. This choice is yours – that you go on saying that light is good. And every book, the Koran and the Gita and The Bible, goes on making parallels between God and light. They go on saying, "God is light."

This is because man is afraid of darkness. Otherwise darkness is more godly than any light because light is always limited, darkness is always unlimited. Light has to be produced, darkness is there eternally, there is no need to produce it. You can bring light in, you cannot bring darkness in. Simply put off the light and you find that the darkness was already there, there is no need to bring it. It is always there, the eternal and always infinite.

Light has a tension with it, that's why you cannot sleep in light. It is difficult to sleep because a tension continues on the mind. Darkness has a relaxation. Darkness absorbs you, it takes you in its womb and relaxes you. Darkness is like death. But we are afraid of death so we are afraid of darkness. No one says that God is darkness. This is because of our mind. But I tell you, God is both. And unless God becomes both to you, you will never enter him.

Don't choose. Accept without any choice. Be choiceless and accepting. Whatsoever falls upon you, accept it and feel grateful for it. Try this – you have tried everything else. When misery comes to you thank God, feel happy that misery has befallen you and now you can experience it. Don't be scared. Try to experience what misery is and you will start enjoying it. You will start feeling new dimensions in it, new depths of which you were never aware.

This is why comedies in literature are never as deep as tragedies. And a person who has not known misery remains always shallow – always shallow. He may be laughing, smiling, but his laugh and smile are always shallow, just on the surface. He has no depth. A person who has passed through miseries, many miseries, gains depth. He knows both the heaven and the hell. And a person who knows both really becomes integrated.

Nietzsche has written many beautiful things, fragments of course. One of the most beautiful things he has ever asserted is that if you want to reach heaven, if you want to touch heaven, your roots must go to hell. It is just as if a big tree arises on the earth: the higher it reaches into the sky, the lower it has to penetrate in the earth. The highest tree must have the deepest roots. And it is proportionate, always the same: if the tree is twenty feet high the roots reach twenty feet down, if the tree is one hundred feet high the roots reach one hundred feet down. A man who really wants to reach a peak of bliss must send his roots deep into sadness, anguish, misery, and the proportion will always be the same.

If you accept both you transcend. Then neither misery can make you miserable nor happiness can make you happy – you remain the same. Misery comes and goes, happiness comes and goes, you remain untouched. Just like day comes and night comes, and they go on moving in a circle and you remain untouched, life comes and death comes and you remain untouched. Until this is achieved your bliss is just a deception. The bliss that exists against misery is no bliss. Only that bliss is called bliss, ananda, which doesn't exist against misery, which transcends happiness, unhappiness, both.

So when the peak has gone and the valley has come, accept it. It will be difficult, but try. Accept it, feel it, be sensitive to it. Allow it to happen and you are changing its quality, and you are changing yourself also through it. And don't divide, don't say happiness, unhappiness; these are two aspects of the same coin. Accept both or reject both; only then tranquility, calmness, peace, become possible.

The fourth question:

Osho,

Do you feel that the hippie way of life – a life of nonachieving, all play and no work, living for the moment, wandering about instead of remaining in one place – is better for a spiritual seeker than the usual life of marriage, family and career?

The first thing: the hippie is not the alternative, he is a by-product. He has always existed in different forms. But remember, he depends on the established society. He is not an alternative, he's just a shadow, a by-product of the society. He can go on moving, wandering, because many are established. If everybody is wandering nobody can be a hippie. A wandering monk, a wandering hippie, needs a society which is established, otherwise where is he going to wander? And he can afford play because others are working.

This is new in the West, because the West has become for the first time affluent. It is one of the ancient traditions in India. Right now five million sannyasins exist in India, wandering. They have been always there. They don't stay in one place, they don't work – they simply exist. They beg, the society supports them. But they can exist only because a society exists, and the better the society is established the better they can exist. That is why only in America is the hippie way of life possible. Because American society is now well established, rich, it can afford a few young men wandering here and there, playing with life. It can afford it. In a poor society hippies cannot exist, a poor society cannot afford them.

So the hippie way of life is not an alternative, it is a by-product. And it happens only when a society has reached a particular point of establishment, richness. Then it can allow a few young men to wander here and there and experiment. This hippie way of life cannot become universal and I never suggest that which cannot become universal because it is useless. And if you have to depend on the society you condemn, then the whole thing seems to be bogus.

I don't say no work and play, I say make your work your play. That is totally different, that can exist universally. Then you are not exploiting; otherwise hippies are exploiting. They may be exploiting their parents, their families, but they are exploiting. Their father and their mother and their brothers are working hard and they are enjoying a hippie way of life. This is sheer exploitation. Somebody has to work, and if somebody has to work it is better you work yourself. But change the work into play. If the work itself becomes the play then the whole world can go hippie, then there is no problem. And unless the whole world goes hippie it cannot become a way of life.

Hippies have always existed and then they have disappeared. Many times they come into existence and then they disappear. Sometimes they were called Bohemians, sometimes other names, but they could not create a permanent way, they couldn't make it universal. It is impossible to make it universal, somebody has to work somewhere. So I don't say only work, I don't say only play – I say make your work your play.

Secondly, wandering, a life of a wanderer, is good for a few, it is not good for all. And that too is good only for a particular period of life, not for the whole life. My feeling is that every young man and woman should be allowed to wander for a few years, wander carelessly, just experimenting with everything that is possible, good and bad both; moving with many types of people, different societies, countries. Before one gets established one should have wandered the whole earth.

This will give a richer family life. Then you are more experienced, more sensitive, multidimensional. And when you have wandered and then you settle your settlement has some meaning. You have known the opposite, and it is always good to know the opposite. It is said that whenever a person comes back to his own home country after wandering long, for the first time he comes to know it. It is true, because unless you have knocked at other doors you cannot recognize your own. So this must be a sort of university, this wandering.

Every young man and woman should be allowed to move for a few years carelessly, without any responsibility, because soon responsibilities will happen, will come. They will have to settle and they will have to carry many burdens. Before this happens they must be allowed a floating life, just to know whatsoever exists on earth – the bad and the good, the establishment and the anti-establishment – they must know everything.

The more you have moved around the richer becomes your consciousness. But this cannot be the whole pattern of life, this can be just a training, because wandering gives many things and then settling in a family life also gives many things that no wanderer can know. Both have their own richnesses.

You may love many women. That has its own significance, because you come to know many types of personalities, and the more you know the richer you are. But then to love one woman has a different significance, because loving many women may be a vast, rich experience, but it is never deep, it is always superficial. Depth needs time, depth needs a deep long contact. So when you love one woman and you have settled, all the wandering of the mind has ceased and now your desire never craves for anyone else, you can move deeply with one person. Now you can relate, now love can flower.

While making friendships and love with many women and men, you may come to know many techniques, many experiences of sex, but you will not be able to know love, what love is, because love needs seasoning. Just a hit-and-run experience cannot be of much depth – it cannot be. When you live with a person, and not only outward but inward wandering also has ceased, and nobody can create the craving in you, now this person is the sole and whole, then a depth starts happening. Then you start mingling, merging into each other, and higher peaks of love will be available to you. And a moment comes when two persons become one.

Both have to be known. So I am neither for this nor against that. I am always for a richer life – the richer the better. But it is better if the first wandering part is done when you are not responsible. It must precede, and the latter part should succeed. And you will have your experience with many persons, many places, which will help you to settle somewhere, to choose the right person.

The first love can almost never be the right love. It is bound to be childish, it is a baby love. You don't know anything about love. When you have loved many persons you know what love is. You know the misery and the bliss both, the expectations and frustrations both, and then you can choose.

I am in favor of many trial love affairs, and then also in favor of a fixed, permanent marriage. But marriage must happen after you have wandered here and there and knocked at many doors, tasted at many wells. Only then allow marriage to happen. Then there will be no divorce; otherwise divorce is bound to be there. The first love is dangerous, one should never marry in the first love. Wait, because you don't know your mind, how it will change. It will change, it may be just a mood. Experiments are good.

But there have been only two types of people. One type says, "Marry. You should remain true forever to the first person you fall in love with." This is nonsense. Then there is the other party, the other extreme, who says, "There is no need for marriage, go on experimenting. Even when you are on your deathbed, go on experimenting." That too is foolish. They are both foolish.

My attitude is absolutely the third. There is a time to experiment; when you are young, experiment. Know many persons, allow many happenings, don't be shy, don't feel guilty, let life flow so you can become acquainted with it. And when you feel that now you are acquainted, you have known, you have a certain experience to settle with, then settle, and then settle forever. Both these things will give you the highest peaks possible.

And this is my attitude in every dimension of life: allow both the opposites to happen. Don't choose between the opposites, allow both the opposites to happen. Then you have depth, then you have height, and you will have a growth which cannot happen to persons who get married and have not known many persons, which cannot happen to persons who go on changing. Both miss.

But these are the two parties: one is known as the orthodox, the other is known as the hippie – and both are wrong. A deep synthesis is needed. There are moments you should be a hippie and there are moments you must be a conformist. And if you can allow both, if you can enjoy both, you will be richer for that.

The fifth question:

Osho,

How is one to overcome boredom? How can one rediscover mystery in things that have become boring, repetitive, demystified?

The first thing to remember is that it is not that things are repetitive – it is your mind, not the things. The sun rises every day, you can say that it is repetitive. It is not, because the sun rises every day in a different way. The colors are different, the mood is different, the sky is different. The sun never repeats, it is always new. It is your mind which says, "This is repetitive, so what is the beauty there?"

Looking at the sun rising every day will create boredom, but the boredom is coming because you are not sensitive enough to see the newness. Everything is new every moment. It looks old because you carry the past in your mind and you look through the past.

You may have lived with a person for thirty years – your wife, your husband, your friend – and you may have noticed that for years you have not seen the face of the person, for years. You may be living with the person but you have not seen those eyes, the face. You think there is no need, you know the person well. The face is changing every day, the eyes are changing every day, the mind is changing every day. Life is a flux. Nothing is old, nothing can be old here. Never is a thing repeated, it is nonrepetitive. And if you think that things are old it is only because you are not sensitive enough to see the newness.

Just try to see a person; observe for twenty-four hours, and see how many persons exist in that one person. And this is not only so with a person, even a rock has its moods. Sit by the side of a rock and feel the mood. Sometimes the rock is happy and then the rock will receive you, will welcome you. And you can feel, you can touch and feel a warmth, a receptive welcome. Sometimes the rock is sad. You touch it and it will be cold. She will not be receiving you, it is as if she is saying, "Go away." In the morning look at the rock, in the evening look at the rock. When the stars have appeared in the night then look at the rock. It is not the same rock because the whole milieu is changing, it is part of a great milieu. When the whole milieu is changing how can this rock remain the same? It goes on changing but you don't have eyes to see.

Your eyes are old, this is the first thing to remember. Nothing is old in the world, everything is new – only your eyes get old. You become fixed, you start seeing patterns. Now scientists say that ninety-eight percent of the information that goes on coming from the outside world is not taken in by your senses, only two percent is taken. And that two percent of information that is taken in by your senses, you have a fixed pattern of taking, you choose it. That's why the thing becomes old.

You come to the house, you look at your wife in a particular pattern that has become fixed. You may not observe – you are not observing many things. The wife may be happy but you have become fixed with an idea: "My wife and happy? – it is impossible!" She may be happy but you cannot see. You have a pattern, you see only that which you believe.

And if the wife sees that you are seeing only unhappiness when she is happy suddenly she will become unhappy, because happiness cannot exist unsupported. She may have been smiling and waiting for you. Then she looks at your face and reads your face and sees that you are seeing that she is unhappy. Suddenly the smile disappears and your pattern is proved right. And the wife is doing the same with the husband....

Everybody has a fixed pattern, that's why things become old, look repetitive. Drop this pattern. Boredom comes because of you, the world is not creating boredom. It is one of the most wonderful worlds possible. Everything is new and everything is changing, nothing fixed, no pattern is followed. It is an alive movement. But you have a dead mind, so you see only those things which you have fixed. Drop this mind and start looking afresh.

What to do? Meditate. Whenever you see a thing which you feel is old, meditate. Look deeper, look again, think twice, feel, touch, be sensitive. Try to discover something new in it and you will always be enriched, you will always find something new there. Sometimes sit with your wife or with your child, with your friend, and look in the eyes, touch the face as if you are meeting for the first time. Close your eyes, put the light off, touch the face of your wife or your husband and feel the lines, the curves, as if for the first time. And suddenly the boredom will disappear, the person will become new. The person has always been becoming new only you never touched, your touch was dead. You never felt, your feeling was dead.

"How is one to overcome boredom?" The first thing to remember, drop your pattern; your mind creates the boredom. And then you will feel mystery all around you. Every day you go to the table, you take your food – it has become a routine. Tomorrow, or this very night when you are eating, close your eyes. First feel the bread with your hands, smell it – you have never smelled it. Touch it on your cheek – you have never touched it. And be slow, so you can feel and you can absorb. And then eat it, then taste it. Chew it as much as possible.

It should be the rule that while drinking water, eat it, and while eating food, drink it. Chew it so much that it becomes just like water and you can drink it. And when you drink water, don't drink it abruptly, don't just throw it down. Taste it. When you are thirsty just feel the water on your tongue, in your throat going down, the thirst disappearing – the feel of it. And even ordinary food can become wonderful. An ordinary woman can give you all the mysteries that any Cleopatra can give. An ordinary man is all – because ordinariness is just in your mind; otherwise everybody is extraordinary, everybody is unique. But you have to discover it.

Life is not given readymade, it has to be discovered. You get bored because you think life is readymade, somebody is going to give it to you. Nobody is there to give it to you. You have to discover it moment to moment, every day. The discovery must continue to the very end. If you stop discovery you will be bored.

You *have* stopped discovery, long ago you stopped discovery completely. Start again. Start feeling things, persons, try to find out something new always. Wherever you look – in the sky, at the trees, at the market, at the shop – wherever you look just be in a search to see something new. And there is enough, you will never feel a failure. Always the new will bubble up, the life will again become a mystery.

And when life becomes a mystery you become religious. A demystified life cannot lead you towards the divine. The divine means the deepest mystery that is hidden in this life.

The last question:

Osho,

Does a buddha ever get bored?

That's impossible, for many reasons. One, a buddha means one who has dropped his past, so he can never feel that anything is old, he can never feel that anything is repetitive. He is new. His mind is fresh and new every moment, he goes on dropping the past, the whole life is a new discovery.

Once it happened, a man came who was very angry with Buddha because Buddha asserted something which was against his creed. The man was very angry, he started abusing Buddha. But that was not enough, so he spat on Buddha's face.

Buddha asked the man, "Okay, have you anything more to say?" He wiped his face and asked the man, "Have you anything more to say?"

The man could not believe his ears, because he expected some reaction – irritation, anger, hatred. Buddha's disciples were very angry. When the man had left they said, "This is too much! And we could not do anything because of you. We could have put this man right in his place."

Buddha is reported to have said, "I was feeling sorry for that man and now I am feeling sorry for you. And that man can be forgiven; you cannot be forgiven so easily. You have been with me for so many years. You have not learned a simple lesson." Buddha said, "I enjoyed that man's anger. It was so authentic, it was so real; it was not bogus. He was a very authentic man. This is how he felt so he expressed it. He was no hypocrite. You are hypocrites. If you were feeling angry, why didn't you express it? You have been suppressing. That man was more innocent than you." Buddha said, "I enjoyed that man's authenticity. It was his childishness of course – but real."

Next day the man came again. The whole night he must have thought about it and he said, "Sorry." He felt that he had done something wrong, he felt guilty. Next morning he came, fell down at Buddha's feet and started crying. Tears were flowing down from his eyes onto Buddha's feet.

Buddha again asked that man, "Have you anything more to say? You are a man of body language; when you were angry you spat – it is a body language. Now you feel sorry, you are crying and weeping and your tears are falling on my feet. But you are authentic and I love your authenticity."

The man said, "I have come just to ask your forgiveness for the wrong act that I did yesterday."

Buddha said, "Forget it. Yesterday is no more. And I am not the same person you spat upon, so how can I forgive you? But I can assure you, the man who was there yesterday was not angry. You were already forgiven at that very moment because I don't carry anything, I close my accounts every moment. And now this is not the same man, because the consciousness is just riverlike."

Buddha is reported to have said, "As the Ganges is flowing...and if you go to the bank today you will not find the same water that you found yesterday. The water has gone. Consciousness is like a river. So," Buddha said, "you have come to the same bank again, but the river is not the same. So who will forgive you? But it is good that you ask, the very asking is enough. I am happy – you are authentic, honest."

You cannot make such a man bored. Everywhere he will find something he can enjoy, even your anger he can enjoy. You cannot make this man bored be-cause out of his riverlike consciousness he creates newness everywhere. He never exists with the past.

Secondly, only the ego can get bored. If you are not, who is going to get bored? For many years I have been living in one room, so many of my friends come and they say, "Don't you get bored just in one room?" Ordinarily I never go out – twenty-four hours in one room, almost only sitting in one chair. Their question is relevant. They ask me, "Don't you get bored? The same room, the same chair – and an empty room, there is nothing in it, nothing even to see – don't you get bored?"

Their question is relevant – but you can get bored only if you are there. So I sometimes tell them, "The room may be getting bored with me – the same person. I am not bored. There is no one who can get bored." And life is so rich, even in an empty room. And every moment the room is changing, it is not the same. Nothing can be the same – even the emptiness goes on changing, it has its own moods.

A buddha has no ego, you cannot bore him. He exists like an emptiness, as if he is not. If you penetrate him you will not find anyone there. The house is vacant, no one lives there really. You can move in a buddha but you will never meet him.

One Zen monk, Bokuju, used to say about Gautam Buddha, his own master, "The whole story of Buddha is false. He was never born, he never died, he never walked on this earth, he never preached a single word." And every day he would go into the temple and bow down before a Buddha statue.

So his disciples said, "Are you mad? You go on saying this man is just a myth – he was never born, never died, never walked on the earth, never asserted a single word – so to whom do you go every day? Before whom do you bow down? And we have heard you even praying there; you do prayers, and we have heard that you say *'Namo Buddhaya'* – so whom do you address?"

Bokuju started laughing and he said, "Nobody. This statue is not of anybody. This statue is just of a nobody, of nothingness. And I say he was never born because he was not an ego, he never walked on this earth because who will walk? He never asserted a single word because who will assert?"

He's not saying that really Buddha was not born, he is simply denying any entity there. You cannot say, "An emptiness is born, an emptiness is walking, an emptiness is speaking, an emptiness is dying." We can say this, this can be said, but there is no substance in it, no ego.

Try – if you cannot do anything else, then only do this: commit suicide as far as your ego is concerned. You will never get bored. You will be like an empty mirror. Whatsoever is reflected is always new because the mirror is empty, it cannot compare. It cannot say, "I have seen this face before."

Become the empty mirror, become egoless. And then there is no boredom – all life is a beatitude, a blessing, a deep ecstasy.

About Osho

Osho defies categorization. His thousands of talks cover everything from the individual quest for meaning to the most urgent social and political issues facing society today. Osho's books are not written but are transcribed from audio and video recordings of his extemporaneous talks to international audiences. As he puts it, "So remember: whatever I am saying is not just for you... I am talking also for the future generations."

Osho has been described by *The Sunday Times* in London as one of the "1000 Makers of the 20th Century" and by American author Tom Robbins as "the most dangerous man since Jesus Christ." *Sunday Mid-Day* (India) has selected Osho as one of ten people – along with Gandhi, Nehru and Buddha – who have changed the destiny of India.

About his own work Osho has said that he is helping to create the conditions for the birth of a new kind of human being. He often characterizes this new human being as "Zorba the Buddha" – capable both of enjoying the earthy pleasures of a Zorba the Greek and the silent serenity of a Gautama the Buddha.

Running like a thread through all aspects of Osho's talks and meditations is a vision that encompasses both the timeless wisdom of all ages past and the highest potential of today's (and tomorrow's) science and technology.

Osho is known for his revolutionary contribution to the science of inner transformation, with an approach to meditation that acknowledges the accelerated pace of contemporary life. His unique OSHO Active Meditations™ are designed to first release the accumulated stresses of body and mind, so that it is then easier to take an experience of stillness and thought-free relaxation into daily life.

Two autobiographical works by the author are available:

Autobiography of a Spiritually Incorrect Mystic, St Martins Press, New York (book and eBook)

Glimpses of a Golden Childhood, OSHO Media International, Pune, India

OSHO International Meditation Resort

Each year the Meditation Resort welcomes thousands of people from more than 100 countries. The unique campus provides an opportunity for a direct personal experience of a new way of living – with more awareness, relaxation, celebration and creativity. A great variety of around-the-clock and around-the-year program options are available. Doing nothing and just relaxing is one of them!

All the programs are based on Osho's vision of "Zorba the Buddha" – a qualitatively new kind of human being who is able *both* to participate creatively in everyday life *and* to relax into silence and meditation.

Location

Located 100 miles southeast of Mumbai in the thriving modern city of Pune, India, the OSHO International Meditation Resort is a holiday destination with a difference. The Meditation Resort is spread over 28 acres of spectacular gardens in a beautiful tree-lined residential area.

OSHO Meditations

A full daily schedule of meditations for every type of person includes both traditional and revolutionary methods, and particularly the OSHO Active Meditations™. The meditations take place in what may be the world's largest meditation hall, the OSHO Auditorium.

OSHO Multiversity

Individual sessions, courses and workshops cover everything from creative arts to holistic health, personal transformation, relationship and life transition, transforming meditation into a lifestyle for life and work, esoteric sciences, and the "Zen" approach to sports and recreation. The secret of the OSHO Multiversity's success lies in the fact that all its programs are combined with meditation, supporting the understanding that as human beings we are far more than the sum of our parts.

OSHO Basho Spa

The luxurious Basho Spa provides for leisurely open-air swimming surrounded by trees and tropical green. The uniquely styled, spacious Jacuzzi, the saunas, gym, tennis courts...all these are enhanced by their stunningly beautiful setting.

Cuisine

A variety of different eating areas serve delicious Western, Asian and Indian vegetarian food – most of it organically grown especially for the Meditation Resort. Breads and cakes are baked in the resort's own bakery.

Night life

There are many evening events to choose from – dancing being at the top of the list! Other activities include full-moon meditations beneath the stars, variety shows, music performances and meditations for daily life.

Or you can just enjoy meeting people at the Plaza Café, or walking in the nighttime serenity of the gardens of this fairytale environment.

Facilities

You can buy all of your basic necessities and toiletries in the Galleria. The OSHO Multimedia Gallery sells a large range of OSHO media products. There is also a bank, a travel agency and a Cyber Café on-campus. For those who enjoy shopping, Pune provides all the options, ranging from traditional and ethnic Indian products to all of the global brand-name stores.

Accommodation

You can choose to stay in the elegant rooms of the OSHO Guesthouse, or for longer stays on campus you can select one of the OSHO Living-In program packages. Additionally there is a plentiful variety of nearby hotels and serviced apartments.

www.osho.com/meditationresort
www.osho.com/guesthouse
www.osho.com/livingin

Books by Osho in English Language
Early Discourses and Writings
A Cup of Tea
Compassion and Revolution
Dimensions beyond the Known
Earthen Lamps
From Sex to Superconsciousness
The Great Challenge
Hidden Mysteries
I Am the Gate
Life Is a Soap Bubble
Nine Sutras
The Art of Living
The Path of Meditation
The Psychology of the Esoteric
Seeds of Wisdom
Work Is Love Made Visible

Meditation
And Now and Here (Vols 1 & 2)
In Search of the Miraculous (Vols 1 &.2)
Meditation: The Art of Ecstasy
Meditation: The First and Last Freedom
The Inner Journey
The Perfect Way

Buddha and Buddhist Masters
The Book of Wisdom
The Dhammapada: The Way of the Buddha (Vols 1-12)
The Diamond Sutra
The Discipline of Transcendence (Vols 1-4)
The Heart Sutra

Indian Mystics
Enlightenment: The Only Revolution (Ashtavakra)
Showering without Clouds (Sahajo)
The Last Morning Star (Daya)
The Song of Ecstasy (Adi Shankara)

Baul Mystics
  The Beloved (Vols 1 & 2)
Kabir
  The Divine Melody
  Ecstasy: The Forgotten Language
  The Fabric of Life
  The Fish in the Sea is Not Thirsty
  The Great Secret
  The Guest
  The Path of Love
  The Revolution
Jesus and Christian Mystics
  Come Follow to You (Vols 1-4)
  I Say Unto You (Vols 1 & 2)
  The Mustard Seed
  Theologia Mystica
Jewish Mystics
  The Art of Dying
  The True Sage
Western Mystics
  Guida Spirituale (*Desiderata*)
  The Hidden Harmony (Heraclitus)
  Reflections on Kahlil Gibran's *The Prophet*)
  The New Alchemy: To Turn You On (Talks on Mabel Collins' *Light on the Path*)
  Philosophia Perennis (Vol. 1 & 2) (*The Golden Verses of Pythagoras*)
  Zarathustra: A God That Can Dance
  Zarathustra: The Laughing Prophet (Talks on Nietzsche's *Thus Spake Zarathustra*)
  The Voice of Silence
Sufism
  Just Like That
  Journey to the Heart
  The Perfect Master (Vols 1 & 2)

The Secret
Sufis: The People of the Path (Vols 1 & 2)
Unio Mystica (Vols 1 & 2)
The Wisdom of the Sands (Vols 1 & 2)

Tantra

Tantra: The Supreme Understanding
The Tantra Experience: The Royal Song of Saraha (same as Tantra Vision, Vol. 1)
Tantric Transformation: The Royal Song of Saraha (same as Tantra Vision, Vol. 2)
The Book of Secrets: Vigyan Bhairav Tantra

The Upanishads

Behind a Thousand Names (Nirvana Upanishad)
Finger Pointing to the Moon (Adhyatma Upanishad)
Flight of the Alone to the Alone (Kaivalya Upanishad)
Heartbeat of the Absolute (Ishavasya Upanishad)
I Am That (Isa Upanishad)
The Message beyond Words (Kathopanishad)
Philosophia Ultima (Mandukya Upanishad)
The Supreme Doctrine (Kenopanishad)
That Art Thou (Sarvasar Upanishad, Kaivalya Upanishad, Adhyatma Upanishad)
The Ultimate Alchemy Vols 1 & 2 (Atma Pooja Upanishad)
Vedanta: Seven Steps to Samadhi (Akshaya Upanishad)
The Way beyond Any Way (Sarvasar Upanishad)

Tao

The Empty Boat
The Secret of Secrets
Tao:The Golden Gate (Vols 1 & 2)
Tao:The Pathless Path (Vols 1 & 2)
Tao: The Three Treasures (Vols 1-4)
When the Shoe Fits

Yoga

Yoga: The Alpha and the Omega (Vols 1-10)
The Path of Yoga (Vol.1)

Yoga: The Science of the Soul (Vol.2)
Yoga: The Mystery beyond Mind (Vol.3)
The Alchemy of Yoga (Vol.4)
Yoga: A New Direction (Vol.5)
Essence of Yoga (Vol.6)
Yoga: The Science of Living (Vol.7)
Secrets of Yoga (Vol.8)
Yoga: The Path to Liberation (Vol.9)
Yoga: The Supreme Science (Vol.10)

Zen and Zen Masters

Ah, This!
Ancient Music in the Pines
And the Flowers Showered
A Bird on the Wing
Bodhidharma: The Greatest Zen Master
The Buddha: The Emptiness of the Heart
Communism and Zen Fire, Zen Wind
Dang Dang Doko Dang
The First Principle
God Is Dead: Now Zen Is the Only Living Truth
The Grass Grows By Itself
The Great Zen Master Ta Hui
Hsin Hsin Ming: The Book of Nothing
I Celebrate Myself: God Is No Where, Life Is Now Here
Kyozan: A True Man of Zen
The Language of Existence
Live Zen
The Miracle
Nirvana: The Last Nightmare
No Mind: The Flowers of Eternity
No Water, No Moon
One Seed Makes the Whole Earth Green
The Original Man
Returning to the Source
The Search: Talks on the 10 Bulls of Zen
A Sudden Clash of Thunder

The Sun Rises in the Evening
Take it Easy
This. This. A Thousand Times This
This Very Body the Buddha
Turning In
Walking in Zen, Sitting in Zen
The White Lotus
Yakusan: Straight to the Point of Enlightenment
The Zen Manifesto: Freedom from Oneself
Zen: The Diamond Thunderbolt
Zen: The Mystery and the Poetry of the Beyond
Zen: The Path of Paradox (Vols 1-3)
Zen: The Quantum Leap from Mind to No-Mind
Zen: The Solitary Bird, Cuckoo of the Forest
Zen: The Special Transmission

Osho: On the Ancient Masters of Zen (7 volumes)*
Dogen: The Zen Master
Hyakujo: The Everest of Zen – With Basho's haikus
Isan: No Footprints in the Blue Sky
Joshu: The Lion's Roar
Ma Tzu: The Empty Mirror
Nansen: The Point Of Departure
Rinzai: Master of the Irrational

Responses to Questions
Be Still and Know
Beyond Enlightenment (Talks in Bombay)
Beyond Psychology (Talks in Uruguay)
Come, Come, Yet Again Come
From Bondage to Freedom
From Darkness to Light
From Death to Deathlessness
From the False to the Truth
From Unconsciousness to Consciousness
The Goose Is Out
The Great Pilgrimage: From Here to Here

The Invitation
Light on the Path (Talks in the Himalayas)
My Way: The Way of the White Clouds
Nowhere to Go but In
The Path of the Mystic (Talks in Uruguay)
The Razor's Edge
Sermons in Stones (Talks in Bombay)
Socrates Poisoned Again After 25 Centuries (Talks in Greece)
The Sword and the Lotus (Talks in the Himalayas)
Transmission of the Lamp (Talks in Uruguay)
Walk without Feet, Fly without Wings and Think without Mind
The Wild Geese and the Water
Yaa-Hoo! The Mystic Rose
Zen: Zest, Zip, Zap and Zing

Osho's Vision for the World

The Golden Future
The Hidden Splendor
The New Dawn
The Rebel
The Rebellious Spirit

The Mantra Series

Hari Om Tat Sat
Om Mani Padme Hum
Om Shantih Shantih Shantih
Sat Chit Anand
Satyam Shivam Sundaram

Personal Glimpses

Books I Have Loved
Glimpses of a Golden Childhood
Notes of a Madman

Interviews with the World Press

The Man of Truth: A Majority of One

For any information about OSHO Books, please contact:

OSHO Media International

17 Koregaon Park, Pune – 411001, MS, India
Phone: +91-20-66019999 Fax: +91-20-66019990
E-mail: distribution@osho.net
Website: http://www.osho.com
For More Information

For a full selection of OSHO multilingual online destinations, see www.OSHO.com/AllAboutOsho

The official and comprehensive website of OSHO International is

www.OSHO.com

You will find more OSHO unique content in multiple languages and formats, for example,

○ plan a visit to the OSHO International Meditation Resort
○ search the open access OSHO library for your favorite topic
○ find a complete presentation of all the OSHO meditations and related music
○ get Facebook updates about events, festivals, OSHO Multiversity courses and media releases
○ wake up to a daily OSHO quote on Twitter
○ access the YouTube OSHO video channel
○ make OSHO available in your local language through the OSHOTalks project
○ listen to OSHO radio or view OSHO tv

For details and links, see www.OSHO.com/AllAboutOsho:
Thank you for buying this OSHO book.